1-23-56

The Pacific Coast Maritime Shipping Industry, 1930-1948

A Joint Publication of the
Bureau of Business and Economic Research, Southern Section
and the Institute of Industrial Relations, Southern Division
University of California

The Pacific Coast Maritim

Volume I

Berkeley and Los Angeles, 19

hipping Industry, 1930-1948

ANALYSIS OF PERFORMANCE

Wytze Gorter and George H. Hildebrand

IVERSITY OF CALIFORNIA PRESS

UNIVERSITY OF CALIFORNIA PRESS
BERKELEY AND LOS ANGELES
CALIFORNIA

CAMBRIDGE UNIVERSITY PRESS
LONDON, ENGLAND

COPYRIGHT, 1954, BY
THE REGENTS OF THE UNIVERSITY OF CALIFORNIA

L. C. CATALOG CARD NO. 52-13855

PRINTED IN THE UNITED STATES OF AMERICA
BY THE UNIVERSITY OF CALIFORNIA PRINTING DEPARTMENT
DESIGNED BY A. R. TOMMASINI

BUREAU OF BUSINESS AND ECONOMIC RESEARCH
Southern Section

◇

INSTITUTE OF INDUSTRIAL RELATIONS
Southern Division

Preface

STATISTICALLY SPEAKING, *the Pacific Coast maritime shipping industry does not bulk large in the American economy. Yet it commands an unusual amount of interest for the economist. It is highly vulnerable to sudden shifts in world politics and trade. It is sharply sensitive to movements of the business cycle and to longer-term developments in the economy of the western states. It is subject to keen competition from land carriers in its coastwise and intercoastal trades. And during the past twenty years its strikes and poisoned labor relations have brought it both unwonted notoriety and very severe economic losses. In a word, Pacific shipping is a sick industry, struggling to survive in the midst of an unrivaled boom and subsisting to an unhealthy degree upon government largesse.*

Many of these basic facts were well known and had long been the subject of public discussion, enlightened here and there by occasional specialized inquiries. However, no one had compiled a comprehensive account of the industry's operations and its difficulties or had undertaken a detailed examination of the causes of its subtle as well as its more obvious troubles. The absence of such investigations provided the principal inspiration for our present study. Moreover, industries in decline are peculiarly fascinating to that perverse group who com-

vii

pose the genus of economists. Last, but not in order of importance, well-conceived industry studies provide a valuable laboratory for putting the hypotheses of economic theory to the test of the facts.

As we got under way with our investigation, we found that it could be divided conveniently in two parts, which we have published separately. In Volume I, "An Economic Profile" (1952), we presented a broad statistical record of primary movements in tonnage, vessel arrivals, and employment over the period 1930–1948. This span was long enough to give adequate perspective. We did not extend it beyond 1948 because this year was the most recent one for which data were available during roughly the first one and one-half years of our research and because important series were discontinued after that date. In a nutshell the profile reveals that during these years the industry suffered long-run decline and violent intermediate fluctuations in the physical volume of its tonnage, with particularly acute impacts in its foreign, intercoastal, and coastwise trades. Furthermore, job opportunities tended to be stagnant for the whole period, though bolstered postwar by a continuing heavy movement of government shipments.

These findings led naturally into the second phase of the inquiry, whose results appear in this volume. In essence, we have attacked here the problem of explaining the long-run decline and violent fluctuations experienced by the industry. Our first step was to get behind the global totals of tonnage in the various trades, to determine their commodity patterns and to isolate on a commodity basis the major movements that account for changes in the global totals. By this means we were able to evaluate the over-all "import" and "export" position of the economy of the western states and to relate changes in that economy to maritime shipping and its traffic markets.

Our next step was to set up an exhaustive group of suspected hypothetical causes believed to have governed the industry's performance, and to test these causes with evidence. As factors in long-run decline, we have considered these: growth of local industry and local markets in the west, which affected exports of primary products and imports of finished goods; increasing world-wide restrictions upon international trade; diversion of traffic to land carriers because of frequent and pro-

longed strikes and resulting unreliable services; and disproportionate increase in the industry's production costs, which placed it at an increasingly serious competitive disadvantage relative to railroads and trucks. To account for the industry's extreme fluctuations, we have examined the impacts of business fluctuations in the United States; World War II; and the disastrous series of costly strikes that originated from an extraordinarily bitter conflict in labor-management relations.

In describing the effects of these influences, we have found that some required more space than others. This should not be taken as a guide to their relative importance. For example, the factor of deep conflict in labor-management relations proved crucial at several points, making it necessary to piece together an involved history that has direct relevance to the performance of the industry. Most of the evidence here was qualitative in nature and demanded much careful interpretation. No account of the plight of Pacific Coast maritime shipping would have been adequate without detailed appraisal of this side of the story. This required much more text than the presentation of our analyses of some other influences that also were of high importance.

A word is also necessary concerning our main approach. We offer here an industry study. On the one side, it is a descriptive account of the major elements in the experience of Pacific maritime shipping during these years, an account that is intended to reveal what happened and to indicate the character of the industry's difficulties. On the other, it is an analysis designed to test and to indicate the impacts of a group of causal influences that together were responsible for the record. Viewed as a whole, the inquiry should not be construed as a study of trade, of transportation, or of labor relations as such, but as an integrated treatment of the industry's experience and problems, one that endeavors to bring together in a common focus a broad group of relevant causal forces.

Thus in undertaking the investigation, we have centered our attention upon the industry, viewed as the scene of action in which these forces played their different roles. The concept of an "industry" is, of course, extremely slippery at best and always tentative in any case.

However, causal analysis in any field requires the establishment of working boundaries if the inquiry is not to wander off into a morass. Actually, there were ample technological, legal, and institutional precedents to justify our treatment of Pacific Coast maritime shipping as a distinct unit for study. But in proceeding on this basis, we have not ignored the fact that, marketwise, maritime shipping is only part of a larger unit, the transportation industry as such. On the contrary, we have paid much attention to the changing position of shipping within this larger complex, but always with the emphasis upon the former. Our orientation lay consistently with Pacific Coast maritime shipping, its history, its performance, and its difficulties. Accordingly, we have not investigated the transportation industry as a whole, or maritime shipping on the Atlantic and Gulf coasts. Nor have we attempted extensive, detailed comparisons of water versus land freight rates, a notoriously treacherous field in any event. And finally, we have viewed Pacific shipping as a coastwide whole, rather than devoting our emphasis to the problems of the particular ports along the coast.

At many points we have found it necessary to supply interpretive analysis, and in some instances analysis of hotly controversial issues. This is most apparent in our explanation of the atmosphere of conflict that enveloped the industry's labor relations for so many years. Conflict means controversy. Issues that are controversial cannot therefore be ignored, in a spirit of false objectivity. They must be faced candidly and honestly, as we have sought to do. In venturing into controversial areas, we have employed the same technique that we applied to the more tranquil domains of our research: to collect and report the facts, and to develop hypotheses for explaining them. We leave it to the reader to judge the soundness of our account, recognizing, of course, that there is more than one way to look at the same set of facts.

Different readers will approach this volume from different points of view. Industry specialists, economic historians, and economists, for example, will (we hope) want to read it through. Trade and regional specialists will find chapters ii–v of primary interest. Labor economists will find Part III and chapters vi and vii of greatest pertinence. Those who have sought in vain in the past for an adequate statistical record of the industry will, we believe, be helped in some degree by the appendix. For the man in a hurry, we offer chapter xii, which summarizes our findings.

In passing we call attention to some important complementary studies which, along with several others, attest to extensive and growing public concern for the industry's difficulties. For the earlier years, there are Eliot G. Mears' Maritime Trade of the Western United States *(Stanford, Stanford University Press, 1935); and Walter Radius'* United States Shipping in Transpacific Trade 1922–1938 *(Stanford, Stanford University Press, 1944). For a more recent study of the transpacific trade, there is a publication by the Stanford Research Institute,* An Economic Analysis of Pacific Coast Trans-Pacific Shipping *(Stanford, Stanford [University] Research Institute, 1950, mimeographed). There now exists also an extensive study of the San Francisco Bay ports, which was prepared by a committee of the California Senate, titled* Final Report of the Senate Fact-Finding Committee on San Francisco Bay Ports *(Sacramento, California State Printing Office, 1951).*

The industry's labor relations problems have also attracted much attention in recent years. Among several accounts, these must be mentioned: Congress of the United States, Joint Committee on Labor-Management Relations, Labor-Management Relations: West Coast Maritime Industry, 80th Cong., 2d sess., S. Rept. 986, part 5 *(Washington, Government Printing Office, 1948); Subcommittee on Labor-Management Relations, Committee on Labor and Public Welfare, hearings concerned with* Hiring Halls in the Maritime Industry, 81st Cong., 2d sess. *(Washington, Government Printing Office, 1950); Paul Eliel, "Industrial peace and conflict: a study of two Pacific coast industries,"* Industrial and Labor Relations Review *(July, 1949); and Clark Kerr and Lloyd H. Fisher, "Conflict on the waterfront,"* Atlantic Monthly *(September, 1949). At the present time, the San Francisco Bay Area Council has under way a study of labor relations in that city's port, to determine their effects upon water traffic.*

For evidence concerning problems of costs and rates in Pacific shipping, we refer to two particular publications of the Interstate Commerce Commission: Ex Parte No. 165, Problems in the Regulation of

Domestic Transportation by Water *(by C. S. Morgan) (Washington, Government Printing Office, 1946); Docket No. 29721,* All Rail Commodity Rates Between California, Oregon, and Washington, *and Docket No. 29722,* Pacific Coastwise Water Rates, *277 I. C. C. 511 ff. (1950).*

Many people have given us invaluable help, though none bears any responsibility for the findings, interpretations, or possible errors that appear here. To Frank P. Foisie, former president of the Waterfront Employers Association of the Pacific Coast, we owe a great debt for much material and for many frank discussions, always tempered by tolerance and understanding, whatever the topic. Ralph Dewey, Jr., now of Pacific Far East Line, gave us our initial orientation to the industry's operations and sources of data. John Cushing, formerly chairman of Matson Navigation Company, and Admiral F. A. Zeusler of the Alaska Steamship Company provided useful information about trade with Hawaii and Alaska, respectively. Captain Harry Johnson, vice-president of the Sailors' Union of the Pacific, gave us valuable insights about labor relations, and Dr. Lincoln Fairley, research director of the International Longshoremen's and Warehousemen's Union, ably presented that union's view of the employers' strike statistics.

To W. B. Harmon and Irwin J. Heinie of the United States Maritime Commission, J. Edward Ely of the Bureau of the Census, Gertrude Searby of the Field Service of the Department of Commerce in San Francisco, and E. C. Lombard, executive secretary of the Panama Canal, we extend generous thanks for access to much unpublished data.

We owe much essential information and many valuable insights to Professor Robert J. Lampman of the University of Washington, for his excellent doctoral dissertation on the Sailors' Union of the Pacific; and to Paul Eliel, formerly an official of the Waterfront Employers Association, for his numerous and very penetrating studies of labor relations in the industry.

We also acknowledge the competent workmanship of four research assistants—Gregory Barlous, Martin Bailey, Lloyd Valentine, and Seymour Lesser. To Mrs. Anne Cook of the Institute of Industrial Relations on the Los Angeles campus we are much indebted for a most thorough editorial criticism of the manuscript.

Among institutional agencies, we wish particularly to acknowledge the help given us by the Maritime Commission, the Bureau of the Census, the Department of Labor, the Department of Commerce, and the public utilities commissions of California, Oregon, and Washington.

The study would not have been possible had it not been for the very generous support afforded to research by the University of California. In this instance, the financing was provided through the Institute of Industrial Relations and the Bureau of Business and Economic Research of the Los Angeles campus of the University. Both organizations served as cosponsors of the project and supplied much valuable aid.

We have benefited from valuable and trenchant professional criticism, in particular that furnished by Professors Armen Alchian, John C. Clendenin, Paul Homan, and Warren C. Scoville. To all of them we extend our grateful appreciation. Also, we acknowledge the indispensable help provided by Glenn Gosling, editor of the University Press on the Los Angeles campus, in preparing the manuscript for publication.

The question will inevitably arise in the minds of some readers as to the relative responsibilities of the two of us as collaborators. As was true of our first volume, the book is strictly a joint product. While we divided the initial tasks of investigation, the work of analysis and exposition was subjected to exhaustive mutual criticism at all decisive stages. Thus the order of our names as authors is maintained as it was in Volume I, where it was originally decided by toss of a coin.

Wytze Gorter
George H. Hildebrand

University of California, Los Angeles

Contents

XV

Part III: THE INFLUENCE OF LABOR RELATIONS

Part IV: AN APPRAISAL

FIGURES

xvii

TABLES

ABBREVIATIONS

ACA	American Communications Association
ARTA	American Radio Telegraphists Association
CMU	Committee for Maritime Unity
IBU	Inlandboatmen's Union of the Pacific
ILA	International Longshoremen's Association
ILWU	International Longshoremen's and Warehousemen's Union
ISU	International Seamen's Union
MCS	National Union of Marine Cooks and Stewards
MEBA	National Marine Engineers' Beneficial Association
MFOWW	Pacific Coast Marine Firemen, Oilers, Watertenders and Wipers Association
MFP	Maritime Federation of the Pacific
MMP	National Organization [of] Masters, Mates and Pilots of America
MSB	Marine Service Bureau
NIRA	National Industrial Recovery Act
NLRB	National Labor Relations Board
NMU	National Maritime Union of America
NWLB	National War Labor Board
PASA	Pacific American Shipowners Association
PMA	Pacific Maritime Association
SAPC	Shipowners Association of the Pacific Coast
SFEC	San Francisco Employers' Council
SIU	Seafarers' International Union of North America
SUP	Sailors' Union of the Pacific
WEPC	Waterfront Employers Association of the Pacific Coast
WEUSF	Waterfront Employers' Union of San Francisco

Part I
Introduction

CHAPTER I

The Inquiry

● *The Industry.*—As we indicated briefly in Volume I, the maritime shipping industry of the Pacific Coast embraces the ocean-borne transportation of freight and passengers originating or arriving at the Pacific ports of the continental United States. Within this complex there are two principal operations: the loading or unloading of ships at these ports and the actual operation of the vessels themselves by the steamship lines. So stated, this definition excludes shipbuilding and repair, lighterage, barging, intraharbor transfers, and local operations along inland waterways.

The major ports involved include Los Angeles–Long Beach and the group lying along the margins of San Francisco Bay; Portland, Oregon; and Seattle, Washington. In addition there are many small ports, usually handling specialized cargoes such as petroleum and lumber. Among these are the clusters on Puget Sound, Washington, and along the Columbia River basin in Oregon; the small harbors along the Oregon shore, and the "redwood" coast of northern California.

In this study we are concerned with the ocean trade of the Pacific Coast as a whole, rather than with the distribution of that trade as among particular ports. There is ample reason for this emphasis,

3

which of course does not ignore the independent importance of other studies of individual ports as such. Comparable statistics are lacking for comparative port studies, and in any case it will soon become evident to the reader that by far the greater interest attaches to the coastwide changes experienced by the industry, rather than to the distribution of the total among the ports themselves.

Vessel operations in the industry may be classed in two main ways. One consists of the division between dry and tanker cargoes, which we shall consider below. The other is according to "trade" or, broadly viewed, the principal market areas for steamship services. Of these, there are four. The *foreign* trade consists of traffic moving between the United States ports of the Pacific Coast and foreign countries.

The *noncontiguous* trade embraces traffic moving between the Pacific ports and the offshore territories and possessions of the United States. Here Alaska and Hawaii are by far the most important and we have confined our analysis to them. Then follow the two "domestic" trades. One, the *intercoastal,* involves traffic flowing between the Pacific ports and those lying along the Gulf and Atlantic coasts of the continental United States. Finally, there is the intraregional *coastwise* trade, which includes traffic moving between the ports of the Pacific Coast itself, but within the continental United States.

Only the foreign trade is open to the competition of foreign flag vessels.[1] The other three are all reserved by law for American operators. In the noncontiguous trade, the operators have the added advantage of being insulated by geography from the competition of railroads and, except for minor competition in Alaska, from trucks.

Operations may also be distinguished as between dry and tanker cargoes, whatever the trade. The tanker lines constitute a separate group, which transports bulk petroleum and gasoline, using specially designed vessels and shore facilities. For the most part, these opera-

---

[1] It is very unfortunate that the available statistics permit no breakdown of the foreign trade tonnage of the Pacific Coast between that carried by foreign lines and that by Pacific Coast operators. The distribution makes no difference as far as the scale of stevedoring operations is concerned. However, it plainly affects the prosperity of the Pacific Coast lines and their personnel. With the rapid postwar recovery of the merchant marine of many foreign nations, there seems little doubt that this competition is becoming increasingly severe.

tions are conducted either by the oil companies themselves or by contract carriers. True, the tankers participate in all of the four main trades, but by the nature of their services they may be considered as noncompetitive with those offered by the dry-cargo lines. Hence they require separate treatment from the market point of view. Tanker operations form a large part of the total tonnage moving in each of the trades, however, and indeed postwar they contributed over half of the total tonnage of all trades together.

From the standpoint of markets and of competition, therefore, it is essential to distinguish between dry and tanker cargoes, and at the same time to center attention upon each of the four main trades, viewed separately. It is also necessary to recognize that competition itself is diversified. In the intercoastal and coastwise groups, the dry-cargo lines compete with railroads, trucks, and to a limited extent with the airplane, as well as among themselves, while the tanker lines have the pipeline as their principal rival. In the foreign trade, competition among the United States dry-cargo lines themselves is sometimes not intense between particular points, but there is often keen rivalry between foreign and domestic vessels.[2] In the noncontiguous, the dry-cargo carriers are relatively well situated, as we have noted. This is especially true in the Hawaiian portion of the trade, where institutional connections in the Islands have long favored the principal operator.

The explanation of short- and long-run tonnage movements in the industry must therefore include analyses of the competitive structure of its markets. At the same time, the changing over-all position of the industry must also be examined. Like steel, maritime shipping on the Pacific Coast is a multiple product, multiple market industry. It is a distinct industry in the technological sense and its output, for our purposes, consists of tons of cargoes moved across Pacific Coast wharves. It is, therefore, an industry from the point of view of service

---

[2] Another form of competition in all the trades involves the scheduled lines versus tramp ships. For many years, the operators in the various trades have established minimum rates by joint "conferences," in an attempt to shift the impacts of competition away from price. Complaints of rate-cutting have long been common, however, especially against tramp operators. Tramp shipping becomes a threat whenever substantial excess carrying capacity exists, as in the depression or following World War II.

output, employment, and contribution to the national income. Institutionally, its steamship firms and stevedoring concerns are rather closely organized, respecting legislative activities, rate-fixing, and collective bargaining.[3] Yet these components, while sharing certain common objectives, have separate individual interests as well. For example, the ports of the Pacific Coast are primarily interested in the total volume of trade passing over their docks and only incidentally in its origin or destination, or whether it is carried by American or foreign lines. The stevedoring firms and their longshoremen, too, have a particular interest in total trade, and this distinguishes their orientation from that of the American carriers and the offshore trade unions which are vitally interested in the competition offered by foreign vessels.

So much, then, for a brief introduction to the industry. We turn next to a sketch of its postwar plight.

● *The Postwar Plight of Pacific Shipping.*—During 1948, the maritime shipping industry of the Pacific Coast found its fortunes at their lowest ebb in more than a decade. In that year it handled about 38 million long tons of commercial cargo in its regular trades and about 4 million long tons of special government shipments, for a total of 42 million long tons. In 1930, commercial traffic accounted for 52 million long tons and government shipments were not significant. Though the Pacific states were well into the postwar boom by 1948, maritime shipping obtained 20 per cent *less* tonnage than it had nearly two decades before. Indeed, if government tonnage is ignored, commercial shipments in 1948 were actually 27 per cent below 1930. These few figures reveal the plight of the industry.

There were many aspects to this plight and they can be clearly set forth by citing some of the highlights of our first volume.[4] First are

---

[3] There are a few independents, particularly for bargaining with the numerous trade unions. Moreover, some of the American steamship lines hire their labor and do their bargaining on the Atlantic Coast or Gulf Coast. Finally, the tanker lines constitute a separate group, for trade union and other matters.

[4] Wytze Gorter and George H. Hildebrand, *The Pacific Coast Maritime Shipping Industry, 1930–1948*, Vol. I, *An Economic Profile* (Berkeley and Los Angeles, University of California Press, 1952). The discrepancy between the total and coastwise cargo tonnages cited here and in Volume I is attributable to the receipt of additional information regarding coastwise oil shipments since the publication of Volume I.

our findings regarding the tonnage of cargoes carried in each of the trades. This is an acceptable measure of the physical output of the industry. During 1946–1948, the water-borne *foreign trade* of the Pacific Coast averaged 9.7 million long tons per year, exactly equal to the level reached in 1933, at the low point of the depression.[5] *Imports* in 1946–1948 barely equaled the 1930–1939 annual average, whereas exports were nearly 30 per cent below the average for the preceding decade. In the *intercoastal trade*, average tonnage in the three postwar years was 3.1 million long tons, one-half the total for 1932, at the bottom of the slump, and less than one-half the annual average for the 'thirties as a whole. *Coastwise traffic* in 1946–1948 averaged slightly over 20 million long tons, about the same as the average for 1930–1939 and 6 per cent below 1935–1939. The postwar coastwise figure, however, was made up almost entirely of petroleum shipments handled by the specialized tanker lines, and so it conceals the almost complete disappearance of the dry-cargo trade after 1939. Last, there is the *noncontiguous trade* with Hawaii and Alaska, which averaged 4 million long tons in 1946–1948, well above the average of 2.5 million long tons for the 'thirties. In fact, this trade was the only one to show postwar growth, and this growth was far from enough to offset the heavy losses experienced in the others.

Turn next to the service offered by the industry. In 1946–1948, the average number of vessel arrivals at all major ports except Portland, Oregon, was substantially below the lowest year during 1930–1939. And despite the introduction of larger and faster ships, the total cargo-carrying capacity represented by these vessels was also well below prewar at all major ports except Portland. Quite clearly, the total volume of service offered by the industry was shrinking in the early postwar years along with the physical volume of its total traffic.

The employment record of the industry is a little more difficult to interpret, because its 1946–1948 behavior seemingly contradicts the evident decline in industry output. In these years, dockside and ship-

---

[5] Gross tonnage in 1946 and 1948 was seriously depressed by three coastwide strikes, and although these losses should certainly be considered part of the industry's record and plight, we have decided here to use a three-year annual average in order to permit a more stable basis for comparison with the prewar decade.

board employment both averaged well above prewar, although a very rapid rate of decline was also revealed. During the war, there had been very large increases in the numbers of longshoremen and shipboard employees. Postwar, the problem promptly became one of drastic reduction in the labor force. There was thus a substantial exodus of men in each year of 1946–1948, but the rate of these withdrawals fell well short of the rate of contraction in tonnage. As a result, average annual hours per regular longshore gang in 1946–1948 fell 7 per cent below the 1935–1939 level. A similar surplus developed among the seagoing group. If this surplus manpower could have been fully overcome in these years, the level of employment in the industry would have been about the same as it was in the latter half of the 'thirties.

What emerges so far from this sketch of the initial postwar position of the industry is far from reassuring. On a long-run basis with the depression decade as a base and with the temporary effects of the war eliminated, Pacific maritime shipping operated during 1946–1948 roughly at an over-all level comparable with the worst years of the slump. It had even failed to hold the gains made during the recovery years of the later 'thirties. Worse still, it had not shared in the unprecedented postwar boom, though the Pacific states themselves had participated most impressively in that expansion. Instead, shipping was in deep trouble; its foreign trade had declined, its intercoastal tonnage had fallen disastrously, and its coastwise dry-cargo traffic was at a negligible fraction of earlier levels.

This, then, was the principal evidence for our verdict that the industry was in long-run decline. But this was not the whole story of the industry's experience during 1930–1948. It also suffered from extremely violent fluctuations in volume of cargo tonnage, number of ship arrivals, and level of employment. It had earned an unenviable reputation as a feast-or-famine industry.

By the end of 1948, the industry had reached a state of crisis and was in a mood for taking serious stock of its entire position. Confronting the operators were some very grave facts. They had just settled their third coastwide strike in three years (the fifth in twelve peacetime years), a tie-up lasting over three months and costing possibly four million long tons of lost cargo. Whatever the cause, their labor relations had been poisoned by conflict ever since 1934. Moreover, the water lines were as desperate for traffic as they had been in the worst years of the depression. Probably much tonnage had been lost forever. In the dry-cargo portions of the coastwise and intercoastal trades, the increasingly severe competition of railroads and trucks led to pessimistic forecasts of the future in these trades. Foreign trade was stifled by political and economic forces over which the operators had no control. Only the exceptional and relatively small noncontiguous trade, coupled with a continuing heavy "emergency" movement of government tonnage, precluded an even more severe slump in total traffic.

What was the explanation of this crisis in the industry? What forces had brought about its decline and its extreme instability? How did it acquire its dubious reputation of having the worst strike record and the worst labor relations in the United States? By what actions of its own, if any, could it reverse its declining fortunes, and replace them with stability and tranquillity, and possibly even with growth?

These are some of the questions we have sought to answer in this volume. At this point it is convenient to describe the methods by which we reached an explanation.

● *The Scheme of the Inquiry.*—To arrive at an explanation of a group of events requires going beyond a description of the events themselves. Actually, description and explanation go together. First, one must formulate preliminary hypotheses regarding the reasons for particular developments. These are indispensable for guiding the collection and organization of the evidence. Second, once the record is obtained, the importance of the suspected causes contained in the initial hypotheses can be gauged.[6]

Viewed from the side of demand, the market for the services of the Pacific Coast maritime shipping industry was strongly affected by forces beyond the control of the operators. Recognition of this fact led

---

[6] By a "cause" we mean any independent factor that affected the performance of the industry. Obviously, performance was influenced by a host of causes, one of which was the Russo-Finnish war in 1939–1940, whose effects were negligible. The primary problem was, therefore, to separate large effects from small, to permit concentration upon major factors.

to a group of questions based upon certain apparently reasonable hypotheses. (1) What were the effects of the policies of governments upon the foreign trade of the Pacific Coast? (2) In what ways did the economic development and growth of the population of the Pacific states influence the volume and composition of incoming and outgoing traffic by water? (3) How did major swings in American production affect the tonnage available to the industry? (4) Of what importance were the impacts of World War II upon maritime shipping?

From the standpoint of both demand and supply, two other questions were of great significance. (5) What were the effects and the underlying causes of the five coastwide and more than fifty major local strikes which plagued the industry for so many years? (6) How did the railroads and trucks affect the traffic available to the water carriers in the intercoastal and coastwise trades, and how successful were the water lines in controlling costs in these operations?

The hypotheses inherent in these questions gave logical structure to our inquiry. Two principal types of evidence were required. The first type involved the industry itself. Broadly, it was composed of a detailed commodity analysis for each of the four trades, an equally detailed record of strikes and of labor relations, and statistics of wages, production costs, and freight rates. The second type involved causal factors affecting the industry from outside. This required data indicating the growth of industry and population on the Pacific Coast, foreign trade policies affecting Pacific shipping, production statistics for industries that were major users of the industry's services, and relevant information about output fluctuations within the American economy.

What emerged, therefore, to become this book was at one and the same time a detailed descriptive history of the recent experience and difficulties of the industry and a causal explanation of this history.

Causal accounts must have limits and are never final. We have deferred to this fundamental truth, as an illustration or two will show. Our commodity analysis for the coastwise trade revealed at once that lumber shipments had seriously declined. At the crudest level, this decline was one important "cause" of the industry's shrunken market.

Yet the "cause" was itself only a descriptive fact, which failed to indicate the reasons why this traffic had fallen off, whether from declining lumber production or from diversion to rival carriers. Proceeding upward in the scale of causes, we found that although lumber output had seriously declined in the early years of the depression, it had recovered again to attain record levels after the war. Coastwise lumber traffic by water had failed to share in this revival, however, whereas lumber tonnage on the railroads had soared to new highs. Thus the primary factors contributing to the decline of the coastwise maritime lumber trade were business fluctuations and increasing competition of land carriers. For our purposes, this was the essential explanation. Obviously, it was unnecessary for us also to proceed to an explanation of the business cycle, which itself was only the effect of still wider causes.[7]

Strikes provide another instance of the principle. In 1934, 1936, 1946, and 1948, maritime operations were tied up for two or three months in each year because of strikes that strongly depressed the tonnage totals. Clearly, these strikes were a direct "cause" of the instability of the industry. But in broader terms, the strikes were not a "cause" but instead the effect of deeper forces which led to conflict in industrial relations within the industry. It was necessary to account for the conflict in developing an explanation of the performance and the difficulties of the industry. However, it was clearly not necessary to push the explanation to include the origins and nature of trade unionism in the United States.

As the primary measure of performance, we have centered attention upon the physical volume of cargo tonnage—in the aggregate and broken up by trades, and by commodities in each trade, and by regions of origin and destination in the foreign trade. Physical tonnage is the

---

[7] In some instances the evidence concerning causes was direct, for example, the fall in total tonnage that was associated with the decline in world production during 1929–1932. In others, the evidence was in part circumstantial, in the sense that once certain essential facts were established, others could be inferred. For example, we proved that movement of some important commodities by water had languished, in spite of large increases in their production, and that their movement by land had greatly increased. We inferred without personal interviews that shippers had shifted to railroads and trucks, hence that water services had become less attractive in the users' minds. Needless to say, circumstantial evidence has a recognized place in analytical research, as much as in juridical proceedings.

most useful common denominator for gauging changes in the actual scope of the industry's operations and for linking those changes to causes. Tonnage figures have the added advantage of not being distorted by changes in prices. True, it would have been helpful to have been able to supplement the tonnage statistics with revenue and profit figures for the operators, but these proved impossible to obtain, either for a continuous period or with a coverage that accurately would have exhibited the changing position of the firms involved. Moreover, it is certain that the major changes in total tonnage available adequately indicate changes in the profitability of operations. In addition we have augmented the tonnage statistics here and there with facts concerning changes in the number of companies and number of ships participating in particular trades.

The tonnage data were of two kinds: that for the regular commercial trades, where the operators and the shippers themselves were principally private firms; and that dispatched by the federal government in its military and civilian aid programs. Government traffic was of no importance before 1940 and owed its existence entirely to the war and its aftermath. Despite the uncertain statistical nature of this traffic, we have not neglected it in our analysis of the record. We have stressed its wartime origins, however, to isolate it from a causal standpoint. In turn this permitted us to consider separately the commercial trades for the entire period, so that the effects of forces other than the war could also be examined. In this manner, it proved possible to obtain an integrated view and explanation of industry performance.

● *Organization of the Book.*—The history of the Pacific Coast maritime shipping industry during 1930–1948 reveals three outstanding phenomena: long-run decline, extreme instability, and bitter internal conflict between management and labor. As the earlier description of our working hypotheses indicates, no simple explanation or single factor can account for these phenomena. Only by detailed description and complex analysis can a satisfactory explanation be obtained.

In Part II, "The Influence of Environment," we consider the effects of a group of forces that were external to the industry itself. In chapter ii we begin this analysis with an account of the principal commodities carried by the industry in its foreign, noncontiguous, intercoastal, and coastwise trades. This enables us to show the kinds of traffic that were most important to the industry, and to isolate the focal points of change in the over-all tonnages handled in each of the trades. Moreover, this commodity pattern yields important clues to the economy of the western states—in particular its dependence upon external areas and its supplies of marketable surpluses.

In chapter iii we describe the foreign trade of the Pacific Coast, to establish the principal geographical sources of imports and markets for exports. By this means we can reveal the influence of geography upon the pattern of foreign trade. In turn this permits us to determine the principal "trading partners" of the coastal states and to consider (in chapter iv) the possible influence of certain international economic and political policies upon Pacific Coast foreign trade.

Chapter v contains our findings regarding the second hypothesis: that the growth of industry, population, and income in the Pacific states affected the volume and composition of incoming and outgoing traffic by water in all the trades. Here we present various indicators of economic growth, and place special emphasis upon the impacts of growth as they affected shipments of two basic commodities in water traffic, lumber and petroleum.

In chapter vi, we consider three more hypotheses: the degree of dependence of shipping tonnage upon business fluctuations in the United States; the impacts of World War II; and the effects of the many strikes upon the volume of cargo tonnage. Admittedly, the strike factor fits a bit awkwardly into the basic plan of Part II, because it was less a true "cause" than an effect whose origins lay within the industry's troubled labor relations. We elected, however, to include it here because it meshes well with the other forces having direct effects upon tonnage.

We complete Part II with chapters vii and viii, in which we examine the last of our environmental factors, the role played by increasing rail and highway competition in diverting traffic from the intercoastal and coastwise trades. In essence this is a problem of relative changes in production costs as between maritime shipping and railroads and trucks. In particular it concerns the inability of the water lines to control their soaring costs, confronted as they were with unusually aggressive and successful trade unions. We thus consider the importance and comparative behavior of wages, the wage policies of the maritime unions, and the productivity of maritime labor, in their collective impacts upon the competitive position of the industry.

In Part III, "The Influence of Labor Relations," we examine the nature and causes of the deeply rooted conflict that so adversely affected the performance of the industry. With chapters ix and x we follow the same principle as in chapters ii and iii on commodity patterns, namely, to reconstruct in detail the essentials of the record, to lay a basis for a tenable explanation. Chapter ix presents the story of the five coastwide strikes. Chapter x describes the development of the industry's peculiar collective bargaining system and considers some less obvious but highly important manifestations of conflict. Together, these chapters underscore the fifteen-year failure of both sides to achieve an acceptable *modus vivendi*. Then in chapter xi we set forth our view of the primary causes of the conflict.

Part IV consists of a single chapter, in which we bring together our major conclusions in a unified account, appraising the postwar position of the industry and assessing tentatively its future prospects.

Probably the central conclusion emerging from our inquiry is that in great part the Pacific Coast maritime shipping industry was the passive victim of causal forces over which it had little or no effective control. In the main, changes in its environment were unfavorable. That environment was *displacing* rather than *adopting* the industry, and so shipping gradually lost an important part of its former position. This was the outcome of a long process. Moreover, shipping managements, viewed as centers of initiative, in important degree proved incapable of *adapting* to that changing environment, though such was vital if the adverse fortunes of the industry were ultimately to be reversed. In part, this inability to adapt to external change may well be attributed to the demoralization and lack of vigorous initiative that usually accompany industrial decline. But in much greater part, more successful adaptation probably was precluded by the institutional ties imposed by unusually strong unionism, coupled with very limited possibilities for influencing the demands for the services of the industry.

If this view is sound, and we are convinced that it is, then the present restricted scope of Pacific Coast maritime shipping and its considerable dependence upon stimulants administered by government should hardly occasion surprise.

Part II
The Influence of Environment

CHAPTER II

Some Clues to the Industry's Plight: The Commodities Carried

● *Introduction.*—The economic fortunes of the maritime shipping industry often depend primarily upon matters largely beyond its control. For example, a change in consumer tastes, or a technological development, may mean larger or smaller cargoes, and financial gains or losses for the shipping trade. A rapidly growing economy experiences many such changes and they will be reflected in its commodity shipping statistics. An analysis of these statistics thus provides the initial insights for an explanation of the factors outside the Pacific Coast maritime shipping industry that contributed to its decline between 1930 and 1948.

In Volume I we presented statistics showing the total cargo tonnage carried in each of the trades—foreign, noncontiguous, intercoastal, and coastwise. In this chapter we present data indicating the commodity breakdown of those separate totals. The accompanying charts that depict these data also show the general behavior of total tonnage in each trade. We therefore simultaneously review the major total tonnage findings for each trade as presented in Volume I and relate the tonnage of specific commodities or groups of commodities to the shifting totals.

Unfortunately, the available statistical data do not permit a com-

19

pletely nontechnical discussion. In some of the trades the shipping statistics of 1930–1948 are broken into three distinct periods using different commodity classifications. The joining of these disparate series required some truly heroic measures, and the critical reader is entitled to know the character of these statistical devices. For the most part, these technical matters are dealt with in footnotes. Some textual discussion is essential, however, even for the casual reader.

● *Foreign Trade.—Exports.* In 1930, four groups of commodities accounted for 94 per cent of the foreign trade export tonnage of the Pacific Coast. They were the following.

Petroleum and products	60.3 per cent
Logs and lumber	18.9 per cent
Grains and grain products	9.8 per cent
Animals, fruits, vegetables, and products	5.0 per cent
Total	94.0 per cent

No other classification of exports contributed as much as 1 per cent of the total export tonnage.

As figure 1 shows, after 1930 Pacific Coast exports remained concentrated largely in extractive and farm products. The western economy thus shipped out items embodying its plentiful resources in exchange for its required imports. The crucial export role of oil, timber, and farm products needs little elaboration. In the prewar years, the oil and lumber industries furnished about three-fourths of each year's export tonnage. Lumber's share of export tonnage displayed a declining tendency while the petroleum and products portion tended upward.

Although farm and extractive products dominated export trade throughout the period 1930–1948, developments in two other export categories merit attention. Exports of metals and manufactures[1] became more important, reflecting the growth of manufacturing in the west.[2] The rise in exports of manufactures was gradual and was inter-

---

[1] Two categories have been combined here—iron, iron ore, and steel and copper manufactures, etc. (See Appendix, table 1.) Together they furnished 1.5 per cent of total foreign trade export tonnage in 1930.

[2] This judgment is based on the finding that most export tonnage originates in the eleven western states because the pattern of freight rates favors shipments to Pacific Coast ports. The Stanford Research Institute found that only 5 per cent of the exports via Pacific Coast

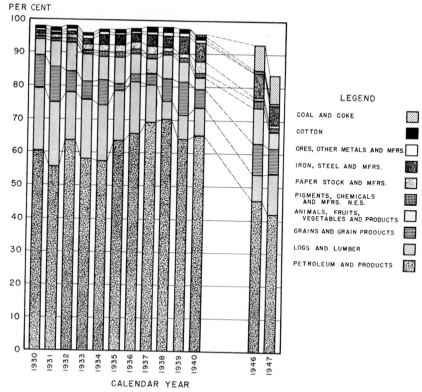

PER CENT

LEGEND

COAL AND COKE

COTTON

ORES, OTHER METALS AND MFRS.

IRON, STEEL AND MFRS.

PAPER STOCK AND MFRS.

PIGMENTS, CHEMICALS
AND MFRS. N.E.S.

ANIMALS, FRUITS,
VEGETABLES AND PRODUCTS

GRAINS AND GRAIN PRODUCTS

LOGS AND LUMBER

PETROLEUM AND PRODUCTS

CALENDAR YEAR

Fig. 1. Distribution of Pacific Coast foreign trade export cargo tonnage by principal commodity groups, 1930–1940, 1946, and 1947. Source: Appendix, table 1.

rupted only during 1934–1936. Though the importance of this export category was small relative to lumber and oil, on several occasions it exceeded that of grains and grain products. In 1939, the leading exports and their shares of total foreign trade export tonnage were as follows.

Petroleum and products	64.3 per cent
Logs and lumber	7.3 per cent
Grains and grain products	9.9 per cent
Animals, fruits, vegetables, and products	6.0 per cent
Metals and manufactures	6.3 per cent
Total	93.8 per cent

ports to the Orient originated outside the western region. (Stanford Research Institute, *Final Report, An Economic Analysis of Pacific Coast Trans-Pacific Shipping* [Stanford, April 15, 1950], p. 6.) For a discussion of the industrial growth of the west, see chap. iv.

In 1946 and 1947, coal and coke shipments suddenly became substantial compared with prewar. Before World War II they never accounted for more than one-half of one per cent of total exports. The first two postwar years show figures of 7.8 and 8.1 per cent. These increases represent the effect of purely transitory postwar conditions that cannot be expected to continue for an extended period.[3]

Although our data do not permit precise comparisons between the prewar and postwar relative importance of export commodities, additional generalizations appear warranted.[4] With appropriate reservations, the figures for 1946, shown below, may be compared with those for 1930 and 1939 presented above.

Petroleum and products	46.0 per cent
Logs and lumber	7.9 per cent
Grains and grain products	9.4 per cent
Animals, fruits, vegetables, and products	10.8 per cent
Metals and manufactures	7.6 per cent
Coal and coke	7.8 per cent
Total	89.5 per cent

Postwar, petroleum and products fell in importance. Combined with logs and lumber, they contributed a little more than half of total export tonnage, as compared with about three-fourths during the 'thirties. This decline may well continue as the local consumption of these commodities rises with increases in population and manufacturing output.[5] The enhanced importance of agricultural exports, particularly in 1946, probably represented war-deferred and relief demands—both temporary forces.

Another useful comparison involves the number of commodity groups, ranked in order of size, required to constitute the major portion of Pacific Coast exports. For example, from 1930 to 1940, three leading commodity groups furnished at least 80 per cent of the tonnage. In 1946, it required the first five groups to yield a total of 80

[3] For example, there were sizable shipments of coal to Italy and France.
[4] See notes to Appendix, table 1, for a discussion of the statistical problems encountered in the construction of the pertinent commodity export series.
[5] For an analysis of trends in manufacturing output, see below, pp. 83–93. The peculiarities of lumber and timber exporting are examined below, pp. 92–99.

per cent of all foreign trade exports. It is likely that the same number or perhaps one or two more groups constituted this fraction of exports in 1947.° Though the tonnage evidence is certainly insufficient to warrant any firm conclusions regarding long-term trends in the commodity pattern of exports, the above comparison itself suggests the likelihood of an important change in the pattern after World War II.

Collateral evidence supports this contention. Between 1940 and 1948, western industry expanded rapidly and this resulted in a greater diversification of output of goods and services. Some of this new industrial output undoubtedly found its way into the export stream. This matches the earlier experiences of other regions and countries that added manufacturing to what originally was an almost wholly agricultural and extractive economy.

To sum up our findings thus far, we can say that between 1930 and 1948 there was a general tendency toward a greater diversification of exports, accompanied by reduced importance of lumber and oil after 1938, and a growth in shipments of manufactures. Undoubtedly, the very sharp contrast between prewar and postwar commodity patterns was primarily attributable to marked changes in conditions of world trade. Some of these changes, however, appear to have been under way during the late 'thirties.

As figure 1 shows, the tendency toward diversification of exports was accompanied by year-to-year changes in the relative importance of the leading export commodity groups. And both these phenomena occurred against a background of varying annual total export tonnage. Obviously, the variations in total tonnage stemmed from the variations of its components, with different commodity groups exerting major influence upon the total from time to time. Accordingly, a study of these relationships provides additional clues as to the probable causes of the shipping industry's instability and decline.

Petroleum and products comprised over 50 per cent of total export tonnage during the 'thirties. Therefore, it is not surprising to find a general tendency for oil and total cargo tonnage to change in the same direction although not in the same degree. Opposing directions of

---

° We cannot be certain because the principal commodity data for 1947 were compiled on different bases. See Appendix, table 1.

change occurred on only two occasions: 1932–1933 and 1935–1936. In the first instance, petroleum and other groups fell while lumber and metallic manufactures rose. In the second, oil shipments rose while over-all tonnage fell. The fall in total tonnage reflected decreased exports of fruit, animal, and vegetable products.

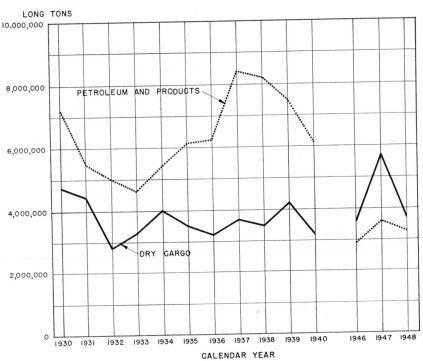

Fig. 2. Pacific Coast water-borne foreign trade exports of petroleum and products, and dry cargo, 1930–1940, 1946–1948. Source: Appendix, table 14; Gorter and Hildebrand, *op. cit.*, Vol. I, Appendix II, table 1.

Sales of petroleum and its products are very sensitive to business conditions.[7] As a result, the heavily "oil weighted" figures for total export tonnage show that the export trade was closely related to the business cycle. This would account for the steep decline from 1930 to 1932, the subsequent rise to 1937, and the fall in 1938. The decreases in 1939 and 1940 represent the effects of war and war preparation. The postwar lack of correspondence between export tonnage and the

---

[7] See, for example, the analysis of the relationship of coastwise oil shipments to gross national product. Pp. 112, 116.

state of economic activity can be explained as constituting, in part, further evidence of a long-term decline in exports, already visible during the 'thirties.

The main elements of this decline are disclosed by subtracting oil shipments from total export tonnage.[8] During the 'thirties, as shown in figure 2, dry-cargo export tonnage fluctuated more often than did petroleum tonnage. The pattern of dry-cargo fluctuations also appears to have been largely cyclically determined. Postwar, 1946 and 1948 were "strike" years and 1947 was without a major work stoppage. But where is the long-term decline? Certainly it is not evident from a casual glance at figure 2, which apparently shows that, aside from 1947, the dry-cargo export trade was primarily stagnant after 1932.

At this point, numbers are more enlightening than charts, as the following statistics clearly demonstrate.

Years		Average annual dry-cargo foreign trade export tonnage
1930–1934		3.9 million long tons
1935–1939		3.6 million long tons
1946–1948	(excluding coal, government relief, and military dry cargoes)	3.7 million long tons[9]
1946–1948	(including coal, but excluding government relief and military dry cargoes)	4.0 million long tons
1946–1948	(including coal, government relief, and military dry cargoes)	8.5 million long tons[10]

[8] Strictly speaking, we have subtracted petroleum and products. We shall refer to the net figure as "dry-cargo" tonnage. The industry prefers to use dry cargo or "general" cargo (dry cargo minus certain bulk commodities such as lumber, grains, and coal) in many of its analyses, on the grounds that more of the industry's facilities are used in dry- and general-cargo handling than in bulk oil shipments. Further, much bulk oil is shipped by producers in their own vessels as part of their delivery service. The shipping industry, accordingly, contends that its welfare depends primarily upon general- and dry-cargo volume. It is appropriate at this point in our study to separate dry and tanker cargo in order to isolate the effects of the tonnage of certain commodities upon the industry's cargo tonnage performance record. Our dry-cargo figures are derived from Appendix, table 1.

[9] To derive this figure we estimated the coal and coke tonnage for 1948 as the average for 1946 and 1947. See Appendix, table 1.

Prewar coal shipments ranged from 300 tons in 1931 to approximately 44,000 tons in 1940. In 1946, 504,000 tons were exported and in 1947 nearly 750,000 tons entered the export stream. As noted above (p. 22), much of the postwar movement in 1946 went to France and Italy. This should not be considered as a permanent factor in postwar trade. We therefore excluded coal from some of our postwar calculations.

[10] We have estimated this figure as follows: (1) Army dry-cargo measurement tons were converted to long tons by using a stowage factor of 70, or 1.75 measurement tons = 1 long

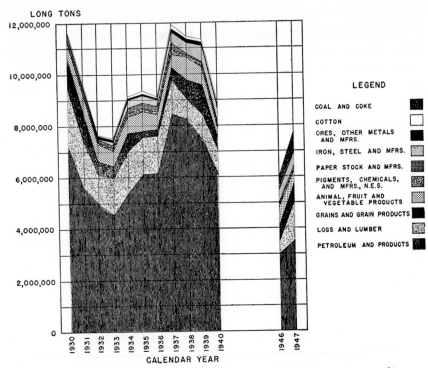

Fig. 3. Pacific Coast foreign trade export cargo tonnage by principal commodity groups, 1930–1940, 1946, and 1947. Source: Appendix, table 1.

Only by including the unusually large coal shipments in the postwar statistics can the private enterprise (nongovernmental) segment of the industry's export dry-cargo tonnage be prevented from showing a decline between 1930 and 1948. The industry's postwar advance over its prewar position in foreign exports, therefore, was almost wholly attributable to government cargoes.[11]

ton (see *Merchant Marine Study and Investigation*, 81st Cong., 2d sess., S. Rept. 2494 [Washington, 1950], p. 11) ; (2) civilian relief shipments for 1946 and 1947 were estimated at 28.5 per cent of total (dry plus tanker) exports on the basis of the known ratio in 1948; (3) civilian relief program exports in 1948 were added to the total of (1) plus (2) above; and (4) the sum of (1) plus (2) plus (3) above was divided by three. The tonnage data are taken from Gorter and Hildebrand, *op. cit.*, Vol. I, pp. 18, 37. The estimate of 4.5 millions tons may be somewhat larger than the actual tonnage mark in those categories because the army figures may include some civilian relief tonnage and the relief program statistics include some petroleum and products.

[11] It should be noted that in 1950, when there were expectations that military cargoes would become quite small compared with 1946–1948, the Korean conflict induced a tremendous growth in outbound shipments.

Presumably the long-term future of the shipping industry lies in private commercial dry cargo unless, of course, governmental relief and military shipments continue to provide over 50 per cent of the export cargo tonnage. It is therefore pertinent to examine what happened to the absolute volume of the tonnage of leading export commodities. Figure 3 provides an almost self-evident answer.

The decline of logs and lumber tonnage stands out as the most significant depressive factor upon the annual volume of export dry-cargo tonnage throughout 1930–1948. In 1930, over 2.25 million long tons, nearly half of Pacific Coast dry-cargo exports, consisted of logs and lumber. Except for brief upsurges, the long-term tendency was downward. In 1947, the last year for which we have data, only slightly more than one million tons of logs and lumber moved in the export channels of foreign trade.

Increasing exports of manufactures, particularly of iron and steel, provided the most important offset to the decline in logs and lumber throughout 1930–1948. Exports of iron, steel and manufactures, which amounted to 96,000 tons in 1930, rose to 612,000 tons in 1939 and were 552,000 tons in 1947.

Exports of grain and grain products varied widely. They amounted to 1.2 million tons in 1930. Subsequently they fell steadily until 1935, when they were only one-fifth of their 1930 level. Then they climbed until 1939, very nearly reaching the 1930 level. In 1940, less than half this volume was exported, and in 1946 and 1947, 600,000 and 700,000 tons, respectively, entered the export stream.[12] Exports of grain and grain products followed the same pattern as logs and lumber until 1935, and then moved upward for three years, to help offset the decline in logs and lumber during this period. The behavior of grain and grain products tonnage thus worked to accentuate the fall in dry-cargo tonnage in the early 'thirties, and then to mitigate the depressive effects of the drop in lumber cargoes between 1936 and 1938. Postwar, grain tonnage conformed to the pattern of most of the other categories.

The export tonnage of other farm products remained fairly steady throughout the entire period.

---

[12] Grain shipments under government relief programs were heavy in the postwar years.

Quickly reviewed, our findings regarding commodity composition and tonnage reveal an over-all decline in total (dry plus tanker) commercial exports from 1930 to 1948, although there was some recovery

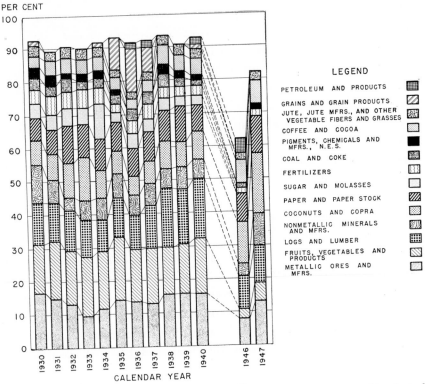

Fig. 4. Distribution of Pacific Coast foreign trade import cargo tonnage by principal commodity groups, 1930–1940, 1946, and 1947. (Amounts less than 1 per cent not shown.) Source: Appendix, table 2.

during the late 'thirties. Even including relief shipments, but not the army cargoes, postwar average annual exports were below the 1930–1934 annual average.[13] Dry cargoes, exclusive of relief and army shipments, increased slightly in the postwar period after falling a little between 1935 and 1940. The postwar figures, however, are considerably bolstered by unusually heavy coal shipments. If these are subtracted, the postwar annual average falls to about the prewar level.

[13] See Gorter and Hildebrand, *op. cit.*, Vol. I, pp. 16–19.

However, adding army and relief shipments to the total commercial cargo tonnage puts 1946–1948 far above 1930–1939.

Oil shipments dominated exports, though postwar they were both relatively and absolutely smaller than prewar. Tonnage of logs and lumber tended downward, also declining in importance relative to other exports. Grain and grain products fluctuated widely, with no long-term tendency to rise or fall. Other farm products showed comparatively small year-to-year variations, and no upward or downward tendencies. Metal manufactures displayed a fairly steady long-term increase in both annual tonnage and share of total exports. All exports were affected by business fluctuations, though their sensitivities varied.

The increasing variety of exports, the growing importance of manufactured exports, and the relative decline in the importance of the products of extractive industries together suggest that the industrial development of the Pacific Coast was a powerful factor affecting the area's export pattern.

Imports. Between 1930 and 1948, Pacific Coast foreign trade import tonnage was nearly all dry cargo. In contrast to exports, imports consisted of a wide variety of commodity groups, with none dominating the picture. This probably accounts for the absence of a striking up or down tendency in import tonnage, although there were sharp annual fluctuations.

The following figures indicate the general behavior of foreign trade import cargo tonnage during 1930–1948.[14]

Years	Millions of long tons per year
1930–1934	2.1
1935–1939	2.7
1930–1939	2.4
1946–1948	2.3

Farm and extractive commodities plus a small measure of manufactures characterized imports. Tonnagewise, therefore, we may say that Pacific Coast foreign trade consisted primarily of the two-way exchange of the products of farm, forest, and mine.

Prewar, though there were occasional yearly shifts in the importance

[14] *Ibid.*, p. 16.

of some of the import categories, there were few marked changes ex-·
tending over several years. As figure 4 shows, logs and lumber imports increased their relative share in the late 'thirties[15] and then suffered a severe decline in the two postwar years. Fruits, vegetables,

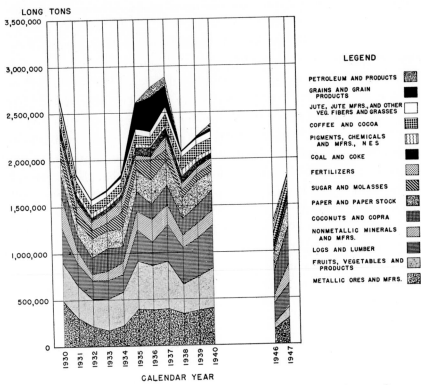

Fig. 5. Pacific Coast foreign trade import cargo tonnage by principal commodity
groups, 1930–1940, 1946, and 1947. Source: Appendix, table 2.

their products, and animal products n.e.s.[16] dropped in significance
during the postwar years. There was a long-term downtrend in the
importance of fertilizer imports, but since this category at its height
accounted for only about 6 per cent of total imports, its influence upon
the total was slight. The large increases in coffee and cocoa in 1946
and 1947, over prewar levels, probably represent a restocking of

---

[15] We cannot be sure of the exact amount of the change, because the figures for 1930–
1948 are based upon three separate statistical series, spliced in 1938 and 1946.
[16] "Not elsewhere specified."

inventories following the restricted wartime trade in these items, and greater regional consumption associated with the rapid growth in population.

The *total* volume of imports generally corresponded closely to changes in business conditions—the postwar period being an important exception. The absolute tonnages of individual commodity groups, however, did not conform so closely to the cyclical pattern. Nor did they all follow the long-term (1930–1948) stagnant or possibly slightly downward tendency. Figure 5 illustrates these divergent behaviors. The width of each band on the chart shows the tonnage contributed by the relevant commodity classification.

Logs and lumber imports increased between 1930 and 1940, as did fruits, vegetables, and animal and vegetable products n.e.s., and coffee and cocoa. The other groups displayed no pronounced tendency to change during these years. As we noted earlier in connection with exports, postwar-prewar comparisons are dangerous because of the differences in basic data. Postwar, the tonnage in all categories except coffee and cocoa appears to have been smaller than prewar. This is partly a "statistical" rather than an actual decline, because the tonnage figure shown for each commodity group does not always include all the tonnage imported in that group, but only the tonnage "trapped" by the sampling technique used.[17] For the postwar years, all that can safely be said is that the six leading commodity groups (by tonnage) were about the same as prewar, except that coffee and cocoa supplanted fruits, vegetables, and animal and vegetable products n.e.s. in this list. We may conclude, then, that the pattern of Pacific Coast foreign trade imports changed very little between 1930 and 1947.

The stability of this import pattern and of the absolute volume of total imports, in spite of the tremendous growth of population and manufacturing on the Pacific Coast, indicates a declining per capita dependence upon foreign imports. The evidence suggests, however, that imports of logs and lumber, at least during the 'thirties, were required for the expanding western economy. Further, increased imports

---

[17] For 1946, the Bureau of the Census reported commodity imports by port. Only commodities involving 1,000,000 pounds and over or $100,000 and over were included in its tabulations. See Appendix, table 2, notes c and d.

of coffee and cocoa then were directly geared to the increase in population. The coffee and cocoa group resumed its gains in the postwar period. By contrast, certain other foreign trade import groups were not sensitive to the growth of the west, either in population or production.

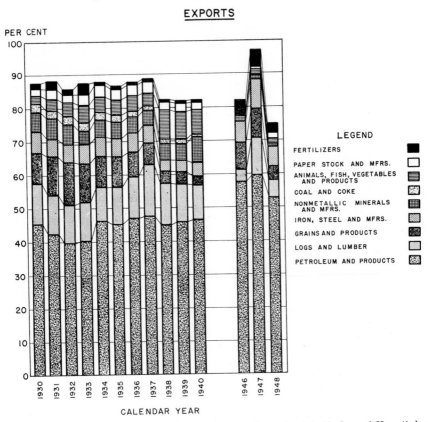

Fig. 6. Distribution of Pacific Coast cargo tonnage in trade with Alaska and Hawaii, by principal commodity groups, 1930–1940, 1946–1948. Imports for 1946–1948 and exports for 1946 and 1947 include Hawaii only. Source: Appendix, table 3.

In addition, some imports were gradually being replaced by domestic substitutes—rubber and fibers, for instance. But this is running ahead of our story. This résumé of import commodity findings can only point the way to the types of production and consumption that must be examined for their influence upon the shipping industry.[18]

[18] See below, especially pp. 83–107.

● *Noncontiguous Trade.*—The difference between foreign and non-contiguous trade is basically political. The noncontiguous territories and possessions of the United States have been grouped together primarily because they have enjoyed preferential tariff treatment by

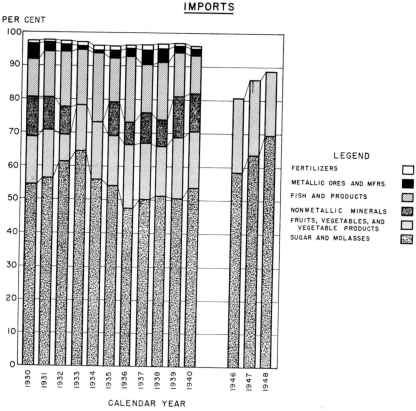

Fig. 6—*Continued*

the mother country. They are not, however, treated exactly the same as the contiguous states in the union and therefore are properly excluded from an analysis of domestic ocean-borne commerce. In fact, trade with noncontiguous areas is very similar to foreign trade. Except for the absence of certain restrictions and the reservation of shipping to United States vessels, the trade *is* foreign in character and involves commodities encountered in bona fide foreign trade.

Because of the shifting official territorial composition of noncontiguous trade throughout the entire period covered by this study, we have confined our analysis to trade with Alaska and Hawaii.[19] Even when noncontiguous is narrowly defined, however, there are serious statistical difficulties. Federal statistics are available for 1930–1940 and 1944–1947 only. The former period is covered by two different series. Data for the latter interval appeared only in unpublished tabular form. Here we were limited by our financial resources to computing only total annual tonnage for exports to Alaska and Hawaii. We have therefore relied upon unofficial sources for postwar commodity breakdowns.[20]

Noncontiguous exports. Figure 6 reveals that, as was true in foreign trade, petroleum and products, logs and lumber, and grain and grain products were the most important outbound commodities during the period bounded by 1930 and 1940. Further, figure 6 shows that during these years there were no long-term shifts or marked year-to-year changes in the share of total exports attributable to any group of commodities. The differences between the 1938–1940 shares and those for 1930–1937 may be largely the result of the statistical splicing of two separate series.[21]

Prewar and postwar export commodity patterns were probably not markedly different, although our statistical data cannot be used to verify this.[22] However, the statistics clearly indicate one difference. Exports of iron, steel and manufactures became more important during

[19] As indicated in Volume I (n. 14, p. 29), trade with Alaska and Hawaii constituted over 70 per cent of total noncontiguous imports and over 55 per cent of noncontiguous exports between 1930 and 1940.

[20] Commodity breakdowns of this trade were obtained from the United States Maritime Commission's *Report No. 275* and *Report No. 2610* for 1930 to 1940. Through the courtesy of the Matson Navigation Company we secured figures for postwar trade with Hawaii. We have some sketchy data regarding postwar shipments to Alaska as furnished by the Alaska Steamship Company. Since trade with Hawaii dominates Pacific Coast noncontiguous trade and the Matson Company dominates the Hawaii trade (except for tanker shipments), our postwar figures are probably representative of the main items entering into noncontiguous trade as we have defined it.

[21] See Appendix, table 3.

[22] Our postwar data, covering Hawaii only (exports, 1946 and 1947), show some apparently marked changes in the importance of certain types of export commodities. These cannot, however, be accepted as reflecting the true status, because the figures are not complete. For example, the basic records used here contained no entry for logs and lumber in 1946, yet they were shipped. We have independently estimated their 1946 tonnage. (See Appendix, table 3, note j.)

1946–1948. The rise in importance of this group during the 1946–1948 period followed the pattern also evident in foreign trade. Part of the sharp rise in fertilizer exports as a percentage of the total may be due to the inclusion of exports from British Columbia, Canada, in

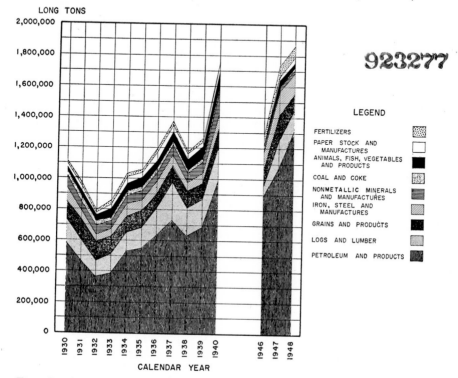

Fig. 7. Pacific Coast exports to Alaska and Hawaii by principal commodity groups, 1930–1940, 1946–1948. Exports for 1946 and 1947 include Hawaii only. Source: Appendix, table 3.

the statistics used to cover the postwar years. Changes in the relative position of the other commodity groups may stem partly from the absence of Alaska data and partly from the factors noted above.

The three leading export commodity groups, petroleum and products, logs and lumber, and grain and grain products, together with iron, steel and manufactures and nonmetallic minerals and manufactures, comprised over 70 per cent of noncontiguous exports in every year but 1948.[23] Nonmetallic minerals (largely cement) and iron, steel

―――――――――

[23] In that year, despite a 25 per cent "all other" group, these items totaled 68.8 per cent.

and manufactures were, percentagewise, more important in the non-contiguous than in the foreign trade. This follows primarily from the small output of these items in Alaska and Hawaii and the nearness of

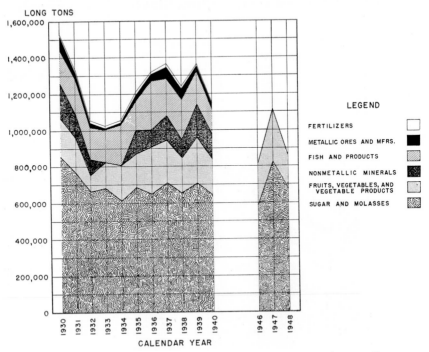

Fig. 8. Pacific Coast imports from Alaska and Hawaii by principal commodity groups, 1930–1940, 1946–1948. Imports for 1946–1948 include Hawaii only. Source: Appendix, table 3.

the Pacific Coast as a source of supply. The less important position of farm products in the noncontiguous as compared with foreign trade probably reflects the small population of Alaska and the relatively abundant supply of these and similar items in the Hawaiian Islands. On the whole, however, Pacific Coast noncontiguous exports fell within the range of the west's important products.

The behavior of the absolute tonnage of noncontiguous export commodity groups is shown in figure 7. Again, the vertical width of each band depicts the tonnage volume of the relevant group. Except for animals, fish, and vegetables, and their products, all categories were adversely affected by the business decline of the early 'thirties. And except for grain and grain products, all categories tended upward during the middle and late years of the decade. Most of the groups

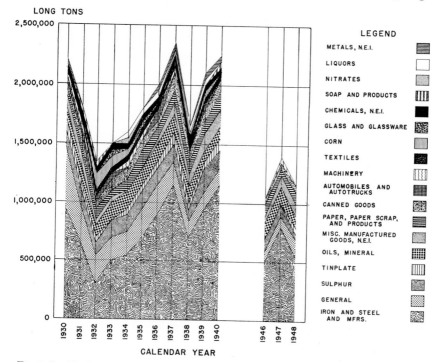

LONG TONS

LEGEND

METALS, N.E.I.

LIQUORS

NITRATES

SOAP AND PRODUCTS

CHEMICALS, N.E.I.

GLASS AND GLASSWARE

CORN

TEXTILES

MACHINERY

AUTOMOBILES AND AUTOTRUCKS

CANNED GOODS

PAPER, PAPER SCRAP, AND PRODUCTS

MISC. MANUFACTURED GOODS, N.E.I.

OILS, MINERAL

TINPLATE

SULPHUR

GENERAL

IRON AND STEEL AND MFRS.

CALENDAR YEAR

Fig. 9. Pacific Coast intercoastal inbound cargo tonnage by principal commodity groups, 1930–1940, 1946–1948. For percentage of total inbound tonnage covered, see figure 11. Source: Appendix, table 4.

declined cyclically in 1938. The exceptions were the food groups and nonmetallic minerals and manufactures.[24]

Postwar, the same commodities dominated the trade. Since our postwar data are largely limited to shipments to Hawaii only as lifted by vessels of the Matson Navigation Company and the prewar figures include cargoes shipped to Alaska as well, we obviously cannot safely infer any long-term (1930–1948) tendencies in tonnage of individual

[24] Fluctuations in the food categories were not unusual since food shipments would not be expected to be as sensitive to business conditions. The nonmetallic minerals increase may be due to the unavoidable difference in the components of this class of exports in 1938 as compared with 1937. See Appendix, table 3.

commodities. However, there appears to have been a substantial rise in exports of iron, steel and manufactures and of fertilizer postwar as compared with prewar. Tonnagewise the other groups appear to have remained nearly the same as prewar or to have dropped. Absence of Alaska statistics may account for this.

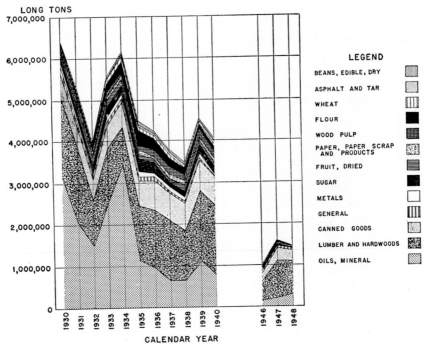

Fig. 10. Pacific Coast intercoastal outbound cargo tonnage by principal commodity groups, 1930–1940, 1946–1948. For percentage of total outbound tonnage covered, see figure 11. Source: Appendix, table 5.

Noncontiguous imports. From 1930 to 1940, over 75 per cent of the Pacific Coast's imports from Alaska and Hawaii consisted of sugar and molasses (mainly the former), fruits, vegetables, and vegetable products (primarily pineapple), and nonmetallic minerals and manufactures (mostly limestone). When fish and products (nearly all salmon) are added, the totals exceed 90 per cent.

As figure 6 indicates, there may have been a slight downward tendency in the import share belonging to sugar and molasses from

1930 to 1940. Fruits, vegetables, and vegetable products maintained a fairly constant share, although there were occasional sharp changes. The percentage of imports attributable to fish and products showed some decline in the late 'thirties while nonmetallic minerals moved in the opposite direction.

Our very limited postwar data permit only the observation that sugar, molasses, and pineapples remained overwhelmingly important in the Pacific Coast's imports from Hawaii.[25] This was probably also true of imports from Alaska and Hawaii combined. We lack data to check this, but a comparison of the postwar (Hawaii only) with the prewar (Hawaii plus Alaska) import commodity shares seems to confirm this contention.

The absolute volume of imports from Alaska and Hawaii is shown in figure 8. Once again the general pattern conformed to the state of business activity—at least from 1930 to 1940. Individual commodity behavior, however, did not conform as closely. The stability of sugar imports probably stemmed from the rigid import and production controls in effect. Fruits, etc. and nonmetallic minerals responded to the growth of the Pacific Coast. The fluctuations in imports of fish and fish products probably reflect variations in the salmon catch. There was some tendency toward decline in the late 'thirties. Postwar, sugar and molasses as well as pineapples were at all-time highs (except for 1930) in 1947. The lower figures for 1946 and 1948 show the effects of waterfront strikes upon shipments of these commodities.

During 1930–1948, noncontiguous (Alaska and Hawaii) traffic as a whole rose from about 2 million long tons in 1932 and 1933 to over 3.5 million tons annually between 1946 and 1948.[26] It consisted primarily of a bilateral exchange of the products of agriculture, mining, and forestry. There was some growth in exports of iron, steel and manufactures. The general character of noncontiguous commerce was very similar to that of foreign trade with the notable exception that the latter included a sizable import volume of metallic ores and manufactures.

---

[25] Matson Navigation Company records (our source of information here) contain only four categories: sugar, molasses, pineapple, and general merchandise. The latter grouping conceals many items of interest.　　　[26] Gorter and Hildebrand, *op. cit.*, Vol. I, p. 31.

● *Intercoastal Trade.*—In 1930, 9.5 million long tons of commodities passed through the Panama Canal in the intercoastal trade of the Pacific Coast. In 1948, this trade totaled approximately 3 million long

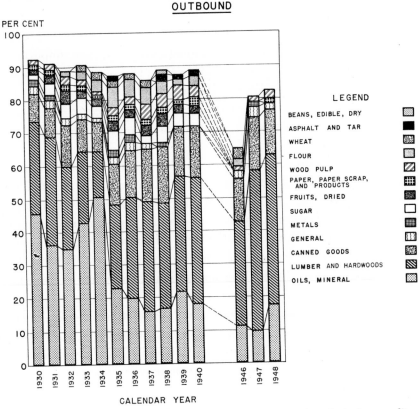

Fig. 11. Distribution of Pacific Coast intercoastal cargo tonnage by principal commodity groups, 1930–1940, 1946–1948. Source: Appendix, tables 4 and 5.

tons.[27] In the late 'thirties, as can be seen in figure 9, inbound (Atlantic to Pacific) cargo tonnage was recovering from depression lows. Following the wartime interruption this traffic revived but did not reach prewar levels during 1946–1948.[28] Outbound (Pacific to Atlantic) traffic tended downward between 1930 and 1940. In the postwar years,

---

[27] Figures used in this section are taken from Appendix, tables 4 and 5.
[28] The average annual prewar inbound tonnage was 2.3 million tons; postwar it was 1.5 million.

outbound cargo tonnage was well below prewar and not far from the position that could have been predicted by extension of a prewar trend line.[29] This is evident from figure 10.

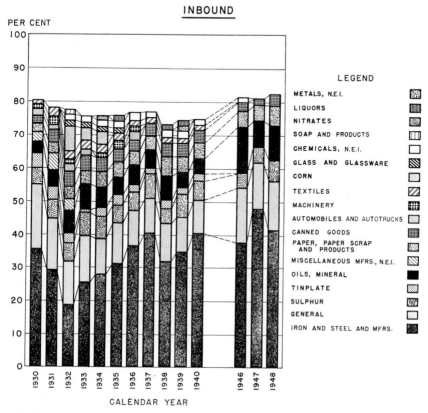

Fig. 11—*Continued*

Pacific Coast intercoastal trade reflected the differences in regional economic development within the United States. Outbound cargoes consisted mainly of food, logs and lumber, and petroleum—the principal items in noncontiguous and foreign export trade. Inbound, the Pacific Coast received metals, chemicals, machinery, and other manu-

[29] Average annual outbound tonnage ran as follows: 1930–1934, 5.9 million; 1935–1939, 4.6 million; and 1946–1948, 1.7 million. From 1930 to 1940, the annual average was 5.1 million long tons.

factures from the highly industrialized eastern seaboard. Unlike foreign and noncontiguous trade, however, there were some almost sensational developments in the commodity structure of intercoastal trade.

Outbound cargoes. The story of outbound intercoastal traffic between 1930 and 1948 revolves almost entirely about three commodity groups—petroleum, lumber, and canned goods.[30] Figures 10 and 11 show clearly that petroleum shipments declined both absolutely and as a percentage of total outbound tonnage. The opposite tendencies appeared in the movements of lumber, although in the postwar years absolute volume was much lower than in the period 1930–1940. Canned goods also displayed some tendency to rise absolutely as well as relatively during the prewar years. In 1946–1948, the share of outbound tonnage accounted for by this category showed little change from the period 1930–1940, but the actual tonnage was far below prewar.

There were sporadic changes in the volume and importance of other outbound commodities but none consistently contributed a sizable portion of the total tonnage. Wheat is an example. Other relatively small tonnage items showed some increase both relatively and absolutely during the 'thirties. Sugar and wood pulp illustrate these. Postwar, however, they shrank in importance along with trade as a whole.

If oil were excluded from the total outbound, how did this trade fare? We noted above that total cargo tonnage tended downward over the entire period 1930–1948. Exclusive of oil, the tendency was only slightly downward, if at all, between 1930 and 1940. The average annual dry-cargo tonnage was nearly 4 million long tons during 1930–1934 and 3.7 million between 1935 and 1939. In 1940, it was 3.6 million tons. However, averages are sometimes deceiving. The figure for 1930–1934 is heavily influenced by a 6.7 million ton entry in 1930 that offsets a very low 2.8 million ton figure for 1932. Yearly tonnage from 1935 to 1939 ranged from 3.3 to 3.9 million. Although

[30] In 1930, they accounted for 82 per cent of the cargo tonnage. They fell as low as 56 per cent in 1946, but by 1948 were back up to 77 per cent. See Appendix, table 5.

outbound dry-cargo tonnage was roughly 10 per cent lower in 1935–1939 than in the preceding five years, it was steadier year to year. Postwar, annual dry-cargo tonnage amounted to less than 50 per cent of prewar—or about 1.5 million tons.

Given this catastrophic fall in postwar tonnage, one can well imagine the consternation felt by operators in this trade. After all, even a simple projection of the declining prewar trend entitled them to expect far more tonnage than they actually obtained.

Inbound cargoes. Even a cursory inspection of figure 11 is sufficient to impress the reader with the growth in relative importance of iron and steel manufactured goods in inbound intercoastal trade. Absolutely, this growth was also impressive, at least from 1930 to 1940, as figure 9 shows. In the postwar years, however, the absolute volume of these items was lower than in the years just before the war, as was the volume of all intercoastal shipping. Little can be said about the other commodity groups because their relative importance was slight.[31] Of some interest, perhaps, was the postwar increase in the importance of petroleum and paper shipments; but here the absolute tonnages were not large.

Inbound intercoastal trade as a whole increased during the 'thirties. From 1930 to 1934, it averaged about 2.1 million long tons per year, rising to 2.5 million tons annually during 1935–1939. In 1940, it was 2.9 million tons. Postwar, it was far below these figures—only 1.4 million tons per year in 1946–1948.

Intercoastal trade in general. Aside from the drastically lower postwar cargo tonnage compared with prewar, two other characteristics of intercoastal trade deserve comment. First, though both inbound and outbound traffic were cyclically sensitive, the former was more so than the latter. This is probably attributable to the preponderance of agricultural commodities in the outbound cargoes and the large volume of manufactured goods included in inbound shipments, since the output of and demand for agricultural food products are generally less sensitive than manufactures are to changes in general business conditions. Second, there is the prewar upward tendency in inbound and down-

---

[31] "General cargo" is a catch-all category, not susceptible to meaningful analysis.

ward tendency in outbound tonnage. This suggests that the industrially developing west needed manufactures from the Atlantic Coast and at the same time required larger amounts of its own output of food and

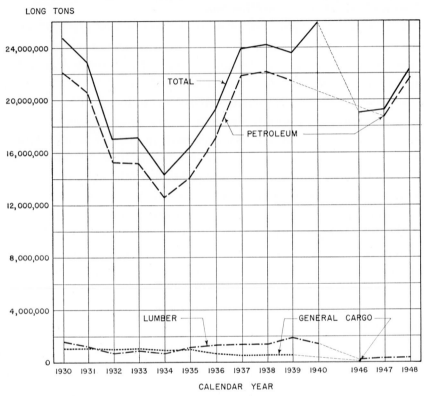

Fig. 12. Pacific Coast coastwise cargo tonnage by principal commodity groups, 1930–1940, 1946–1948. Source: Appendix, table 6.

raw materials to take care of its increasing population and industrial activity.[32]

● *Coastwise Trade.*—In 1930, nearly 25 million long tons of waterborne cargo moved between the ports of the Pacific Coast.[33] By 1934, the volume of coastwise traffic had fallen to about 14 million long tons. Then there followed a period of recovery ending in 1940, when tonnage again almost reached the 25 million ton mark. From 1946 to

[32] This is discussed further in chap. v, on the economic development of the Pacific Coast.

[33] All figures used in this section on coastwise trade, unless otherwise noted, are taken from Gorter and Hildebrand, *op. cit.*, Vol. I, Appendix II, tables 6 and 8, and pp. 24–29.

1948, annual tonnage, according to our estimates, averaged about 20 million long tons.

The tremendous tonnage volume of coastwise shipping is deceptive. About 90 per cent of it was contributed by tanker cargoes—petroleum. Of the remainder, lumber was the most important single item. All the rest can conveniently be classified as general cargo with no individual commodities standing out as worthy of special investigation.[34]

As figure 12 reveals, both lumber and oil movements were severely hit by the business depression of the early 'thirties and both recovered strongly thereafter, dipping slightly only in 1939. The postwar years, however, found oil tonnage only moderately below prewar peaks, while lumber traffic dropped far below the lowest prewar level. General cargo tonnage tended downward between 1930 and 1939, and this tendency appeared to be unbroken in the postwar years.[35]

Prewar, coastwise dry-cargo tonnage was fairly stable, except for the cyclical decline characteristic of all trades in the early 'thirties. This stability was maintained by rising shipments of lumber, which offset declining general cargoes.[36] Common carriers of general cargo

---

[34] Commodity information on coastwise traffic is sketchy. Some is available in *Stenographers' Minutes Before the Interstate Commerce Commission, Docket No. 29721 and 29722: in the Matter of All-Rail Commodity Rates Between California, Oregon, and Washington; Pacific Coastwise Water Rates* (Washington, Alderman Reporting Service, April 28, 1947); and United States Maritime Commission, *Exhibits Before the Interstate Commerce Commission in re Ex Parte 164, Water Competitive Railroad Rates and Practices; Docket No. 29721, All-Rail Commodity Rates Between California, Oregon, and Washington; and Docket No. 29722, Pacific Coastwise Water Rates* (Washington, April 28, 1947), Exhibit 1.

[35] The magnitudes shown in figure 12 are approximations. Available commodity data do not permit accurate, clear-cut derivation of the relevant tonnage figures. For example, we have only two official tonnage figures for petroleum shipments—for 1947 and 1948. The others we derived by subtracting lumber and general-cargo tonnage from the official figures for dry-plus-tanker coastwise tonnage. The lumber tonnages are for shipments from Washington and Oregon to California and do not include intrastate movements for any of the three coastal states or shipments between Oregon and Washington, or shipments from California to Oregon and Washington. General cargo (all commodities other than lumber and bulk oil) is limited to movements in and out of Portland and Seattle on the one hand and to and from California on the other. Shipments within Oregon, Washington, and California, and between Oregon and Washington are not included. Our oil figures for the period 1930–1939, therefore, include some general cargo and lumber tonnage. This means, then, that our lumber and general-cargo figures are somewhat smaller than those actually carried. In spite of these admitted weaknesses in the derived figures, we are quite certain that the general tendencies indicated are correct. Collateral evidence such as the demise of a number of coastwise general-cargo shipping companies supports this view.

[36] Data limitations forced us to confine our analysis to trade between Oregon and Washington on the one hand and California on the other. Intrastate coastwise traffic is excluded.

were therefore being squeezed out while lumber carriers were improving their position a bit. World War II brought a halt to coastwise water traffic and the trade did not recover after the war's end. Thus most of the lumber carriers were also finally driven out with the drastic reduction of this important dry-cargo trade.

● *General Summary.*—The imports and exports of an area tell much about its economic development and its role in the world economy. Both, of course, are vital to shipping. To assess their impact upon maritime shipping requires adequate statistical data covering the quantity of each good shipped into and out of the region in all of the trades *combined.* Unfortunately, our information is inadequate for this purpose. Commodity classifications are not uniform for all the trades. This blocks the possibility of deriving grand total tonnages for shipments of groups of commodities in all the trades taken together.

Nevertheless, the data do permit some useful generalizations. In a broad but sketchy, though convincing, way they reveal the pattern of the economic development of the Pacific Coast. Though this pattern was partly determined by ocean shipping rates, other factors were important. To the extent that they were, the maritime shipping industry had to adapt itself to forces beyond its control.

Products of the farm, forest, and mine dominated all the outbound and coastwise water-borne commerce of the Pacific Coast. This is not surprising. The resources of the region provide it with ample comparative advantage in the output of these types of products.

What may be surprising to some, however, is that shipments of logs and lumber declined in importance relative to other outbound items, except in the intercoastal trade. (*Absolutely* they were far lower postwar than prewar in the intercoastal trade.) A further surprise may be that, except for movements to Alaska and Hawaii, petroleum shipments fell in importance after 1938. The importance of food products relative to other exports changed very little.

If intrastate lumber shipments declined in the late 'thirties, then total coastwise dry-cargo trade (inter- plus intrastate) may have declined. Two observations suggest that this may have occurred. First, after 1934, rail shipments of California redwood increased. Second, officials in the California lumber industry expressed the belief that water-borne shipments declined during this period.

In the purely intraregional coastwise trade, shipments of lumber showed little change in importance between 1937 and 1940, after recovering from the depression low of 1932. Postwar, lumber shipments appear to have been far below prewar both absolutely and relative to total coastwise shipments of all commodities. Our evidence indicates that shipments of petroleum and products increased in relative importance in this trade.

The relative and absolute decline in the importance of lumber in the foreign and noncontiguous trades, and its sharp absolute drop, postwar, in the intercoastal and coastwise trades, suggest at least two possibilities. The first is that the expanding Pacific Coast economy needed increasing amounts of lumber, and the second, that railroads and trucks hauled larger quantities intraregionally. These possibilities are also suggested by the stability of the share of outbound shipments attributable to farm products. For petroleum, only the first one seems to be a valid inference to be drawn from the declining importance of oil shipments in all but the Alaska-Hawaii and coastwise trades. These inferences are verified in chapters v and viii, below.

The small but rapidly growing importance of exports of iron, steel, and metallic manufactures in the foreign and noncontiguous trades is evidence of the industrialization of the Pacific Coast states.

Inbound cargoes were more diverse than outbound. Industrial products—mainly metals, machinery, and chemicals—flowed in from the east coast of the United States. Foods, metallic ores and manufactures, agricultural raw materials, and logs and lumber dominated foreign and noncontiguous imports. There was little change in the relative importance of these groups, except that logs and lumber apparently declined sharply after the war and some food items (coffee and cocoa, for example) increased coincidentally with the rise in population.

Our findings regarding the commodities that comprised the cargoes of the vessels calling at Pacific Coast ports reveal the need for additional investigations to determine, if possible, the causes for the behavior of the tonnage of oil, lumber, farm products, food, and iron, steel and manufactures. It is indeed tempting, at this stage of our study, to proceed immediately to track down the probable causes. To do so, however, would be unwise. Additional background information is required before we can undertake an assessment of the importance of the various factors apparently contributing to the industry's performance. This background consists primarily of a knowledge of the geographic distribution of Pacific Coast foreign trade and the part played by commercial policies in shaping this distribution. We turn next to a consideration of these matters.

CHAPTER III

Changes in the Geographic Pattern of Pacific Coast Foreign Trade

● *Introduction.*—There is no need to stress the importance of geographic factors in determining the course of international trade. Geographic accident binds countries together through trade; and their industries become interdependent, with maritime shipping often providing the most important link joining them together. Shipping prosperity thus depends in a large measure upon the perpetuation and further development of this interdependence.

The "accident of geography," by determining an area's trading partners, exposes each partner, and therefore the shipping industry as well, to the effects of the others' political and economic ambitions. It is therefore appropriate to find out the geographic pattern of Pacific Coast foreign trade and so to disclose the principal trading partners. Variations in total cargo tonnage can then be traced to geographic origin or destination, and investigation made of the relevant tariff, commercial, and other policies and their possible effects upon this commerce.

The essentials of the geographic distribution of Pacific Coast foreign trade cargo tonnage can readily be understood from table 1.[1] It

---

[1] For a more detailed breakdown see Appendix, table 7, and figures 13–15 below.

49

shows that trade with the Pacific basin nations dominated the water-borne foreign commerce of the Pacific Coast, and that after the war the relative importance of trade with the Far and Middle East and of imports from Europe fell. Substantial gains were registered in the percentage of total commerce attributable to trade with Canada and Latin America and to exports to Europe.

TABLE 1

Geographic Distribution of Pacific Coast Water-Borne Foreign Trade Cargo Tonnage, 1930–1939, 1946, and 1947 [a]

Period	Foreign trade region and per cent of Pacific Coast import or export tonnage							
	Latin America		Europe Mediterranean, Black Sea		Australasia, Antarctica, India, Persian Gulf, Red Sea, East Indies, East Asia		Canada	
	Imports	Exports	Imports	Exports	Imports	Exports	Imports	Exports
1930–1934....	17.1	12.9	16.5	20.5	41.2	56.2	25.2	10.1
1935–1939....	23.0	13.1	16.3	16.3	33.8	60.7	26.9	9.5
1930–1939....	20.1	13.0	16.4	18.4	37.5	58.4	26.0	9.8
1946–1947....	30.7	11.7	4.1	26.4	32.6	40.7	32.6	20.0

[a] South, east, and west Africa have been omitted because imports from those areas were negligible and exports never exceeded 3 per cent of total Pacific Coast export tonnage. Only in 1948 was the 3 per cent figure attained. In eleven of the remaining thirteen years for which figures were compiled, less than 1 per cent of Pacific Coast exports went to these regions.

Source: Appendix, table 8.

All of these developments were in some measure produced by World War II and some appear to have been the culmination of factors already at work even before the war. Isolating the effects of these factors calls for a more detailed examination of the evidence. We turn first to exports.

● *Exports.*—Between 1930 and 1940, the outstanding feature of the geographic distribution of Pacific Coast foreign trade exports was the steady growth in the volume and relative importance of the *East Indies and East Asia* segment of this trade.[2] The rise and fall of exports to this area can be quickly grasped from the following figures.

[2] "East Indies" includes Straits Settlements, Thailand, French Indochina, Netherlands East Indies, British Malaya, Burma. "East Asia" primarily includes China, Japan, Asiatic Russia, and the Philippines.

Year	Millions of long tons
1930	4.3
1934	5.0
1939	6.7
1940	5.6
1947	2.1

From 1933 until 1940 this area absorbed over 50 per cent of the export cargo tonnage of the Pacific Coast, reaching 59.6 per cent in 1940. It took only 23 per cent of total export tonnage in 1947—the peak postwar (1946–1948) year.[3]

Next in order of importance in 1930 were exports to the *United Kingdom*. As the data below indicate, exports to the United Kingdom never recovered sufficiently after the world-wide depression to regain their absolute and relative importance as of 1930. The 1938 figure represents a recovery from the depression low of 789,000 long tons in 1934.

Year	Millions of long tons	Per cent of Pacific Coast export tonnage
1930	2.0	18.0
1938	1.2	10.2
1940	0.5	5.6
1947	1.2	13.1[4]

Turning to the Western Hemisphere, we find that exports to the *Caribbean–Mexican–Central American* region were marked by considerable year-to-year fluctuations in tonnage volume. This is evident from figures 13 and 14. The chief characteristics of the export trade with

---

[3] Our figures for 1948 are incomplete and not included in Appendix, table 7. However, total tonnage of exports was greater in 1947 than in either 1946 or 1948; therefore it seems reasonable to assume that 1947 was probably the peak postwar (1946–1948) year for shipments to the Orient. Our figures include commercial cargoes only.

[4] In the first two months of 1948, about 9 per cent of Pacific Coast exports went to the United Kingdom.

Limited funds precluded completion of the laborious, time-consuming task of transcribing, sorting, and checking the information for 1948 taken from the monthly code sheets furnished by the Bureau of the Census. Any inferences drawn from 1948 export tonnage data are therefore presented with extreme reservation. Nevertheless, the distribution of trade in January and February of 1948 as compared with earlier years suggests that the 1948 figures are probably representative of 1948 as a whole.

Source of 1948 figures is the same as for July–December figures for 1947. See source note, Appendix, table 7.

EXPORTS

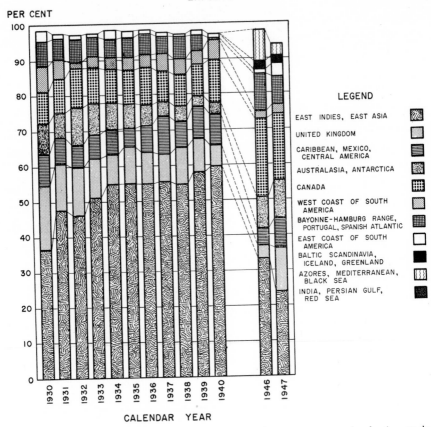

Fig. 13. Distribution of Pacific Coast foreign trade cargo tonnage by foreign trade regions, 1930–1940, 1946–1948. Only imports shown for 1948. See notes to source table. Source: Appendix, table 8.

this area are apparent from the statistics that follow. The tonnage for 1947 was about equal to the average annual tonnage during the last half of the 'thirties.

Year	Millions of long tons	Per cent of Pacific Coast export tonnage
1930	1.1	9.1
1932	0.5	6.3
1937	1.2	10.2
1940	0.8	8.9
1947	0.8	8.5

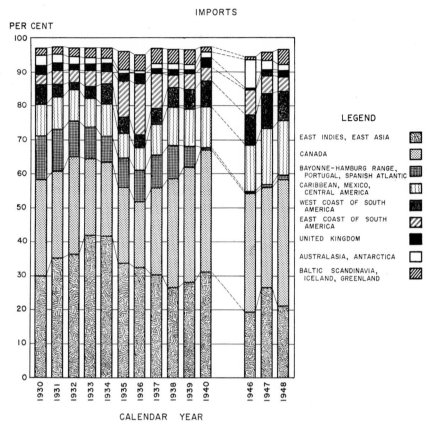

IMPORTS

Fig. 13—*Continued*

South America received nearly 10 per cent of Pacific Coast export tonnage in 1930. The major fluctuations in the relative importance of South America to Pacific Coast exporters can be seen from the figures below.

Year	Per cent of Pacific Coast export tonnage	Per cent to east coast	Per cent to west coast
1930	9.7	2.5	7.2
1932	2.5	0.9	1.6
1940	6.6	1.2	5.4
1947	6.3	3.7	2.6

Though exports to the west coast of South America recovered some after falling from 857,000 long tons in 1930 to 125,000 tons in 1932, they never again equaled the 1930 figure. In 1937, they reached a maximum of about 610,000 tons, and in the last prewar years they

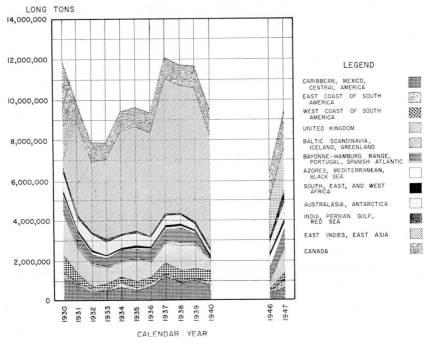

Fig. 14. Pacific Coast foreign trade export cargo tonnage by foreign trade regions, 1930–1940, 1946, and 1947. Source: Appendix, table 7.

hovered around the 500,000 ton mark. In 1947, they amounted only to about 244,000 long tons.

Exports to the east coast of South America seldom exceeded 100,000 tons in the prewar period following 1930. In 1930, they amounted to 293,000 long tons of cargo. After the decline in the early 'thirties, they tended upward slightly, particularly during 1938–1940; but they did not return to the high set in 1930. Postwar, in 1947, exports surpassed the 1930 level. About 342,000 tons of export cargo were sent to the east coast of South America.

Exports to *Canada* showed marked long-term growth. In 1930, she received about 9 per cent of Pacific Coast export tonnage and during the next nine years between 9 and 11 per cent annually. Her share grew to 12.5 per cent in 1940, and in the postwar years, to 20 per cent. Except for the period 1932–1935, prewar exports to Canada were fairly steady at around 1 million tons per year. In 1946, the export cargoes destined for Canadian ports totaled 1.4 million long tons, and in 1947, 1.7 million long tons.

The story of exports to *Australasia and Antarctica* is one of gradual decline in the prewar years. In 1930, exports to this region amounted to a little over 1 million long tons of cargo (9 per cent of Pacific Coast export tonnage). By 1940, they had fallen to a low of about 296,000, or 3.2 per cent of Pacific Coast exports. Postwar, this trade revived. In 1946, about 580,000 tons (9.1 per cent) of exports went to the "down-under" countries, and in 1947 the total was 983,000 tons (10.6 per cent).

Continental Europe, included in what we shall call, for purposes of abbreviation, the "Bayonne-Hamburg range," accounted for about 7 per cent of Pacific Coast export tonnage in 1930.[5] This was the prewar high. This region's share of export tonnage tended downward between 1930 and 1940. In 1940, under the impact of World War II, it was less than 1 per cent—a considerable drop from its 1930–1939 annual average of about 6 per cent. It was well above this figure in 1946 and 1947, averaging about 9.4 per cent in those years. The following figures outline the outstanding features of the volume of exports sent to this range.

Year	Thousands of long tons
1930	862
1932	522
1938	775
1940	64
1946	661
1947	775

● *Imports.*—In 1930, 86.2 per cent of the import tonnage of the Pacific Coast originated in five of the eleven foreign trade regions

[5] This range includes the ports lying along the Atlantic Ocean or North Sea in Spain, Portugal, France, Belgium, the Netherlands, and Germany. See Appendix, table 7.

shown in figures 13 and 15.[6] About 58 per cent came in from two regions alone—East Indies and East Asia, and Canada. We therefore shall confine our analysis to the five leading import foreign trade regions.

During the prewar years the volume of imports from *East Indies and East Asia* underwent two violent drops followed by sharp up-swings. As a result, there was no clearly evident tendency up or down during these years. The high and low points of the major upswings and downswings in this period were the following.

Year	Thousands of long tons
1930	869
1932	626
1936	967
1938	597
1940	802

Postwar (1946–1948), import tonnage from this foreign trade region reached a peak of 543,000 tons in 1947. The prewar share of Pacific Coast import tonnage attributable to East Indies and East Asia was usually between 30 and 35 per cent, except for 1933–1934, when it rose to 42.2 per cent, and in 1938 and 1939, when it fell to about 27 per cent. Postwar, it furnished roughly a quarter of the import tonnage.

Canada also loomed large in the import picture of the Pacific Coast. Unlike the behavior of the volume of import tonnage from East Indies and East Asia, the volume of imports from Canada showed a sharp, though occasionally interrupted, upward tendency after 1932. In fact, in 1938–1940, Canada supplanted the Orient as the leading exporter to the west coast of the United States. And it retained this position in the postwar years. The behavior of import volume from Canada can be stated briefly. Tonnage fell from 815,000 long tons in 1930 to 409,000 tons in 1933. It then rose in every year, except for declines in 1936 and 1938, to 928,000 tons in 1940. Postwar, it began at 519,000 tons in 1946 and rose to 929,000 tons in 1948. The story of

---

[6] They were East Indies and East Asia (30 per cent), Canada (28.1 per cent), Bayonne-Hamburg range (13.2 per cent), Caribbean, Central America, and Mexico (9.1 per cent), and west coast of South America (5.8 per cent). No other foreign trade region contributed more than 3 per cent to Pacific Coast import cargo tonnage. See Appendix, table 8.

Canada's share of imports by the Pacific Coast may also be put briefly. It tended downward from 1930 to 1936, falling from 28.1 per cent to 19.6 per cent. It then rose each year until it was 36 per cent in 1940. In 1948, it was 37 per cent. Clearly, between 1930 and 1948, Canada

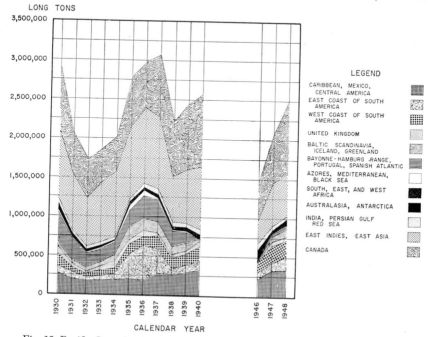

Fig. 15. Pacific Coast foreign trade import cargo tonnage by foreign trade regions, 1930–1940, 1946–1948. Source: Appendix, table 7.

had increased both its relative and absolute status as an exporter to the Pacific Coast.

Imports from the *Bayonne-Hamburg* range ranked third in importance in 1930. Slightly more than 13 per cent (approximately 385,000 tons) of the Pacific Coast's import tonnage originated there. Imports from this part of continental Europe tended downward, both absolutely and relatively, between 1930 and 1948. In 1934, tonnage had fallen to 157,000 long tons and the share attributable to this range to 7.8 per cent. Both then rose, reaching a maximum of 286,000 tons and 9.3 per cent in 1937. A decline followed; and in 1940 the tonnage was about 8,000 tons and the share 0.3 per cent. Despite the rise in the middle 'thirties, the over-all tendency was downward, since the 1930 peak was never exceeded. Postwar, this trade accounted for less than 1 per cent of Pacific Coast imports in 1946 and 1947 and only 1.5 per cent in 1948.

The *Caribbean countries, Central America, and Mexico* sent about 265,000 long tons of goods (9.1 per cent of total imports) to the Pacific Coast in 1930. After a fall of over 100,000 tons between 1930 and 1932, imports from this area tended upward, rising to 318,000 tons (12.3 per cent of total imports) in 1940. In 1946–1948, the Pacific Coast increased its imports from these neighboring nations from 205,000 tons in 1946 to 388,000 tons in 1948. During those three years 15.2 per cent of Pacific Coast import tonnage moved in this trade.

The general tendencies in the absolute and relative volume of imports from the west coast of *South America* were similar to those in imports from the Caribbean, Central America, and Mexico, as the following figures indicate.[7]

Year	Thousands of long tons	Per cent of Pacific Coast import tonnage
1930	168	5.8
1932	38	2.2
1940	191	7.4
1946	130	8.8
1947–1948 (average)	215	9.5

● *Summary.*—What were the outstanding characteristics of the geographic distribution of Pacific Coast foreign trade as revealed by our analysis? Prewar, exports to the East Indies and East Asia region far overshadowed shipments to any other area. Further, there was definitely an upward tendency in the annual volume of cargo tonnage destined for these Oriental countries both absolutely and relative to total Pacific Coast exports. In 1930, 4.3 million tons of cargo went to this foreign trade region, and in 1940, 5.6 million tons. The share of

---

[7] Though there was an upward tendency during the late 'thirties, only in 1938 and 1940 did the percentage exceed the 1930 figure. From 1930 to 1936 the volume of import trade with the west coast of South America exceeded 5 per cent of Pacific Coast import tonnage in only two years—1930 and 1934. See Appendix, table 8.

total exports unloaded in these Oriental ports amounted to 36.2 per cent in 1930 and 59.6 per cent in 1940. Postwar (1946–1948), our figures indicate that the maximum cargo tonnage was shipped in 1947. It was less than half the 1940 total and accounted for only 23.1 per cent of the Pacific Coast's export tonnage.[8] Postwar reëstablishment of trade relations had not, at least by 1947, brought about a restoration of this trade to prewar levels.

With the exception of exports to Canada, which exceeded the 1930 level as early as 1937 and showed a distinct upturn in 1940 over 1939, prewar exports to other areas during 1930–1940 either displayed no up or down tendency or tended downward.[9]

Postwar, annual exports to Canada were well above prewar; both 1946 (1.4 million long tons) and 1947 (1.7 million tons) exceeded the prewar high (1.2 million tons in 1940). In addition, Canada's share of Pacific Coast exports rose to 20 per cent as compared with a prewar peak of 12.5 per cent in 1940. Exports to the United Kingdom and the Bayonne-Hamburg range were higher in 1947 than in most of the prewar years. There was a revival of exports to Australasia and Antarctica. The behavior of export volume to Latin America varied: in 1947 the Caribbean, Mexico, and Central America region took about the same as during the late 'thirties, while the east coast of South America took more in 1947 than in any other year.

The net effect of these opposing changes in postwar export tonnage as compared with prewar was insufficient to offset the tremendous decline in shipments to East Indies and East Asia. In 1947, total Pacific Coast export tonnage was 2.7 million lower than in 1930. Exports to East Asia and East Indies were 2.2 million tons lower.[10] The loss of this tonnage, then, seems to have been primarily responsible for the sharp difference between postwar and prewar export tonnage.

Pacific Coast imports originated mainly in five foreign trade re-

---

[8] Only commercial cargoes are included. Obviously, military and relief shipments increased the total tonnage going to the Orient. These should not, however, be included in the postwar-prewar comparison.

[9] This refers only to exports to foreign trade regions included in our textual discussion. This excludes four areas accounting for a total of 2 per cent of Pacific Coast export cargo tonnage in 1930.

[10] See Appendix, tables 1 and 7.

gions: East Indies and East Asia; Canada; Bayonne-Hamburg range; the Caribbean, Mexico, and Central America; and west coast of South America. These regions furnished 86.2 per cent of the imports in 1930.[11] No other foreign trade area provided more than 3 per cent.

Until 1938, East Indies and East Asia provided the greatest share of Pacific Coast import tonnage (35.2 per cent or 838,400 long tons annually). There were four wide fluctuations in the volume of import tonnage from this area in the prewar years but no marked up or down tendency appeared from 1930 to 1940, though from 1937 to 1940 tonnage tended downward a bit. Postwar imports from the Orient were well below prewar (455,300 tons annually or roughly 25 per cent of Pacific Coast imports). The figures for 1948 indicate some revival in this trade.

In contrast to East Indies and East Asia, prewar imports from Canada tended sharply upward after 1933 and surpassed those from the former region in 1938. In the postwar years, Canada retained its leading position, and in 1948 its exports to the Pacific Coast barely exceeded the prewar high. Its share of Pacific Coast imports fell from 28.1 per cent in 1930 to 19.6 per cent in 1936 and then recovered to pass the 30 per cent mark in 1938. Postwar it continued above this figure, averaging 34.1 per cent for 1946–1948. There can be no doubt of Canada's growing importance to the economy of the Pacific Coast.

Imports from two other Western Hemisphere areas also tended upward in the 'thirties. Our postwar data indicate that imports from the Caribbean, Mexico, and Central America and west coast South America regions resumed their war-interrupted climb. Imports from these areas in 1948 exceeded the prewar highs set in 1940 (600,500 tons *vs.* 508,900 tons or 24.2 per cent of Pacific Coast imports *vs.* 19.7 per cent).

Bayonne-Hamburg range exports to the Pacific Coast displayed an over-all declining tendency from 1930 to 1940, although there was some recovery from 1934 to 1937. Postwar, Pacific Coast imports from this part of western continental Europe totaled less than 1 per

[11] In 1948, these areas furnished 84.1 per cent of the import tonnage.

cent of all imports—quite a change for a region that produced 13.2 per cent of the imports entering Pacific Coast harbors in 1930.

For the most part, imports from the remaining areas showed no distinct rising or falling tendencies throughout the 1930–1940 period. Imports from two of these regions, however, showed substantial increases in the mid-'thirties. They were the east coast of South America and the Baltic-Scandinavia-Iceland-Greenland range. In the former, imports jumped from less than 100,000 tons annually to over 300,000 tons in 1935–1937 and then settled near the 100,000 ton mark. In the latter, the rise during these years was from about 56,000 tons annually to roughly 150,000 tons.[12] Postwar, imports from all these remaining areas together were nearly the same as in the early 'thirties.

This completes our analysis of the total tonnage statistics presented in Volume I and, briefly, in this volume. We have exposed some of the superficial "causes" of the fluctuations and decline in Pacific Coast water-borne commerce between 1930 and 1948 by showing how the total figures were affected by changes in the magnitudes of their commodity components and by changes in the volume of cargo tonnage originating in and destined for the principal foreign trade regions. We shall now proceed to utilize the clues provided by our detailed study of cargo tonnage to determine, if possible, the influence of certain factors upon the performance of the Pacific Coast maritime shipping industry. We shall first consider certain aspects of the relationships between international politics and national commercial policies, on the one hand, and Pacific Coast shipping, on the other.

---

[12] For an explanation of these phenomena, see below, pp. 69–71.

CHAPTER IV

Politics and
Commercial Policies

⌐⌐⌐⌐⌐⌐|⌐⌐⌐⌐⌐⌐⌐⌐⌐⌐⌐⌐⌐⌐

● *Introduction.*—Every country regulates its
foreign trade. Regulations, stringent or lax,
limited or extensive, are imposed to further what each nation conceives
to be its national interest. Pacific Coast maritime shipping has both
suffered and benefited as a result of these regulations.

During the prewar years, many nations adopted commercial policies designed to help combat the local effects of the world-wide business depression. Some of these policies hurt maritime shipping while
others helped it. Most observers agree that the United States Tariff Act
of 1930 (Hawley-Smoot) properly belongs among those that hurt,[1]
whereas the Reciprocal Trade Agreements Program (1934) should
be included in the group that helped. The currency devaluations of the
'thirties often provided a temporary stimulus to exports from each of
the devaluating countries, while at the same time checking the flow of
imports. However, the over-all effect of all the devaluations, including
the devaluation of the United States dollar in 1933, was probably a
contraction of international trade and therefore detrimental to maritime shipping. Later, after the outbreak of World War II but before

[1] Other examples abound: for instance, the British Imperial Preference System adopted
in Ottawa in 1932 and the Australian tariff of 1931.

62

December, 1941, the policies adopted in the economic warfare affected operations in the shipping industry.

World War II required a huge expansion of the entire United States shipping industry. As a result the industry was favored by the policy-makers. On the Pacific Coast, shoreside facilities were sorely taxed as the large peacetime excess plant and equipment were put to work to aid in the conflict with the Axis powers.

After the war, some commercial policies were beneficial to shipping and others not. On the one hand, the generous aid and relief programs of the United States and the tariff reductions made under the General Agreement on Tariffs and Trade stimulated shipping. On the other hand, the so-called "dollar shortage," the almost universal adoption of export and import quantitative restrictions, and the growth in the number of Soviet satellites contributed to increased state intervention in foreign trade. This was detrimental to shipping.[2]

Unfortunately, it is impossible to establish clearly the precise effects of the removal or imposition of most trade barriers. There are too many other factors at work simultaneously. Thus, though there can be no doubt that a tariff restricts trade, the amount of restriction attributable to the tariff alone cannot be determined. In the early 'thirties, for example, the depression reduced the volume of foreign trade. Tariff rates were increased. How much of the reduction of trade was due to the tariff increase? There is no way to find out. Similarly, during the upswing that followed, the United States and other countries reduced tariffs. Foreign trade increased. Again, it is not possible to determine the amount of the increase resulting from the tariff reductions.[3]

In spite of our inability to measure the effects of trade policies, political decisions, and other factors upon the volume of cargo ton-

---

[2] The Korean conflict occurred after the period covered by our study. Here, a political decision proved profitable to the shipping industry.

[3] Admittedly, inconclusive attempts have been made to determine the effects of the United States Reciprocal Trade Agreements Program. See William Diebold, Jr., *New Directions in Our Trade Policy* (New York, Council on Foreign Relations, 1941) ; J. M. Letiche, *Reciprocal Trade Agreements in the World Economy* (New York, King's Crown Press, 1948) ; and United States Tariff Commission, "Operation of the Trade Agreements Program, June 1934 to April 1948," *Report No. 160*, Second Series, Part V (Washington, Government Printing Office, 1949).

nage, we believe that it is worth while to point out possible connections between certain general developments in commercial policies and international politics, on the one hand, and major fluctuations in the volume of cargo tonnage moving between the Pacific Coast and certain foreign trade regions, on the other. To those tempted to forecast the future of Pacific Coast shipping, this will provide additional data for their speculations. We shall confine ourselves here to an attempt to explain the past.[4]

● *1930–1940.*—We noted earlier that Pacific Coast exports to the East Indies and East Asia region tended markedly upward from 1930 to 1940. In addition, their volume was far greater than that going to any other foreign trade region. What did United States tariff policy contribute to the rise in exports? Probably very little.

To begin with, the first trade agreements with countries in this area did not become effective until 1936. These covered only trade with the Netherlands East Indies and French colonies, dependencies, and protectorates. The United Kingdom and the United States signed an agreement in 1938, effective in 1939, including trade with the British Colonial Empire. China and Japan concluded no trade agreements with the United States.

Briefly sketched, the prewar tariff histories of Japan and China were as follows.[5] In Japan, some duties were lowered in 1929 only to

---

[4] Before proceeding further, another limitation of our analysis must be mentioned. We have not shown the volume of cargo tonnage by commodity for trade with each foreign trade region. The reason for this is simple. For the period 1930–1937, this information appeared in a United States Maritime Commission report (*Report No. 42*) on a fiscal year basis by foreign and domestic ports by principal commodities handled in each port. For 1938–1940, the Maritime Commission segregated commodity imports and exports by United States and foreign trade regions (*Report No. 2610*). For 1946, the information can be obtained from the Bureau of the Census' *Foreign Commerce and Navigation of the United States.* For 1947 and 1948, it is available on a United States port, foreign country basis in the unpublished machine record tabulations of the Bureau of the Census. Aside from the problems involved in attempting to match fiscal and calendar year statistical series in the prewar years, our limited financial resources precluded our consolidating the foreign and domestic port statistics into foreign trade region and Pacific Coast region totals. Since our primary interest is in the *changes* in the volume of tonnage of commodities shipped to and from certain foreign trade regions, the periods for which these data are available by foreign trade region are not extensive enough to warrant compilation and analysis of the data.

[5] Unless otherwise noted, references to the trade policies of foreign countries have been drawn from Asher Isaacs, *International Trade, Tariff and Commercial Policies* (Chicago, R. D. Irwin, 1948). Professor Isaacs has done yeoman work and provided students of international commercial policies with an invaluable collection of the facts and source refer-

be followed by increases in 1932. By 1934, exchange control and other restrictive devices were employed to reduce imports. Their war with China, which began in 1937, imposed further restrictions. In China, tariffs were increased in 1933 and 1934.

In our commodity analysis of Pacific Coast foreign trade exports we found that the over-all rising tendency in exports after 1932 apparently resulted from the increase in petroleum and products shipments that more than offset the marked decline in lumber exports. There was also a steady increase in exports of metals and manufactures.

The foregoing array of facts suggests that the 1930–1940 expansion of exports to the Orient resulted largely from two developments: first, the Sino-Japanese war, and, second, in a minor way, the Reciprocal Trade Agreements Program. The first development called for increased shipments of oil, machinery, and scrap metal. Despite higher tariffs and increased restrictions on foreign trade, the importation (by China and Japan) of these items probably grew. The second development probably helped to stimulate exports from the Pacific Coast of the United States to the Asiatic sections of the British, French, and Dutch empires.[6]

Exports to Canada, the fifth largest (tonnagewise) foreign market for Pacific Coast exports in 1930, were subject to four negotiations under the Reciprocal Trade Agreements Program. The effective dates of the agreements were January 1, 1936, January 1, 1939, January 1 and December 20, 1940. Exports to Canada increased about 100,000 long tons over the previous year in each of the years an agreement

---

ences. Further, he has furnished many interesting and provocative insights into the relationship between politics, economics, and commercial policy.

[6] The effect of the Reciprocal Trade Agreements Program upon trade with the British Colonial Empire could hardly have been very great in the prewar years, because the agreement became effective in 1939. As to the effect of the 1936 trade agreements with the French and Dutch possessions in this area, little can be inferred from the dollar volume figures for United States exports to these countries. These show an increase over 1935. The total cargo tonnage of exports to East Indies and East Asia from the Pacific Coast was lower in 1936 than in 1935. In 1937, both the aforementioned tonnage and the dollar volume of exports to Netherland and French possessions rose sharply. This resulted primarily from the business recovery of 1937. (For the dollar volume figures referred to in this chapter, see United States Tariff Commission, "Operation of the Trade Agreements Program, June 1934 to April 1948," *op. cit.*, pp. 9–36.)

became effective. In 1934, however, Canadian exports were also up about 100,000 tons over the 1933 figure, and yet the United States and Canada had no trade agreement in 1934. Again, it is difficult to assess the effect of United States commercial policy upon this trade. There were marked rises in the value of exports to Canada from the United States as a whole following each agreement. But in one "non-agreement" year (1934), there was a larger increase than in the "agreement" year of 1936. In other years (1939, 1940, 1941), there were very substantial increases. Here, however, export-value figures were probably influenced by exports of war supplies to England via Canada. Thus the rise in exports from 1934 to 1940 seems to have resulted from the growth of Canada as a market for Pacific Coast products, from the Reciprocal Trade Agreements Program that provided for a removal of some restrictions, and, in the later years, from the preparedness and war programs of the allied powers.

Between 1934 and 1939, the United States concluded reciprocal trade agreements with seven nations in the Caribbean, Mexico, and Central America foreign trade region.[7] The volume of cargo tonnage moving from the Pacific Coast to this region tended upward after 1932. Except for a sharp rise from 1936 to 1937—a rise consistent with the general marked upswing in total Pacific Coast exports—the annual changes in cargo tonnage do not suggest that the trade agreements produced a pronounced or evident effect. Again, the conclusion is that the general recovery in business activity from 1933 to 1937 played the decisive role in the increase in export tonnage shipped to this area.[8]

Turning to commercial policy relations with Europe, we find that not until January 1, 1939, did a trade agreement become effective between the United States and the United Kingdom. By then, war was imminent and the subsequent fall in export tonnage bound for the United Kingdom from the Pacific Coast was primarily attributable to

[7] Cuba, Haiti, Honduras, Guatemala, Nicaragua, El Salvador, and Costa Rica.

[8] For example, exports from the United States to Cuba rose from $24.8 million in 1933 to $44.8 million in 1934 (the agreement became effective on September 3, 1934). Perhaps the agreement did encourage part of this increase. In 1938, however, exports to Cuba were down to $75.7 million as compared with $90.8 million in 1937. Here a large change occurred primarily because of the 1937–1938 business recession. This suggests that the 1933 to 1934 increase might also have resulted primarily from a change in general business activity. (For source see above, p. 65, n. 6.)

the stepped-up war preparedness program that diverted vessels from the Pacific Coast to the faster turn-around Atlantic runs. In common with exports to other regions, there had been a slow recovery during the middle and late 'thirties, but it had failed to restore annual export volume to the peak reached in 1930. The imperial preference tariff system may well have contributed to this result, for it was intended to discriminate against exports from the United States.

Exports to continental Europe,[9] averaging 579,000 long tons per year from 1932 to 1936, varied little from year to year and showed no up or down tendency. We may therefore infer that the trade agreements with Belgium, Sweden, Netherlands, Switzerland, Finland, and France—which became effective during this period—had little effect upon Pacific Coast shipments to this region. The tariffs, exchange controls, and bilateral trading arrangements of other European countries all helped to prevent a rise in exports during these years. There was, however, a marked rise in exports in 1937 and 1938.[10] Then they fell off sharply. In 1940, they were down to 108,000 tons. War and its preparation no doubt were principally responsible for the decline.

How were imports affected by national commercial policies? Here several generalizations must be kept in mind. The volume of imports is closely related to the level of income of the importing region. An increase in income usually leads to an increase in imports, although the proportion of income spent upon imports may not remain the same. United States import volume is very sensitive to changes in domestic business activity.[11] This comes about primarily in two ways. First, the

[9] Continental Europe here refers to the countries included in the Baltic, Scandinavia, Iceland, and Greenland region and the Bayonne-Hamburg range including Portugal and Atlantic Spain. See Appendix, table 7.

[10] One other European country—Czechoslovakia—concluded a reciprocal trade agreement with the United States in 1938. Its effective date was April 16, 1938. This agreement alone could hardly have been responsible for the rise in exports. Once again, general business conditions appear to have been the controlling factor.

[11] In a study covering the period 1922–1937, J. H. Adler found that for the United States the average income elasticity of imports was .97. This means that "... within the range of observed real income, a 10 per cent increase in real income resulted in a 9.7 per cent increase in real imports." (J. H. Adler, "United States import demand during the interwar period," *American Economic Review* [June, 1945], p. 421). Kindleberger states that there is general agreement that the income elasticity of the United States demand for imports is very near 1. See C. P. Kindleberger, *The Dollar Shortage* (Boston and New York, The Technology Press and Wiley, 1950), pp. 39–41.

rise or fall in domestic incomes leads to a rise or fall in the volume of imports because there is more or less income available for purchases of all kinds. Second, a fall in income and employment brings with it a clamor for protection from the competition of foreign sellers. Legislators have not been insensitive to this demand. The Hawley-Smoot tariff of 1930 and the dollar devaluation of 1933 are examples of the results of these demands. Each gave further impetus to the tendency toward reduced imports, as induced by the fall in national income, by raising the price of imports. A rise in income, however, increases the willingness of domestic producers to permit foreign competition, as indicated by the adoption of the Reciprocal Trade Agreements Program in 1934. It helped to reduce the prices of imports and strengthened their tendency to increase as national income rose. Politics thus reinforces the underlying economic tendencies.

The sharp drop in imports from the East Indies and East Asia region during the early 'thirties resulted from a combination of industrial depression in the United States and the high tariff of 1930.[12] The marked rise from 1933 to 1937 mainly reflected the business recovery in the United States. As noted earlier, reciprocal trade agreements were limited to trade with the French and Dutch possessions in this area, so their effect was probably small. In 1937–1938, the recession in the United States reduced imports from the Orient. In 1939 and 1940, imports rose sharply once again. This time the stockpiling of strategic raw materials, as part of the preparedness program, and the expansion of business activity provided the stimuli. About all that can be said concerning the influence of United States commercial policy, therefore, is that from 1934 onward it strengthened the basic tendency of imports to expand.

Imports from Canada display the familiar decline in volume during the early 'thirties—a decline precipitated by a combination of depres-

---

[12] Adler notes that duty-free imports into the United States retained their relationship to income after 1930 with no downward shift. From this he infers that the restrictive effects of the 1930 tariff were more pronounced than was generally conceded. (Adler, *op. cit.*, pp. 419–420.) Hal B. Lary and Associates reached a similar conclusion. See United States Department of Commerce, Bureau of Foreign and Domestic Commerce, *The United States in the World Economy*, by Hal B. Lary and Associates, Economic Series, no. 23 (Washington, Government Printing Office, 1943), pp. 53–54.

sion and higher tariff rates and dollar devaluation.[13] From 1934 to 1940, they clearly show the effects of economic recovery in the United States. The pronounced upswing in import tonnage also indicates the growing dependence of Pacific Coast industries upon Canadian raw materials (pulpwood to supply the rapidly expanding paper and paper products manufacturers, for example).

What were the effects of the reciprocal trade agreements signed with Canada? The swift rise in import tonnage suggests that the agreements were important. Nevertheless, in 1940, import tonnage was only about 120,000 long tons greater than in 1930. There is no way to determine whether the recovery in the import trade would have been as great without the reciprocal trade agreements. The presumption is that it would not have been.

Between 1934 and 1939, twelve Latin American and Caribbean nations signed reciprocal trade agreements with the United States. Eleven went into effect before 1941.[14] These agreements partly account for the rising tendency in import cargo tonnage from each of the three Latin American foreign trade regions—east coast of South America, west coast of South America, and the Caribbean, Mexico, and Central America—from 1938 to 1940.[15] The imports consisted primarily of

[13] Although the effects of the tariff of 1930 cannot be measured accurately, the approximate 50 per cent decrease in import cargo tonnage originating in Canada in 1933 as compared with 1930 suggests that something more than a depression was at work. The gross national product of the United States (in constant 1939 dollars) was down about 21 per cent from 1930. A more than two to one ratio for the fall in tonnage to the fall in gross national product is substantial. Further light on this matter comes from statistics covering Unied States imports of softwood lumber from Canada. These show that in 1929 the United States imported 1,353,000,000 board feet of lumber; in 1930, 1,062,000,000 board feet; in 1931, 675,000,000 board feet. In 1932, when additional restrictions were imposed, imports totaled only 316,000,000 board feet. (Import statistics obtained from United States Bureau of Foreign and Domestic Commerce as cited by I. M. Elchibegoff, *United States International Timber Trade in the Pacific Area*, p. 214.)

[14] Argentina concluded an agreement on October 14, 1939, which became effective on November 15, 1941.

[15] A comparison of the annual volume of import tonnage from the Caribbean–Mexican–Central American region, on the one hand, with the west coast of South America region, on the other, reveals strikingly similar patterns. There was a drop from 1930 to 1932 and then a fairly steady rise to a bit above the 1930 peak, in 1940.

Imports from the east coast of South America fell much less from 1930 to 1932. In 1934, they were still down near the low volume of 1932. In 1935, they shot up from 69,000 long tons in 1934 to 308,000 tons. In 1936, they were up again, this time to 437,000 long tons. They then fell, in 1937, to 326,000 tons before getting back to a more "normal" figure of about 80,000 tons in 1938.

This tremendous rise in imports during the middle 'thirties appears to have been largely

foods and industrial raw materials. They reflected the demand for food by the increasingly populous Pacific Coast and its growing need for raw materials for manufacturing purposes. The Good Neighbor Policy as it found expression in the Reciprocal Trade Agreements Program no doubt contributed to making these demands effective.

Imports from Europe and the Mediterranean generally went through three phases: the fall in the early 'thirties, the rise until 1936 or 1937, and the subsequent fall until 1940. Between 1935 and 1939, eight trade agreements became effective with countries in these foreign trade regions. The agreements were designed to overcome the harmful effects of the retaliatory trade policies adopted by European nations in response to the unfortunate United States high tariff of 1930 and to counteract the restrictive effects of United States dollar devaluation upon imports. Unfortunately for the analyst, the impact of the reciprocal trade agreements upon imports from the European and the Mediterranean countries was obscured by the economic recovery in the United States and the outbreak of hostilities in Europe in September, 1939.[16]

---

attributable to a very great increase in tonnage originating in Argentina. Dollar volume of imports by the United States as a whole rose from $29.4 million in 1934 to $63.8 million in 1935. In 1936 they amounted to $65.3 million, whereas in 1937 they reached $136.3 million. In 1938, they dropped down to $41.7 million. Although the increases were spread over a large number of commodities, they were very large in the following: canned beef, cattle hides, corn, flaxseed, and carpet wool. The value of corn imported increased by more than $14 million in 1935 over 1934; and by over $38 million in 1937 over 1936. The value of flaxseed imports increased from $8.2 million in 1934 to $14 million in 1935. In 1937, it was $34.1 million as compared with $14.3 million in 1936. Carpet wool imports rose swiftly, going from $2.3 million in 1934 to $11 million in 1937. Canned beef (the 1934 figure is for canned meat—canned beef not shown separately) increased from $1.2 million in 1934 to $2.4 million in 1935 and stood at $4.5 million in 1937. The value of cattle hides went up from $2.8 million in 1934 to $6.1 million in 1935, and by 1937 amounted to $8.4 million. The drought in the United States undoubtedly played a substantial part in bringing about these sizable increases in imports. (For a confirmation of this view, see United States Tariff Commission, "The foreign trade of Latin America," *Report No. 146*, Second Series, Part II, Vol. I [Washington, Government Printing Office, 1942], pp. 32–33.)

It should be noted that there was also a substantial increase in imports of combing wool from Uruguay. They rose from $500,000 in 1935 to $4.7 million and $5.9 million in 1936 and 1937, respectively. In 1938, they were back to $500,000 again.

Note: The source for the dollar volume statistics is United States Department of Commerce, Bureau of Foreign and Domestic Commerce, *Foreign Commerce and Navigation of the United States* (Washington, Government Printing Office, 1935, 1938, 1940), pp. 354–355 (Vol. I, 1934) ; pp. 415–416, 419 (Vol. I, 1936) ; pp. 398, 402 (1938).

[16] We noted earlier that imports from the Baltic-Scandinavia-Iceland-Greenland range moved up sharply in 1935. (See above, p. 61.) Unfortunately, we can throw little light on

● *1946–1948.*—Pacific Coast exports in 1946–1948 were far below prewar, primarily because of the drastic decline in shipments to the East Indies and East Asia region. In 1940, these amounted to about 5.6 million long tons as compared with 2.1 million tons in 1947—a "good" year for Pacific Coast shipping. Exports to other areas were near 1940 levels. These figures, however, do not include military cargoes. The addition of these shipments increases the total markedly.[17] Even so, the essential fact remains that ordinary commercial tonnage fell off sharply postwar as compared with prewar.

National commercial, diplomatic, and military policies favored shipping. In fact, the maintenance of the volume of exports (all kinds—military and civilian) above the lowest prewar level was attributable to the political necessity for the shipment of food and supplies to war-torn countries and former enemy powers. This meant substantial movements of cargo to the Orient under the sponsorship of the army and certain civilian relief organizations. It also meant some shipments to European countries, but there the need was so urgent that the eastern United States ports—far closer to Europe—were favored.[18]

As noted earlier, the total annual volume of imports was not far below the prewar average. Imports from the East Indies and East Asia region were well below their prewar peaks. This depressive effect upon total tonnage was to a large extent offset by the recovery of the import trade with the Latin American and Caribbean countries and the small increase in imports from Canada. Imports from Europe were low because of the low productivity there and the inability to spare ships

this phenomenon. Trade agreements certainly did not account for the rise. Agreements were signed with only two of the fifteen nations included in this region—Sweden (effective August 5, 1935) and Finland (effective November 2, 1936).

The dollar volume of United States imports from this area increased about 15 per cent over 1934, and almost every nation in the region participated in the rise. This suggests that improved economic conditions accounted for the rise in imports by the Pacific Coast. This inference is strengthened by the fact that in 1938–1939 average annual Pacific Coast imports from this region totaled 103,000 long tons as compared with a 56,000 ton average for 1930–1934. Thus, in spite of the drop from the 1935–1937 average of 153,000 tons, imports from this area showed considerable improvement.

Note: Percentage increase in dollar volume of imports computed from *Foreign Commerce and Navigation of the United States*, Vol. I (1934, 1936), table 3.

[17] See above, pp. 25–26.

[18] As we showed in Volume I, the Pacific Coast's share of total United States export tonnage of commercial cargoes was far below prewar. See Vol. I, Appendix II, table 2.

from the transatlantic run where, because of the shorter turn-around time, their annual carrying capacity was far greater.

During the years 1946–1948, there were several important developments affecting maritime shipping—some beneficial to the industry and others not. The world eagerly sought the products of the United States. War-deferred demand was so great that the United States imposed restrictions upon exports. Even so, the industry prospered. Much of the demand came from the United States government through its armies of occupation and civilian relief and reconstruction agencies. This was favorable to shipping. The rest of the demand stemmed from foreign governments and civilians. And this, too, for a time, was favorable to shipping.

However, as foreigners developed import balances with the United States, their dollar and gold reserves dwindled. This development plus inflation induced country after country to resort to exchange control, bilateral agreements, quantitative restrictions, and a host of other devices designed to protect their foreign exchange reserves. Inevitably, international trade became dominated by governments. The large volume of governmental cargoes passing through Pacific Coast ports was an aspect of this development. Ordinary commercial shipping suffered, as the statistics reveal.

To counteract the tendency toward increased restrictions, the United States and a number of other nations concluded the General Agreement on Tariffs and Trade in Geneva in 1947. This favored shipping. Its effects cannot be confidently assessed because the agreement itself permitted a number of restrictive practices to continue and, on occasion, even to be introduced. Then, in April, 1948, the European Recovery Program was inaugurated and United States shipping was again benefited. Pacific Coast shipping felt some of the impact of this program, but its influence was far greater on the eastern seaboard of the United States.

Thus, in common with the entire United States shipping trade, the Pacific Coast maritime shipping industry found itself alternately the victim or the beneficiary of policies over which it could exert little influence.

● *Conclusions.*—Not much can be said about the influence of national commercial policies upon the fortunes of the Pacific Coast maritime shipping industry during the period 1930–1948. Business fluctuations and World War II so obviously affected the volume of foreign trade that it is not possible to isolate the effects of changes in tariffs and other trade restrictions that also occurred during these years. In the first few years covered by this study, there were both a business depression and a world-wide recourse to the protective tariff. In addition, quotas, exchange controls, and other discriminatory policies were introduced. Exports as well as imports were hampered by these developments. In the mid-'thirties, economic recovery and the adoption of a more liberal trade policy by the United States occurred at about the same time. Foreign trade increased. Again, commercial policy helped to reinforce a tendency based upon underlying economic conditions. However, the business recession of 1937–1938 brought with it a sharp drop in foreign trade cargo tonnage during a period when the United States was reducing trade barriers. We must therefore conclude that general (world-wide) business conditions rather than national commercial policies were primarily responsible for major fluctuations in the volume of foreign trade from 1930 to 1938.

World politics as expressed through preparation for war, war itself, and its aftermath appear to have been the dominant factor in the development of Pacific Coast trade after 1938. To some extent, of course, politics were important before then—particularly in commerce with the East Indies and East Asia area. Here the requirements of the Sino-Japanese war apparently overrode the restrictive policies of the belligerents, and Pacific Coast exports to the Orient increased. After 1938, and until the United States entry into the war, fluctuations in trade with the Orient and Europe and to some extent with Canada seem to have been closely related to war preparations and finally to the war itself. United States participation in the war in the Pacific entailed an enormous expansion of maritime shipping on the Pacific Coast. And 1946–1948 saw world politics—now expressed through civilian aid and military occupation—sustain the shipping industry.

Further, the growth of state trading, as nations sought to solve their balance of payment difficulties throughout 1930–1948, brought a substitution of the government administrator for the private business man in the conduct of world trade. Under these circumstances, the volume of foreign trade came to depend increasingly upon government plans and was therefore subject to fluctuations arising from decisions of the planners and not necessarily from conditions in the markets of the world.

International politics and national commercial policies were in some measure responsible for the *fluctuations* in the volume of Pacific Coast *foreign* trade. Thus they primarily affected only one sector of the shipping industry's activities and contributed to only one aspect of its experiences—the alternative periods of "feast or famine." An explanation of the long-term (1930–1948) decline in the industry requires an examination of the factors that affected not only foreign trade but noncontiguous, intercoastal, and coastwise trade as well. Therefore, an analysis of the economic development of the Pacific Coast and its effects upon maritime shipping follows.

CHAPTER V

A Declining Industry in an Expanding Economy

CLEARLY, the demand for transportation service in a given region is strongly affected by population growth and changes in the pattern of economic activity. For that matter, regional growth itself is in turn directly influenced by shifts in transportation technology. Though together these developments are often slow and subtle in operation, they are nevertheless basic in shaping the destinies of all carriers—railroads, trucks, pipelines, airlines, and water lines. Now we already know that during 1930–1948 the western states enjoyed great growth, but maritime shipping on the Pacific Coast lagged sadly behind. What were the reasons for this paradox? Was there anything inherent in regional development that may have worked against the water lines and in favor of their rivals? Why was maritime shipping being displaced from its earlier position?

To determine the effects of regional growth upon the industry, we shall first consider the nature of population changes on the Pacific Coast, and follow with an examination of shifts in its production pattern. In this way we can appraise the impacts of growth upon ocean shipping.[1] Then we shall test the implications of our analysis by study

---

[1] Before proceeding further, a word of caution is appropriate. The easy identification of

of two very important water-borne cargo commodities, lumber and petroleum.

● *The Growth and Geographic Distribution of Population.*—On first thought, it would seem reasonable to expect that the spectacular growth in the population of the western states during 1930–1948 would have been beneficial to maritime shipping; but maritime trade declined. Was there any causal relation between these opposing developments, or was the fall in water-borne cargoes wholly explained by other factors?

Certainly no one would contend that ocean shipping and population are unrelated. Some might argue that the increase in population on the Pacific Coast was favorable to shipping but that other forces, unfavorable to shipping, proved more powerful and occasioned its decline. This view may seem correct, particularly in the light of the rise in rail and truck traffic. Perhaps, it may be argued, this shift occurred mainly because costs, and hence rates, rose more in maritime shipping than in railroading and trucking. This opinion is common in the industry. In fact, it has led to pleas that rail rates be raised to enable shipping to regain its "rightful" place among the forms of transportation.

It is true that the rate differentials favoring ships became narrower, particularly after the war.[2] But this probably hastened rather than

the factors in economic development that have influenced maritime shipping belies the difficulties involved in determining, precisely, the effects of each upon ocean-borne commerce. The influence of a single factor cannot be isolated, because other factors are always at work simultaneously. Under these circumstances, the analyst can only guess what might have happened if a particular event had not occurred, and then by inference attribute causality because it did occur. Therefore, in our study of economic development and the decline of this industry, we were unable to determine unequivocally the influence of any single factor. Fortunately, however, plausible inferences can be supported by the evidence at hand. And, though we lack precision in the individual case, the effects of all factors combined are quite clear.

[2] According to findings of the Interstate Commerce Commission, the rate differential that traditionally favored vessels over trains in the coastwise trade almost disappeared after World War II. The Commission reported, "Thus, on most of the movements shown an advantage of 7 cents or more [per 100 pounds] in favor of the water movement, when the movement rates only are considered, is entirely eliminated or converted into a disadvantage of as much as 14 cents. The only instances in the table in which the total charges for the water movements are lower than the rail rates are those on paper bags, and on beer and ale, and for the movement to Seattle of dried fruit and rice." (Interstate Commerce Commission, "All rail commodity rates between California, Oregon and Washington," *Interstate Commerce Commission Reports*, vol. 277 [Washington, Government Printing Office, 1950], p. 557.)

initiated the shift from water to land carriers, especially in the coast-wise trade.[3] The growth and changing geographic distribution of population, coupled with the concurrent industrialization of the west, probably provided the basic impetus in this direction. The answer as to why this shift finally occurred lies in the growing inability of water carriers to meet the region's changing transportation needs. Back of these changing transportation requirements lay population and industrial developments.

Except for the noncontiguous, all the trades were apparently adversely affected by the growth and redistribution of population. Foreign and intercoastal trade appear to have suffered from the increased local consumption of export goods (particularly lumber and oil), coupled with the discovery and greater utilization of resource sites outside the Pacific states. This is borne out by a study of the product composition and tonnage of outbound shipments in both trades.[4] Coastwise commerce fell sharply, except for oil shipments, in part because of the growing advantage of carriage by land over carriage by water.[5] Noncontiguous trade with Hawaii and Alaska prospered primarily because these territories required larger amounts of our exports as they became more populous; and the mainland's demand for raw materials and fruit (sugar cane and pineapple, for example) rose. Further, Pacific Coast shipowners prospered in the noncontiguous trade because foreign competition in this phase of commerce was not permitted by the federal government.

We have alluded to the growth and geographic distribution of population in California, Oregon, and Washington. What are the facts? The absolute increase between 1930 and 1948 amounted to slightly more than 6 million, or about 75 per cent of approximately 8 million residents in 1930.[6] For the United States as a whole, the increase was almost 23 million, nearly 16 per cent over 1930. The three western states therefore contributed slightly more than one-fourth (26 per

[3] Of course, there are instances in which a change in rail rates was decisive—almost the prime cause of the decline of water-borne transport. Rates and costs are discussed in chap. viii, below.

[4] See above, pp. 20–29, 40–42.

[5] See below, pp. 155–165.

[6] The population statistics are from Appendix, table 9.

cent) to the increase in total United States population. Exclusive of the Pacific Coast, United States population gained about 15 per cent of the comparable figure for 1930, or about 17 million people.

Part of the growth in western population resulted from natural increase. Immigration accounted for the rest. Nearly five million people moved to California, Oregon, and Washington between 1930 and 1948.[7] The ratio of net change (6,145,000) to natural increase (1,325,000) in population was approximately 4.6.[8] Since a ratio of 1 indicates that population rises only by the amount of natural increase, immigration was more than three and a half times as large as the natural increase.

The great migration to the Pacific Coast brought with it a marked change in the distribution of population in the United States as a whole. In 1930, the west contained about 6.7 per cent of the total population of the United States, as against 9.7 per cent in 1948.[9] This growth occurred mainly after 1940. A special study of the Department of Commerce shows that in 1929 the Pacific Coast held nearly 6.6 per cent of the total population of the United States. In 1940, the west's share had risen to about 7.5 per cent, and in 1949 it was roughly 10.1 per cent.[10] California, which included 70 per cent of the west's population in 1930 and 73 per cent in 1948, moved from sixth place among the states in the United States in 1929 to second in 1949.[11]

Pacific Coast rural population increased both absolutely and as a percentage of total Pacific Coast population. In 1930, rural residents accounted for 32.5 per cent of all residents; by 1940, 34.7 per cent; and in 1950, 37.1 per cent.[12] Rural population rose from about 2.7

[7] Computed from United States Department of Commerce, *Economic Development Atlas* (Washington, Government Printing Office, 1950), p. 7.

[8] *Loc. cit.*

[9] Computed from Appendix, table 9.

[10] *Economic Development Atlas*, p. 9.

[11] Percentage computed from Appendix, table 9. Other data from *Economic Development Atlas*, p. 9.

[12] Computed from Appendix, table 10. We have used the 1940 Bureau of the Census rural-urban definitions. (Urban areas generally consist of cities and incorporated places of 2,500 or more population. See United States Department of Commerce, Bureau of the Census, *Sixteenth Census of the United States*, Vol. I [Washington, Government Printing Office, 1942], p. 10.) In 1950, these definitions were changed. For comparative purposes the Bureau published 1950 figures based upon the 1940 as well as the 1950 definitions. We have used

million in 1930 to nearly 5.4 million in 1950. During this same period urban population increased from approximately 5.5 to 9.1 million.[13]

Urban population underwent a redistribution in favor of intermediate-size communities. There was a fall in the proportion of urban residents in cities of 100,000 or over and in cities under 10,000, while cities in the 10,000 to 25,000 and 25,000 to 100,000 groups increased their shares of total urban population. The sharpest changes were in the 100,000 and over class, where the percentage of total urban population fell from 60.3 per cent in 1930 to 57.3 per cent in 1950; and in the 10,000 to 25,000 group, which included 11 per cent of the 1930 total and 14.7 per cent of the total for 1950.[14]

The number of urban places jumped from 221 in 1930 to 313 in 1950.[15] Part of this increase resulted from the incorporation of previously unincorporated places (classified as being in rural territory) that exceeded 2,500 in population. The rest reflected the growth of incorporated rural cities and the establishment of new communities. Unfortunately, the available statistics do not permit an analysis of these shifts. Cities from 10,000 to 25,000 population showed the greatest absolute and relative gains during this period—going from forty-two in 1930 to ninety in 1950 and increasing their share of the total number of urban places from 19 to nearly 29 per cent. For the 5,000 to 10,000 group there was a small gain (seven) in number of cities but a loss in relative status from 27.6 to 21.7 per cent of the total. The other groups of urban places increased in number but displayed no large changes in percentage of total places.

Between 1930 and 1950, unincorporated places increased their

1950 figures because the rural-urban breakdown is available for the census years only. For further information, see the publications referred to in Appendix, table 10, note b.

[13] See Appendix, table 10. Between 1940 and 1950, while United States urban population increased 18.7 and rural 7.4 per cent, urban population along the Pacific Coast went up by 43.3 and rural by 59.3 per cent—a radically different growth pattern. (United States figures from United States Department of Commerce, Bureau of the Census, "Population of the United States, urban and rural, by states, April 1, 1950," *1950 Census of Population, Preliminary Counts*, Series PC-3, no. 10 [Washington, February 16, 1951], p. 3; Pacific Coast percentages computed from Appendix, table 10.)

[14] Computed from Appendix, table 10.

[15] The figures cited in this paragraph are either quoted or computed from Appendix, table 10. "Places" is a collective term used by the Bureau of the Census to denote all types of communities (cities, towns, etc.) included in their urban or rural enumerations.

share of total rural inhabitants from 85.7 to 92.3 per cent, and the share going to the group of towns from 1,000 to 2,500 fell from 8.8 to 5.2 per cent. The percentage of rural inhabitants living in incorporated towns of under 1,000 in population decreased from 5.5 to 2.5.[16] This means that rural population, under the 1940 Census definition, resided primarily in unincorporated places, some of which were fringe areas near metropolitan centers.

Between 1930 and 1950, the total number of incorporated rural towns fell. A slight gain (from 154 to 169) in number of towns with from 1,000 to 2,500 inhabitants was more than offset by a loss (from 498 to 450) in the under 1,000 classification.

The highlights of the foregoing analysis of the community-size-group distribution of population can be summarized briefly. Cities having between 10,000 and 100,000 inhabitants grew both relatively and absolutely in population. The 10,000 to 25,000 group showed the largest gains in share of total urban population. It also had the greatest absolute growth in number of cities and percentage of total urban places. Cities over 100,000 population enjoyed the largest absolute gain in number of inhabitants but suffered the greatest loss in percentage of total urban population. Rural population tended to drift into unincorporated communities. The number of towns of under 1,000 inhabitants dropped sharply between 1930 and 1950, and the number ranging in size from 1,000 to 2,500 people fell by about 10 per cent. Rural population as a whole increased its share of total population.

Some observations regarding the *geographic* distribution of population remain to be made. Analysis of the location of urban places reveals, first, that many fast-growing cities are clustered about San Francisco and Los Angeles; and, second, that a sizable number are located in the Sacramento and San Joaquin valleys and in the interior of Oregon and Washington. Some of the communities on the fringes of the clusters are over one hundred miles from the metropolitan centers noted.

Had the tremendous growth in the population of the Pacific Coast been confined primarily to the coastal port cities, domestic water-borne

---

[16] Computed from Appendix, table 10.

commerce would probably have prospered, for maritime shipping is usually superior for the long haul of bulk commodities between port cities. The influx of people into rural areas, even though some of these areas were not far from port cities, and the spectacular increase in the number of relatively small cities located far from the ports apparently increased the demand for short- and long-haul land transportation relative to the demand for long-haul water transport service.[17] Further, the larger number of residents consumed more of the locally produced products. Domestic as well as foreign trade was affected by this. Consequently maritime shipping was doomed to play a decreasingly important role.

This was a gradual development. In the early days of the west, with the population largely concentrated in the seaport cities, ships provided the simplest and cheapest transportation linking these centers.[18] These ports became business centers and transshipment points for goods destined for inland consignees. Wholesalers often provided warehouses to which inbound shipments flowed. From these coastal points, inland redistribution was made to retailers in the vast, sparsely populated regions surrounding the ports. Most important, the ships got most of the tonnage.

As land travel from the east became less arduous, migration to the Pacific Coast grew. Though the migrants continued to go mainly to the relatively populous port cities, more and more of them found their way to the interior and took up farming, mining, and logging.

Products of the farm, forest, and mine furnished the exports of the region. These were for the most part bulk commodities readily handled by ship. Imports, consisting mainly of manufactures, flowed first

---

[17] Interport rail and truck shipments also increased. To some extent this was attributable to the more reliable and frequent service provided by the railroads and trucks. Rates and costs to the shipper also played a part in the shift from water to rails and trucks. There is much evidence, however, that the port and transshipment charges for the delivery of merchandise to and from outlying districts within the metropolitan areas as well as the nearby cities and towns were very important factors in the decline of coastwise and intercoastal water-borne commerce. Part of the increase in the local delivery or transshipment expense occurred because of the greater distances between dockside and ultimate destination or origin of the shipments. For a discussion of rates and costs, see chap. vii.

[18] For an interesting account of some pioneers in the shipping and lumber industries, see E. T. Coman, Jr. and H. M. Gibbs, *Time, Tide and Timber* (Stanford, Stanford University Press, 1949).

around South America and later through the Panama Canal. The long haul predominated and water-borne transport filled the need. This was the golden age of the Pacific Coast maritime shipping industry.[19]

As population increased, new towns and cities were served by the big cities in the traditional way. After a time, however, these newer towns became centers with their own clusters of satellite communities. Gradually it became profitable for wholesalers to set up warehouses in these centers. Goods now began to be shipped to and from the region directly via these new hub cities. This reduced the importance of the large seaports, though they were still very active in domestic trade and water-borne commerce.

The very large influx of population between 1930 and 1948 flowed to both the cities and the rural areas.[20] Manufacturing, formerly concentrated in a few localities, became much more widespread. These two developments—the heavy in-migration with its accompanying increase in the number of urban centers, and the growth of manufacturing—increased the demand for short-haul transportation.

In-migration provided a further impetus to the growth of short-haul transportation through increasing the west's consumption of locally produced food.

These developments also stimulated the demand for intraregional long-haul transport services. Why, then, did maritime carriers find their position deteriorating in the coastwise trade? The answer lay in certain disadvantages in the intraregional shipment of commodities via the water lines.

So long as most of the smaller satellite cities were located very near the large seaports, the transshipment of goods to smaller towns involved relatively little expense. However, with the extension of the boundaries of port-city metropolitan areas and the growth of new metropolitan areas a considerable distance from the ports, the haul from dockside to a local warehouse and then to the ultimate destina-

---

[19] Of interest is the fact that farm products, timber, and oil—all directly dependent upon the natural resources of the west—also dominated exports during the period 1930–1948. See above, pp. 20–28.

[20] Nearly five million people moved to the three Pacific Coast states during this period. See above, p. 78, and Appendix, table 9.

tion became more expensive. This difficulty was partly overcome through bypassing the port wholesaler or warehouseman by shipping direct to the interior and nonport coastal cities. As long-haul trade developed between interior areas within the western region, however, the roundabout movements of goods from the interior to a port, then by water to another port, and then by transshipment to another inland town became more expensive than direct rail or truck movement between consignor and consignee cities.[21]

Shipments by rail and truck were simplified as the railroads extended their rail network throughout the region and as hard-surfaced main highways and adequate farm-to-market roads were developed. Then, too, there were the great strides made in the durability and carrying capacity of the trucks themselves, enabling them to carry large loads on long hauls. The development of pipelines for the transmission of crude petroleum from northern California to the San Francisco Bay area also cut into the cargo potential of the vessel operators. All of these phenomena worked to the disadvantage of maritime shipping in its battle for traffic.

● *Industrial Development of the Pacific Coast, 1939–1947.*—Industrialization is usually hailed as a sign of progress and increased welfare. On the Pacific Coast industrialization proceeded rapidly. Yet the maritime shipping industry declined. Could it be that industrialization was actually detrimental to the shipping industry? To answer this requires a study of the character of the industrial development. Let us first look at some facts. Much can be learned about industrialization from a study of the shifts in the occupational distribution of the population and the value added by manufacture in a selected group of industries.

Our figures are limited to two annual observations—1939 and 1947.[22] These show that the number of manufacturing production

---

[21] See below, pp. 155–165.

[22] Only the statistics for 1939 have been adjusted by the U. S. Department of Commerce to make them comparable with the available census year nearest the end point of our study. Pre-1939 figures are comparable with neither 1939 nor 1947. We shall, therefore, ignore pre-1939 data. This is not disastrous to our analysis since we know that manufacturing increased throughout the period 1930–1948, and very rapidly between 1939 and 1947. The lack of information, however, obviously precludes our discussing any annual or short-period

workers was 410,000 in 1939 and 745,000 in 1947—an increase of nearly 82 per cent. The national difference between the two years amounted to 53 per cent. Measured in this way, the west's manufacturing development was truly prodigious. But the increase was not evenly divided among the states. Oregon's 50 per cent increase fell short of the national figure, and Washington registered a gain of 61 per cent. California enjoyed the largest absolute increase, 259,000, and the largest percentage increase over 1939—96 per cent.[23]

Though the rise in the number of manufacturing production workers was impressive, the west lagged behind the nation as a whole in what the Department of Commerce calls the "degree of industrialization as measured by manufacturing workers per 1000 population."[24] The United States figure for 1939 was 59.7. In 1947, it was 83.1, an increase of 39.2 per cent. California led the west in gain over 1939, but its 35.3 per cent gain was below the national growth. Oregon and Washington trailed far behind, with 12.9 and 9.2 per cent, respectively.[25] The great increase in manufacturing, therefore, was not commensurate with the growth of population. If the national ratio of manufacturing production workers to total population is considered optimum, then the industrial development of the Pacific Coast was

---

relation between water-borne commerce and the growth of manufacturing as shown by the index.

For a discussion of the procedure used to render certain of the 1939 and 1947 statistics comparable, see United States Department of Commerce, Bureau of the Census, *Census of Manufactures, 1947*, Vol. III (Washington, Government Printing Office, 1950), p. 90.

[23] Only three states exceeded California's relative growth—Nevada and New Mexico with 100 per cent increase and Nebraska with 106 per cent. In these states the absolute growth was very small. California's absolute increase was the sixth largest. New York, Pennsylvania, Illinois, Michigan, and Ohio all had more manufacturing production workers than California in 1939 and grew more absolutely though far less relative to 1939 than did California.

The above data are computed from Department of Commerce, Bureau of the Census, *Census of Manufactures, 1947* as found in Department of Commerce, *Economic Development Atlas*, p. 15.

[24] *Ibid.*, p. 13.

[25] The west was also well below the total United States absolute "degree of industrialization." In 1939, Oregon, Washington, and California, respectively, had 52.7, 47.8, and 39.9 manufacturing workers per 1,000, and in 1947 these figures were 59.5, 52.2, and 54.

Degree of industrialization data were computed from *Census of Manufactures, 1947* final state reports and from *Current Population Reports*, P-45, no. 9 (for 1939 population), and P-25, no. 12, p. 7 (for 1947 population), by the Department of Commerce, *Economic Development Atlas*, p. 13.

inadequate between 1939 and 1947. This would appear to favor the contention of those who claim that the growth of the west should have substantially increased the volume of water-borne commerce. Surely insufficient industrialization combined with a phenomenal expansion of population should spell prosperity in maritime commerce. How can we believe otherwise? Let us consider the evidence further.

Superficially, it seems reasonable to infer that if the "degree of industrialization as measured by manufacturing workers per 1000 population" in a given state or region is below that of the United States as a whole, the state or region is not as industrially advanced as the nation as a whole and is therefore a net importer of manufactures from the rest of the United States. In short, the region is not as "self-sufficient" as the whole country in the production of manufactures.[20] Further, if the change in a regional or state ratio fails to match the national percentage gain over the same period, it can be inferred that the region has lost ground in the race for "self-sufficiency." The Pacific Coast fared badly on both counts between 1939 and 1947.

Was the west, in fact, becoming less self-sufficient, rather than more self-sufficient, as we have contended? Certainly, the index above suggests so. But is the measure foolproof? And what does the other evidence suggest?

The measure is crude. Though partly indicative of the position of the west, it does not provide all the information necessary to determine whether the west was becoming more or less self-sufficient, manufacturingwise, between 1939 and 1947. The index is a composite; all industrial production workers are added together to yield the final figure. In some Pacific Coast industries, workers per thousand population exceeded the national total in 1939 and in others they were well below. The industries reporting a figure higher than the national level may have manufactured "export" commodities for shipment out of the region, whereas those employing less than the national number

---

[20] This does not imply that the United States is self-sufficient vis-à-vis the rest of the world. It means only that the region may import, relative to its own output, more from the rest of the world (including the rest of the United States) than the United States may import, relative to *its* output, from the rest of the world.

may have produced items that were also "imports" from the rest of the country.[27]

A study of the number of production workers by industry groups reveals that between 1939 and 1947 there was, in addition to an increase in the number of workers in each industry group, a decline in the relative importance of certain "export" industries and a growth in the relative importance of "import" industries.[28] Regardless of what the over-all crude index shows, the Pacific Coast might well have been increasing its self-sufficiency.

Moreover, the index tells nothing about productivity. A lag in the growth of number of production workers per thousand population may reflect an increase in productivity per worker. Then the increase in output will be greater than the rise in the number of employees. In relatively undeveloped areas, unhampered by old or obsolete capital equipment, this often occurs, since the most modern layouts and equipment are installed. A simple crude index of number of industrial

[27] This is borne out by our calculations of number of production workers per 1,000 population, by industry. These show that in food and kindred products, lumber and products except furniture, and in transportation equipment, the 1947 Pacific Coast figure for number of production workers per 1,000 population exceeded the national figure for that year. As the trade commodity analyses show, these are important "export" industries for the Pacific Coast. For the United States, the relevant number of production workers per 1,000 population in 1947 is 7.7, 4.2, and 6.9 for food and kindred products, lumber and products, and transportation equipment, respectively. For the Pacific Coast, the respective figures are 9.4, 8.9, and 7.7. (Computed from Appendix, table 9, and United States Department of Commerce, Bureau of the Census, *Census of Manufactures, 1947*, Vol. III, pp. 22, 92, 505, 627.)

[28] The percentage of *total* production workers in a given industry group is a rough measure of the relative importance of that industry. For example, in 1939, the food and kindred products and the lumber and products (except furniture) industry groups employed 43.7 per cent of all production workers in California. In 1947, these industries used only 34.2 per cent of the total. This drop accounted for a large percentage of all the declines in shares of total production workers and was very nearly balanced by gains in five other industry groups. These were the primary metals, fabricated metal products, machinery (except electrical), electrical machinery, and transportation equipment industries whose combined share of total production workers rose from 21.8 per cent in 1939 to 34.7 per cent in 1947. A large part of the transportation group growth was in aircraft manufacture—hardly an important item in Pacific Coast consumption. The industrial manufacturing groups noted are therefore not all "import" industries. (Computed from Department of Commerce, Bureau of the Census, *Census of Manufactures, 1947*, Vol. III, pp. 92, 505, 627.)

For the Pacific Coast as a whole, food and kindred products and lumber and products also fell in importance as measured by number of production workers per 1,000 population. The food and kindred products category figure was 9.8 in 1939 as compared with 9.4 in 1947. In lumber and products, production workers per 1,000 population fell from 9.8 to 8.9. Gains occurred in the metals and metal-working industries as noted above. (For source of calculations, see above, p. 84, n. 25.)

workers per thousand population conceals these developments. It is therefore unwise to rely exclusively upon this index of industrialization.

Other measures that can be used are the number of manufacturing establishments, the total number of employees (production plus non-production workers), their salaries or wages, and the value added by manufacture. Under these measures, how did the west compare with

TABLE 2

INDEXES OF NUMBER OF MANUFACTURING ESTABLISHMENTS, TOTAL NUMBER OF
EMPLOYEES IN THESE ESTABLISHMENTS, THEIR TOTAL SALARIES AND WAGES,
VALUE ADDED BY MANUFACTURE, UNITED STATES, PACIFIC COAST, CALIFORNIA,
OREGON, AND WASHINGTON, 1947

(1939 = 100)

State or region	Number of establishments	Total number of employees	Total wages and salaries[a]	Value added by manufacture[a]
United States.............	138.6	150.0	312.4	303.9
Pacific Coast[b].............	147.9	174.6	330.6	358.4
California................	152.7	185.9	386.8	355.9
Oregon..................	161.6	157.1	361.4	430.8
Washington..............	119.3	145.6	307.2	326.5

[a] Not adjusted for price level differences.
[b] California, Oregon, and Washington.
SOURCE: Computed from United States Department of Commerce, Bureau of the Census, *Census of Manufactures, 1947*, Vol. III (Washington, Government Printing Office, 1950), pp. 21, 90, 504, 626.

the United States as a whole? Table 2 shows that in 1947 Pacific Coast manufacturing relative to 1939 exceeded the national growth. The Oregon and California performances were well ahead of all the states taken together, whereas Washington failed to keep up except in value added by manufacture.

A breakdown, by industry, of value added by manufacture and number of production workers shows that, for both the United States as a whole and the three Pacific Coast states, the largest gains over 1939 were in the production of metals, machinery, and transportation equipment.[29] This similarity, however, hides certain important differences.

First, on the Pacific Coast as compared with the United States as a whole, the increase in these manufacturing activities entailed a greater

[29] See Appendix, table 11.

1939 1947

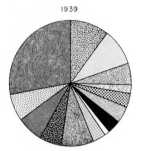

UNITED STATES

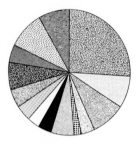 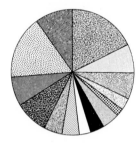

LEGEND

FOOD AND KINDRED PRODUCTS

APPAREL AND RELATED PRODUCTS

LUMBER AND PRODUCTS, EXCEPT
MANUFACTURES

FURNITURE AND FIXTURES

PAPER AND ALLIED PRODUCTS

PRINTING AND PUBLISHING
INDUSTRIES

CHEMICALS AND ALLIED PRODUCTS

PETROLEUM AND COAL PRODUCTS

STONE, CLAY, AND GLASS
PRODUCTS

PRIMARY METALS INDUSTRIES

FABRICATED METAL PRODUCTS

MACHINERY, EXCEPT ELECTRICAL

TRANSPORTATION EQUIPMENT

OTHER

CALIFORNIA

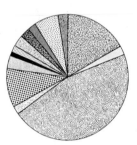 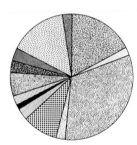

WASHINGTON

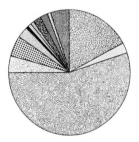 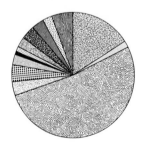

OREGON

rise in their importance relative to total industrial activity.[30] Second, on the Pacific Coast the shifts in the distribution of production workers among the manufacturing groups were more drastic. Likewise, the Pacific Coast groups underwent more drastic changes in their relative contributions to value added by manufacture.[31] Third, there were differences between the national and regional decline in the relative importance of some industries. And fourth, different industries declined in importance, to some extent, in the United States as compared with the Pacific Coast.

To avoid laborious, detailed descriptions of changes in the relative status of industries locally and nationally, we have summarized the relevant data in figures 16 and 17. These show that the relative decline in the importance of the food and kindred products group was greater in the Pacific Coast states than in the United States as a whole. Nevertheless, this industry remained far more important regionally than nationally.[32] The lumber and products (except furniture) group

[30] This was determined as follows. We computed the percentage of total value added by manufacture and number of production workers attributable to each Census industry group in 1939 and 1947. Next, we compared the 1939 and 1947 percentages of each group. If the 1947 percentage was larger, the difference between 1947 and 1939 was recorded as positive; if smaller, as negative. Obviously, the algebraic sum of these differences was zero—the loss in some industries being offset by the gains in others. If an industry's share of total value added by manufacture in all industries rose from 10 per cent in 1939 to 20 per cent in 1947—a difference of + 10 in "per cents"—this represented a greater gain in status relative to total value added by manufacture than a rise from 1 to 2 per cent during the same interval.

Using this measure, we found that for value added by manufacture in the metals, machinery, and transportation equipment industries (Census industry groups no. 33 to 37, inclusive) the Pacific Coast gain in 1947 over 1939 was 8.0 in "per cents," and the national gain was 4.0. This indicates that relative to total value added by manufacture in all industries together, there was a greater relative gain in the Pacific Coast states than in the United States as a whole. For number of production workers, the Pacific Coast score was + 12.9 as compared with + 8.0 nationally.

[31] Using the measure described above (n. 30), there were changes totaling 9.8 (in "per cents") in value added by manufacture and 14.6 in number of production workers on the Pacific Coast between 1939 and 1947. The respective national changes were 9.4 and 6.6. Thus, in the Pacific Coast economy there were more extensive shifts of workers and value added by manufacture than in the nation as a whole. This was to be expected in a rapidly developing area.

[32] It absorbed 17.5 per cent of the production workers in the three western states in 1947 and 22.9 per cent in 1939. It contributed 20 per cent of value added by manufacture in

Fig. 16. Distribution of number of production workers by selected industries, United States, California, Oregon, and Washington, 1939 and 1947. Source: Appendix, table 12.

1939 1947

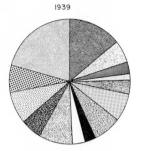

UNITED STATES

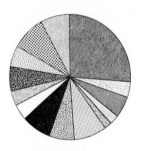 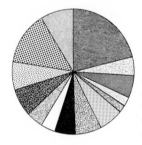

LEGEND

FOOD AND KINDRED PRODUCTS

APPAREL AND RELATED PRODUCTS

LUMBER AND PRODUCTS, EXCEPT
MANUFACTURES

FURNITURE AND FIXTURES

PAPER AND ALLIED PRODUCTS

PRINTING AND PUBLISHING
INDUSTRIES

CHEMICALS AND ALLIED PRODUCTS

PETROLEUM AND COAL PRODUCTS

STONE, CLAY, AND GLASS
PRODUCTS

PRIMARY METALS INDUSTRIES

FABRICATED METAL PRODUCTS

MACHINERY, EXCEPT ELECTRICAL

TRANSPORTATION EQUIPMENT

OTHER

CALIFORNIA

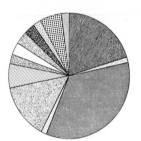 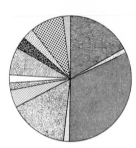

WASHINGTON

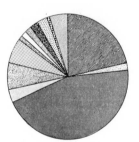 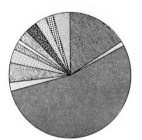

OREGON

showed a sharp decline in percentage of total regional production workers, yet a larger increase in value added by manufacture than was true for the entire United States. At the regional level, this group also was much more important relative to the regional total of value added by manufacture and number of production workers than it was at the national level relative to the corresponding national totals.[33]

Figures 16 and 17 also show the gains in metals, machinery, and transportation equipment manufacturing referred to above.[34] Further, they show that there were intraregional divergencies in shifts in the relative importance of industry groups.[35]

From our brief survey of industrial developments on the Pacific Coast, certain inferences may now be made. First, the rapid rise in metals, machinery, and transportation equipment production called for increased shipments of steel and manufactures to the Pacific Coast. Heavy structural steel and other bulk fabrications of steel and iron were shipped from the east coast via the Panama Canal in increasing amounts during the 'thirties, as our analyses of tonnage have shown. Pacific Coast industrial development also called for the inbound movement of components needed in various fabrication processes. Many of these were no doubt relatively higher valued and less bulky than those moved by vessel. Here, transcontinental rail service was increasingly utilized.

1947 and 24.7 per cent in 1939. The relevant figures for the United States were 9.2 per cent of production workers in 1947 and 10.3 per cent in 1939; for value added by manufacture, the figures were 12.1 in 1947 and 14.2 in 1939.

[33] On the Pacific Coast, 16.6 per cent of production workers were employed in this industry in 1947 and 22.8 per cent in 1939. Nationally, these figures were 5 per cent and 5.4 per cent, respectively. The percentage of total value added by manufacture was 15.7 in 1947 and 14.4 in 1939 on the Pacific Coast, and 3.4 and 3, respectively, nationally.

[34] Though the Pacific Coast gains were greater than the national, these industries remained smaller relative to total number of production workers and value added by manufacture in the region than in the nation. In 1947, the Pacific Coast industries used 34.7 per cent of the regional total of production workers and the national industries employed 39.5 per cent of the national total. In value added by manufacture, the percentages were 30.4 regionally and 37.9 nationally.

[35] Note, for example, the large increase in share of value added by manufacture going to lumber and manufactures in Oregon, as compared with the experience of this industry group in California and Washington.

Fig. 17. Distribution of value added by manufacture in selected industries, United States, California, Oregon, and Washington, 1939 and 1947. Source: Appendix, table 12.

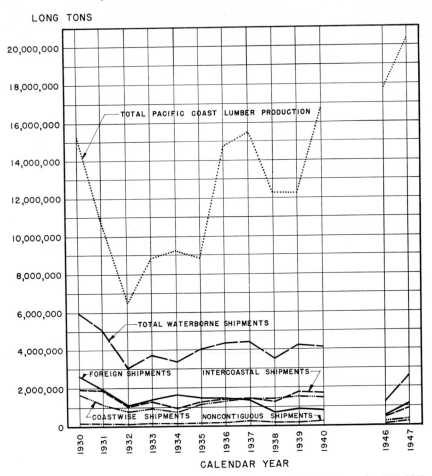

Fig. 18. Pacific Coast production and water-borne shipments of lumber by trade, 1930–1940, 1946, and 1947. Source: Appendix, table 13.

Second, the distribution of the finished products manufactured in the west undoubtedly required predominantly short-haul and long-haul land transportation to intraregional points. This reinforced the increasing demand for this type of service for the movement of other commodities, occasioned by the growth in size and number of smaller cities in the three Pacific Coast states.

Third, the decline in importance of the lumber industry in Washington and its increase in Oregon, where many timber stands are not as near adequate coastal ports as they were in Washington, reduced the demand for coastwise lumber schooner and vessel service.

Fourth, growing industrialization together with increasing population meant a rise in the local consumption of products normally exported from this predominantly agricultural and raw material producing area. Among these products were two very important commodities—lumber and petroleum. We next examine the shipping industry's experience with these two items.

● *Lumber.*—Little needs to be said about the importance of lumber production to the economy of the Pacific Coast and, in particular, to its shipping industry. Lumber and logs were important in all the ocean trades. The story of lumber and maritime shipping tells much about the industry's difficulties. It has a "barometric" value. Pacific Coast lumber had to be hauled long distances. Water transportation appeared ideal for this cheap bulk commodity. What happened to the lumber trade?

As figure 18 shows, annual lumber production tended sharply upward after 1932. In contrast, total annual water-borne lumber shipments never again attained their 1930–1931 levels and varied little in the prewar years.[36] Over 40 per cent of total Pacific Coast lumber production was shipped by water during the years 1930–1935. Thereafter, until 1940, it was below 30 per cent;[37] and in 1946 and 1947 the percentages were 7 and 12.6, respectively. The tendency was clearly downward after 1931, with only a sharp rise in 1935 and a very small increase in 1938, interrupting the decline. Statistics of total shipments, however, conceal important differences in the behavior of the separate components (foreign, noncontiguous, intercoastal, and

[36] Total shipments refers to the sum of foreign, noncontiguous, intercoastal, and coastwise shipments. Our data for coastwise movements of lumber include only the movement of Douglas fir from Oregon and Washington to California. The coastwise shipment of other varieties of lumber is therefore excluded. Intra-California lumber movements are also not included. Information obtained from the Southern Pacific Company, the California Redwood Association, the Pacific Maritime Association, and certain California lumber companies indicates that after 1934 intra-California and California to Oregon and Washington water-borne lumber shipments all declined. The same sources stated that though this water trade revived after World War II, the volume was far below prewar.

[37] Percentages computed from Appendix, table 13. Shipments include logs as well as lumber. It is therefore possible that some of the fall in percentage of total lumber production shipped by water was attributable to a decline in log shipments.

coastwise shipments). The behavior of these components must therefore be analyzed to forestall unwarranted inferences.

Figure 18 reveals that the relative stability of the total tonnage of
water-borne lumber shipments during the period 1935–1940 resulted
primarily from a sharp fall in exports of lumber in foreign trade,
which was offset by a rise in shipments in the other trades, particularly intercoastal and coastwise. Until 1937, annual exports of lumber
in foreign trade exceeded either coastwise or intercoastal shipments.
From 1937 to 1940, they were well below those in either of the domestic trades. Postwar, they resumed their leading position.

Three facts strongly show increasing demand for Pacific Coast lumber within the United States: increased output after 1932, increased
domestic water-borne shipments, and falling foreign exports.[38] At the
same time, there was a decline in the foreign demand for Pacific Coast
lumber.[39]

From the available statistical data, we cannot determine the distribution of the increased lumber shipments to domestic markets. Rail
movements of lumber are shown only by number of carloads and tons
originating and terminating by states without information as to actual
destinations or origins. We can thus find out the number of carloads
of lumber, for example, entering and leaving Oregon, Washington,
and California, but we cannot find out where they originated or went.[40]

---

[38] Noncontiguous shipments may be ignored. They were less than 2 per cent of total
production throughout the period under consideration.

[39] I. M. Elchibegoff, an authority on lumber production and trade, states that the volume
of lumber exports depends primarily upon the ability of domestic producers to sell their
output in the United States. According to Elchibegoff, when their domestic sales relative to
output are small, they seek foreign outlets for their lumber. He points out that in the early
'thirties the United States increased its restrictions on lumber imports. Other nations,
notably many countries in the British Empire, retaliated by granting each other preferential rates that discriminated against United States exports of lumber. Thus the demand for
domestic lumber by the United States increased and the foreign demand decreased. Of
course, the world-wide depression also contributed to the fall in foreign demand. See I. M.
Elchibegoff, *United States International Timber Trade in the Pacific Area* (Stanford, Stanford University Press, 1949), pp. 212–221.

[40] See Interstate Commerce Commission, Bureau of Transport Economics and Statistics,
"Tons of freight originated and tons of freight terminated in carloads by groups of commodities and by geographic areas—Class I, steam railways," *Statement No. Q550 (SCS)*.
The carload waybill studies of the Commission provide such regional data but the time-
span covered is too short for our purposes. The cost of an adequate waybill study was
beyond our limited financial means.

Nevertheless, it seems reasonable to assume that the Pacific Coast demand for lumber rose more than commensurately with the rise in lumber output. The rapid growth of population and industry, as compared with the rest of the United States, probably had this effect.[41]

There is no doubt, therefore, regarding increased domestic consumption of lumber within the United States, and there is good reason to suspect that within the west the increase was relatively larger than it was nationally. How did these changes affect Pacific Coast maritime shipping?

Both intercoastal and coastwise shipments increased absolutely. (See figure 18.) Intercoastal tonnage, however, was only about 11 per cent of total lumber production during 1935–1939 as compared with 14.2 per cent for the period 1930–1934; coastwise tonnage went from 10.2 per cent in the 1930–1934 period to 10.6 per cent in the next five-year span. And this happened despite the decline in the percentage of total lumber production entering foreign trade from 16.7 per cent during 1930–1934 to 9.2 per cent in 1935–1939.

This analysis reveals that in the 'thirties the shipping industry merely maintained its total absolute volume of lumber tonnage by a shift from foreign to the domestic trades, and failed to share in the increased volume of lumber production; the greater share of the increase in the domestic demand for lumber movement went to the railroads and trucks.[42] One indication of the increased share going to the railroads is that the average annual tonnage of California and Oregon lumber handled by the Southern Pacific and Northwestern Pacific railroads increased by 50 per cent, or about 600,000 tons, in 1935–1939 over 1930–1934, while the shipping industry's gain in the coastwise and intercoastal movement of lumber was 17 per cent, or about 400,000 tons.

During the war years, coastwise shipping was almost completely shut down. As a result, the volume of lumber shipments handled by the railroads rose sharply. As table 3 shows, the Southern Pacific and

---

[41] See above, pp. 77–87.

[42] Figures provided by the Southern Pacific Company and the Northwestern Pacific Railroad Company indicate the gains made by the railroads. Table 3 shows the divergent experiences of the railroads and the Pacific Coast maritime shipping industry.

Northwestern Pacific railroads carried 4.1 million long tons of lumber annually during the period 1940–1945 as compared with 1.8 million tons per year during the preceding five-year span.

In the three postwar years, 1946–1948, coastwise and intercoastal water-borne lumber shipments averaged about one-third of their 1935–1939 volume, while the railroads mentioned handled about three and one-half times their average annual tonnage in 1935–1939. In fact,

TABLE 3

Average Annual Tonnage of Lumber Originating in Oregon and California Carried by Southern Pacific Company and Northwestern Pacific Railroad Company, and of Pacific Coast Lumber Shipped by Vessel in the Coastwise and Intercoastal Trades, 1930–1948

(in millions of 2,240-lb. tons)

Years	Shipments carried by SP and NWP (Oregon and California only)	Shipments by vessel
1930–1934..	1.2	2.4
1935–1939..	1.8	2.8
1940–1945..	4.1	3.2[a]
1946–1948..	6.2	1.0

[a] 1940 only. Shipments negligible during the war period, 1941–1945.
Source: For rail shipments, *Annual Report of the Southern Pacific Company to the Public Utilities Commission of the State of California; Annual Report of the Northwestern Pacific Railroad Company to the Public Utilities Commission of the State of California; Annual Report of the Southern Pacific Company to the Public Utilities Commission of the State of Oregon* (San Francisco, Offices of the Southern Pacific Company), unpublished copies of the reports submitted. For water-borne shipments, Appendix, table 13.

these companies alone handled almost twice the 1935–1939 average annual water-borne intercoastal and coastwise lumber tonnage. And it must be remembered that their statistics are confined to lumber originating in California and Oregon only.

The maritime shipping industry's "lumber experience" from 1930 to 1948 falls into three segments. The first was the period of the middle and late 'thirties, when the share of lumber production shipped by water to domestic destinations failed to increase markedly, despite a drop in water-borne shipments to foreign countries and despite increased lumber output. The second was the war period, when the industry was effectively excluded from competing with the railroads and trucks. The third was the postwar years, when maritime shipping recaptured some of its lumber traffic but fell far short of its prewar volume although lumber production was well above prewar levels.

Basically, the plight of the industry resulted from its apparent inability fully to satisfy the increased demand for domestic lumber transportation.[43] There were five main reasons for this. First, sailing schedules were very erratic because of numerous strikes. Second, World War II shut off the supply of coastwise and intercoastal ocean services, giving the railroads and trucks opportunity to invade the market. Third, the shutdown during World War II hastened the extinction of many coastwise lumber carriers whose floating equipment had been allowed to become obsolete during the slump of the 'thirties, and was judged not worth the risk of replacement in the unpromising postwar market. Fourth, the tremendous postwar increase in local demand for lumber involved many points relatively remote from seaports but near railroads. Fifth, there was a shift to timber stands farther inland which were not readily or cheaply accessible to lumber schooners.

Next to the manufacture of foods and kindred products, the production of lumber and its products (except furniture) was the most important industrial activity on the Pacific Coast. But, while the number of establishments involved in food production declined absolutely between 1939 and 1947, the number increased in the lumber industry. Value added by manufacture (not corrected for price changes) tripled in the food industry and nearly quadrupled in the lumber industry. There can be no doubt that the lumber industry was a leading factor in the tremendous upsurge in the output of the Pacific Coast economy—an upsurge that carried the value added by manufacture in all industries from about $1.5 billion in 1939 to $5.5 billion in 1947.[44]

For the shipping industry, too, lumber was important. In every trade it was at least the second leading outbound commodity. However, relative to the increased output, water-borne shipments of lumber

---

[43] In 1934, the railroads were granted permission to charge lower rates on lumber. This probably encouraged a shift to the use of railroads. The nearly simultaneous increase in domestic demand and possible decrease in foreign demand complicate the picture so that we can make no clear-cut inference regarding the effect of the rail rate reduction.

[44] For source of figures cited in this paragraph, see Appendix, table 11.

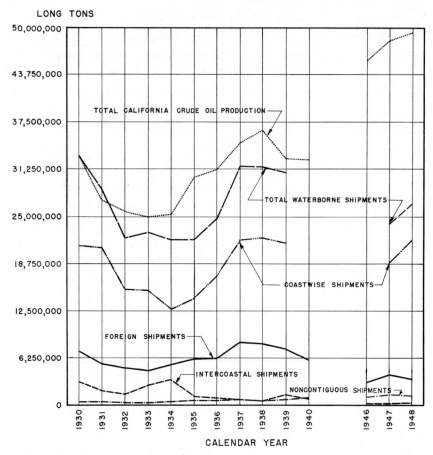

Fig. 19. Pacific Coast water-borne shipments of petroleum and products by trade, and California crude oil production, 1930–1940, 1946–1948. Source: Appendix, table 14.

steadily declined in importance. The tonnage of annual water-borne shipments varied little from 1935 to 1940 and was well below prewar during the years 1946 and 1947. The water lines were the victims of an adverse shift in demand, which cut deeply into their tonnage. Moreover, as we shall point out in chapter vii, they were also victims of a disproportionate increase in operating costs, which cut further into their tonnage by reducing the supply of domestic water services.

The strikingly divergent behavior of lumber output and water-borne shipments of lumber, together with the sharp fall in exports to foreign countries, shows clearly that there was an increased domestic demand for lumber. The shipping industry's failure to expand its lumber tonnage points to a vital weakness in the position of the industry. It was unable to benefit from the expansion of lumber production. Railroad and truck competition was insurmountable.[45] Ocean-going vessels could no longer adequately fulfill the transportation requirements arising from the increased domestic demand for lumber.

● *Oil.*—There is no need to recount the turbulent history of the California oil industry.[46] In common with the industry elsewhere, there has been a series of important discoveries of oil fields in the past two decades. Production, while rising secularly, has been sensitive to business conditions and war in the short run. This is evident even during the relatively short period covered by this study. California crude oil production fell from about 33 million long tons[47] in 1930 to 25 million long tons in 1933, averaging a little over 27 million tons during the period 1930–1934. As figure 19 shows, crude output rose during the next four years—averaging 33 million tons annually. Postwar (1946–1948), average annual production was about 48 million long tons.[48]

From 1930 to 1939, the annual pattern of total outbound Pacific Coast water-borne shipments of petroleum and products conformed very nearly to that of California annual crude oil output. (See figure 19.) Coastwise, foreign, and noncontiguous shipments displayed a rising tendency in the late 'thirties, whereas intercoastal tonnage of outbound petroleum and products fell off sharply after 1934.

Annual outbound intercoastal oil tonnage fell from 3.2 million long tons during the period 1930–1934 to the extremely low level of 0.9

[45] Additional evidence of the effectiveness of rail competition comes from the records of the Pacific Lumber Inspection Bureau. These show that the ratio of rail to water-borne shipments of lumber certificated by the Bureau rose from .016 in 1930 to .032 in 1939. In 1947, a "strike-free" year for the maritime industry, the ratio was .137. In 1946 and 1948, the ratios were .297 and .279, respectively. (The Bureau's figures include some shipments from British Columbia, Canada.)

[46] For an excellent account of the operations of the California oil industry, see J. S. Bain, *The Economics of the Pacific Coast Petroleum Industry* (Berkeley, University of California Press, 1944–1947), 3 vols.

[47] Oil production is usually stated in barrels. We have converted the output statistics to long tons to facilitate comparisons between output and shipments. For conversion methods employed and source of the oil production data, see Appendix, table 14.

[48] During the war years (1940–1945), California crude oil production amounted to a little more than 39 million long tons per year.

million tons in the 1935–1939 interval. The percentage of total California crude oil output represented by this tonnage[49] dropped from 9.3
per cent in the first period to 2.8 in the second. This decline continued
in the postwar years when average annual intercoastal tonnage was
.23 million tons and amounted to only 0.5 per cent of annual California crude oil production. The discovery and exploitation of oil
fields nearer the east coast of the United States undoubtedly contributed importantly to this decline.

Unfortunately, our information about total petroleum and products
tonnage for the period 1946–1948 is incomplete. We have complete
data only for 1947 and 1948. These show that water-borne outbound
movements of petroleum and products averaged about 25.4 million
long tons—higher than during the mid-'thirties but well below the
figures for the earlier and later years of that decade.[50] Coastwise shipments in 1947 and 1948 were slightly above the 1935–1939 annual
average.

Intercoastal movements during 1946–1948, as noted above, continued the downward tendency of the early 'thirties. Noncontiguous oil
tonnage was higher than prewar, and in line with the modest tendency
for this trade to rise during the 1930's. Exports of petroleum and products to foreign countries during 1946–1948 were only about half as
large as annual average prewar tonnage. Had the prewar average annual volume of foreign trade exports of oil been maintained in 1947–
1948 then *total* oil shipments from the Pacific Coast during these years
would have exceeded the prewar annual average.

We have shown that from 1935 to 1939, except for intercoastal
trade, annual water-borne tonnage of petroleum and products tended
to increase. A similar divergence occurred in the behavior of the ratio
of tonnage shipped in each trade to total California output of crude oil.
In all trades except intercoastal, the ratio showed some tendency to

---

[49] We cannot say that shipments during a given period *were* a certain percentage of output during that *same* period because some of the oil produced during that period may have
been stored. In this case, total shipments by all means of transportation would fall short
of total output. Conversely, if oil had been moved out of storage then shipments would
exceed production for the period. This apparently happened in 1931. (See fig. 19.)

[50] If coastwise shipments in 1946 were the same as the average annual tonnage for 1947–
1948, then the postwar average was 25.2 million long tons—well below the annual average
for 1938–1940.

rise during the late 'thirties, after falling in the earlier years. Foreign trade absorbed a fairly steady percentage of California crude oil in the form of petroleum and products, as did noncontiguous trade. Coastwise trade was subject to the widest absolute variations in the percentage, falling from about 76 per cent in 1931 to 47 per cent in 1935, and subsequently rising to 66 in 1939. Intercoastal trade fell from a high of about 13 per cent in 1934 to a low of approximately 2 per cent in 1938.[51] Except for the years 1935 and 1936, the prewar water-borne share hovered around 90 per cent in all trades combined.[52]

Postwar, the available figures indicate that all trades except noncontiguous did not carry as great a percentage of total annual California crude oil production in the form of petroleum and products as they did prewar. In fact, only about 51 per cent of output in 1947–1948 appears to have gone out by vessel.[53]

Our brief survey of the relationship of oil output and water-borne shipments of petroleum and products reveals four important developments. First, except for 1935 and 1936, there were no large changes in the prewar percentage of total California crude oil production appearing as shipments of petroleum and products. Second, total shipments were about 10 per cent lower in 1947–1948 than the annual average for 1935–1939, and the percentage of total output shipped by tanker vessel was far lower than prewar. Third, there was a tendency for the ratio of total oil shipments by water to total California output to vary in the same direction. Finally, outbound intercoastal oil tonnage dropped precipitously after 1934.

Prewar, the Pacific Coast maritime shipping industry apparently maintained its share of oil shipments, except for the years noted. The volatility of the percentage of total oil production shipped by tanker vessel in the coastwise trade suggests that from time to time pipelines, railroads, and trucks offered severe competition. A cut in oil production apparently meant a more than commensurate reduction in the

---

[51] Officials of the Standard Oil Company of California stated that the sharp rise in intercoastal shipments in 1934 occurred because of the disposal of a large accumulation of petroleum and products in storage in California.

[52] It was 100 per cent in 1930 and 104.7 in 1931. See p. 100, n. 49 for explanation.

[53] If we assume that coastwise shipments amounted to 20.3 million long tons in 1946 (see above, n. 50), only 53 per cent would have moved by vessel.

use of tanker vessels. Conversely, a rise in output led to a more than proportionate increase in the use of tankships. Ocean-going tankers therefore provided the necessary elasticity in transportation facilities. Greater local consumption, coupled with the discovery of oil east of California, accounts for the drop in intercoastal trade.

Postwar, the absolute fall in annual water-borne oil tonnage, though substantial, was not unusual. In the prewar period, total water-borne tonnage had fallen by as much as 6 million tons in a single year. Relative to postwar output, however, the decrease was startling. The rapid growth in oil production both elsewhere in the United States and in foreign countries reduced the need for shipments from California. Simultaneously, the expansion of population and industrial output within the Pacific Coast region boosted the local consumption of petroleum and products.

Once again the maritime shipping industry failed to get an increase in cargo tonnage, despite a big rise in the output of a commodity well suited to long-haul water transportation. And once again, as in the case of lumber, the growth of local regional consumption was an important factor contributing to this failure. Apparently pipelines and trucks end, to a limited extent, railroads were better able to handle the transportation to intraregional destinations, which were rapidly growing in importance. Regional economic development had worked against the expansion of maritime shipping.

● *Summary.*—From 1930 until the end of World War II, there was a fairly close correspondence between fluctuations in business activity and fluctuations in the volume of cargo tonnage handled by the Pacific Coast maritime shipping industry.[54] During this period, however, the growth of population and production worked in favor of a decidedly upward tendency in general business activity. Yet these very forces gave rise to a stagnant, if not declining, tendency in water-borne commerce. Though their operation was discernible in the 'thirties, their long-term effects were concealed by violent short-term shifts in economic prosperity. In the 'forties, the increase in the magnitudes of these factors was obvious to all. But here the war intervened and ob-

---

[54] See below, chap. vi.

scured their possible long-term effects upon ocean shipping. In the postwar years, the initial shock of readjustment after the war was followed by realization that recovery of peacetime cargoes was not simply a matter of presenting the potential customer with the opportunity to ship by vessel once again. Something basic had happened to decrease the demand for shipping services.

A mere influx of a large number of people into a given area does not necessarily mean prosperity for *all* lines of business activity. The ultimate geographic distribution of the people affects some forms of transportation favorably and others unfavorably. Maritime shipping was adversely affected by the growth in both the number and size of the smaller cities lying well inland from the deep-water harbors of the Pacific Coast. These same population phenomena encouraged extension of the rail and road network that subsequently redounded to the benefit of the railroads and the rapidly improving trucks.

Further, an increase in population, though often associated with a rise in output, does not mean that interregional and international trade must necessarily expand. The Pacific Coast is primarily a producer of food and raw materials. In recent decades, it has been shifting resources to manufacturing. The increases in population and in manufacturing production have meant increased local consumption of locally produced food and raw materials. In part, this contributed to the reduction in outbound shipments of oil and lumber relative to the output of these commodities. The failure of outbound cargo tonnages of food to rise commensurately with the rise in production can probably also be attributed to increased local consumption. Increasing population and business activity did not, therefore, generate substantially larger cargoes for the maritime shipping industry.

At the same time, however, much larger cargoes went by rail and truck.[55] The growth of population, its shifting geographic distribution, and the rise in the volume of regional business increased the need for both short-haul and long-haul land transportation.

The effects of population growth and relocation upon maritime shipping were reinforced by the industrial development of the Pacific

_____
[55] See chap. viii.

Coast. The volume of assembly work (automobiles, for example), light manufacturing (small engines, for example), and aircraft manufacturing increased rapidly. Many of these industries received high value component parts from east of the Rockies. Inbound intercoastal cargoes reflected this. There was a steady rise in the tonnage of iron, steel and manufactures flowing into Pacific Coast ports. The railroads, however, offered superior point-to-point service for the movement of semimanufactured items and parts required by Pacific Coast industries.

Much of the output of western factories was apparently sold to nearby customers or to those who received their purchases by rail and truck transportation. Our study of water-borne trade shows that only in the noncontiguous and foreign export trade was there a significant rise in the volume of metal manufactures exports. To this very limited extent, then, water-borne commerce was helped by the growth of manufacturing, and here only perhaps because land carriers were not available.

Only the volume of noncontiguous trade showed the generally upward tendency characteristic of production on the Pacific Coast. Alaska and Hawaii furnished imports not highly competitive with products of the mainland—sugar, pineapple, and fish. And the needs of the Pacific Coast for these imports grew as population increased. Exports to these territories involved items best purchased on the Pacific Coast—petroleum, food, and some manufactures. These close economic relationships between Alaska and Hawaii on the one hand, and the Pacific Coast on the other, make the territories a part of the Pacific Coast region, economically at least. Between 1930 and 1948, intraregional trade increased. In the Alaska and Hawaii trade, maritime shipping was bound to prosper.

In the coastwise sector of the intraregional trade, the shipping industry did not fare so well. Bulk commodities—petroleum and lumber—constituted about 90 per cent of the tonnage carried in the trade. Total volume of coastwise trade increased during the 'thirties, but the volume of general cargo declined drastically. In part, this decline must be attributed to the shifting nature of the region's transportation requirements following from the rise in the number and population of interior cities. Movements of general cargo by rail and truck rose sharply.[56] Lumber shipments increased, but the percentage of lumber output shipped in coastwise vessels did not vary much throughout the 'thirties. And this happened in spite of a substantial drop in foreign export shipments during a period of rising lumber production. As we have shown, the *total* tonnage of water-borne shipments in all trades together did not increase. With the decline in foreign shipments, domestic shipments (coastwise plus intercoastal) rose, but there was no increase in the percentage of lumber output shipped by water in the coastwise and intercoastal trades. Railroads and trucks, obviously confined almost entirely to coastwise and intercoastal trade, thus increased their share of the total lumber output shipped. We know that for coastwise and intercoastal shipments combined the railroads increased their movement of lumber more than did the vessel operators. It seems safe, therefore, to infer that in the coastwise trade alone the same occurred. Again, shipments to interior points probably account for a considerable amount of the gains by railroads and trucks. Postwar, the water-borne coastwise movement of lumber was far below prewar both in absolute volume and as a percentage of total output.

Coastwise water-borne oil shipments increased in volume and as a percentage of total crude oil output from 1934 to 1939. Our postwar figures are not complete; however, in 1947–1948 a far smaller percentage of total output was shipped by water in all trades. This suggests a greater distribution by pipeline, trucks, and railroads.

Our analysis indicates that as the Pacific Coast developed, the shipping industry lost ground in long haul of general cargo and of an important bulk commodity—lumber. Both of these phenomena resulted partly from the changing transportation needs of the region and partly (as we shall discuss in chapter viii) from the superior port-to-port service offered by the railroads and trucks.

Prewar, three aspects of intercoastal water-borne commerce reflected the industrial development of the Pacific Coast. First, the prewar rise in inbound cargoes of iron and steel and manufactures—

---

[56] See chap. viii.

particularly structural steel, pipe, and other bulk items—indicated regional need arising chiefly from construction activity. Second, the absence of a marked rise in tonnage of other inbound commodities may be attributed to the growing importance of western production, coupled with increased shipments to the west via rail and truck. Third, the stability of annual dry-cargo tonnage and the fall of petroleum tonnage in the outbound trade were probably due to increased regional consumption of these commodities and to the successful invasion by producers in other areas of the markets served by Pacific Coast producers.

To some extent, the decline in outbound intercoastal traffic postwar as compared with prewar was probably a continuation of the tendency already noticeable in the late 'thirties. However, much of the sharp fall here as well as in the inbound trade occurred because the war had interrupted service, and so permitted the railroads and trucks to invade this trade. Nevertheless, the shipping industry's failure to regain more of its prewar volume of cargo tonnage may well have occurred because it was unable to provide the cheap and flexible services that the growing and increasingly self-sufficient postwar Pacific Coast economy required.

As we noted in our commodity analysis of foreign trade, the Pacific Coast's foreign trade consisted primarily of a two-way exchange of products of field, forest, and mine. Annual import volume was fairly steady between 1930 and 1948, indicating a smaller volume per capita. The substitution of domestic output for foreign probably accounted for part of this. However, tariff and trade policies, and war and its aftermath, were undoubtedly overriding factors of considerable importance.[57] Exports of lumber fell. After 1937, oil exports also decreased. There was some rise, though the absolute amount was small, in exports of manufactured goods. Dry-cargo exports, generally, showed little change. The growth in the output of the Pacific Coast did not result in a commensurate increase in the volume of exports. Again, the verdict must be that increased local consumption was partly responsible.

---

[57] Some of these matters are discussed in chap. iv.

Initially, one might reasonably have expected maritime shipping to expand with regional growth and industrialization. The facts show quite the opposite. Apparently this growth actually contributed to the decline of the industry. The evidence that it did so is not conclusive, but it furnishes support for the inferences we have drawn. We intend to show in later chapters that regional development was not the only factor in that decline.[58] In fact, it is *possible*—although to us it seems *unlikely* on the basis of the data available—that the decline was entirely attributable to other factors.

---

[58] The reader may wish to compare our findings with the forecast made by Professor E. G. Mears in 1935. His was temperately optimistic and saw, in the development of the western United States, expanding opportunities for ship operators. In fairness to Professor Mears, it must be pointed out that he was careful to posit a continuation of the relatively peaceful conditions of the 'thirties. See E. G. Mears, *Maritime Trade of the Western United States* (Stanford, Stanford University Press, 1935), pp. 422–448.

CHAPTER VI

Business Fluctuations, War, and Work Stoppages

~~~~~~~~~~~~~~~~~~~~~~~~~~~~~~~~~~~~~~

● *Introduction.*—Two central facts emerge from the economic profile of Pacific Coast maritime shipping during 1930–1948: *instability* from year to year and long-run *decline* for the whole period. In this chapter, we shall consider the primary causes responsible for the short-run instability of the industry.

Three main causes are sufficient: general business fluctuations, World War II, and strikes. First, maritime shipping depends directly upon the volume of total national production. Hence movements of general business ought to show up in shipping statistics. Was this true during these years, and if so, how close was the relationship?

Second, World War II temporarily thrust aside the forces making for persistent decline in Pacific Coast maritime shipping—forces already evident in the late 'thirties. As a global conflict, the war required an unprecedented expansion of overseas shipping. What were the impacts of this expansion for shipping on the Pacific Coast? What happened to the domestic trades? And what kind of legacy did the war bequeath the industry?

Third, it is hardly questionable that strikes depressed the annual totals of shipping volume in certain years. Indeed, there is no dearth of claims that these strikes alone explain the present plight of the industry. How important and how frequent were these strikes, and how great was their influence?

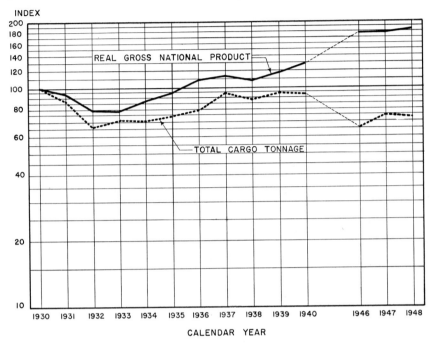

Fig. 20. Indexes of real gross national product and total cargo tonnage of the Pacific Coast maritime shipping industry, 1930–1940, 1946–1948 (1930 = 100). Source: Appendix, table 15.

We shall begin by examining the effects of business fluctuations. ● *The Influence of Business Fluctuations.*—As a service industry engaged in the movement of cargoes and passengers by water, maritime shipping is directly affected by changes in the level of national production and income. The causal relation is direct: shipping volume depends upon total production—among other factors. Total national production, in contrast, clearly does not depend in any important degree upon shipping volume.

However, certain qualifications are in order at the outset. First, the level of national production is only one of several influences simultaneously affecting shipping volume. None of these influences can be wholly isolated for analysis. The degree of correspondence between shipping tonnage and national output will therefore vary from time to time. Second, only in a literal sense was World War II a "business fluctuation." Rather, it was primarily an irregular or erratic force of very great magnitude that originated from outside the American economy. Hence we shall treat the war as a separate influence. Last, the volume of exports to foreign countries—which averaged between a fourth and a fifth of total Pacific Coast tonnage—need not move directly or closely with American production. After all, exports are a relatively small part of American output, and their volume moves mainly with foreign demand.

The influence of business fluctuations may be explored on two levels: total cargo tonnage in all trades combined, and tonnage in specific trades. We shall consider each of these in turn.[1]

Total trade. Comparing changes in "real" gross national product with changes in Pacific Coast water-borne cargo tonnage will indicate the correspondence of maritime shipping activity with business fluctuations. We have used "real" gross national product because it is the most inclusive index available, hence probably the most sensitive to actual changes in the level of total production.[2]

Figure 20 illustrates the comparative behavior of the indexes of total tonnage (not including government emergency or army dry-cargo tonnage) and real gross national product (1930 = 100). In eight out of the twelve peacetime years for which annual changes can be observed, both series moved in the same direction. In two of the four years of contrary movements (1934 and 1948), it seems likely that major coastwide shipping strikes distorted the tonnage series. If

---

[1] To the reader not especially interested in the details of the relationships between general business conditions and the volume of cargo tonnage in each trade we suggest that he read the following section on total trade and then turn to the summary, pp. 127–128.

[2] "Real" gross national product is derived from gross national product (the market value of the nation's output of goods and services before deduction of depreciation charges and other allowances for business and institutional consumption of durable capital goods) by correction of the original magnitudes for changes in the price level, which yields a more accurate measure of actual changes in physical production, not magnified by changes in the value of money. The "real" gross product series used here is expressed in 1939 prices, and was taken from United States Department of Commerce, *Survey of Current Business*, supplement, "National income and product of the United States, 1929–1950" (Washington, Government Printing Office, 1951), table A, p. 146.

there had been no protracted strike in 1934, tonnage probably would have increased, instead of almost equaling 1933; and if there had been no lengthy strike in 1948, tonnage in that year probably would not have fallen relative to 1947. So far as *direction* of annual changes is concerned, there is a fair amount of parallelism in the behavior of the two series. This parallelism, however, is lessened when we compare *percentages* of change between successive years. For six particular years the conformity is reasonably close, particularly in the 1937–1939 recession and partial recovery. After 1939, all correspondence between the two series ceases.[3]

How did tonnage and national output correspond for periods longer than one year? The Burns-Mitchell reference cycle for the American economy places the trough of the 1929 depression in 1932, which was followed by unbroken recovery to a peak in 1937. The year 1938 began a new decline, and with 1938 their data end.[4] With the exception of the 1934 strike year, Pacific Coast shipping during 1930–1938 fits this reference pattern perfectly. This is also true for the gross national product series, except that its depression low fell in 1933 instead of 1932.

Further examination of the tonnage and gross product series reveals certain facts of high importance. First, although their 1930–1939 patterns are similar in general conformation, shipping shows a markedly

---

[3] A statistical test of the degree of association of annual changes in total tonnage with changes in real gross national output during 1930–1940 yields an adjusted coefficient of linear correlation of .75 and an index of determination of .565. The first measure means that the two series were fairly closely associated; and the second, that about 56 per cent of the changes in tonnage were linked to changes in total output, with 44 per cent attributable to all other influences. On a priori grounds, we interpret these relationships as showing some dependence of tonnage upon national production, and not merely chance association or mutual dependence upon some unknown third factor. (See above, pp. 109–110.) More important, however, the correlation loses all significance when the 1946–1948 observations are included with the values for 1930–1940. This means that during 1946–1948 other causal factors clearly outweighed any continuing influence exerted by total output upon the movement of cargo tonnage. (See below, pp. 113–114.)

The standard error of estimate for the estimating equation was 4.8 million tons.

We are fully aware of the pitfalls inherent in correlation analysis of time series. Our purpose was simply to test the observed association of the two series, in which dependence was assumed on good theoretical grounds. We do not propose the findings for use as an equation for prediction of future behavior; the 1946–1948 divergence is too obvious to warrant it, not to mention more technical difficulties.

[4] Arthur F. Burns and Wesley C. Mitchell, *Measuring Business Cycles* (New York, National Bureau of Economic Research, 1946), p. 78.

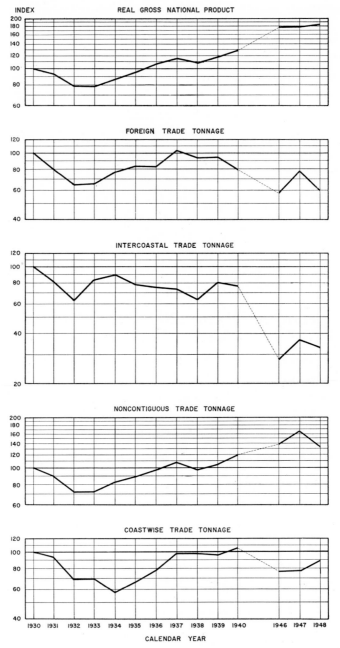

Fig. 21. Indexes of real gross national product and foreign, intercoastal, noncontiguous, and coastwise trade cargo tonnages, Pacific Coast maritime shipping industry, 1930–1940, 1946–1948 (1930 = 100). Source: Appendix, table 15.

greater relative decline during the 1930–1932 slump, and a clearly weaker recovery to the 1937 peak. In that year, national product was nearly 13 per cent above 1930, whereas shipping was 5 per cent lower. By 1940, this divergence was even greater: output was 28 per cent

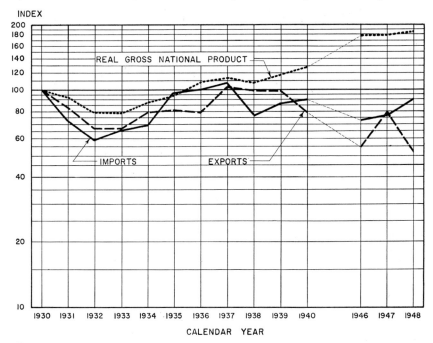

Fig. 22. Indexes of real gross national product and of imports and exports in foreign trade, Pacific Coast maritime shipping industry, 1930–1940, 1946–1948 (1930 = 100). Source: Appendix, tables 15 and 16.

over while tonnage was 7 per cent below 1930. Without doubt, shipping during the 'thirties was feeling the adverse effects of other influences, whose collective impact increasingly offset the stimulus of increasing national output after 1933.

Second, this protracted weakness in prewar shipping performance recurs with undeniable clarity during the first postwar years. Even in the best of those years (1947) tonnage was 25 per cent below 1930; national output was 80 per cent higher. So far as shipping was concerned, the depressive forces had clearly gained the upper hand despite unprecedented prosperity in the country as a whole.

We therefore conclude that, although during the 'thirties changes in business conditions and total tonnage were rather closely paralleled by derived movements in tonnage, the correspondence was cyclical and certainly not secular in character. Other factors became increasingly important and, in the postwar years, clearly dominant.

Foreign trade. As figure 21 indicates, total Pacific Coast foreign trade in the main followed the conformation of the gross product series up through 1938. Even in these years, however, foreign trade showed pronounced weakness, falling much further relatively during 1930–1932, and subsequently failing to recover as fully as total production. This weakness became painfully apparent after 1938, when the movements of the two series were markedly divergent. By 1946–1948, this divergence was very great, with foreign tonnage at about 35 per cent less than 1930 and total production about 80 per cent larger than 1930.

Since exports during 1930–1948 accounted for about three-quarters of total Pacific Coast foreign trade they were the more important element in changes in the volume of this trade. Exports often reflected the influence of policies of foreign governments toward imports from the United States—a factor to some extent independent of business fluctuations in this country.[5]

Comparison of the exports and gross product series (figure 22) bears this out. In a rough way, exports did follow the pattern of the product series through 1938, but thereafter the divergence was extreme. And even before 1938, the export series lagged well behind. Clearly, the poor performance of total foreign trade was mainly attributable to the behavior of exports.

Imports were of lesser importance. Movements in their volume showed much greater volatility than did exports, as figure 22 indicates. Imports fell 40 per cent between 1930 and 1932, when total output dropped 20 per cent. By the 1937 peak, imports recovered to

---

[5] No doubt there was some interconnection: the fall of United States imports during the depression, for example, by drastically reducing the supply of dollars for foreign exchange, induced restrictive policies. In some instances, however, these policies also had independent origins. Whatever their origins, their continuing effect was cumulatively to check United States exports, notwithstanding recovery in this country. See above, pp. 64–67.

107 per cent of their 1930 level, and total production was about 13 per cent above 1930. Yet in the 1938 recession, import volume fell drastically (almost 25 per cent below 1937) as compared with a decrease of about 4 per cent in output. During 1939 and 1940, imports and output recovered by about the same percentage. As expected, imports were much more sensitive to movements in domestic production and income than were exports from the Pacific Coast.[6] Even in 1947 and 1948, the volume of imports expanded. Here, however, the postwar divergence between the behavior of cargo tonnage and national output once more was evident. The high level of domestic production (80 per cent over 1930) was associated with an import volume that averaged 20 per cent below 1930. As noted in chapter iv, factors other than general business were at work—some domestic, some foreign.

Intercoastal trade. Between 1930 and 1934, intercoastal trade and gross national product changed in the same direction except that the former reached its low point in 1932 and the latter in 1933. Their relationship is shown in figure 21. However, intercoastal tonnage fell further (relative to 1930) during the 1930–1932 downswing, and rose further (relative to 1932) in the 1933–1934 upswing. After 1934, the only remaining correspondence in the behavior of the two series turns up in the 1938 recession and 1939 revival, and there in both directions the relative change was greater for intercoastal traffic.

Beyond doubt, the most important fact revealed by figure 21 is the widening gap between the two series after 1934, a gap of astonishing size by 1946–1948. Instead of sharing in the slow but generally persistent recovery in national output after 1933, the intercoastal trade was slowly declining through the later 'thirties, after which the decline became a collapse. Granting that volume in this trade showed some dependence upon the level of general business during 1930–1934 and again in 1938–1939, two inferences are clearly suggested. First, that the general pattern of the intercoastal series cannot be explained by fluctuations in the American economy; and second, that other causal influences were therefore dominant in accounting for the behavior of

---

[6] This is generally true of United States imports. See above, pp. 67–70, for a discussion of import-income relationships.

this trade. We shall only suggest these other more powerful influences noted in chapters v and viii: substitution of land transport, industrialization of the west, and the shifting patterns of trade, output, and consumption of locally produced raw materials such as petroleum and lumber.

Coastwise trade. With the exception of two years, tonnage in the coastwise trade parallels rather closely the pattern of the gross product series, as figure 21 shows. Looking at the larger aspects of the pattern, however, we find persistent weakness in coastwise tonnage relative to general business. It failed to recover from its low to the same degree, and so began in the 'forties at about the same level as in 1930; total production in 1940 was 28 per cent above 1930. This persistent lag in coastwise trade was even more marked by 1946–1948, when tonnage averaged about 20 per cent below 1930, while national output was running 80 per cent above. As with the other trades, then, we must recognize the increasingly powerful effects of additional causes, to account fully for the behavior of the coastwise series. Among these causes, we suggest that diversion of traffic to rival carriers—trucks, railroads, and pipelines—was probably the most important.[7]

It should be noted that petroleum tonnage carried in tankers strongly dominated the coastwise trade throughout the period, accounting for 91 per cent of all tonnage in 1939 and 98 per cent in 1947–1948.[8] Tankship traffic is handled either by the oil companies themselves or by specialized contract carriers. If we consider the commercial dry-cargo tonnage alone, we find some measure of recovery between 1933 and 1935 (interrupted by the 1934 strike) and stable behavior through 1939. After 1939, business conditions markedly improved in the United States, and 1946–1948 saw the emergence of a well-defined boom. Yet the coastwise dry-cargo trade shrank close to the point of extinction in these postwar years.

Noncontiguous trade. The tonnage pattern for noncontiguous (Alaska-Hawaii) trade conformed remarkably well with movements in gross national output during 1930–1940. Year-to-year changes in

---

[7] Tests of this factor are presented in chap. v.

[8] Appendix, table 22, for coastwise dry cargo; Gorter and Hildebrand, *op. cit.*, Vol. I, Appendix II, table 8, for total coastwise tonnage, including petroleum.

both series were identical in direction and very close in relative amounts, as figure 21 shows. The dependence of this trade upon the volume of general business was clearly indicated—in the 1930–1933 contraction, the 1934–1937 recovery, the 1938 recession, and the 1940–1941 revival.

For 1946–1948, the correspondence in the two series is less apparent. During these years, noncontiguous tonnage ran well above

TABLE 4

COMPARATIVE PERCENTAGE CHANGES IN GROSS NATIONAL PRODUCT AND CARGO
TONNAGE, FOR PERIODS OF MAJOR BUSINESS MOVEMENTS, 1930–1948[a]

Period	Real gross national product	Total tonnage	Trades			
			Foreign	Inter-coastal	Coast-wise	Non-contiguous
1930–1932.........	−20.7	−33.6	−35.6	−37.5	−31.5	−28.6
1932–1937.........	42.0	42.2	59.5	18.4	40.7	50.0
1937–1938.........	−4.4	−6.7	−8.5	−15.5	1.2	−10.0
1946–1948.........	3.7	10.8	3.5	15.0	16.7	−5.2
1930–1948.........	83.7	−27.3	−40.3	−67.7	−10.6	32.1

[a] Percentage changes calculated from first year of designated period. Figures for total tonnage and for foreign trade tonnage for 1946–1948 do not include cargoes for the army or for emergency government relief programs.
SOURCE: For real gross national output, see above, p. 110, n. 2; for all cargo tonnage series, see Gorter and Hildebrand, *op. cit.*, Vol. I, Appendix II, table 8. Figure for 1948 coastwise and total tonnage revised. See Appendix, table 6.

prewar levels, averaging 45 per cent above 1930, while national output was 80 per cent larger. In this respect, the two series moved together. However, they were seriously divergent during the three postwar years themselves. The tonnage values are strongly humped around 1947, whereas output showed small but steady growth in all three years. Major coastwide strikes in 1946 and 1948 were the main reason for the humped behavior of noncontiguous tonnage.

We conclude, then, that business fluctuations were the major factor determining the behavior of noncontiguous trade during 1930–1948. Considering the nature of the trade, this conclusion is not surprising. Operations are reserved by law for domestic carriers. More important, there is no rivalry with carriers using land routes. Air competition is a recent development, limited to low bulk cargoes of high value, and so could have had little impact upon tonnage. Alaska and Hawaii, furthermore, are primarily exporters of raw materials to the continental United States. American demand for these products directly reflects the volume of domestic production and consumption. In turn, proceeds from these exports directly influence imports into Alaska and Hawaii from the mainland. Thus the volume of noncontiguous trade can be expected to move directly with domestic business conditions. By reason of their protected position, the water carriers in the trade will share fully in tonnage changes.

Summary. Although there is no reason to expect a one-to-one correspondence between movements of general business and changes in cargo tonnage, there is ground for expecting that there will be some direct correspondence between the two series during pronounced swings in national production. More accurately, when correspondence in the latter sense is poor or lacking entirely, we then must look for the presence of other factors affecting the volume of shipping.

In table 4, the comparative performances of national production and cargo tonnage are summarized.

● *The Effects of World War II.*—As a causal influence upon the economic behavior of Pacific Coast maritime shipping, World War II should be classed as an erratic and powerful force. Like general business movements, the war shows up in statistics of the industry as a well-defined cycle of expansion and decline. The cycle began with 1942, reached its crest in 1945, and by 1948 had sharply receded but was still not fully completed.

Lacking, as we do, over-all tonnage figures for 1942–1945, our appraisal here must rest upon incomplete data. These data are sufficient, however, to indicate the main outlines of the war cycle in Pacific Coast shipping.

On the negative side, the American entry into the war led to a complete shutdown of the coastwise and intercoastal trades for more than three years. This development is examined more fully at a later point in this discussion. On the positive side, the war brought about a great expansion of military tonnage moving mainly between the Pacific Coast and the Pacific theaters of the conflict. At their peak in 1945,

United States Army dry cargoes alone aggregated 10.5 million long tons. At the same time total gang-hours worked by longshoremen rose 70 per cent over 1935–1939 by 1945, and the number of registered men increased by two-thirds. Seagoing personnel increased fivefold. As of January, 1941, the Pacific American Shipowners Association reported twenty-one member companies, operating 146 vessels, and employing 8,881 seagoing personnel. By August, 1945, PASA had twenty-nine member companies, 1,100 ships in service, and 49,343 seagoing workers.[9]

The expansion phase of the war cycle got under way in 1942. By 1945, cargo tonnage and all of the employment series reached their peaks. Contraction followed in 1946–1948. By 1948, army dry cargo had fallen 80 per cent below 1945. This tonnage, however, still remained substantial (2.5 million long tons in 1948) and also was strongly supplemented by emergency government relief cargoes arising as an aftermath of the war. Compared with 1945, the input of gang-hours had fallen over 50 per cent.[10] Offshore, the Pacific American Shipowners Association reported only 340 ships in service in 1948, a decline of nearly 70 per cent. Seagoing personnel had fallen by over 75 per cent in the same period. In short, although the war cycle was not fully completed by 1948, the phase of contraction had largely eliminated the enormous wartime gains in tonnage and employment.

For the tonnage and employment series of the industry, then, the war was felt in two major ways. First, it imposed a special kind of cycle that was not fully complete after seven years' duration. Second, the war intensified the scale of year-to-year movements of expansion and decline, increasing the instability of the industry in the short run.

Moreover, World War II exerted powerful effects in other ways as

---

[9] Data for longshoremen were taken from Gorter and Hildebrand, *op. cit.*, Vol. I, pp. 44–47.

The PASA data were obtained from a mimeographed tabulation entitled "Offshore Employment," prepared by the Pacific Maritime Association (San Francisco, Feb. 21, 1950). The PASA statistics cover almost all steamship lines having headquarters on the Pacific Coast.

[10] The 1948 strike undoubtedly depressed the total, but even by 1947 gang-hours had fallen about one-third; registered longshoremen in 1948 were nearly one-fourth fewer in number.

well. Price inflation, which was temporarily suppressed during the war, occurred in the postwar years, much to the disadvantage of American lines faced with foreign competition. Increases in the costs of shipbuilding made vessel replacements very expensive. In the domestic trades, sharp increases in loading and operating costs drove the water carriers into a ruthless competitive squeeze relative to rail and truck rivals. In all instances, this inflationary pressure had much to do with the two protracted coastwide strikes in 1946, which proved so costly in direct losses as well as in the greatly increased operating expenses resulting from settlement terms.

When the intercoastal lines resumed peacetime operations at the end of 1945, they were confronted at the outset with the task of rebuilding their former customer relationships. Practically speaking, this involved recapture of customers from the railroads and truck lines. In this attempt, the vessel operators were forced to compete at rates that were insufficient to cover soaring costs. Even though rail and water rate increases went into effect between 1946 and 1948, the water carriers were unable to compete as effectively as in the prewar years.[11] As a result, the postwar intercoastal trade was severely crippled. It resumed operation only on a limited scale, with about 55 ships in service in 1948 as against 143 ships in 1939.[12] Tonnage moved was far below prewar, and the competitive squeeze became even worse with the passage of time.

The coastwise lines fared no better. They, too, were closed down during the war years. In reviving their services after the war, they, too, were caught between rising costs and unremunerative competitive rates. Consequently, as of 1948, only one common carrier and seven contract lumber operators had survived in the dry-cargo portion of this trade.[13] By contrast, in 1938 there were thirteen common carrier coastwise dry-cargo lines, offering a broad array of frequent sailings.[14]

---

[11] See below, pp. 160–164.

[12] U. S. Senate, *Final Report of the committee on interstate and foreign commerce . . . pursuant to S. Res. 50: A resolution authorizing the committee on interstate and foreign commerce to investigate problems relating to the United States merchant marine*, 81st Cong., 2d sess. (Washington, Government Printing Office, 1950), p. 14.

[13] *Ibid.*, p. 15.

[14] Compiled from schedules published in the *Pacific Shipper*, a trade paper, for the last quarter of 1938. For further discussion, see below, pp. 166, 168, n. 29.

The almost total extinction of this once great trade cannot, of course, be attributed to the war alone. But there is no doubt that the war dealt it a crippling blow.

It is clear, therefore, that the impacts of the war were powerfully felt in many directions. The unique cycle it imposed increased the instability of the industry and, even more, created very difficult problems of adjustment to extremely rapid rates of expansion and decline in scale of operations.

Yet the war cycle favored the industry in some ways. Many operators formerly starved for working capital emerged financially stronger than at any time since the 'twenties. War-induced shipbuilding enabled the carriers to acquire a whole fleet of larger and faster ships, backed by an ample reserve. Finally, the postwar military and relief cargoes provided desperately needed cargo tonnage at a time of badly depressed private foreign trade. For some American lines in this trade, these cargoes meant survival in place of extinction. For longshoring and seafaring workers, postwar government tonnage furnished needed employment at a time of greatly excessive labor supply.

● *The Influence of Work Stoppages.—Summary of the record.* To say that Pacific Coast maritime shipping has been the most strike-ridden industry in the United States is not to indulge in an overstatement.[15] In chapters ix and x we present a detailed account of this record of extreme conflict. At this point we shall limit ourselves to a survey of its major outlines, in order to assess its impacts upon the industry's operations during 1930–1948.

The record properly begins in 1934; before that year independent unionism had been made impotent by disastrous defeats in 1919 and 1921. With 1934, there began the series of five bitter and protracted coastwide strikes that have brought such notoriety to the industry.[16]

---

[15] Following the practice of the United States Bureau of Labor Statistics adopted in 1935, we use the term "strike" in the "generic sense to include all stoppages of work due to labor disputes," without regard to initiating causes. This would therefore include lockouts. United States Department of Labor, Bureau of Labor Statistics, *Handbook of Labor Statistics, 1941 Edition*, bull. no. 694 (Washington, Government Printing Office, 1942), Vol. I, p. 317.

[16] These coastwide strikes sometimes involved the longshoremen or the seafaring unions separately; other times both were involved. Where two or more strikes coincided in time, we have counted them as one. Where separated in time, each was counted as one coastwide strike for the whole industry, since its effect was a total shutdown.

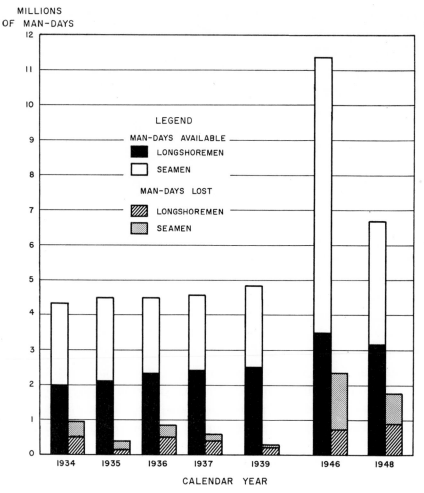

Fig. 23. Man-days lost in thirty-one coastwide and major local strikes compared with man-days available, longshoremen and seamen, Pacific Coast maritime shipping, selected years, 1934–1948. Source: Appendix, tables 21 and 23.

The 1934 shutdown lasted 83 days; that in 1936–1937 lasted 98 days; the sailors' strike in 1946 lasted 21 days, and was followed by a 52-day longshore strike in the same year. Then in 1948, the longshoremen closed down the entire coast for 95 days.[17] Thus these five coastwide strikes cost the industry 349 calendar days of working time in

---

[17] We calculate the length of the strike as the total calendar days the industry was actually shut down, even if formal settlement had been reached earlier.

fifteen years.[18] For the eleven peacetime years in which these strikes actually occurred, nearly one full year or almost 9 per cent of all calendar days was lost in coastwide shutdowns.

There is still more to the record. Between 1934 and 1948, there were twenty-eight major port strikes known to involve 1,000 men or more for one shift or more, and fifty port-wide shutdowns of unknown length.[19] In addition, there were 152 minor local strikes known to involve at least one gang (eleven or twelve men) for at least one shift. Last, there were 1,103 other minor local strikes of unknown length but involving more than one man.[20] In total, then, the industry suffered from 1,338 strikes in the fifteen-year period of 1934–1948, and eighty-three of these strikes were particularly serious in their impacts.

There is another dimension to the industry's strike record—the ratio of man-days lost to man-days available for each year. This can be calculated for the five coastwide shutdowns and for twenty-six of the twenty-eight major port strikes of known length.[21] Figure 23 sharply reveals these losses. Longshoring operations are the pivot on which the whole industry turns. In 1934, 22 per cent of available longshore working time was lost in major strikes; in 1936, nearly 18 per cent; in 1937, 12 per cent; in 1946, nearly 21 per cent; and in 1948, nearly 27 per cent. Parallel calculations to include time lost by seagoing workers in these strikes yield closely corresponding percentages for these same years. There can be no doubt that the industry was hurt badly by these strikes.

Impacts of the strikes. Admittedly, there is no precise way to determine how much tonnage was lost to the industry from strikes. There are too many unknowns in the problem. On the one side, operating delays from short strikes often can be made up with overtime work, and losses of new business will usually be negligible. As for the coast-

[18] Maritime shipping is continuous, working day and night, seven days a week.

[19] A "shift" is a working day of eight hours.

[20] A tabulation of these figures, with indicated sources, may be found in Appendix, tables 17 and 18.

[21] The calculation assumes that each man involved would be available fifty five-day weeks in a given year, and that each man-day normally represents one eight-hour shift. This means that the length of a given strike in calendar days had to be corrected in the conversion to man-days lost by each man in the force. A tabulation, with description of method and indicated sources of data, is provided in Appendix, tables 20 and 21.

wide shutdowns, they were events whose occurrence was expected some time in advance by shippers and operators, because they were preceded by extended negotiations and public controversy, and because it was known (except in 1934) that the contract would expire on a given date. Gang-hour records therefore show pronounced "bulges" for the two weeks immediately preceding and following these strikes. In some part, at least, the actual losses were offset in this manner.

To some extent, moreover, the coverage of the particular strike will directly influence the magnitude of tonnage loss. A lengthy coastwide strike induces diversion of traffic from Pacific Coast maritime shipping as a whole. In contrast, a port-wide strike may partly be offset by diversion to other Pacific Coast ports, without complete loss of tonnage by water carriers. Still more, a strike affecting a local stevedoring concern may be overcome by substituting the services of competitors at the same port, without complete loss to the water carriers. Finally, a strike involving a single carrier may only mean diversion of tonnage to competitors in the trade, again without complete loss to the industry as a whole.

These, then, are the unknowns that tend to reduce the losses resulting from strikes. On the other side, there are powerful intangibles that together preclude complete recovery of lost tonnage. Overtime longshore operations before and after long strikes become very costly.[22] High charges and lengthy delays tend to drive away new business and to restrict the scope of such operations. Moreover, there are practical limits to the use of overtime as a means of offsetting time lost. It is not feasible to increase the industry work force to make up for losses from brief strikes, while after a long strike the existing force is physically unable to provide the amount of overtime that would be required to replace fully the strike loss. For example, a longshoreman out for

---

[22] With the 1934 award, overtime pay rates were established for work after 5:00 P.M. and before 8:00 A.M. on weekdays and for all work between 5:00 P.M. on Saturday and 8:00 A.M. the following Monday and on all legal holidays. Overtime was also established for work in excess of six hours during the period 8:00 A.M. to 5.00 P.M. on weekdays, and for work exceeding thirty hours per week in any four-week period. In 1946, the overtime practice was extended further with the provision that work between 5:00 P.M. Friday (rather than Saturday) and 8:00 A.M. Monday was to be at overtime rates. In addition, the *rate* of overtime pay was increased through these years from 41 per cent over the straight-time rate in 1934 to 50 per cent above the base in 1941 and thereafter.

ninety-five days in 1948 could not make up his lost time even by working seven days a week for the remaining thirty-eight weeks in a hypothetical year.[23]

Finally, some business is irrevocably lost as a result of long strikes.
In the coastwise and intercoastal trades, shippers can and do divert
traffic to land carriers, particularly when delivery dates are important,
as with seasonal or perishable merchandise. Shippers forwarding tonnage between the mainland and Hawaii, or the Far East, or Austral-

TABLE 5

ESTIMATED MAN-DAYS LOST IN STRIKES, SELECTED YEARS, PACIFIC
COAST MARITIME SHIPPING INDUSTRY, 1934–1948

Year	Man-days lost		
	Longshoremen	Seagoing workers	Total
1934.	465,000	493,000	949,000
1936.	411,000	388,000	799,000
1937.	348,000	211,000	559.000
1946.	743,000	1,624,000	2,367,000
1948.	847,000	928,000	1,775,000

SOURCE: Appendix, table 21.

asia, can and do divert traffic to Vancouver, or to the Atlantic or Gulf
ports, to avoid delays.

All things considered, therefore, strikes involve some permanent
losses in tonnage, especially when they are coastwide and last a long
time. As an indirect measure of this lost tonnage, we have used man-
days lost in strikes. Table 5 presents our estimate of these losses for
the five most critical years.

We estimate that man-days lost in strikes in these five years ranged
from 12.2 per cent of available working time in 1937 to nearly 27
per cent in 1948. Losses of these magnitudes cannot be wholly made
up by overtime operations, and extensive losses of tonnage for the
Pacific Coast were the result.

How important were tonnage losses in these particular years? There

---

[23] The example is generous, for in fact the industry does not have a year to make up the
delays involved in a three-month strike.

is no way to measure them precisely, but in table 6 we have presented a rough test. It assumes that major changes in national output will give rise to corresponding changes in the same direction, though not necessarily of the same degree, in dry-cargo tonnage.[24]

In the year 1934, national output rose 10 per cent over 1933, while dry cargo increased only 4.3 per cent. The lag in tonnage is large

TABLE 6

COMPARATIVE YEAR-TO-YEAR PERCENTAGE CHANGES IN REAL GROSS NATIONAL PRODUCT AND DRY-CARGO TONNAGE IN PACIFIC COAST MARITIME SHIPPING, FOR SELECTED YEARS, 1934–1948

Year	Real gross national product (1930 = 100)	Total dry cargo (million long tons)	Per cent change from preceding year	
			National product	Dry-cargo tonnage
1933..........................	78.7	13.9	....	....
1934..........................	86.9	14.5	10.4	4.3
1935..........................	94.6	16.5	....	....
1936..........................	107.4	16.4	13.5	−0.6
1937..........................	112.6	17.5	4.8	6.7
1946..........................	177.2	10.9	....	a
1947..........................	177.5	14.5	0.2	33.0
1948..........................	183.7	11.1	3.5	−23.4

a No dry-cargo figure is obtainable for 1945. The year 1947 was almost free of strikes. It was included to provide a bench mark for comparison with tonnage totals for 1946 and 1948, when serious strikes occurred.
SOURCE: Appendix, tables 15 and 22.

enough to suggest that the long coastwide strike in that year was primarily responsible. In 1936, output rose 13.5 per cent over 1935, while dry cargo declined slightly by 0.6 per cent. Almost 18 per cent of available working time in that year was lost in strikes, which again were mainly responsible for the disappointing performance in tonnage. The year 1937 presents a somewhat different story. Strikes cost the industry about 12 per cent of available working time. Although this loss was large, it was well below that for 1936. For this reason primarily, dry-cargo tonnage could increase 6.7 per cent over 1936.

[24] We have used dry-cargo, rather than total, tonnage because longshoremen do not handle tanker movements of petroleum and its products, and the tanker lines were not organized by the maritime unions until the late 'thirties, when they came under separate bargaining agreements. These operators were therefore exempt from the major strikes.

Yet total tonnage (including petroleum and its products) rose by 18.6 per cent at the same time. Had the strike loss in 1937 been even lower, dry cargo might have attained an even higher level over 1936.

From the standpoint of strike losses, the years 1946 and 1948 were the worst in the series. We cannot determine the change in dry-cargo tonnage from 1945 to 1946, but we can compare 1946 with 1947. The year 1947 was almost entirely free of strikes; in 1946, however, about 20 per cent of available working time was lost in stoppages. Moreover, national production in 1947 was almost identical with 1946. Yet dry-cargo tonnage increased by one-third in 1947 over 1946. Clearly, strikes depressed the 1946 total. In that year, strikes caused a loss of 2,367,000 man-days of work, as against only 33,000 man-days in 1947.

In 1948, dry cargo fell 23.4 per cent below 1947. Economic conditions were prosperous nevertheless, and national output rose 3.5 per cent in the same year. Once more, strikes accounted for the large loss in tonnage. In 1948, nearly two million man-days were lost, over a quarter of available working time. Compare these figures with the loss of a mere 33,000 man-days in 1947 and the conclusion is unavoidable that strikes in 1948 badly crippled the industry.[25]

In five out of eleven peacetime years between 1934 and 1948, then, strikes caused significant losses of tonnage, even if the precise amounts cannot be determined. The short-run effect of these strikes was to increase the annual fluctuations in the tonnage handled and in the work opportunities afforded by the industry. In addition, the strikes made scheduled services highly unreliable for shippers. Thus it is probable that over the long run some traffic was permanently lost to the industry.

● *Summary.*—The three causal factors reviewed in this chapter—business fluctuations, the war, and strikes—by no means wholly explain the economic performance of the industry during 1930–1948. The declining trend in operations is still to be accounted for. What these influences do explain is the year-to-year instability of the industry and its pronounced cyclical swings over the whole nineteen-year

[25] Annual man-days lost in strikes, compared with man-days available, are presented in Appendix, tables 21 and 23.

period. Together they show that demand for the industry's services (exerted mainly through general business movements and the war) was crucially important in producing the characteristic "feast-or-famine" pattern. Here the industry had to adapt itself to externally imposed forces, quite beyond its control. The third factor—strikes—also produced instability. In one sense these strikes, too, were an externally imposed force. In the postwar years they reflected the effects of inflation upon the demand for labor in all industries, and the political pressures upon the leaders of the maritime unions "to keep up with the procession." To this degree, the strike factor also was beyond the control of the industry.

In another sense, however, the industry's strike record was an internally created influence. It had its origins in the bargaining structure developed by the parties and, more important, in the unusually intense conflicts peculiar to Pacific Coast shipping. Here lies the main explanation of the coastwide strikes, and of the frequency and great length of the shutdowns during the period. In this respect, the parties in the industry had some potential control over strikes as a causal influence. From the extreme strike record, it is clear that management and labor in the industry were largely unable to compose their differences peacefully. Their failure to do so imposed heavy losses all around. To round out our explanation of maritime shipping's performance during 1930–1948, in chapters ix-xi we shall explore more fully the area of industrial conflict and its basic causes. Before doing so, however, we shall first consider, in the next two chapters, the impacts of rising costs upon competitive relationships between the water carriers and the railroads and trucks.

CHAPTER VII

Wages and
Productivity

~~~~~~~~~~~~~~~~~~~~~~~~~~~~~~

● *Introduction.*—Between 1934 and 1937,
the Pacific Coast maritime shipping industry
found itself confronted by the challenge of several highly aggressive
unions, determined to achieve major gains in wages and working conditions. Thus began a protracted fifteen-year conflict. Part of this conflict was forcefully revealed in the enormous strike losses described in
the last chapter. (We defer to Part III the full story of the struggle, its
underlying causes, and its broad impacts upon the industry.) In this
chapter and the next we shall explore two important problems, both of
which were closely related to the development of labor-management
relations but which have independent interest in themselves. First,
what were the effects of renewed collective bargaining upon wage rates
and labor productivity in the industry, between 1935 and 1948?
Second, what happened to production costs and how did changes in
costs affect the competitive position of the industry? Before attacking
these problems, let us make clear the assumption and scope of our
analysis.

To test the economic success of unionism, we have calculated indexes of basic wage rates for the seven principal occupational groups
separately and for all of them together. These indexes measure relative

changes in the pure price of labor as derived from basic job rates. Since they do not include the effects of premium pay for overtime or penalty work, they understate the actual increases in hourly earnings. They also fail to reflect changes in annual wage earnings arising from increases or decreases in total time worked, and they do not indicate improvements in working conditions, such as increased provisions in kind for shipboard personnel. Hence the indexes are conservative in their implications, despite the large gains that they reveal. For this very reason, there is ample warrant for using them as approximations, for comparisons with changes in the cost of living and with indexes of hourly earnings of employees in manufacturing, in railroading, and in motor truck transportation. Moreover, given rather substantial evidence attesting against any marked growth in the productivity of Pacific Coast maritime labor, we regard the over-all index of wage rates as a reasonable, conservative measure of changes in unit labor cost for tonnage handled.

It would be a serious but hardly novel error to regard collective bargaining in all situations as a separate and isolated causal force, having some mysterious power of its own to influence wages, and acting quite independently either of the surrounding economy or of the given firm or industry. Obviously, the bargaining environment normally imposes its own limits. Yet there are exceptions. By closure of entry and control over labor supply, a trade union can successfully defy the penalty of reduced job opportunities, and therefore can invoke an aggressive cost-increasing wage policy. In general, this was what occurred in Pacific Coast maritime shipping; the monopolistic accouterments of the closed shop, closed entry, and union rationing of available work all emerged between 1934 and 1937.[1] With these powers the unions were able to impose large increases in wage costs, notwithstanding what became in the long run an unfavorable labor market. Indeed, this very policy was an important *contributing* cause of the decline of the industry. As we shall subsequently see, the rise of costs imposed by unionism was most keenly felt in the highly competitive

---

[1] The origins, development, and range of the unions' control over labor supply are described in chaps. ix and x. See also below, pp. 144–146.

coastwise and intercoastal trades. At this point we merely desire to emphasize our view that in maritime shipping, bargaining power had a basis in fact and functioned as an important cause of economic change.

Ambitious unionism drove up production costs in four major ways: basic wage rates and ancillary wages (overtime and penalty rates); resistance to increased physical productivity; weakened managerial control over selection, direction, and discipline of personnel; and strike losses leading directly to lower volume and probably to some permanent losses of tonnage. It has not been possible to assess increases of cost stemming from strike losses and weakened managerial control of personnel.[2] Thus we have limited ourselves to a quantitative analysis of changes in wage rates and an over-all test of the productivity of longshoremen.

It is conventional to separate production costs into two classes, fixed and variable. Within the former are grouped the familiar elements of overhead expenses; within the latter are included wage outlays and expenses for materials and supplies. Now it may be objected that since wages, or more accurately unit labor costs, are not the whole of average cost either for the short or the long run, it is misleading to place much emphasis on them. Although we recognize that wages are never 100 per cent of all costs, we do hold that in maritime shipping they were the most important single variable working from the side of costs to weaken the industry's competitive position. It has been estimated that for shipping lines in the domestic trades (those reporting to the Interstate Commerce Commission) employee compensation constituted about 40 per cent of total operating expense.[3] For stevedoring alone

[2] A qualitative analysis of the decline of the employers' authority in personnel matters and of the "quickie" strike problem is presented in chap. x. The issue of efficiency (and indirectly of productivity) of longshoremen is also reviewed in chap. x.

[3] Total operating expenses included the following types of expenses: maintenance, depreciation and amortization, transportation (line service, terminal service), casualties, traffic, general, insurance, operating rents, taxes other than federal income taxes. This breakdown obtained from Interstate Commerce Commission, Bureau of Transport Economics and Statistics, *Selected Financial and Operating Statistics from Annual Reports of Carriers by Inland and Coastal Waterway and Maritime Carriers, 1948*, Statement No. 4940 (Washington, Oct., 1949), table 1, pp. 4–27.

Of interest is the Commission's finding that the employee compensation amounted to

the percentage was much higher. These high proportions made maritime shipping vulnerable to aggressive unionism.

The water lines of the Pacific Coast face two important kinds of competition, that of foreign flag vessels in the foreign trade, and that of land-based carriers in the coastwise and intercoastal trades. In the foreign trade, on trade routes classified as essential, cost pressure can be largely absorbed by federal operating subsidies without recourse to substantial rate increases. In other instances, cargoes not carried by United States flag vessels because of higher rates or less desirable service will often shift to foreign vessels and result in no loss of cargoes moving across Pacific Coast wharves and hence no decline in cargo tonnage moving to and from the Pacific Coast by ocean-going vessels. In the coastwise and intercoastal trades, however, this is not so. Here, then, is the zone in which rising costs have exerted their greatest influence upon the industry's competitive position.

In this chapter, we present our analysis of wage rates and productivity, and in the next, our appraisal of changes in costs and their impacts upon the competitive position of the water lines.

● *Maritime Wage Rates, 1935–1948.*—As used here, basic job rates refer only to the payment per unit of straight time spent on the job— for longshoremen, the hour, and for seagoing personnel, the month.[4] Figure 24 shows the behavior of an index (simple average) of basic pay rates for twenty-two key occupations of the seven maritime crafts, from 1935 to 1948. There were three distinct upswings—1937, 1940– 1941, and 1945–1948. The first occurred during the peak year of the

---

about 60 per cent of total operating expenses for Class I line-haul railroads and approximately 40 per cent for Class I motor carriers of property.

Figures based on computations made by the Interstate Commerce Commission from its *Selected Financial and Operating Statistics* (for water carriers), *Statistics of Railways in the United States,* and *Statistics of Class I Motor Carriers* as published in Interstate Commerce Commission, Bureau of Transport Economics and Statistics, *Ex Parte 165, Problems in the Regulation of Domestic Transportation by Water,* by C. S. Morgan (Washington, Government Printing Office, 1946), p. 310.

[4] Our measure therefore excludes all overtime premiums and penalty pay for certain kinds of work or for handling of certain types of cargo. The latter elements would appear in a measure of gross average hourly earnings, which would rise and fall more readily than would an index of basic rates alone. The latter is only a first approximation to actual movements in wage costs, but was the only index that could be derived from the available evidence. It really understates the actual increase of labor costs to the industry in spite of the very large relative increases it reveals,

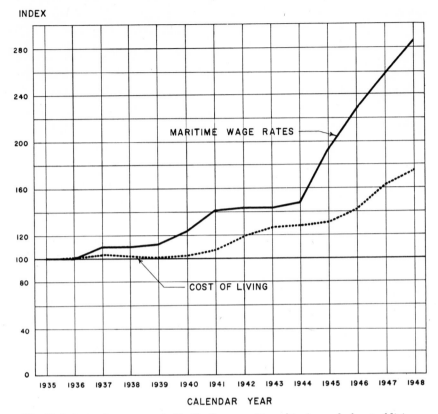

Fig. 24. Indexes of wage rates in Pacific Coast maritime shipping and of cost of living, 1935–1948 (1935 = 100). Source: Appendix, tables 24 and 25.

post-1932 shipping recovery and was facilitated by increasing demand for maritime labor. The second coincided with the early phase of World War II, when demand was again increasing, this time following the 1938 shipping slump. The third (1945–1948) followed three years of rather effective federal wage control and is more difficult to interpret. By late 1945, the demand for maritime labor had started its precipitous decline. Yet wage rates began an unprecedented rise. The primary reason seems to have been the general postwar inflation. The pull of increasing money demand made it possible for unions throughout the economy to obtain large wage increases without the penalty of reduced employment. In spite of increasing unemployment in the

INDEX

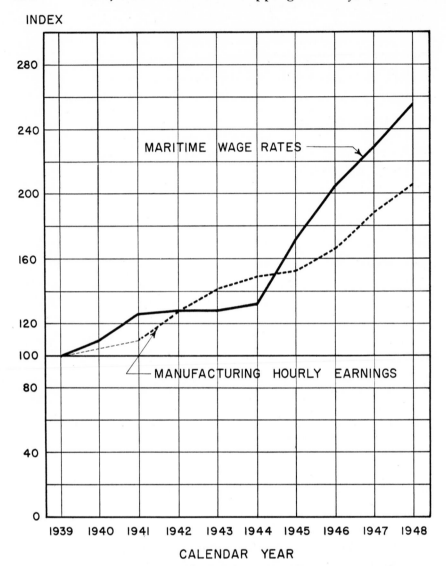

CALENDAR YEAR

Fig. 25. Indexes of wage rates in Pacific Coast maritime shipping and of average hourly earnings of production workers in manufacturing, 1939–1948 (1939 = 100). Source: Appendix, table 26.

shipping industry, the leaders of the maritime unions were under great pressure from the rank and file to match these increases. Moreover, their unusual monopoly power enabled them to meet the problem of unemployment by refusing to admit men to the unions, by expelling wartime temporary men, and by reducing the work quotas in the rotation of jobs.[5] Furthermore, the maritime employers offered relatively little resistance to wage pressure, probably because to a considerable extent their operations were on federal account or subject to various kinds of federal aid.

For 1935–1948 as a whole, the trend of maritime wage rates was strongly upward. In a nutshell, the operators in 1948 were paying basic rates that exceeded the 1935 rates by about 185 per cent.[6] This was not all. Overtime pay for the seagoing group was greatly increased after 1945, and the longshoremen gained rather extensive penalty rates of about ten cents an hour after 1937. Indeed, the operators consider the "extras" in the wage bill rather than the increases in basic wages to have been more important in raising labor costs.

As figure 24 shows, maritime workers on the Pacific Coast kept well ahead of the cost of living as measured by the index of prices of consumers' goods. That is, these workers turned the "terms of trade" sharply in their favor. To illustrate, the average maritime worker could earn 60 per cent more goods with an hour's work in 1948 than in 1935. He would have had to pay much higher taxes in 1948, however, but so would many others whose real wages had actually fallen. Moreover, the worker's plane of living rests on his total earnings rather than upon the relative value of an hour's work. Postwar, the total work opportunity in the industry fell close to the levels of the late 'thirties, and the number of workers failed to fall as fast—which depressed annual work time per man at a time when wage rates were

---

[5] See chap. x for a description of the development of these controls.

[6] As appears subsequently in the text, there was considerable dispersion in the actual gains, by craft groups. On a 1935 base, the longshoremen gained only 89.6 per cent by 1948, whereas at the other extreme were the sailors, who gained 285.4 per cent. Our index is constructed on a simple average for the seven groups. About half the personnel consists of longshoremen, half seagoing personnel. Thus, on a weighted average basis, the over-all increase between 1935 and 1948 would amount to just under 150 per cent, as against 185.2 per cent on the simple average actually used.

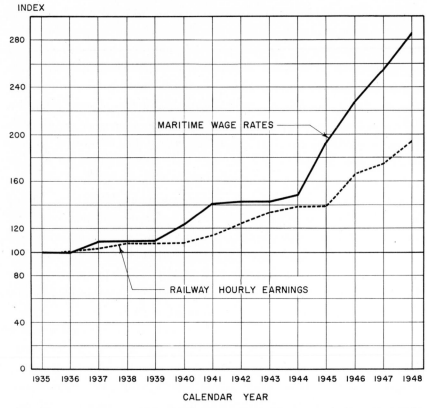

Fig. 26. Indexes of wage rates in Pacific Coast maritime shipping and of average straight-time hourly earnings of Class I railway employees, 1935–1948 (1935 = 100). Source: Appendix, table 25.

rapidly rising. The maritime unions nevertheless placed great stress upon increases in basic rates "to conform to national 'wage patterns,' " "to keep up with the cost of living," and "to share in increasing productivity." That productivity increased is questionable for this industry, but there is no doubt whatever that its workers had beaten the rising cost of living by an impressive margin.

Nor is there any doubt that they had done better than certain other groups of workers. For example, as figure 25 shows, wage rates in Pacific shipping from 1945 have risen more rapidly than the straight-time hourly earnings of production workers in manufacturing industry.[7] On a 1939 base, maritime rates were 156 per cent higher in 1948, while straight-time hourly earnings in manufacturing increased only 107 per cent.

Or, to compare forms of transportation, consider the railways. Railways and ocean shipping are close competitors in the shipment of certain kinds of merchandise. Wages are a high proportion of total costs in both industries, and there is considerable similarity in the structure of labor skills required by both. Also, both have strongly entrenched craft unions. Again, the workers in Pacific Coast maritime shipping did far better, as figure 26 shows. For all of 1935–1948, maritime wage rates rose faster than the straight-time hourly earnings of railway employees.[8] As of 1948, Pacific Coast maritime rates were 185.2 per cent higher than in 1935, while straight-time hourly earnings in railroading had advanced only 93.6 per cent. Between 1945 and 1948, maritime wages rose 47.6 per cent as against an increase of only 39.5 per cent for the railway series. Undoubtedly, this differential gain in maritime wages placed ocean shipping under a serious handicap in its domestic trades. By the same token, the railroads acquired a distinct competitive advantage in the coastwise and intercoastal trades, implications of which are considered later in this chapter.

Though the evidence is much less satisfactory, it appears that soaring wage rates in Pacific shipping also placed the industry at a disadvantage relative to motor trucking. During the ten years between 1937 and 1947, hourly wage rates of truck drivers advanced only 69.2 per cent, while maritime rates increased 158.3 per cent.[9]

On all of these standards of comparison, the rise of basic wage rates in Pacific Coast shipping was indeed remarkable. Wages there markedly exceeded the inflationary rise in the cost of living. Maritime workers gained much more than the average production worker in

---

[7] There is no index of pure wage rates in manufacturing, and instead we have had to use an index of hourly earnings exclusive of overtime, as a substitute. The latter index may overstate the rise in pure wage rates to some extent; if so, it reinforces our conclusion.

[8] The railway data exclude the earnings of executives, officials, and staff assistants. They were computed by dividing total annual payments for straight time by known straight-time hours worked by railway employees.

[9] Wage rates in motor trucking were obtained from United States Department of Labor, Bureau of Labor Statistics, *Handbook of Labor Statistics* (1947), bull. no. 916 (Washington, Government Printing Office, 1948), table C-8, p. 100.

manufacturing. Quite likely they even held their own with some of the most fortunate groups, in terms of wage rates, in the whole economy— skilled crafts in the building trades and bituminous coal miners. And relative to their closest competitors—railway workers and truck drivers—maritime workers gained far greater wage increases.

● *Relative Changes in Maritime Wage Rates.*—How did the different crafts in Pacific shipping fare relative to one another between 1935

TABLE 7

INDEXES OF BASIC WAGE RATES BY CRAFT GROUPS, PACIFIC COAST MARITIME
SHIPPING INDUSTRY, 1935–1948

(1935 = 100)

Craft	1935	1939	1940	1945	1948
Longshoremen...................	100.0	100.0	100.0	142.6	189.6
Sailors.........................	100.0	119.0	135.9	241.6	385.4
Firemen........................	100.0	115.9	131.7	230.9	356.5
Cooks and stewards.............	100.0	112.8	128.0	207.8	297.0
Radio officers...................	100.0	108.7	119.6	189.1	281.2
Engineers......................	100.0	108.5	122.7	171.5	254.2
Officers (deck).................	100.0	117.4	129.2	184.8	268.5
All crafts[a].....................	100.0	111.4	123.3	193.1	285.2

a Represents an average of the annual relatives for twenty-two occupations, and not an average of the craft group relatives shown above.
SOURCE: Appendix, table 24.

and 1948? Were there significant differences in the rates of increase in basic wages?

Table 7 summarizes the evidence. Two groups—the sailors and the firemen—clearly led the field. The pay rates of sailors rose 285.4 per cent over the whole period, and nearly 60 per cent from 1945 to 1948. For the firemen, the gains for the corresponding dates were 256.5 per cent and 54.4 per cent. On the basis of these results, Harry Lundeberg of the Sailors' Union of the Pacific was the champion gain-producer in the industry. Indeed, there were few unionists in the entire country who could claim as much so far as basic wage rates were concerned.[10]

[10] Admittedly, unionism was late in being reëstablished in the Pacific Coast shipping industry; the event occurred in 1934, in the depths of the depression. Even skill rates were therefore very low in the base year (1935), and relative increases were probably larger than in those parts of the economy where strong unions had been long established. Even so, the maritime record remains impressive, especially when gauged from a 1945 base.

In contrast, the longshoremen fell far behind the sailors as to basic rates, though much less so when all benefits are considered. For 1935–1948 as a whole, their rates rose 90 per cent—only 8 per cent more than the cost of living. During the postwar inflation, longshore wage rates advanced only 33 per cent, while those of sailors went up nearly 60 per cent. However, exclusive reference to longshore wage rates would understate Harry Bridges' achievements during these years. First, the longshoremen actually obtained the six-hour day in 1934—a much more liberal overtime standard than was prevalent in the rest of the economy, and far in excess of overtime premiums later gained by the seagoing crafts.[11] As a result, the actual money earnings of longshoremen rose more than their basic rates.

Second, the 1937 contract provided for the adoption of a uniform system of differential or "penalty" rates to be added to the basic rates for working certain kinds of cargo. Although some of these rates antedated 1934, their effect was to place the actual earnings of longshoremen somewhat above the standard rate.[12] Third, maximum sling-load limits were incorporated in longshore contracts beginning with 1938. These reduced the input of human effort per man-hour for which basic wage rates were paid, and in a sense increased the real wages of longshoremen, though the magnitude of this increase is unknown.

Although the longshoremen clearly fell behind the six offshore groups so far as basic wage rates were concerned, their true position was thus somewhat better than their wage rates indicate. At the same time, however, the lag was large. Offshore wage rates as a whole ad-

---

[11] Even the old-line AFL crafts generally had only a forty-hour week–eight-hour day standard in these years.

The origins of the six-hour longshore day are somewhat obscure. Apparently, the 1934 National Longshoremen's Board believed that the shorter day would help relieve unemployment. Since longshoring is a round-the-clock, seven-day operation, the main effect was to increase wage earnings and stevedoring costs disproportionately to the wage rate. In 1946, Saturday was added to Sundays and holidays as an overtime day.

[12] In 1938, the average penalty premium was ten cents per hour over the base rate—approximately 10 per cent. In 1948, the premium had not risen significantly, while basic rates had nearly doubled. Cargoes requiring penalty rates were not changed during the period, but their actual importance in total tonnage is unknown. (Data computed from coastwide agreements between the International Longshoremen's and Warehousemen's Union and the Waterfront Employers Association of the Pacific Coast, 1938–1948. See chap. x.)

vanced 206.5 per cent during the entire period, while longshore rates rose only 89.6 per cent.[13] Why?

In part, the answer may lie in what economists call the elasticity of demand for labor.[14] There is some reason to believe that the demand elasticity for longshoremen is considerably greater than that for all the offshore groups taken together, or for any one of them, say the sailors, taken separately. First, wage costs are a very high proportion of stevedoring costs, which means that rising wages would have a relatively large direct effect upon the rates charged shippers for loading or unloading cargoes, and thus upon the volume of cargoes offered the water lines over time. Second, these costs for stevedore services have mounted rapidly in recent years, to become a high proportion of all freight costs assessed to cargoes moving by water. In 1949, for example, Liberty (EC-2) ships operating on bareboat charter in the intercoastal service had an average of 78.6 per cent of total voyage expenses and 45.9 per cent of total expenses attributable to stevedoring and cargo-handling costs. For Victory (VC-2) ships in this service, stevedoring and cargo-handling costs were 77.4 per cent of voyage expenses and 44.4 per cent of total expenses.[15]

Third, operating subsidies have been available since 1936 to American ships in foreign trade. These subsidies have meant that rises in expenses for vessel operation—*not* stevedoring services—would not necessarily be reflected in freight rates, if these rates would otherwise be thrust above those of lower cost foreign competitors. By contrast, the commercial stevedore concerns were not directly subsidized, and so their charges rose steadily with the higher wage costs for longshore work.

The other factors affecting demand elasticity for labor involve possibilities for capital substitution, elasticity of demand for steamship

---

[13] Appendix, table 24.

[14] The elasticity of demand measures the responsiveness of quantity of man-hours "sold" to changes in the price of labor, when the changes are relatively small. Normally, the relation is inverse. That is, a rise in the price of labor will reduce the volume of man-hours worked, given time for certain adjustments to occur.

[15] *Merchant Marine Study and Investigation*, Hearings Before a Subcommittee of the Committee on Interstate and Foreign Commerce, United States Senate, 81st Cong., 2d sess., pt. 6, April 11, 13, 14, and 18, 1950 (Washington, Government Printing Office, 1950), pp. 1222–1227.

services, and supply of capital to the industry. However, these do not seem to have been strongly divergent as between longshore and off-shore labor. Accordingly, it is reasonable to infer that the cost ratios and operating subsidies jointly brought about a considerably higher elasticity of demand for longshore labor than for the offshore crafts taken together or separately. The higher elasticity means that the long-shoremen were relatively much more vulnerable to unemployment, be-cause higher wages for them would have had a much greater effect upon total freight charges and thus upon available tonnage than would have been the case for the offshore groups. In the postwar years in particular, the potential unemployment effects may have restrained the wage demands of the longshoremen. By contrast, the offshore unions could make large demands with less concern for the adverse conse-quences, especially since each of them bargained separately and could point to the relatively small portion of shipping costs attributable to their wages alone.

Finally, the ship operators themselves may well have deliberately followed a policy of generous wage concessions to Lundeberg (head of the Sailors' Union of the Pacific) in hopes of weakening the political position of Bridges (head of the International Longshoremen's and Warehousemen's Union) within the union group as a whole.[16] Eco-nomically, it was easier to make concessions to the SUP, as we have just shown. Ideologically, there was every reason for doing so.

In any event, a rather wry conclusion suggests itself. Lundeberg, who had abandoned an anticapitalist strategy to become the head of a strong and practical "business" union, was able to make this approach pay off economically, and pay off handsomely. Bridges, who continued to stress ideological hostility and a tough and unrelenting policy toward the employers, proved much less successful. That is, he was less successful in terms of the conventional rank-and-file standard of economic gains for the membership. Yet Bridges possessed great power in bargaining relations with the employer. However, this power was not sufficient, nor of the kind, to overcome the limitations imposed by the market itself.

---

[16] There is evidence to support this hypothesis, beginning with the SUP settlement in December, 1936. See chap. xi, p. 267, n. 8.

● *Some Economic Implications of the Wage Policies of the Pacific Coast Maritime Unions.*—As we have shown, basic wage rates of the maritime crafts on the Pacific Coast nearly tripled between 1935 and 1948. What happened to employment? It expanded greatly during the war, but following V-J Day it began a rapid contraction. By 1948, the average number of shipboard employees was about 22 per cent above 1935–1939. The total input of longshore gang-hours (which measures the scale of the work opportunity) in 1948 was actually 17 per cent lower than in 1935–1939. The long strike in 1948, however, undoubtedly depressed the input for that year. If this effect is statistically removed, gang-hours input in 1948 would have been perhaps 12 per cent above the prewar base.[17] In any case, the postwar employment record of the industry was not bright. Large decreases in available work occurred in each successive year between 1945 and 1948, and by 1948 these decreases would have been even more severe had it not been for the sustaining influence of army and emergency cargoes. Moreover, the "ration" of available work per longshoreman fell seriously because the union was unable to reduce the number of registered men as rapidly as the decline in the total volume of available work.

While wage rates were rapidly rising postwar, employment was rapidly falling. And for 1935–1948 as a whole, while wage rates almost tripled, employment opportunities showed little long-term increase.

Two questions thus emerge: (1) Was there a connection between rapidly rising wage rates and long-run stagnation in the number of jobs offered by the industry; and (2) what kind of wage policy were the maritime unions following, in particular after V-J Day?

There is strong reason to believe that the very rapid rise in maritime wages was an important factor contributing to the long-run decline in tonnage handled by the industry, exerting its main influence upon the coastwise and intercoastal trades. As we have suggested in earlier chapters, there were other forces contributing to decline—among them, the economic development of the west, the unreliable services because

---

[17] These calculations were based upon data presented in Gorter and Hildebrand, *op. cit.*, Vol. I, p. 47; Appendix II, table 20.

of frequent and protracted strikes, and the disruptive effects of the war.[18] Recognition of their presence does not belie the importance of soaring wage costs as an important collaborating influence.

First, maritime wage rates on the Pacific Coast rose nearly twice as fast as did railway wage rates between 1935 and 1948 and truck drivers' wages between 1937 and 1947. Wages are a high proportion of costs in all three branches of the transportation industry. This warrants the inference that ocean shipping in the coastwise and intercoastal trades was very severely handicapped vis-à-vis its close competitors. There, the steamship operators faced two alternatives in 1945: either to restore service and try to regain whatever tonnage they could still profitably handle (bulk items not requiring rapid transit), or not to resume operations at all. Both courses were followed, and relative to prewar each meant reduced tonnage and fewer jobs. Postwar, the pulse of the intercoastal and coastwise trades was much feebler than it had been even in the depressed 'thirties.

Second, the foreign and noncontiguous trades were largely insulated from this cost pressure. The former enjoyed the support of substantial government tonnage plus operating subsidies, and the latter was protected from competition of land carriers or foreign flag vessels and so could raise rates with little threat to its available tonnage. Accordingly, the wage squeeze probably had its greatest effects upon the coastwise and intercoastal trades, in which rail and truck competition was severe.[19]

This, in fact, is exactly what happened. In 1947, when there were no strikes to confuse the story, intercoastal dry-cargo tonnage amounted to only 3.2 million long tons, as compared with an annual average of 6 million in 1935–1939—a decline of 46.6 per cent. Coastwise dry cargo in 1947 amounted to only a half-million long tons, as against 2.1 million in 1935–1939—a drop of over 75 per cent.[20]

---

[18] These are discussed in chaps. iv, v, and vi.

[19] Rail and truck transportation since 1940 has also enjoyed great technological advances, which have increased output per worker and so have absorbed part of the cost pressure from rising wage rates. Ocean shipping cannot point to equally impressive technological advances; its gains were limited almost wholly to larger and faster vessels.

[20] We have cited dry rather than total cargo because longshore costs are negligible in the tanker trade. The corresponding figures for dry-plus-tanker cargo, 1947 as against the

Certainly, there is warrant for the inference that the extreme rise in maritime wage rates contributed to the catastrophic decline of dry-cargo tonnage in these two domestic trades.[21] Had maritime wages risen less rapidly, hence in closer conjunction with railroad and truck wages, ocean transportation would have suffered less cost pressure. Accordingly, it might well have regained part of the lost tonnage.

How, then, are we to interpret the wage policy of the maritime unions on the Pacific Coast? To begin with, it would appear that the unions were either ignorant of the effects of rapidly increasing wages upon the competitive position of their industry, or indifferent to the possibility of long-run stagnation in the number of available jobs. Probably the truth is a mixture of both. Craft unions traditionally have advocated the "lump-of-labor" doctrine: that there is always a fixed amount of work to be done, regardless of the level of wages.[22] Although the doctrine is demonstrably false, it is still an article of faith, hence an idea guiding practical action. More important, perhaps, the Pacific Coast maritime unions were in a position to be indifferent to stagnation in job opportunities. The question is: Why?

The answer is that since 1937 all the unions except the licensed crafts have operated under what in fact were closed shops, coupled with a rotation system. Consider the longshoremen and the sailors as typical examples. To be eligible for assignment, a longshoreman has to be registered at the port. To gain registration, he must have the approval of a majority of the port committee, half of whose membership consists of union representatives. This gives the ILWU control over the supply of longshoremen, and it is no accident that today all registered men are members of the union. Finally, the union also controls the distribution of available work, by the rotation system. By control of registration and rotation, the union can regulate both the long-run supply of labor and the short-run amount of work available per man.

1935–1939 average, are: intercoastal, 3.5 million long tons versus 7 million (down 50 per cent) ; coastwise, 19.2 million long tons versus 21.5 million (down about 11 per cent).

Dry-cargo figures were taken from Appendix, table 22; dry-plus-tanker-cargo tonnages are from Gorter and Hildebrand, *op. cit.*, Vol. I, Appendix II, table 8.

[21] In chapter v we present an indirect test of the question, by reference to tonnage handled by land carriers.

[22] Bridges has implied the idea in the past (see chap. xi, p. 273, n. 10).

The sailors have a similar system. Only union members are eligible for voyages, and the union assigns the work on a rotation basis. Again, the union can control the long-run supply of labor, and the distribution of the work in the short run. Parallel arrangements exist for the cooks, the firemen, the radio officers, and—more recently—the engineers and deck officers.

In short, the maritime unions from 1934 onward acquired monopoly power over the supply of labor available to the industry.[23] They have used this power in three major ways. First, and most important, when work was slack the unions restricted the number of men eligible to work in the industry, thus at times barring the entrance of new workers. They were able to do this by denying the newcomers admittance to the union and, in the case of the longshoremen, by refusing to add them to the registered list of eligible workers. Then at other times, when men were scarce, the unions admitted the newcomers under a temporary permit system, to facilitate their eventual elimination after the shortage was over. Second, at all times the unlicensed unions allocated the available jobs by rotation, to equalize the distribution of work opportunities. When work was slack, the unemployment was absorbed or "disguised" by rotation, which reduced the work ration per eligible man. When men were scarce, the ration was increased. If the scarcity were persistent, then numbers were ultimately increased, but the insiders were safeguarded by the permit system. Third, the unions used the weapon of the coastwide strike with unusually telling effect, to back up their demands.[24]

By monopoly control over labor supply, then, the unions could cope effectively with unemployment arising from shifts in the demand for labor. In the short run, unemployment could only be met by cutting the work ration per man. For longer periods, however, temporary

---

[23] In a narrow sense it may be argued that no union has monopoly power if the concept of monopoly is defined as price manipulation to maximize profits. The union neither receives profits nor attempts to maximize what it does not receive. Generically, however, "monopoly" refers to any single seller who is able to raise his price by restrictive control over the supply of whatever he has to sell. Certain unions possess this control over the supply of labor-services, and they use it to raise price (wages). To them, the term monopoly may accurately be applied.

[24] The development of union control of admissions and of rotation of work is described in chap. x. The major strikes are recounted in chap. ix, and the minor ones in chap. x.

workers could be eliminated and newcomers excluded from the industry.

Before 1939, fluctuations of labor demand were not great and supply was adapted mainly by the rotation system. Numbers were kept relatively constant by the exclusion of new men. With the onset of World War II, the demand for labor rose enormously. The supply of labor was increased by raising the work ration through rotation and by extensive use of the permit system to expand the number of eligible workers. Also, some permanent men were added. During these years, the rise of labor demand fortunately coincided with rising wage rates, and there was no unemployment problem. Accordingly, restriction of labor supply was unnecessary.

With the end of war, however, the demand for labor rapidly fell for the next three years. Yet at the same time the unions used their monopoly power to push wage rates up even faster than before, thereby accentuating the decline of available work. Heavy and increasing unemployment resulted. During 1946–1948, the unions combated this unemployment in two ways. First, they rapidly eliminated the temporary employees and closed their ranks to the entry of new men. This policy met with some success. Practically speaking, it meant the higher wages were being reserved for the inner core of long-time union members, to the exclusion of outsiders. Second, however, the unions could not reduce their numbers rapidly enough to keep pace with falling demand, and some unemployment did develop. This was absorbed by rotation, with a reduced ration of work per eligible man.

In other words, what might seem to have been a recklessly shortsighted policy of extreme postwar wage pressure (and compared with the far greater portion of the trade-union world, it *was* extreme) makes considerable sense from one particular point of view. This point of view was that of the dominant insiders in control of the unions. As long as they could conserve their own long-run job opportunities in a shrinking market, the large wage gains ultimately would pay off. The losses could be shifted to others: the wartime temporary men, the new postwar candidates for jobs in the industry, the operators, and the consuming public.

The wage policy, then, was the outcome of a high degree of union power to control the supply and allocation of labor to the industry. This power, however, was never absolute, because the unions could not control the demand for maritime labor. In order to force wages upward to an extreme degree, the unions had to accept a declining industry, with a rapid postwar drop in the demand for labor. For the long run, job opportunities were stagnant. Whether the union members were fully aware of these consequences makes little difference. They had to adapt to them in any case.

A final word of caution must be added, however. First, the wage policy alone—although of great importance—was not the sole factor in the decline of the industry. It aggravated the shrinkage already induced by collateral causes. Second, the fact that the maritime unions acquired an unusual degree of monopoly power had other implications as well. This power overcame some of the undesirable social and economic effects of the pre-1934 casual labor system, especially at San Francisco. As Frank P. Foisie, one of the few farsighted leaders in the industry, had been arguing since 1921, there was a strong case for stabilizing the eligible work force, in the interests of both management and labor. By control of supply, available earnings could be protected from extreme short-run declines and in this way a reliable permanent force of loyal men could be developed. From this point of view, the main problem concerned management's loss of authority in personnel relations, rather than restriction of entrance and job rotation themselves. From the public point of view, a strong case may also be made for short-run stabilization through control of supply, but since the attainment of this stabilization places strong discretionary power in the hands of the unions, or management, or both together, there is the obvious attendant danger that the power will be abused. Essentially, the issue concerns the reconciliation of the interests of the workmen already in the industry, the men who would like to work in the industry, management and investors in the industry, and the public as buyers of shipping services. Freedom from all stabilization, as in a purely casual labor market, would, and did, impose extreme hardships on workers in the trade, as the price of free admission for newcomers.

Full union control would, and did, mean considerable sacrifice of the interests of buyers, of management, and of workers excluded from the trade.

Although there is no precise or ideal solution possible, the balance might have been redressed more in favor of buyers, management, and potential employees if the maritime unions had not gained exclusive power to regulate entrance and to distribute available work. As our historical account in chapters viii and ix indicates, what actually emerged was a shift of power of radical type—from a casual market largely dominated by the employers to a monopolistically controlled market largely dominated by the maritime unions.

● *The Productivity of Longshoremen.*—To be complete, the analysis of maritime labor costs should combine movements in wage rates with changes in physical output per man-hour, or labor productivity. If during 1935–1948 productivity had almost tripled along with wage rates, there would have been no significant cost pressure from the side of wages, which represented the dominant element in shipping costs.[25] Indeed, if productivity had only risen enough to offset the differential gain in maritime wage rates over railroad and truck wages either between 1935 and 1948 or between 1945 and 1948, some part of the drastic postwar collapse in the intercoastal and coastwise trades might well have been averted.

Unfortunately, it is easier to acknowledge the importance of labor productivity than it is to gauge its impacts with precision. Although trends in productivity have long been extensively studied by government agencies and private investigators, relatively little has been accomplished in the "nonmanufacturing" sphere in which ocean transportation belongs.

We have not had sufficient funds to undertake a detailed study of labor productivity in Pacific Coast maritime shipping. This has precluded our developing precise facts regarding ton-mile output per hour of vessel labor. All we can say is that after 1940 larger and faster ships were gradually introduced. Although it may have been necessary to increase manning complements with the newer ships and under suc-

---

[25] See above, pp. 131–132.

ceeding labor agreements, the productivity of shipboard labor may well have risen. Nevertheless, it seems quite safe to say that the gain was not large, and certainly not large enough to check fully the adverse competitive pressure of rapidly rising wage rates.[26]

What happened to the productivity of longshoremen? Here again our inquiry was necessarily limited. Ideally, the investigation should consider particular operations—the tonnage of a given commodity handled per gang-hour over several years. Lacking resources for this kind of investigation, we have attempted instead an indirect test. This is to compare inputs of total gang-hours with total dry-cargo tonnage handled over several years. Obviously, an aggregative test of this kind is deficient in two respects: The commodity composition of the tonnage handled will change over the years, altering the input of gang-hours required; and the capital equipment and work methods can also change. The latter factor should properly show up in productivity statistics, but its presence makes it impossible to determine precisely whether there was a slowdown on the part of the men, as the employers frequently charged during these years.

Notwithstanding these limitations, this measure offers direct evidence of the relationship between the input of gang-hours and the output in tons of dry cargo handled. Hence it will indicate whether productivity in this sense changed significantly over the years, and through this, whether the increase in wage rates as a factor in labor cost was partly offset or not.

Table 8 presents the findings in summary form.

It appears that output per gang-hour ("productivity" as used here) fell slightly during 1938 and 1939, at the time the matter became an issue between the employers and the union.[27] At the same time, the prewar figures indicate strong over-all stability, with productivity averaging 27.9 long tons per longshore gang-hour. Alternatively, we reach the negative conclusion that there was no increase in longshore productivity during the latter half of the 'thirties.

For 1946–1948, the picture is not so clear. Productivity was well

[26] Between 1945 and 1948, offshore wage rates rose over 50 per cent.

[27] For a history of the issue, see chap. x, pp. 242–250.

below 1935–1939 levels in 1946 and 1947 but appears to have fully recovered by 1948. Our postwar tonnage figures are less reliable than prewar, however, for it was necessary to include within them estimates of tonnage moved in emergency relief programs and of tonnage shipped for army account.[28] Even if we exclude them entirely, we know

TABLE 8

Dry-Cargo Tonnage Handled per Longshore Gang-Hour,
Pacific Coast Maritime Shipping Industry,
1935–1939, 1946–1948

Year	Total dry-cargo tonnage handled (million long tons)	Total input of gang-hours (in thousands)	Output per gang-hour (long tons)
1935...............	18.7	667	28.0
1936...............	18.4	653	28.2
1937...............	19.6	677	28.9
1938...............	17.3	621	27.9
1939...............	19.7	736	26.8
1946...............	15.6	764	20.4
1947...............	21.0	874	24.0
1948...............	15.8	556	28.4

Source: Total dry-cargo tonnage from Appendix, table 27; total input of gang-hours from Gorter and Hildebrand, *op. cit.*, Vol. I, p. 55.

that productivity increased in each year of 1946–1948, as was also true if they are included.[29]

Working, then, from tonnage totals that include these estimates, we find that postwar the productivity of longshore gangs was 12.9 per cent below 1935–1939. For 1947, when there were no serious strikes, longshore productivity was 14 per cent below the 1935–1939 average.

Two conclusions are suggested. First, it appears that longshore productivity actually declined significantly after 1938. However, we

[28] The emergency tonnage is an arbitrary figure, explained in Appendix, table 27. The army tonnage was converted from measurement to weight tons by using a stowage factor of 70.

[29] Excluding the estimated figures for emergency and army tonnage, the output per gang-hour then becomes 14.5 long tons in 1946, 17.1 long tons in 1947, and 20.6 long tons in 1948—in all instances well below prewar, but indicating a strong tendency to increase. However, the estimated tonnage must be included, for we know that both types of this tonnage were actually handled and that gang-hours were used in handling it.

cannot make a firm assertion that it declined by a specific percentage, because of the uncertain nature of the estimated portion of postwar tonnage. Second, we can assert with confidence that between 1935 and 1948 the productivity of Pacific Coast longshoremen did not increase.

The latter finding is of great importance. It means that the 90 per cent increase in longshore basic rates between 1935 and 1948 was not offset by increased productivity. Hence the full amount entered into increased stevedoring costs. Very probably, wage costs in stevedoring advanced by much more than the full amount of the increase in basic rates, for two reasons. (1) Overtime and penalty rates were of high importance. (2) The evidence suggests that longshore productivity actually fell.

CHAPTER VIII

Costs, Rates, and Competition

HARD PRESSED BY rapidly rising labor costs, the Pacific Coast maritime shipping industry could seek relief by attempting to reduce other costs, altering freight rates, and successfully pleading for increased construction and operating differential subsidies. As indicated earlier, increased subsidies were available only to United States shipping companies operating vessels over foreign trade routes classified as essential by the United States government. However, the fortunes of these companies in foreign trade are not pertinent to our study except insofar as they affected the employment of American seamen. If the American lines lost traffic to their foreign competitors, this did not change the volume of cargo crossing Pacific Coast docks and hence handled by the industry as we view it.[1]

---

[1] It may well have been true that at times the *rates* charged by both domestic and foreign lines inhibited the movement of merchandise between Pacific Coast and foreign ports. It would be difficult, if not impossible, to isolate the effects of rate changes from those attributable to other factors simultaneously at work. Further, the industry's declining cargoes were centered primarily in the coastwise and intercoastal trades. We therefore will not attempt an analysis of the effects of changes in freight rates *or* costs upon the volume of Pacific Coast foreign trade.

In passing, however, it should be noted that with particular reference to trade with East Asia, the Stanford Research Institute found that despite the greater distance between Atlantic and Gulf Coast ports and the Orient the cost to shipper was greater from the Pacific

152

We have also noted that in the noncontiguous trade the industry was insulated from foreign flag competition. Here the adjustment of rates as costs increased was not as difficult as in the intercoastal and coastwise trades where the vessel operations competed not only with each other but also with the railroads and trucks. And it was in these latter trades, particularly in the postwar years, that the industry suffered its greatest long-term decline in cargoes. The cost increases hit hardest in these trades basically because adequate rate or other compensatory adjustments were impossible.[2]

Prewar competition and its effects upon coastwise shipping were described by the Interstate Commerce Commission as follows:

Competition progressively became more keen, especially as the depression of the thirties relatively lessened the available traffic for each type of carrier. In the endeavor to gain traffic, rate reductions made by one type of carrier (or by individual carriers in a class) were met, and more than met, by their competitors. This was the situation at the outbreak of the late war, tempered by such general rate increases as we had permitted and by amendments to our outstanding fourth-section authorizations. The margin between profit and loss was narrowing for all of them, when war broke out and the situation changed radically.

Even before Pearl Harbor, coastwise shipping had become handicapped by rising costs, labor disturbances and disputes, and the menace of submarine warfare. The trend in tonnage was gradually downward from 1929, to 86 per

Coast ports on about 25 per cent of the items listed in the Pacific Westbound Conference tariff. This was attributed to the addition of handling and wharfage charges to the basic freight rates on the Pacific Coast, charges not added to the Atlantic and Gulf rates. This no doubt led to some diversion of cargoes away from Pacific Coast ports to Atlantic Coast and Gulf Coast ports. The Institute found that without the addition of these charges, a comparison of the Pacific Westbound Conference tariff with the Far East Conference tariff showed that 4 per cent of the items in the former were higher than the latter, 13 per cent the same, and 83 per cent lower. (Stanford Research Institute, *An Economic Analysis of Pacific Coast Trans-Pacific Shipping* [Stanford, Stanford (University) Research Institute, 1950], p. 42.)

Only an exhaustive study of individual shipments, rates, and shipper-costs would reveal the extent of the diversion of shipments away from the Pacific Coast to ports on the other coasts. This was beyond our limited financial resources. For a good analysis of rates, see Stanford Research Institute, *op. cit.*, Appendix 2.

[2] The reader should not infer that upward rate adjustments were necessarily the result of a "cost-push," especially during the war and postwar years when inflation was an important factor. Yet railroad freight rates, controlled by government regulatory agencies, ordinarily cannot be raised unless a "cost-push" can be demonstrated. The inflation, by exerting a "demand-pull" on labor prices and other costs, put shipowners in the position of being squeezed as costs rose faster than freight rates.

cent thereof for 1932, 79 per cent for 1934, 62 per cent in 1936, and 54 or 55 per cent thereafter until the World War.[3]

Postwar, rates were raised sharply, but not enough to offset the tremendous increases in maritime wages and other costs. A question thus arises: How badly did shipping fare compared with its rivals—trucks and railroads?

The answer is not easy to formulate, for cost comparisons are always difficult undertakings, especially when they encompass firms in different branches of industry. Nevertheless, such comparisons can be highly informative, when presented in broad terms and based upon a reasonably secure underlying rationale. We have attempted to observe these requirements fully in what follows, and accordingly have limited our comparisons to percentage movements in major types of costs. The evidence obtained shows most convincingly that, compared with its rail and truck competitors, Pacific Coast maritime shipping suffered marked deterioration in its relative cost position.

Wage rates rose far more in Pacific Coast maritime shipping than in either trucking or railroading.[4] Our independent findings are substantiated by a study made by the Interstate Commerce Commission. This investigation showed that, between 1936 and 1945, the average hourly earnings of Pacific Coast line vessel employees aboard ships subject to the Commission's regulations increased 80.6 per cent. For the train and engine employees of western district railroads the rise amounted to only 32.1 per cent. Drivers for over-the-road motor carriers in the Pacific Coast states received 52.1 per cent higher average hourly earnings in 1945 than in 1936.[5] The wage increases after 1945 obviously worsened the competitive position of the vessel operators, particularly when it is recalled that the ratios of labor expenses to total operating expenses were quite comparable among the three types of competition.

All the available evidence indicates that the wages of maritime

[3] I.C.C. Docket No. 29721, *All Rail Commodity Rates Between California, Oregon, and Washington*, 268 I.C.C. 525–526 (1948).

[4] See above, pp. 136–137.

[5] Interstate Commerce Commission, Bureau of Transport Economics and Statistics, *Ex Parte No. 165, Problems in the Regulation of Domestic Transportation by Water*, by C. S. Morgan (Washington, Government Printing Office, 1946), p. 466.

labor increased more rapidly than did wages in railroading or trucking, whether the base chosen is 1935, 1940, or 1945. However, if labor productivity had increased sufficiently and if other increased expenses had been offset by greater operating efficiency, the rise of maritime wages and other direct costs need not have meant a commensurate rise in cost per voyage, per nautical mile, per vessel day, or per ton. Unfortunately, this was not the case. Quite the contrary, as the Interstate Commerce Commission discovered in a cost comparison for 1939–1940 with 1946 that involved privately operated vessels in the coastwise and intercoastal trades. According to the Commission's calculations, the total expense (including depreciation and return on depreciated cost of vessel) per round voyage of operating a vessel in the intercoastal trade in 1946 increased over 1940 as follows: average per voyage, 70.4 per cent; average per nautical mile, 70 per cent; average per vessel day, 87 per cent; average per cargo ton, 83 per cent.[6] In the coastwise trade, 1946 total expenses exceeded those for 1939 by even greater percentages. There the increases amounted to 186.3 per cent per voyage, 179.9 per cent per vessel nautical mile, 206.6 per cent per vessel day, and 339.4 per cent per ton of cargo.[7] All these figures include shoreside as well as vessel costs.

Thus the Commission reached the following unhappy conclusion regarding the changed position of the water carriers.

From study and comparison of the estimates of rail and water costs, in the light of their known deficiencies and limitations, we cannot conclude, as contended by the water lines, that the Pacific Coast steamship line is still the low cost operator; but must conclude that (1) generally between San Francisco and Portland, (2) on most commodities between Los Angeles and Portland and between San Francisco and Seattle, and (3) on many commodities between Los Angeles and Seattle, the advantage of lower costs lies with the rails.[8]

Table 9 shows the Commission's findings regarding the postwar costs of moving certain commodities port-to-port by rail and water.

---

[6] *Ibid.*, p. 284. The cost per ton is based on the assumption that 12,827 tons were carried per round voyage in 1946. For 1940, the figure per round voyage is 13,780 tons. (*Ibid.*, p. 283.)

[7] *Ibid.*, p. 289. The higher cost per ton in 1946 is partly attributable to the smaller number of cargo tons per voyage—3,905 as compared with 6,000 in 1939. (*Ibid.*, p. 288.)

[8] I.C.C. Docket No. 29721, *All Rail Commodity Rates Between California, Oregon, and Washington,* 277 I.C.C. 563 (1950).

TABLE 9

Comparison of Water and Rail Costs along Pacific Coast
(Estimated Full Costs Including Return) [a]
(in cents per 100 lbs.)

Commodity or weight[b]	Route and type of transportation							
	Between San Francisco and Portland		Between Los Angeles (Long Beach) and Portland		Between San Francisco and Seattle		Between Los Angeles (Long Beach) and Seattle	
	Rail	Water	Rail	Water	Rail	Water	Rail	Water
80,000 lbs.	31.2	....	45.0	....	40.1	....	54.0	....
Bulk wheat (southbound)	....	38.1	....	41.7	....	41.5	....	43.2
70,000 lbs.	33.9	....	48.8	....	44.1	....	59.0	....
Iron and steel (northbound)..	....	44.4	....	48.3	....	48.3	....	49.2
60,000 lbs.	37.8	....	53.9	....	48.9	....	65.1	....
Sugar (northbound)	....	55.5	....	61.0	....	61.3	....	64.0
50,000 lbs.	43.0	....	61.1	....	55.8	....	74.0	....
Canned goods (northbound)...	....	64.1	....	70.4	....	71.2	....	74.3
40,000 lbs.	50.9	....	71.9	....	66.3	....	87.4	....
Lumber (southbound)	....	67.0	....	70.2	....	75.9	....	79.6
30,000 lbs.	64.1	....	88.0	....	84.0	....	109.7	....
Newsprint (southbound)	....	76.3	....	79.5	....	74.8	....	75.9

[a] Rail costs include also average freight contribution to taxes and passenger deficit.
    The water costs are based upon prewar loads—1,095 tons northbound and 4,367 tons southbound. These figures represent 40 per cent of cargo-carrying capacity northbound and 100 per cent southbound for vessels in operation during the prewar years. For the larger postwar vessels these tonnages are 20 per cent of capacity northbound and 50 per cent southbound. The water overhead costs are prorated on a measurement (cubic feet of cargo space occupied) basis.
    The costs were incurred in 1948 and 1949, before the start of the Commission's hearings in February, 1949. The water costs, furnished by the Coastwise Line, are based upon twenty-two round voyages completed before that date. See 277 I.C.C. 550.
    [b] The representative rail weights are, according to the Commission, ". . . within the range of minimum loads in this territory of the commodities shown in this table." The rail and water costs are thus roughly comparable.
    Source: I.C.C. Docket No. 29721, *All Rail Commodity Rates Between California, Oregon, and Washington,* 277 I.C.C. 560–561 (1950).

The Commission noted that high port costs (cargo handling) imposed a burdensome competitive handicap upon the vessel operator. For example, for shipments of canned goods between Portland and San Francisco the port costs alone amounted to 37.5 cents per 100 pounds.[9] In contrast, the rail *full* average cost including taxes, return, and con-

---

[9] *Ibid.*, p. 560.

tribution to the passenger deficit was, as table 9 shows, only 43.0 cents per 100 pounds for a 50,000 pound load and 37.8 cents for a 60,000 pound load.

Here the Commission made a highly pertinent finding: that rail costs per carload tend to fall rather rapidly as actual loads increase over the minimum loads cited in table 9. This fact accentuates the cost handicap of the water carriers, in some instances converting their few cost advantages to actual disadvantages as the weight of rail loads rises.

Wheat shipments provide a good example. Here one would have expected the water carriers to have had the advantage, for wheat can be easily handled in bulk at relatively low port costs, given highly mechanized operations. True, such was the case when rail loads were low. Thus at 50,000 pounds of wheat to the car, the rail disadvantage in 1948–1949 would have been between 4.9 and 30.8 cents per 100 pounds, depending on the ports involved. At 80,000 pounds, however, rail costs per pound would have been below water costs in two out of four formerly favorable hauls cited in table 9. Worse yet, the Commission found that the average rail load of wheat moving in the Mountain-Pacific territory at this time was actually 103,520 pounds per car.[10] On this general principle, then, many of the hauls cited in the table as indicating a cost advantage to the water lines proved to be illusory, because the comparisons were predicated upon minimum rail loads only.

Furthermore, the Commission found that if the actual weights of water cargoes were also increased, the cost economies obtained would have been generally less pronounced than they were for the rails. The average reduction in the costs in table 9 would have amounted to 20 per cent if water-borne cargo tonnage were to have been increased by 100 per cent. On this basis a 10 per cent increase in cargoes would have reduced costs per ton by 3.6 per cent; a 20 per cent increase, 6.7 per cent; 30 per cent, 9.2 per cent; 40, 11.4; 50, 13.3; 60, 15; 70, 16.5; 80, 17.8; and 90, 18.9.[11] In some instances, then, it would have

[10] *Ibid.*, pp. 562–563.
[11] *Ibid.*, p. 562.

TABLE 10

COMPARISON OF WATER AND RAIL RATES, IN CENTS PER 100 POUNDS (INCLUDING EX PARTE NO. 162 AND 166 INCREASES),[a] PACIFIC COASTWISE TRADE

Commodity	From	To	Rail rate	Charges for water movement		
				Port-to-port rate	Accessorial charges	Total charge
Northbound						
Beverages.........	San Francisco.........	Portland	64	49	17	66
		Seattle	67	50	17	67
Canned goods.........	San Francisco	Portland	65	52	18	70
		Seattle	72	56	18	74
Cement, building.........	Redwood City.........	Portland	41	34	10[b]	44[c]
					18	52
Fruit, dried.........	Oakland	Portland	80	71	16	87
		Seattle	91	74	16	90
Glassware.........	East Oakland	Portland	52	42	24	66
		Seattle	61	44	24	68
Salt, in packages.........	Newark, Cal.	Portland	44	33	17	50
		Seattle	49	39	16	55
Sugar.........	Crockett, Cal.	Portland	55	46	11	57
		Seattle	59	49	11	60
Rice.........	San Francisco	Portland	53	36	17	53
		Seattle	62	40	17	57

Southbound

Commodity	Origin	Destination				
Bags, paper	Port Angeles, Wn.	San Francisco	72	50	13	63
	Port Angeles, Wn.	Los Angeles Harbor	83	59	13	72
	Camas, Wn.	San Francisco	66	52	13	65
	Camas, Wn.	Los Angeles	78	64	13	77
Beer and ale	Seattle	San Francisco	71	50	17	67
	Seattle	Los Angeles	92	72	18	90
Canned goods	Hillsboro, Ore.	San Francisco	65	52	23	75
	Hillsboro, Ore.	Los Angeles	86	73	22	95
Boxboard, pulpboard	Port Townsend, Wn.	Antioch, Calif.	48	37	12	49
	Port Townsend, Wn.	Stockton	48	37	14	51
Tin scrap	Portland, Ore.	So. San Francisco	36	41	13	54
Wood pulp	Port Townsend, Wn.	Pomona, Calif.	59[d]	50[e]	20	70
	Port Townsend, Wn.	Pomona, Calif.		60[f]	20	80

a These *Ex Parte* increases became effective in 1946 and 1948. See 266 I.C.C. 614–618; 270 I.C.C. 81–105, 412–413.
b For a shipment of 500 tons or more there are no wharfing or switching charges at point of origin.
c Figure corrected from "45," as it appears in source.
d Minimum 80,000 lbs.
e Minimum 100 tons.
f Minimum 30,000 lbs.
SOURCE: I.C.C. Docket No. 29721, *All Rail Commodity Rates Between California, Oregon, and Washington*, 277 I.C.C. 556 (1950).

taken a substantial increase in water-borne tonnage to have equalized water and rail costs.

Increases in wages were the most important factor in the rise of shipping costs. Labor costs were the largest single item of expense and increased in importance. For example, the Interstate Commerce Commission found that, in 1935, the employee compensation (offshore and onshore) of Pacific Coast water carriers subject to its jurisdiction was equal to 30.6 per cent of operating expenses and 29.8 per cent of total operating revenue. In 1945, the figures were 41.2 per cent and 37 per cent, respectively.[12] Between 1945 and 1948, wage rates (all crafts) rose almost 50 per cent, and probably the ratio of wage costs to total costs increased even further.

As a result of these large increases in cost, vessel operators found that despite the substantial increases in freight rates charged by their land-based competitors, they were unable to compete successfully for coastwise and intercoastal cargoes.[13] Their plight was made clear when they indicated to the Interstate Commerce Commission that they desired to increase their coastwise rates by 50 per cent *plus* whatever increases the Commission granted the railroads. They would accept these increases, however, *only* if the rail rates were then raised *again* so that the new water rates would be sufficiently below the ultimate level of rail rates to attract new traffic.[14] In short, the water carriers sought the equivalent of a protective tariff against the railroads, to wipe out their competitive handicap.

---

[12] *Ex Parte No. 165, Problems in the Regulation of Domestic Transportation by Water, op. cit.*, p. 265. The 1945 figure for percentage of operating expenses does not apply to all companies under I.C.C. jurisdiction but only to those that were required to report that year.

We recognize that the comparison of 1935 with 1945 figures is subject to serious question, because 1945 was partly a war year. A comparison of 1935 with 1940, however, shows the same tendencies. In 1940, employee compensation was 32.4 per cent of total operating revenue as compared with 29.8 per cent in 1935; and 36.3 per cent of operating expense as compared with 30.6 in 1935.

[13] Coastwise water rates increased markedly. For example, between 1936 and 1947 commodity rates for shipments between Portland and Los Angeles rose as follows: canned goods, 84.8 per cent; wood pulp, 100 per cent (and minimum weight increased from 30,000 pounds to 40,000 pounds) ; newsprint, 65.6 per cent. (Computed from *Exhibit 16* [Witness: Nickerson] and *Exhibit 20* [Witness: Burley], *Before the Interstate Commerce Commission, in re* I.C.C. Docket No. 29721, *All Rail Commodity Rates Between California, Oregon, and Washington;* and I.C.C. Docket No. 29722, *Pacific Coastwise Water Rates.*)

[14] For a complete statement of this significant plea and the findings of the Commission, see I.C.C. Docket No. 29721, *op. cit.*, 277 I.C.C. 511–566.

TABLE 11

INCREASES NECESSARY IN RAIL RATES TO EQUAL THE WATER PORT-TO-PORT COSTS
PLUS ACCESSORIAL CHARGES IN PACIFIC COASTWISE TRADE
(in cents per 100 lbs.)

Commodity	From	To	Water costs plus accessorial charges	Rail rate	Increase necessary to equalize total charges
Northbound					
Beverages........	San Francisco	Portland	85.4	64.0	21.4
		Seattle	93.0	67.0	26.0
Canned goods	San Francisco	Portland	82.1	65.0	17.1
		Seattle	89.2	72.0	17.2
Fruit, dried.......	Oakland	Portland	82.5	80.0	2.5
		Seattle	89.6	91.0	−1.4[b]
Salt, in packages..	Newark, Cal.	Portland	69.0	44.0	25.0
		Seattle	73.3	49.0	24.3
Sugar.............	Crockett, Cal.	Portland	66.5	55.0	11.5
		Seattle	72.3	59.0	13.3
Southbound					
Beverages........	Port Angeles, Wn.	San Francisco	92.2	70.0	20.2
		Los Angeles Harbor	88.5	83.0	15.5
	Camas, Wn.	San Francisco	84.7	66.0	18.7
		Los Angeles	84.0	78.0	6.0
Canned goods.....	Hillsboro, Ore.	San Francisco	90.4	65.0	25.4
		Los Angeles	90.3	86.0	4.3
Wood pulp........	Port Townsend, Wn.	Pomona	95.9	59.0	36.9

[a] Although the Interstate Commerce Commission did not specify the precise period during which the costs and rates were applicable, it was 1948 and possibly January, 1949. See note a, tables 9 and 10, above.
[b] Reduction necessary.
SOURCE: I.C.C. Docket No. 29721, _All Rail Commodity Rates Between California, Oregon, and Washington,_ 277 I.C.C. 558.

TABLE 12

RAIL RATES, WATER RATES AND COSTS,[a] SELECTED COMMODITIES SHIPPED BETWEEN PACIFIC COAST CITIES, 1948

(in cents per 100 lbs.)

Commodity	From	To	Rail rate	Port-to-port water rate	Water costs	Difference between water rate and costs
Northbound						
Beverages................	San Francisco	Portland	64.0	49.0	68.4	−19.4
		Seattle	67.0	50.0	76.0	−26.0
Canned goods............	San Francisco	Portland	65.0	52.0	64.1	−12.1
		Seattle	72.0	56.0	71.2	−15.2
Fruit, dried.............	Oakland	Portland	80.0	71.0	66.5	+4.5
		Seattle	91.0	74.0	73.6	+0.4
Salt, in packages........	Newark, Cal.	Portland	44.0	33.0	52.0	−19.0
		Seattle	49.0	39.0	57.3	−18.3
Sugar...................	Crockett, Cal.	Portland	55.0	46.0	55.5	− 9.5
		Seattle	59.0	49.0	61.3	−12.3
Southbound						
Canned goods............	Hillsboro, Ore.	San Francisco	65.0	52.0	67.4	−15.4
		Los Angeles	86.0	73.0	68.3	+4.7
Wood pulp...............	Port Townsend, Wn.	Los Angeles	59[b]	50.0[c]	75.9	−25.9
				60.0		−15.9

[a] Costs estimated on basis of 1,095 tons northbound and 4,367 tons southbound.
[b] Minimum 80,000 lbs. for shipment to Pomona, Cal.
[c] Applies to minimum of 100 tons.

All Rail Commodity Rates Between California, Oregon, and Washington, 277 I.C.C. 554, 556.

The Commission found that, in general, the rail rates covered full cost. It also found that, though the port-to-port water rates were generally below the corresponding rail rates, the addition of accessorial charges[15] often pushed the cost to the shipper above what he would pay for comparable shipment by rail. The high importance of the handicap imposed on the water lines by these accessorial charges is illustrated in table 10.

These charges had to be borne by the shipper. They were added to the basic port-to-port water rate that included the charges for loading and unloading the vessel. In table 10 the accessorial charges include the following: wharfage (1.25 or 0.75 cents), marine insurance (0.2 to 4.1 cents), carloading at destination (1.9 to 12.4 cents), switching at destination (3.0 to 5.2 cents), and line-haul charges to Stockton, Antioch, and Pomona, California (8.0 to 13.0 cents).[16]

Shippers, however, need not have incurred all the accessorial expenses indicated here. If they used their own facilities or employed alternative methods of handling shipments to and from the wharves, such as their own trucks, then their accessorial costs were lower than those in table 10. The accessorial charges were nevertheless an important factor bringing about the loss of a substantial margin of tonnage to railroads and trucks.

Further evidence of the weak competitive position of the coastwise shipping companies appeared in the Commission's tabulations as reproduced in table 11. These show that rate increases ranging from —1.5 per cent to +62.5 per cent of the then (1948) rail rates would have been necessary merely to equalize rail rates and the costs to the shipper who preferred to use water rather than rail transportation service. On the items shown in table 11 the average rail rate increase would have amounted to 27.2 per cent.

However, the equalization of rail rates and costs to the shipper by vessel would not have helped the ship operators very much. The costs to shipper by water must be lower than the rail rate in order to com-

---

[15] Accessorial charges include amounts paid for switching, wharfage, marine insurance, loading into rail car or truck at dock for movement of cargo to final destination.

[16] I.C.C. Docket No. 29721, *op. cit.*, 277 I.C.C. 556.

pensate for the lower frequency of service, the irregularity of arrivals and departures of vessels, and the longer transit time.[17]

Table 12 provides a comparison of water and rail rates for a selected group of commodities. It also shows water costs. Comparing these costs with the port-to-port rates reveals the cost-rate squeeze experienced by the vessel operators. The water lines, however, lost their case because the Commission concluded that the rail rates at issue were not unreasonably low. In its own words,

The record shows that because of the incidental costs to the shipper who uses coastwise water service, and also because of the intangible disadvantages of such service, water rates for transportation from dock to dock must be substantially lower than the corresponding rail rates or the water lines cannot secure the traffic. It follows that if the water rates are to be low enough in their relation to the corresponding rail rates to attract competitive traffic, and at the same time be high enough to cover the increased water costs shown and yield some profit to the water lines, a further radical increase in the rail rates would be necessary. But such pronounced increases cannot be justified on any broad scale when at least 80 percent of the rail rates on minimum carloads between the ports yield more than the estimated full costs, with an average allowance for taxes, fair return, and passenger deficit. The levels of only a few rates on eight different commodities were found to be low in relation to cost, and this was predicated on minimum carloads, without regard to actual loadings or commercial or competitive conditions which might justify these levels.[18]

Yet, postwar railroad freight rates were far above prewar levels, as indicated by the figures in the Appendix, table 28. Here it is noteworthy that the rates fell precipitously in the early 'thirties after the Interstate Commerce Commission granted the railroads permission to meet the low rates established by the water and truck lines. After 1934, rates generally moved upward, and then in 1948 averaged nearly double their 1931 level.

Port-to-port water rates for the movement of certain commodities are shown in the Appendix, table 29. They more than doubled between 1929 and 1948 but remained lower than the appropriate rail rates.[19]

---

[17] See below, pp. 166–168.

[18] I.C.C. Docket No. 29721, *op. cit.*, 277 I.C.C. 564–565.

[19] For a discussion of rail-water rate differentials throughout the period covered by our study, see I.C.C. Fourth Section Application No. 13457, *Pacific Coast Fourth Section Ap-*

It should be recalled, however, that in the postwar years the *total* charge to the shipper, after the addition of accessorial charges to the port-to-port rate, was frequently greater by water than by rail on port-to-port shipments. (See table 10.)

These cost and rate developments effectively reduced—and often eliminated—the traditional long-haul advantages of the vessel operators in the coastwise trade. Although we do not have detailed information on costs and rates in the intercoastal trade, similar, though not as drastic, changes occurred there.[20] We can conclude that they were not as drastic because in the postwar years the volume of dry-cargo tonnage hauled did not fall as much relative to prewar as it did in the coastwise trade.

We have noted[21] that an increase in water-borne cargoes would have reduced costs per ton and enabled vessel operators to have shown profits at some of the then existing rates. However, gaining traffic even at the lower prewar rates was apparently difficult. Though average annual water-borne intercoastal and coastwise dry-cargo tonnage increased from 7.4 million long tons in 1930–1934 to 8.1 million long tons in 1935–1939, a rise of about 10 per cent, railroads and trucks gained even more. In California, railroad traffic within the state averaged 26 million short tons annually during 1930–1934 and 31.7 million tons in 1935–1939—an increase of nearly 22 per cent. Similar gains occurred in Oregon and Washington. For trucks required to report to the Public Utilities Commission of the State of California the tonnages were 1.6 million short tons per year for 1930–1934 and 2.5 million tons for 1935–1939—an increase of 56 per cent.[22]

---

plications, and Docket No. 21918, *Los Angeles Chamber of Commerce vs. Southern Pacific Et Al.*, 165 I.C.C. 373–417 (1930) ; and I.C.C. Docket No. 29721, *All Rail Commodity Rates Between California, Oregon, and Washington*, 268 I.C.C. 515–546.

[20] The I.C.C. reported in 1947: "The figures for 10 voyages [in the intercoastal trade] show that, since 1938, voyage and vessel expenses have increased an average of 175 per cent while average revenue per voyage was only about 145 per cent greater than it was in 1938. Stevedoring costs per ton have increased 235 per cent since 1938. The basic wage rates for seamen in June 1947 is [*sic*] 152 per cent higher than it was in 1938. The ratio of terminal expense to total voyage and vessel expense, which was 43 per cent in 1938, is now about 60 per cent." (I.C.C. Docket No. 29663, *Transcontinental Rail Rates*, 268 I.C.C. 572 [1947].)

[21] See above, pp. 157–160.

[22] Statistics computed from Appendix, tables 22, 30, and 31. Tables 30 and 31 also contain data for Oregon and Washington.

Maritime shipping volume in the postwar years was far below pre-war, whereas the volume of traffic handled by its domestic competitors was far above. The maritime shipping dry-cargo tonnage figure for coastwise and intercoastal trade is 3.2 million long tons per year (a *decrease* of 61 per cent from 1935–1939). Railroads in California carried 57.8 million short tons annually (an *increase* of 82 per cent over 1935–1939), and trucks carried 6 million short tons per year (an *increase* of 140 per cent over 1935–1939).[23]

Why did gains in intercoastal water-borne cargo tonnage during the late 'thirties fail to match gains in railroading and trucking?[24] And why, aside from higher costs to the shipper, did maritime shipping find itself with even less traffic than it had carried in the depression years? From discussions with leaders in the industry we conclude that the findings of the Pacific Coast Association of Port Authorities, though strictly applicable to 1951, effectively sum up the long-standing disadvantages of shipping by water and certain deficiencies in the management of the shipping companies.

The Association sent a questionnaire to 589 managers of companies shipping and receiving intercoastal water-borne cargo and received

---

[23] Statistics computed from Appendix, tables 22, 30, and 31.

[24] Unfortunately, the data available do not permit comparisons between intercoastal rail and water-borne shipments. The following figures, however, are indicative of the comparative performances of maritime shipping and the railroads. Average annual revenue tons of freight originated by Class I, II, and III railroads in the United States were about 7.3 per cent greater during 1935–1939 than during 1930–1934. (For Class I railroads the figure is 7 per cent.) Average annual coastwise and intercoastal water-borne dry-cargo tonnage increased by only 1.1 per cent. In absolute terms the contrast is far more impressive. Class I, II, and III railroads originated about 56 million long tons of revenue freight more annually during 1935–1939 than in the preceding years. For the vessel operators, the increase amounted to about 90,000 long tons annually. (Railroad figures computed from United States Department of Commerce, Bureau of the Census, *Historical Statistics of the United States, 1789–1945* [Washington, Government Printing Office, 1949], p. 203. Coastwise and intercoastal figures computed from the Appendix, tables 4–6.)

Our cost and rate discussions are confined primarily to the coastwise operations. This is because more detailed figures are available for the coastwise trade than for the intercoastal. Reports of hearings held by the Interstate Commerce Commission indicate that the intercoastal vessel operators were plagued by the same difficulties though sometimes not to the same extent as the coastwise operators. Similar findings were made by the Committee on Interstate and Foreign Commerce of the United States Senate. (See *Merchant Marine Study and Investigation*, Hearings Before a Subcommittee of the Committee on Interstate and Foreign Commerce, United States Senate, 81st Cong., 2d sess., pt. 6, April 11, 13, 14, and 18, 1950. Washington, Government Printing Office, 1950.)

235 replies.[25] It found that low frequency of service, long transit time, loss or damage to shipments, and unstable labor conditions were important factors preventing the greater use of intercoastal shipping service. Many shippers also indicated that the savings in freight charges when using water instead of rail or truck were insufficient to justify shipping by vessel in view of the disadvantages of water-borne carriage. In addition, they cited the incidental charges such as wharfage and insurance as militating against shipping by vessel.

Intercoastal water-borne traffic would be stimulated, the Association reported, if the shipping companies would establish through rates, joint rates, and through bills of lading to and from inland points. This would "encourage the use of intercoastal service by shippers and consignees not located at seaboard."[26] Also revealed by the survey was the opinion that steamship operators had not advertised their service properly, particularly to prospective shippers located inland from the ports of the Pacific Coast.

It is interesting to note that in 1930, twenty-one years before the Association's report, the Interstate Commerce Commission listed many of the same disadvantages suffered by the vessel operators in their competition with the railroads.[27] By 1941, according to the Commission, coastwise water service had seriously deteriorated. Transit time had increased and the number of sailings per week northbound from Los Angeles had fallen from twenty-seven before 1931 to seven or eight in 1941.[28]

---

[25] The results of the survey are summarized in the *West Coast Shipper*, December, 1951, p. 9.

[26] *Loc. cit.*

[27] They were as follows: (1) the absence of reconsignment, diversion, or transit privileges such as provided by the railroads, (2) the danger of loss or damage of shipments by boat not covered by marine insurance or the claim policy of the water lines, (3) the additional handlings required when using water transport, (4) the daily rail service as compared with the delays while waiting for the ship to sail, (5) the more stringent packing and mailing requirements for water-borne shipments, (6) the greater time and trouble necessary on the part of the shipper using water transportation, (7) the ten cents per ton charged by the rail lines for checking contents and issuing a clear receipt when a switching movement is required on water-borne freight, and (8) the greater dependability of rail service. (I.C.C. Fourth Section Application No. 13457, *Pacific Coast Fourth Section Applications* and I.C.C. Docket No. 21918, *Los Angeles Chamber of Commerce vs. Southern Pacific Company Et Al.*, 165 I.C.C. 402 [1930].)

[28] The Commission noted further: "The transit time is about 7 days, but the boats stop at San Francisco Bay points, where additional freight is loaded; frequently it is loaded on

The failure of intercoastal and coastwise water-borne commerce to increase more than it did during the late 'thirties and its failure to return to prewar levels in the postwar years are partly attributable to the inadequate quality and frequency of service as well as to rising costs to the shipper. The sharp increases in wage rates, the growing network of restrictive working rules that further increased costs, the frequent interruptions of sailing schedules by work stoppages and "quickie" strikes, and the debilitating effects of the long coastwide strikes all effectively discouraged the shipping companies from whole-hearted, industry-wide attempts to provide the frequency of sailings and the other improvements that would have been required to boost traffic.[29]

Postwar, the vessel operators replaced their obsolete ships with larger and faster vessels but were still unable to overcome the enormous cost increases that had proved to be a gravely increasing handicap since the beginning of World War II. To make matters worse, they found that, during the war-enforced suspension of normal coastwise

top of freight from Los Angeles, resulting in delays of 1 or 2 days in unloading. Freight received at Los Angeles for shipment on nonsailing days may not reach its destination in less than 9 to 11 days. The rail service is 5 days a week; the motor carriers operate one or more trucks daily. The testimony is to the effect that shipments from Los Angeles by rail are delivered at Portland on the fourth and fifth days, by motor carriers on second and third days, and by the forwarder on the fourth and fifth days, respectively." (I.C.C. Investigation and Suspension Docket No. M-1230, *Motor-Water Commodity Rates Between California and Oregon-Washington,* 30 MCC 339 [1942].)

[29] Additional evidence of the unattractiveness of coastwise and intercoastal vessel operations generally during the 'thirties can be found in a report by the Maritime Commission in 1939. It noted that in 1938 the average age of freight vessels in the coastwise and intercoastal trades fleet (consisting of vessels operated by forty-two common carrier lines classified as intercoastal or coastwise carriers required to file annual financial reports with the Commission) was twenty years and that it was sixteen and a half years for combination freight and passenger vessels. The Commission pointed out that its investigation showed that from reports filed with it as of December 31, 1937, the coastwise and intercoastal vessel operators were unable to replace their earning assets out of reserves, even assuming they could replace them at the low prices originally paid for them. In addition, these reports showed that though there was a wide range of earnings on investment, the average for the operators reporting amounted to 2.81 per cent for the period 1928–1937, inclusive. (United States Maritime Commission, *Economic Survey of Coastwise and Intercoastal Shipping,* 76th Cong., 1st sess., H. Doc. 209 [Washington, Government Printing Office, 1939], pp. 12–13.)

For a brief discussion of coastwise and intercoastal shipping problems, see also *The Use and Disposition of Ships and Shipyards at the End of World War II,* a report prepared for the United States Navy Department and the United States Maritime Commission by the Graduate School of Business Administration, Harvard University (Cambridge, Harvard University Press, 1948), pp. 71–95.

and intercoastal services, the railroads and trucks had become firmly entrenched in the markets of these trades. In consequence, many water lines never resumed operations in these services during the postwar years. In the intercoastal trade, usually served by about 150 vessels between World Wars I and II, there were only fifty to fifty-five vessels in service as of June, 1947.[30] In the coastwise trade, in February, 1949, four companies operated ten ships totaling 51,700 dead weight tons, as compared with thirty-one companies operating sixty-two vessels totaling 222,983 dead weight tons in 1939.[31]

● *Summary.*—These facts regarding costs and others presented in earlier chapters enable us to account for the great decline in the coastwise and intercoastal dry-cargo trades during 1930–1948. For this decline, there were four principal reasons. (1) The water carriers suffered an extreme rise in operating costs, which was relatively much greater than that experienced by their land competitors. Wages were the major element in this increased cost, which was not offset by gains in productivity. (2) Shippers were diverted from the water carriers by unreliable services, which resulted from the great number of strikes, some of which were of long duration. (3) Economic development of the west, coupled with greatly improved technology in land transport and its greater convenience to the shipper, worked to divert tonnage to more efficient competitors. (4) The war disrupted water services and gave opportunity for these competitors to entrench themselves permanently in these trades. Accordingly, many vessels were diverted to more profitable operations, and services were only resumed on a restricted basis.

Viewed in proper perspective, therefore, increasing outlays for labor and other items were certainly important as a factor contributing to the industry's difficulties between 1930 and 1948, but they were not the only factor. Had the demand for maritime shipping services increased sufficiently as wage and other expenses rose, the larger cargoes would at least have helped to arrest the tendency for costs per ton to rise and shipping might have been able to maintain its position. How-

---

[30] I.C.C. Docket No. 29663, *Transcontinental Rail Rates*, 268 I.C.C. 572 (1947).

[31] I.C.C. Docket No. 29721, *All Rail Commodity Rates Between California, Oregon, and Washington*, 277 I.C.C. 523 (1948).

ever, the demand for transportation favored the railroads and trucks. Inevitably, then, maritime shipping lost in the battle for coastwise and intercoastal traffic.

In the next three chapters we shall endeavor to lay bare some of the causes of the rapid rise in wage rates and labor costs, and the factors behind the many work stoppages that interrupted shipping service and contributed importantly to the industry's decline. In a sense, this will be an analysis of "internal" factors in the industry's development as contrasted with the "external" factors discussed so far.

For the reader not interested in labor relations we suggest that he skip the next three chapters and proceed to chapter xii for the conclusions of this study. The reader desiring a brief summary of the main issues and conclusions to be drawn from chapters ix and x should proceed to chapter xi.

Part III
The Influence of Labor Relations

CHAPTER IX

Major Strikes

● *Introduction.*—In our analysis and explanation of the poor economic performance of the Pacific Coast maritime shipping industry during 1930–1948, we have attacked the problem from two sides, both of which were essential for an adequate account. With reasonable accuracy one side might be called "demand" and the other, "supply." Clearly, both demand and supply factors were at work. Together they governed the behavior of tonnage handled and so lay back of the statistical record. At bottom, therefore, our explanation of that record turns upon an appraisal of the forces of demand and supply. It must be admitted, however, that these two concepts of demand and supply suggest a simplicity of explanation that would be quite misleading. They merely permit a convenient logical division of a group of causes that was broad in range and complex in nature.

In Part II we examined in some detail the behavior of tonnage and the influence of a group of forces that affected tonnage mainly from the side of demand. As we indicated in the last two chapters, however, strikes and wage costs were of great importance in bringing about both the extreme instability and the long-run decline of the industry. They not only weakened demand directly, by driving away business;

173

they also reduced the supply of water services, directly in the case of strikes, and less obviously by forcing up costs and rates relative to those of land competitors in the coastwise and intercoastal trades. Yet frequent strikes and soaring wage costs were themselves the effects of deeper causes, originating within the troubled labor relations of the industry. This fact makes these relations a necessary subject for inquiry.

The question to be considered is what lay back of the industry's extraordinary record regarding strikes and labor costs, which from 1934 onward proved to be one of the dominant difficulties of shipping management. To develop an explanation, the next three chapters are on labor relations in the industry. "Conflict" most aptly describes those relations. The conflict was complex in origins, however, and it changed in form over the years. It was intimately connected with the revival of collective bargaining in 1934. Yet collective bargaining is not necessarily a synonym for conflict. It can also serve as a means of constructive problem-solving. Indeed, as the situation developed, conflict ceased to figure so far as some of the unions were concerned. Moreover, many good things emerged from collective bargaining: a safety code for longshoremen, greatly improved working conditions at sea, wage and hour standards comparable with those in American industry, and greater regularity in employment. But in spite of these achievements, the industry failed to stabilize its relations with the unions. Conflict, rather than coöperation, in the main described those relations for fifteen years. To account for it, we first review the principal facts and then present our interpretation of those facts.

In this chapter we shall review briefly the story of the five great coastwide strikes, in which labor-management difficulties were made obvious to the public. In chapter x we shall look into the development of the industry's peculiar system of collective bargaining and examine some more subtle forms of conflict, which grew out of the administration of collective agreements. Then in chapter xi we shall bring together the implications of the evidence, to develop our explanation of the causes of the struggle which cost so much to both sides.

Probably no other American industry in recent history has such a record of bitter disputes and bad bargaining relationships as that of Pacific Coast maritime shipping. On this many observers agree.[1] Between 1934 and 1948, Pacific Coast shipping suffered five protracted coastwide strikes, seventy-eight port-wide strikes, and 1,255 local stoppages. The five coastwide strikes alone closed down the industry for 349 calendar days during these fifteen years.

What lay back of these coastwide strikes? Why were they two or three times as long as the average shutdown? What were the issues that so deeply divided the parties? Why, at the end of fifteen years, did labor relations in some respects seem to be no better than they were at their beginning in 1934?

The answers to these and other questions require careful examination of a quite complex story. Its beginning really goes back fifteen years before the first great strike, that of 1934.

● *The Situation before 1934.*—Between 1919 and 1921, the maritime employers on the Pacific Coast succeeded in eliminating independent unionism from the industry. Thereafter, a closed antiunion shop prevailed, known to colloquial usage as an "open shop," which latter term we shall also employ. With the introduction of the open shop, well-organized shipping management acquired sole authority in the administration of labor relations, checked only by the relatively weak competitive limits imposed by a casual labor market. Within those limits, management obtained considerable discretionary power in fixing wages, hours, and working conditions.[2] The power was never abso-

---

[1] See, for example: Joint Committee on Labor-Management Relations, *Labor-Management Relations: West Coast Maritime Industry*, 80th Cong., 2d sess., S. Rept. 986, pt. 5 (Washington, Government Printing Office, 1948) ; Paul Eliel, "Industrial peace and conflict: a study of two Pacific Coast industries," *Industrial and Labor Relations Review*, vol. 2, no. 4 (July, 1949), 477–501; Clark Kerr and Lloyd Fisher, "Conflict on the waterfront," *Atlantic Monthly* (Sept., 1949), 17–23.

[2] For evidence concerning this period, we have relied upon the following: Committee on Labor and Public Welfare, Subcommittee on Labor-Management Relations, *Hiring Halls in the Maritime Industry*, Hearings . . . , United States Senate, 81st Cong., 2d sess., March 13, 14, 16, 21, 22, 23, and 28, 1950 (Washington, Government Printing Office, 1950) ; Eliel, *op. cit.*; Paul Eliel, *The Waterfront and General Strikes, San Francisco, 1934* (San Francisco, Industrial Association of San Francisco, 1934), pp. 1–5; Robert James Lampman, *Collective Bargaining of West Coast Sailors, 1885–1947: A Case Study in Unionism* (Ph.D. dissertation, University of Wisconsin, 1950), pp. 124–150; Richard Alan Liebes, *Longshore Labor Relations on the Pacific Coast, 1934–1942* (Ph.D. dissertation, University of California, Berkeley, 1942), pp. 35–41, 50; and Dwight Livingstone Palmer, *Pacific Coast*

lute, because men could still enter or leave the market. As matters worked out, however, entry tended to exceed exodus, and the pressure on wages and working conditions was consistently downward until 1934. Moreover, the mobility of labor is never perfect, and there were many ways in which management could act arbitrarily without fear of a shortage of workers.

Paul Eliel, at one time a leading official of the stevedoring employers' association in San Francisco, has described the situation as this: "... the Pacific Coast water fronts were ... operating, to all intents and purposes, on an open shop basis, but in some ports there were independent unions that were considered by old-time unionists to be employer dominated."[3]

Before 1919, the longshoremen and the sailors had worked under agreements established by collective bargaining.[4] Employer negotiations with offshore unions were conducted either by the Shipowners Association of the Pacific Coast, an organization formed in 1904 for the coasting trade, or by the separate steamship lines in the other trades. The stevedoring firms were organized on a port basis. Naturally, there was much common action among all these management groups.[5]

In 1919, the Riggers' and Stevedores' Union of San Francisco, affiliated with the International Longshoremen's Association (AFL), struck unsuccessfully and was destroyed. Shortly after, a new organization appeared, known as the Longshoremen's Association of San Francisco and the Bay District.[6] This organization was said to be independent, but among the men it had the reputation of being manage-

Maritime Labor: A Study in Industrial Relations before and under the N.R.A. (Ph.D. dissertation, Stanford University, 1935), pp. 65–328.

[3] Eliel, "Industrial peace and conflict...," p. 484.

[4] The longshoremen were originally organized by the Longshoremen's Union of the Pacific, which affiliated with the International Longshoremen's Association (AFL) in 1908. The sailors were represented by the Sailors' Union of the Pacific, formed in 1885 and in this period affiliated with the International Seamen's Union (AFL). At this time, ISU also included two other distinct unions: the Pacific Coast Marine Firemen, Oilers, Watertenders and Wipers Association, and the National Union of Marine Cooks and Stewards. Liebes, *op. cit.*, p. 35; Lampman, *op. cit.*, p. 83.

[5] The Waterfront Employer's Union of Puget Sound was formed in 1908, followed by the Waterfront Employers' Union of San Francisco in 1914. Lampman, *op. cit.*, p. 136.

[6] Eliel, *The Waterfront and General Strikes...*, pp. 2–3.

ment-controlled. In any event, the longshoremen were eliminated from collective bargaining and an open shop was introduced.[7] In 1921, the stevedore employers introduced company-controlled hiring halls at Seattle and San Pedro. A similar hall existed at Portland, Oregon. At San Francisco, however, hiring after 1919 was done at the docks under the "shape-up" system. Under this system, the companies supplemented their "steady" gangs of high-productivity longshoremen with casual labor that was assembled each day as needed. At the other major ports, however, efforts were made by means of the management halls to control the supply of eligible men in order to build a trained force of regular employees.

In 1921, the Sailors' Union of the Pacific (AFL) called a futile strike, which ended in expulsion of the union from further collective bargaining. Once more an employer organization was substituted, the Marine Service Bureau, allegedly to promote the interests of the seamen and to protect the industry from radical unionism. Subsequently, the Bureau undertook exclusive registration of seagoing personnel and began the operation of employer-controlled hiring halls.[8]

The elimination of independent unionism made possible employer job-control. In part, this development was associated with the nationwide "American plan" (open shop) movement following World War I. A more immediate factor lay in the economic problems of ocean shipping after 1919. The industry thereafter was plagued with excess capacity, cutthroat rate-cutting, and keen competition from low-cost foreign lines. Wages and working conditions became a focal point for competitive pressures. This was natural. On the docks, longshore wages were almost 100 per cent of handling costs. At sea, labor costs were the major item in vessel expenses. By means of job-control, the employers gained the freedom to take advantage of a casual labor mar-

---

[7] The Longshoremen's Association of San Francisco and the Bay District was known colloquially as the "Blue Book Union" and was viewed by the men as company-dominated. In the ensuing years, there was little evidence of genuine collective bargaining. In 1921, the Waterfront Employers' Union of San Francisco explained its refusal to bargain further with the ILA by referring to violence and radicalism. See Full and By, *A Message from the Waterfront Employers' Union*, pamphlet (San Francisco, Waterfront Employers' Union, 1921), p. 6.

[8] Lampman, *op. cit.*, pp. 139–141.

ket, dropping standards formerly imposed by collective bargaining. Wage rates were cut, overtime premiums dropped, and hours lengthened. Work was speeded up. At sea, working conditions deteriorated steadily. With the onset of depression in 1929, downward pressure against labor costs increased in intensity, under the twin impacts of reduced demand for maritime labor and increased supply of men seeking work.[9]

In the years after 1919, the port of San Francisco played a peculiarly strategic role. There were good reasons for this fact. Most of the water lines of the Pacific Coast had their headquarters in that city. These carriers also dominated stevedoring operations at the port. Following World War I, there developed among San Francisco business groups a particularly intense determination to replace trade unionism with the open shop, no doubt inspired in part by the growing competitive rivalry of Los Angeles, where unions were very weak. The shipping industry in San Francisco was closely connected with an extreme form of the open-shop movement, and some steamship lines gained the reputation among seamen as notoriously "bad" employers. The shape-up system operated on the docks, provoking bitter discontent among the longshoremen. In marked contrast stood the system of management halls at the other ports.

Thus the ultimate revolt of Pacific Coast maritime labor in 1934 had its origins and at all times its inspiration and direction in San Francisco. In fact, the guess might even be hazarded that if the policies of San Francisco management had not been so extreme, the revolt would have been much less radical.

Many grievances developed among maritime workers after 1919. At their core was this system of employer job-control. Both the longshoremen and the seamen charged that the system included a black list against active unionists. Both the steamship lines and the stevedore firms at San Francisco were accused of bribery and favoritism in allocating jobs. There were wage cuts and worsened working conditions at sea, and some lines were said to have used Oriental labor to beat down standards. Under the shape-up at San Francisco, favored "star

---

[9] *Ibid.,* pp. 124–135.

gangs" were used as pace-setters to speed up cargo-handling. The casual groups were maintained as reserves, often unable to make subsistence earnings.[10] And there is little doubt that the companies frequently displayed small interest in building up a loyal and steady work force, or in developing modern employee relations programs and grievance procedures.[11]

Granted that the operators themselves were under increasingly severe economic pressures, it seems clear that under the open-shop policy they pushed their advantage to unreasonable excess. They had acquired considerable discretionary power and they used it extensively.[12] They therefore planted the seeds of bitter discontent, whose harvest they were to reap in 1934.

● *The 1934 Coastwide Strike.—Developments before the strike.* With the passage of the National Industrial Recovery Act in the spring of 1933, independent unionism at last began to revive in the industry. This statute provided for the creation of "self-governing industry codes" covering prices (in this instance, rates), wages, hours, and working conditions. It also proclaimed the right of employees to bargain collectively, without discrimination against such activity. No enforcement powers were provided to protect this right, however.

In the summer of 1933, the International Seamen's Union (ISU-AFL) began an active organizing campaign among the seagoing crafts. However, it avoided resort to strike for many months. Instead it pinned its faith to the adoption of the proposed shipping code, hoping that the operators would ultimately recognize the union as a bargaining agent for negotiating the labor provisions of the code. This the operators were in no hurry to do, and as late as May, 1934, the proposed code was still under discussion, while the ISU was still unrecognized and bereft of strike plans.[13]

---

[10] Halls were operated by the employers at Seattle, Tacoma, Portland, and San Pedro. Restriction of labor supply and rotation were both practiced. At Seattle, the registered men had an equal voice in these policies. However, they had no independent coastwide union at this time.

[11] These factors of employee discontent are summarized from Lampman, *op. cit.*, pp. 141–146; Palmer, *op. cit.*, pp. 65–328; and William S. Hopkins, "Employment exchanges for seamen," *American Economic Review*, XXV, no. 2 (June, 1935), 250–258.

[12] Eliel, "Industrial peace and conflict . . . ," *op. cit.*, p. 486.

[13] Lampman, *op. cit.*, pp. 151–153.

Thus the initiative for the 1934 strike lay with the longshoremen. Following the enactment of NIRA, the International Longshoremen's Association (ILA-AFL) sent organizers to the Pacific Coast ports. New locals were created, and among these was Local 38-79 in San Francisco, chartered in September, 1933, and destined to play a key role in future events. In the ensuing months, the Pacific Coast ILA program began to crystallize into the following demands: (1) recognition as exclusive bargaining agent in each of the ports; (2) a closed-shop agreement for ILA members; (3) a coastwide bargaining unit in place of port-by-port settlements; (4) a thirty-hour week and a six-hour day, after which work was to be at overtime rates; (5) a system to dispatch all men through jointly controlled hiring halls; and (6) a basic straight-time rate of $1.00 an hour, and $1.50 overtime.[14]

At first, the employers resisted the ILA on the grounds it was not representative of the men. In district convention, the union countered by agreeing to strike if the employers refused to bargain as a coast-wide unit. The employers in San Francisco resisted by claiming that they could not bind the other port associations. They did reach tentative agreements, however, regarding recognition of the union in San Francisco and the establishment of a jointly controlled hall for that port. The union's demand for a *coastwide* settlement led to a deadlock. On March 7, 1934, all coast locals by majority vote approved a strike for March 23. This strike was delayed by the union on request of President Roosevelt, who, on March 22, appointed a fact-finding board to investigate the dispute and to make recommendations for settlement.[15]

Ultimately, this board failed to avert the strike because it could not get agreement that the bargaining unit was to be coastwide, or that wages and certain other conditions were to be made uniform for all ports. The San Francisco local had originally agreed to negotiate for San Francisco separately. Later it was overruled by the district ILA representing the entire coast. In addition, left-wing pressure against

---

[14] Palmer, *op. cit.*, p. 312; Eliel, *The Waterfront and General Strikes*..., pp. 4–8.

[15] Palmer, *op. cit.*, pp. 313–325; Eliel, *The Waterfront and General Strikes*..., pp. 6–8. This original board was composed of Dr. Henry F. Grady (Berkeley), chairman, Charles A. Reynolds (Seattle), and Dr. J. L. Leonard (Los Angeles). Each member was chairman of a regional labor board established under NIRA.

the San Francisco ILA leadership developed. This originated with a prostrike group and culminated in the removal of Lee Holman as president of Local 38-79. On April 30, the ILA informed the employers that unless a satisfactory agreement were reached by May 7, negotiations would end.[16] Some progress was made in the revision of working rules at San Francisco thereafter, but the union's coastwide demand became the rock upon which negotiations ultimately foundered. On the morning of May 9, the coastwide longshore strike began.

The strike itself. The employers attempted with some early success to continue operations, although as the shutdown wore on its effectiveness increased. Between May 16 and May 20, the offshore crafts joined the strike—among these, the Pacific Coast locals of the National Marine Engineers' Beneficial Association (MEBA), the National Organization of Masters, Mates and Pilots of America (MMP-AFL), the Sailors' Union of the Pacific (SUP) (ISU-AFL), the Pacific Coast Marine Firemen, Oilers, Watertenders and Wipers Association (MFOWW) (ISU-AFL), and the National Union of Marine Cooks and Stewards (MCS) (ISU-AFL).[17]

With the addition of these unions to the strike the Pacific Coast ship operators became parties to the dispute, together with the four stevedoring employer associations at each of the major ports which were involved with the ILA in the original strike. The seagoing crafts also demanded recognition and collective bargaining. The SUP and the MFOWW added the demand that the Marine Service Bureau (which operated the shipowners' hiring hall) be abolished. The MEBA and the MMP included among their demands that the employers must reach a satisfactory agreement with the longshoremen, in this way introducing the principle of solidarity among the crafts, the lack of which had proved fatal to the strikes of 1919 and 1921. On the same principle, the ILA announced on May 26 that its strike would continue until satisfactory settlements had been reached with all crafts participating.[18]

---

[16] Eliel, *The Waterfront and General Strikes* ..., pp. 10–11; Palmer, *op. cit.*, pp. 326–328. Palmer dates the union ultimatum as of May 5 rather than April 30.

[17] Lampman, *op. cit.*, p. 154; Palmer, *op. cit.*, pp. 336–339.

[18] Palmer, *op. cit.*, pp. 337–339.

From beginning to end, however, leadership in the strike belonged to the longshoremen, and the center of that leadership lay in the San Francisco local. As the situation developed, the goals of the San Francisco group became clear: (1) to obtain if possible a closed-shop agreement, or at least to eliminate all nonunion longshoremen; (2) to obtain union-controlled hiring halls in each of the ports; (3) to force the employers to concede a coastwide unit for purposes of collective bargaining; and (4) to lay the basis for the ultimate creation of an industrial union in which all existing maritime crafts would be consolidated. In this manner, the power of the employers over job-control could finally be broken.

The union strategy consisted of four parts: (1) to insist upon ratification by the full membership of all proposals emanating from negotiations;[19] (2) to stand firm on the principle of no return to work until all participating crafts had reached satisfactory settlements; (3) to bring into being a joint strike committee empowered to negotiate for all crafts, superseding the national or district officers already involved;[20] and (4) ultimately, to bring about a general strike in order to achieve solidarity and to force the employers to surrender on the unions' terms.[21]

During the first six weeks of the strike, a struggle for power within the ILA rapidly developed. On the one side was Joseph P. Ryan, national president of the ILA, who was active in the negotiations from April until the middle of June. Ryan's position was a vacillating one: in the beginning he was ready to settle for recognition without the closed shop; later, for the closed shop, a jointly controlled hall, and

---

[19] This measure reflected distrust of the national ILA leadership under President Joseph P. Ryan. Harry Bridges' name first appeared in the press on May 19, in support of this proposal. (Eliel, *The Waterfront and General Strikes . . .*, pp. 24–25.) Significantly, the group favoring this principle consistently opposed secret ballots in membership voting. (*Ibid.*, pp. 36–75.) In this way, the Bridges group proved able to control the strike.

[20] The Joint Marine Strike Committee came into being on June 19, with Bridges as an active leader. (*Ibid.*, p. 81.)

[21] First mention of the "possibility of a general strike along the Pacific Coast . . . as almost a certainty" occurred on May 29, in a public statement of the longshoremen's strike committee, of which Bridges was a leading member. At a mass meeting in San Francisco on June 19, members of the Joint Marine Strike Committee called for a general strike as the only means to victory. (*Ibid.*, pp. 35, 83.) The strike did not actually occur until July 16, 1934.

a coastwide bargaining unit; later still, for a nondiscrimination clause without the closed shop and with port-by-port bargaining. On the other side was Harry Renton Bridges, who began as a member of the strike committee of Local 38-79, became the leader of a rank-and-file faction in the local, then emerged as chairman of the Joint Marine Strike Committee, and ultimately wrested the leadership of the strike away from Ryan and the officials of the Pacific Coast district of the ILA. The goals and strategy outlined above were those of the Bridges group. From mid-May until the finish, they clearly dominated the course of action followed by the ILA on the Pacific Coast. Quite clearly, too, the Bridges philosophy was a radical and uncompromising one, immediately centered upon the conquest of job-control for the union.[22]

By the nature of their position, the employers' objective throughout the dispute was containment. Hence their strategy was one of defense, limited concessions, and counterattack. So far as the stevedoring employers were concerned, active leadership for the whole coast lay with Thomas G. Plant, president of the Waterfront Employers' Union of San Francisco. At a later point, the Industrial Association of San Francisco was to enter the dispute, with an attempt to reopen the port.

In the beginning, the employers refused to recognize the ILA locals for collective bargaining. Later, they were willing to bargain, but insisted that the bargaining would have to be on a port-by-port basis, and that they could not accord ILA members either a closed shop or preferential status in hiring. In this connection, the San Francisco group also offered to set up a jointly controlled hiring hall.[23] The employers thereafter held fast to the principle of joint control of the hall.

---

[22] The culmination of the Bridges program was the later withdrawal of all but three small Washington locals from the ILA, to become the International Longshoremen's and Warehousemen's Union, which, with Bridges as president, affiliated in 1937 with the then Committee for Industrial Organization.

There is evidence of some restiveness during the 1934 strike on the part of Andrew Furuseth, venerable president of the ISU, and certain officials of the AFL in San Francisco, concerning Bridges' rise to power. At issue was whether Bridges was under Communist influence and was pursuing a long-run program that clashed with the more conservative "business unionism" of the AFL unions. At this time, however, a good case can be made that Bridges' effort to gain job-control was consistent with orthodox trade unionism, whatever its larger implications.

[23] These proposals, in essence, represent the position taken by the San Francisco group in an offer to the original mediation board on March 28, 1934, when bargaining by port was still in being. (*Ibid.*, pp. 7–8.)

With the onset of the strike, the stevedoring companies attempted to maintain operations and, to do so, employed strikebreakers. The status of these new nonunion men, together with a substantial number of permanent nonunion men who had not gone out on strike, was to complicate the closed-shop issue. Here the employers claimed, with legal exactitude, that the NIRA required nondiscrimination in employment; therefore, that (1) a closed shop could not legally be granted, and (2) these nonunion longshoremen would have to be equally eligible for work under any settlement of the hiring hall issue.

As the strike progressed, the employers found themselves compelled to make further concessions. On May 28, they offered recognition to the ILA at all ports except Los Angeles and arbitration of all issues concerning wages and hours.[24] Under Bridges' leadership in the San Francisco local, the proposal was rejected all along the coast. At this time, business groups in San Francisco initiated discussion of plans to reopen that port.[25]

On June 16, a second "agreement" was reached between the employers and top officials of the ILA (who lacked power to settle), in what was to prove the final act of the original mediation board. This time the employers conceded coastwide bargaining in principle, and offered jointly controlled halls at all ports, under the administration of a joint labor relations committee that would pass on all registrations of men hired after 1933 and would deal with wages, maximum hours, and grievances. However, in this offer the employers stood fast on local wage and hour negotiations and nondiscrimination relative to permanent nonunion men.[26]

Again, the settlement was rejected by the coast ILA membership, although Los Angeles favored it in a referendum vote.[27] Ryan thereupon withdrew from negotiations. The Bridges group emerged in full control. They stressed that they would not settle until all striking unions had reached agreement. On June 19, they brought about the formation of the Joint Marine Strike Committee, to conduct all further

---

[24] Palmer, *op. cit.*, pp. 345–346; Eliel, *The Waterfront and General Strikes* . . . , pp. 33–35.
[25] Eliel, *The Waterfront and General Strikes* . . . , p. 43.
[26] *Ibid.*, pp. 70–71; Palmer, *op. cit.*, pp. 351–356.
[27] Palmer, *op. cit.*, p. 354.

negotiations. As a result, the strike formally became a general maritime strike, and the employer organizations found themselves compelled to bargain as a unit.

At this point, the employers shifted their strategy to an attempt to open the ports. Considerable community pressure had already developed in this direction, aided by incidents of pitched battles between police, strikebreakers, and pickets, together with increasing erosion of economic life all along the coast. Charges were heard that Communists had gained control of the strike, and that they desired not to settle but to bring about open war between civic authority and the strikers in order to produce a general strike and to further a "class war" psychology.

With negotiations at a breakdown after June 16, and with the employers publicly preparing to open the ports, President Roosevelt on June 26 appointed a National Longshoremen's Board, composed of Archbishop Edward J. Hanna (San Francisco), chairman, Edward F. McGrady (Assistant Secretary of Labor, Washington, D.C.), and O. K. Cushing (San Francisco). The new board's first act was to obtain from the Industrial Association of San Francisco, an employer organization, an agreement to postpone its plan to open the ports. From the Joint Marine Strike Committee, the board obtained the unions' demands: (1) all unions were to be recognized; (2) union-controlled halls were to be introduced for all crafts; and (3) wages, hours, and working conditions were to be arbitrated, if necessary. The employers offered arbitration of wages, hours, and conditions, but refused to extend recognition beyond the ILA or to concede a union-controlled hall.[28]

On July 3, the Industrial Association began moving cargo from Pier 38 in San Francisco, in an attempt to break the strike. On July 5, two longshoremen were killed in a clash with police. Governor Frank F. Merriam then put into operation his plans to have the waterfront strip occupied by the National Guard, to protect the operation of the Belt Railroad of California. Bridges, as chairman of the Joint Marine Strike Committee, called for a general strike. Sentiment in San Fran-

[28] *Ibid.*, pp. 361–368.

cisco for this move was crystallized by a dramatic funeral procession for the two longshoremen.[29]

During this time, the board held hearings to learn the demands of the other maritime unions. As representative of the unions affiliated with the ISU, Paul Scharrenberg testified that the steamship operators had a black list, that they used an employer-controlled hall, that they had reduced wages 50 per cent after 1921, and had lengthened hours and eliminated overtime pay. The ISU demanded recognition on a district basis, or representation elections; negotiations immediately following a return to work; and arbitration of all remaining issues, with retroactive pay. The ISU did not, however, stipulate a refusal to return to work until all crafts had reached agreements.[30]

The Masters, Mates and Pilots (MMP) offered similar testimony concerning conditions after 1921, and also demanded recognition, no discrimination, and immediate negotiations with arbitration of un-solved issues. However, the MMP declared it would refuse to settle finally until the other unions were also satisfied. The Marine Engineers (MEBA) presented a similar record concerning wages and working conditions, made the same demands, and declared that the longshore-men must reach a satisfactory agreement. Bridges, representing the longshoremen, took the same position, but refused to arbitrate the issue of the hiring hall.[31]

Speaking for the employers, Plant declared that the WEUSF lacked authority for bargaining with the offshore crafts, and that the solidar-ity principle placed the whole dispute at an impasse. He also ques-tioned the representation of the men by the offshore unions and offered aid in holding elections on the question.[32]

The general strike in San Francisco became a certainty when officials of the powerful Brotherhood of Teamsters (AFL) announced that if the longshore dispute were not settled by July 12, they would walk out. This they did, and during the next three days several other unions followed. The climax was reached on July 15, when the San

---

[29] Eliel, *The Waterfront and General Strikes . . .*, pp. 108–128.
[30] Palmer, *op. cit.*, pp. 370–372.
[31] *Ibid.*, pp. 372–378.
[32] *Ibid.*, pp. 379–381.

Francisco Labor Council voted to "request" all unions that had voted for a general strike to go out at 8:00 A.M., June 16.

The Bay area general strike lasted three days, ending early in the afternoon of the 19th. From the beginning, the Strike Strategy Committee found it necessary to adopt a permit system for the provision of essential goods and services. This practice steadily widened as paralysis developed. Implicitly, a general strike is a challenge to civic authority that inevitably ranges the power of the state against the unions. Thus, as the full implications of the unions' position became clear, the conservatives in their ranks began to prevail, and the resulting pressure to end hostilities finally triumphed.

Two factors seem powerful in explaining the general strike. One lay in a deep-seated conviction among the union rank and file that the longshoremen were in the right. The belief was general that the employers were hostile to unionism, and that the longshoremen's demands for a closed shop and their own dispatching hall constituted elementary justice. Accurate or not, this belief was fortified by the conviction that it was the employers who were really uncompromising, and not the union.[33] The other element was a strong feeling of blind resentment against the employers and civic officials, inspired by the "battle of Rincon Hill," in which two longshoremen were killed by the police. On this count, the general strike in a sense was an act of revenge, not grounded upon rational analysis.

On July 21, in a meeting in Woodside at the home of John Francis Neylan, a prominent San Francisco attorney, representatives of the stevedoring companies, the shipowners, and the press agreed on a program to break the deadlock. If the ILA would agree to arbitrate *all* issues as the board earlier had proposed, the shipowners would arbitrate all unresolved issues involving the offshore crafts.[34] For Bridges, this required abandonment of his earlier stand that the union hall and closed shop were not arbitrable. For the waterfront employers, it meant that the jointly controlled hall and nondiscrimination against the per-

---

[33] Actually, the employers had steadily retreated from their original position and, so far as the longshore dispute was concerned, were ready to arbitrate all issues before the general strike had begun.

[34] Eliel, *The Waterfront and General Strikes . . .* , p. 172.

manent nonunion longshoremen now became arbitrable issues. For the
shipowners, it meant that if the offshore crafts were to gain representation rights in elections, the operators for the first time since 1921
would have to bargain collectively and, further, would have to submit
the issue of hiring halls for the seagoing crafts to arbitration.

This move by the operators broke the stalemate, for the board then
was able to induce the ILA to vote on arbitration of all issues, and the
measure carried by more than 4 to 1. In the hearings that followed,
Bridges, representing the ILA, argued for a jointly controlled hall,
elimination of all strikebreakers, and elections to determine the seamen's wishes as to union representation. The waterfront employers
offered to eliminate the temporary strikebreakers but asked for retention of the permanent nonunion men. These employers also proposed
that, until the board had made its award, the present management-
controlled halls should be supervised by board representatives with
ILA observers present, and the shape-up system be continued at San
Francisco.[35]

Representatives of the forty-two steamship operators proposed the
discharge of all temporary men hired after May 16, except those who
normally followed the sea as an occupation. They guaranteed no discrimination against union men, with right of referral of any such
grievance to the board for decision. They also proposed temporary
supervision of the management-controlled halls by board representatives. In addition, the Shipowners Association of the Pacific Coast,
operating steam schooners in the coastwise trade, recognized the ISU
as representative of the unlicensed personnel.[36]

With this crystallization of the employers' position, the ILA District
Executive Board on July 29 voted to order the longshoremen back to
work at 8:00 A.M., July 31. Following the ILA's action of July 29, the
MMP and MEBA on the same day voted to quit the strike and, in effect,
to rest their hopes upon arbitration. On the day following, the three
ISU affiliates (SUP, MCS, and MFOWW) voted to end the strike,
since they were now "high and dry." Subsequently, wireless returns

---

[35] *Ibid.*, pp. 175–179; Palmer, *op. cit.*, pp. 395–396.
[36] Eliel, *The Waterfront and General Strikes . . .* , pp. 178–180; Palmer, *op. cit.*, pp. 396–
397.

from ships at sea made it possible for the board to tabulate the representation vote for these three ISU groups, and the ISU won by more than 8 to 1.

However, at the point when the ILA leaders ended their strike, the five seafaring crafts were still unrecognized except in the coasting trade. This independent action by the ILA provoked considerable bitterness among the offshore men, for as matters eventually worked out, their position was much weaker than that of the ILA.[37]

The results of arbitration. On October 12, 1934, the National Longshoremen's Board handed down its decision in the longshore case. This award became the basic contract between the parties, and in certain essentials was maintained in succeeding contracts over the ensuing years. The award itself carried an expiration date of September 30, 1935, and the wage increases provided by it were made retroactive to July 31, 1934. All the waterfront employer associations along the coast were parties to the decision, and in effect the ILA obtained a coastwide agreement—one of their primary objectives.

The award defined longshore work and the occupations involved, a matter important for the long-standing jurisdictional conflicts between the ILA and SUP in steam-schooner work in the coastwise trade. In addition, the longshoremen obtained the six-hour day; a normal straight-time day from 8:00 A.M. to 5:00 P.M., Mondays through Saturdays; overtime pay for work in excess of six hours during the straight-time day, and at night or on Sundays. The basic hourly rate was increased from eighty-five to ninety-five cents, and overtime was fixed at $1.40 per hour.

More important, the award established jointly controlled dispatching halls for all ports, with the dispatcher to be selected by the ILA. Control of the dispatcher actually gave the union control of the hall, despite the joint arrangement contemplated. As conceived by the board, each hall was to be administered by a port labor relations committee of six members, three from the union and three from the employers. In case of disagreement, the committees were either to choose their own arbitrator or to accept one assigned by the Secretary of

---

[37] Lampman, *op. cit.*, pp. 158–159.

Labor. Each committee was to prepare a list of "registered" longshore-men eligible for work. To qualify, a man had to have at least twelve months' service during the three years before May 9, 1934—a provision that eliminated the temporary strikebreakers but not the permanent nonunion men. In fact, the award specifically prohibited discrimination of any kind concerning union membership. Thus the ILA did not get a closed shop.

The labor relations committees were also given the task of making the rules for dispatching and rotation of men. Here the employers, subject to the system, were allowed to call for the best qualified men, although beyond this, the dispatching was to equalize earnings as far as practicable. Last, the committees were charged with deciding all grievances originating either from the men or the employers. The latter were given a qualified right to discharge, and also to increase the efficiency of operations by labor-saving devices and new cargo-handling methods compatible with health and safety.[38]

Following the ISU elections, special arbitration boards undertook hearings relative to the coastwise and offshore-intercoastal disputes. In January, 1935, the coastwise board awarded preferential hiring to members of the three ISU affiliates—SUP, MCS, and MFOWW. The old halls of the Marine Service Bureau were abolished. Employment was to be offered either through the unions or on the docks. These men, therefore, did not get a jointly controlled hall. However, the wages of sailors and firemen were raised to $70.00 a month, and an eight-hour day and fifty-six hour week were established, with overtime at seventy cents per hour.[39]

In February, 1935, the offshore and intercoastal board rendered its decision in the ISU cases. Again, the unlicensed men gained a preferential shop, but not a jointly controlled hall. The employer could obtain men at the union offices or on the docks. Shortly after, the Alaska operators settled with the ISU on the same basis.[40]

In the ultimate outcome of the bitter 1934 strike, certain things are of high importance. (1) The employer groups were forced to recog-

[38] Abstracted and summarized from a copy of the award of October 12, 1934.
[39] Lampman, *op. cit.*, p. 162.
[40] *Ibid.*, p. 163.

nize four unions and to concede the principle of coastwide bargaining. (2) The ILA did not gain a closed shop, but did win what was supposed to be a jointly controlled hall which through their control of the dispatcher became, in fact, a union-controlled hall. (3) The unlicensed seafaring personnel won recognition and preferential hiring and obtained the elimination of the employer-controlled halls. These crafts, however, did not gain a jointly controlled hall or clear-cut rotation system. (4) Both the ILA and the three ISU groups won substantial wage increases and penalty rates for overtime work. (5) The licensed officers in the MMP and MEBA emerged empty-handed. They did not even win recognition.

● *The Coastwide Strike of 1936–1937.*—The settlement in 1934 brought peace of a kind to the industry for the next two years. In one sense, it was not peace at all, but a truce during which both sides laid plans for the next battle. For the operators, the objective was to obtain modification of the longshore agreement while retaining if possible their present advantage over the offshore unions. For the unions, the immediate goal was to reëstablish the unified command temporarily provided by the Joint Marine Strike Committee in 1934. By a united front, the gains of 1934 could be protected and the seafaring crafts could be advanced to similar status. Since the attempt of the unions to create this united front was basic to the 1936–1937 strike, we shall begin our account at this point.

The formation of the Maritime Federation of the Pacific in 1935. At the end of the 1934 affair, though the ILA leaders had violated their own principle of joint action, they remained firm advocates of this principle as the essential road to victory. This was logical. Crucial strikes had been lost in 1916, 1919, and 1921 when the unions had acted independently; and there is little doubt that solidarity in the critical stages of the 1934 battle had wrested important concessions from the employers. Moreover, Bridges and his colleagues hoped ultimately to achieve one big industrial union of the maritime workers. Joint action was a necessary first step.

Accordingly, the Bridges group in 1935 initiated action to bring about a formal organization of the maritime crafts into a permanent federation. A series of meetings, starting at Seattle on April 15, 1935, resulted in the formation of the Maritime Federation of the Pacific. Participating were representatives from the ILA, the three Pacific Coast affiliates of the ISU (SUP, MCS, and MFOWW), the MEBA, MMP, and the American Radio Telegraphists Association (ARTA). The Bridges group wished to assign the Maritime Federation sovereign powers concerning negotiations and strikes of all crafts, but the SUP insisted upon their traditional autonomy. The SUP finally prevailed, but the Bridges group was successful in achieving the election of a slate of officials chosen from the rank and file. Harry Lundeberg, Seattle member of the SUP, became the first president of the MFP, and, significantly, the entire slate was chosen from the seafaring crafts.[41]

From the end of the 1934 strike until the strike in October, 1936, the ILA and the SUP in particular had developed a deliberate program of job-action or "quickie" strikes, to bring about additional gains not provided by the original awards and to enforce their interpretations of certain provisions of those awards. In addition, these stoppages included many "hot cargo" or sympathetic strikes as well, involving refusals to work ships manned by Atlantic Coast or Gulf Coast crews, or cargoes emerging from or destined to ports on local strike. Analysis of employers' records reveals 470 such "incidents" during 1934–1936 alone: 353 of these were attempts either to improve the original awards or to enforce the unions' interpretations of them. The remainder (117) were sympathetic strikes.[42]

To some extent, these "quickie" strikes were spontaneous actions of the rank and file, though there is no doubt that both Bridges and Lundeberg favored the tactic. Bridges in 1935 was still himself a rank-and-file leader, working to gain official leadership of the Pacific Coast ILA. Lundeberg was in a similar role in the SUP, which was developing a revolt against the old-line ISU leadership of Andrew Furuseth and Victor Olander.

---

[41] *Ibid.*, pp. 164–167.

[42] The data were presented in mimeographed form by the four port associations of the waterfront employers, with brief notes as to coverage and cause. We regrouped the data as to cause, eliminating all known "one-man" cases.

Recognizing that job-action could get out of hand, the leaders of the MFP adopted a resolution at the 1935 convention that is important for two reasons: (1) it formally endorsed the tactic; but (2) job-action was to be confined to purely local actions and where the action threatened to spread, the district council of the MFP was to have strategic authority.[43]

Internal conflict within the SUP led in July, 1935, to the expulsion of Paul Scharrenberg, editor of the *Seamen's Journal* (ISU) and member of the ISU executive board, from SUP membership—an action that, together with the union's job-action policy, was to bring the SUP into direct clash with the ISU officials. In November, 1935, Harry Lundeberg was elected secretary-treasurer of the SUP and came into control of that organization. Then, in January, 1936, the SUP rank and file struck the steam schooners and incurred attacks by both the ISU leaders and the ILA.[44] In this same month, the ISU held its first convention since 1930. The basic issue was revocation of the SUP charter. Furuseth and Olander charged the SUP with dual unionism, violation of its agreements, refusal to reinstate Scharrenberg, and an illegal schooner strike. As a result, the SUP became an orphan, compelled to fight for its very existence.[45]

Events were now moving toward a second strike, in the fall of 1936. The MFP had been formed. The job-action program was in full swing. Lundeberg now controlled the SUP, and early in 1936 Bridges had become district president of the ILA on the Pacific Coast.

The employers made the first move by serving notice on July 30, 1936, that they wished to modify the ILA contract. They proposed arbitration of all issues unresolved by September 1. They demanded: penalties for violations of the contract; neutral administration of the hiring halls; an increase in the number of registered men, so that the

---

[43] Lampman, *op. cit.*, p. 169, n. 2.

[44] In November, 1935, Lundeberg was openly attacked by the *Western Worker*, a publication of the Communist party, for following "individualistic" ideas. Lundeberg at this time was an advocate of job-action, and stood for the autonomy of the unions affiliated with the MFP. (*Ibid.*, pp. 170–173.)

[45] In February, 1936, Lundeberg quit the presidency of the MFP, and William Fischer, a Portland longshoreman who was sympathetic to Lundeberg rather than Bridges, became head of the MFP. (*Ibid.*, pp. 174–177.)

six-hour day could become a reality instead of a device to increase earnings; wage increases to be related to increases in working efficiency; a pledge that the men would work as directed; and restriction of travel-time allowances.[46]

The ILA response revealed a defensive strategy, though this was coupled with solidarity with the seagoing trades, whose aim was to obtain union-controlled halls (SUP, MFOWW, and MCS) or preferential employment (MEBA and MMP). Thus the ILA itself sought to widen the definition of longshore work to include "indirect transfers" between rail car and warehouse; uniform coastwide penalty rates, working rules, and sling loads; the right to respect picket lines of other crafts without being in violation of their contracts; and more liberal overtime provisions plus an increase in the basic wage. Finally, the ILA rejected arbitration, probably fearing losses relative to the 1934 award.[47]

Negotiations proved futile. The United States Maritime Commission succeeded in getting delays until October 29, 1936. Then all crafts walked out under the leadership of the MFP.

The strike itself. With the shutdown, the employers made no attempt to operate, and both sides settled down for a long siege. Again, the central issue was job-control, this time for the offshore crafts. The SUP, MCS, MFOWW, and ARTA demanded union-controlled halls, while the MMP and MEBA asked for recognition for bargaining purposes and preference in employment.

The first major break in the strike occurred in December, when the operators summoned Lundeberg to their offices for separate negotiations. These parties announced an agreement on December 18, and Bridges thereupon accused Lundeberg of "sabotaging" the strike. In defense, Lundeberg argued that the SUP had won almost "100 per

---

[46] Liebes, *op. cit.*, pp. 136–139. During 1935–1936, the stevedoring employer organizations underwent certain changes: (1) in January, 1935, the office of Coast Coördinator was established, and Frank P. Foisie, long-time manager of the Seattle hall, was appointed to the post; (2) the old San Francisco Waterfront Employers' Union became the Waterfront Employers' Association of San Francisco; and (3) in 1936 the old San Pedro Marine Service Bureau became the Waterfront Employers of Southern California. (*Ibid.*, pp. 166–168.) These moves, and others that followed, reflected a tendency toward the creation of a coastwide, multiple-employer bargaining unit, to match the new-found power of the ILA.

[47] *Ibid.*, pp. 136–139.

cent" of its demands (dispatching exclusively from the union hall under strict rotation of opportunities, a pay increase, and more liberal overtime). Lundeberg also declared that the SUP had no intention of returning to work until the other MFP crafts had reached satisfactory settlements.[48] Some years later, in a lengthy recital of grievances against Bridges, the SUP publication, *West Coast Sailors,* also charged that all crafts could have settled in December for what they obtained on February 4, 1937, and that Bridges had deliberately prolonged the strike to get credit for the ultimate victory.[49]

This episode highlighted the growing differences between Lundeberg and Bridges—differences that began to appear as early as 1935 and became obvious by the time of the second MFP convention in December, 1936. In part, the conflict was ideological: Lundeberg adhered rather closely to classical syndicalist ideas—job-action, contempt for the employer, and exclusive reliance upon the strike as the means for betterment of the workers' conditions. This was popular doctrine in the sailors' ranks, since many of the men themselves had originally been "Wobblies."

In contrast, Bridges' position from the time of his original emergence as a leader in the 1934 strike closely paralleled that of the Communist party. His basic aim was not job-control alone but the ultimate creation of a single industrial union of maritime workers. A highly centralized Maritime Federation of the Pacific was to be the first step. Thus Bridges and his followers sought strategic control of all unions in the Maritime Federation and fought against Lundeberg's doctrine of craft autonomy at the 1935 convention. With the expulsion of the SUP from the ISU in January, 1936, Bridges attempted to commit the MFP to the ISU position: that the SUP was bound to arbitration of the steam-schooner dispute of that time.[50]

Then, in the 1936 convention the Bridges and Lundeberg groups clashed on several points: the latter questioned the value of publicity campaigns to win public support, and opposed "political action" to

---

[48] Lampman, *op. cit.,* pp. 191–192.
[49] *West Coast Sailors,* X (Nov. 26, 1948), 1, 3, 5.
[50] *Loc. cit.*

endorse the Farmer-Labor party; the former criticized the principle of exclusive reliance upon job-action and the strike.[51]

In addition, there had been a long-standing jurisdictional dispute between the sailors and the longshoremen concerning certain work in the coastwise schooner trade. For many years these vessels had carried extra sailors to work cargo, under an arrangement made by the AFL back in 1908. Following 1934, the ILA attempted to reduce the scope of the SUP concerning this work, which brought the two groups into conflict.[52]

Finally, the SUP felt that the ILA had left them in the lurch at the end of the 1934 strike, and the residue of this bitter feeling was not dissipated by the later clashes between Lundeberg and Bridges.

Nevertheless, the MFP managed to hold together and to see the 1936–1937 strike through to victory in the settlements of February 4, 1937. In essence, the longshoremen retained all of their 1934 gains. They won preferential hiring over the nonunion registered men. More important, they progressed toward coastwide uniformity in working conditions, when the employers agreed to the creation of joint committees to fix maximum sling-load limits and uniform coastwide penalty rates. In return, the employers obtained agreement that job disputes were to be settled without stoppages, with work to continue at previous prevailing conditions. The employers, however, lost their attempt to make the union responsible for infractions of discipline. According to the agreement the union in the first instance, and the port labor relations committee in the second, were to administer disciplinary penalties. Although the employers could initiate grievances, the committee and the arbitrator were given no power to impose penalties.[53]

---

[51] It is significant that William Schneiderman, a top official of the Communist party in California at the time, attacked Lundeberg on these points and gave unreserved support to Bridges, in a pamphlet issued by the party after the strike (William Schneiderman, *The Pacific Coast Maritime Strike* [San Francisco, Western Worker Publishers, 1937], cited in Lampman, *op. cit.*, p. 189, n. 1). Similar unqualified support for Bridges and criticism of Lundeberg may be found in Mike Quin, *The Big Strike*, with a postscript by Harry Bridges (Olema, California, Olema Publishing Company, 1949), pp. 213–231. Quin was a contributor to the *Western Worker*, the Communist party paper on the Pacific Coast.

[52] Liebes, *op. cit.*, pp. 204–205. This issue has never been resolved.

[53] *Ibid.*, pp. 150–152; Joint Committee on Labor-Management Relations, *Labor Management Relations: West Coast Maritime Industry*, p. 46.

Of greater importance, the seafaring crafts in the main won advances paralleling those obtained by the longshoremen in 1934. The three unlicensed crafts—the sailors, the cooks, and the firemen—in effect obtained a union-controlled hiring hall that was to be the exclusive source of all men in these crafts. In these groups, job-control and rotation of employment were for the first time secured by contract. The mates, engineers, and radio telegraphists had to be content with less: recognition for collective bargaining. Moreover, the MMP and MEBA did not obtain preference in employment, and so emerged in a weaker position relative to the unlicensed men.[54]

● *The Coastwide Strikes of 1946.*—For nearly a decade after 1937, the industry was able to operate without a coastwide strike. This is not to say that conflict had disappeared with the 1937 settlements. Far from it. More accurately, the conflict was fought out in other ways. In addition, there were important changes in the bargaining system and in the alignments within the union group. (These form the subject of the following chapter.) For purposes of the present account, we shall hurdle an interval of nearly ten years, in order to place the five coastwide strikes in their proper continuity.

V-J Day in August, 1945, ushered in a period of unprecedented turbulence in labor-management relations in the United States. Back of these events were several factors. For five years, serious inflationary forces had been suppressed by federal wage and price ceilings. Now that the imperative of winning the war was gone, the federal controls became a nuisance rather than a patriotic duty, and their destruction was inevitable. In fact, the restoration of collective bargaining depended upon their destruction. The situation was explosive in several senses: the inflationary potential was severe and promised extreme wage and price adjustments; the appearance of new and inexperienced union leaders and managers in American industry meant that it would not be easy to revive the technique of private bargaining.

---

[54] The MMP and MEBA at some point in this period did obtain preference in employment in the Alaska trade alone, but not elsewhere. The Pacific Coast operators have consistently opposed the preferential shop for these licensed men on the ground that their work was supervisory, hence a part of management. Accordingly, the operators have desired full freedom of selection and the right to make individual terms for these men. (Joint Committee on Labor-Management Relations, *op. cit.*, pp. 28–29.)

Obviously, Pacific Coast shipping was a part of this general environment and necessarily was influenced by it. True, the leaders and organizations on both sides were the same as before the war, and most of the bargaining issues in the industry centered upon large "compensatory" wage increases. Within the industry, moreover, there emerged a serious political conflict between the AFL unions, led by Lundeberg, and the CIO groups, led by Bridges. The resulting jockeying for advantage was to complicate negotiations and to intensify the strike problem.

Bridges and the Committee for Maritime Unity. By directive order, the National War Labor Board had amended the 1944 contract between the International Longshoremen's and Warehousemen's Union (formerly the ILA) and the Waterfront Employers Association of the Pacific Coast (now agent for the four port associations). The order was dated August 18, 1945, and the amended contract itself expired on September 30 following. Six weeks before the board's order, the ILWU had already given notice for negotiations for the 1945–1946 contract. At a late hour, the WEPC had agreed to extend the amended contract during these negotiations.[55]

In these negotiations, Bridges initially asked for a five-day, thirty-hour week at $1.75 per hour straight time, later modifying the wage demand to $1.50 per hour. The $1.50 rate had been awarded the New York longshoremen (ILA) in December, 1945, by arbitration. The employers countered with a small wage offer, predicating it upon a guarantee by the union to end illegal work stoppages.[56]

For six months these negotiations made little progress, and early in January, 1946, Bridges began the preparation of strike strategy by addressing a letter to seven crafts—ILWU, MEBA, MFOWW, MCS, the National Maritime Union (NMU), the American Communications Association (successor to the ARTA), and the Inlandboatmen's Union (IBU)—proposing a February joint meeting to develop plans. Meanwhile, Bridges informed President Truman on January 21 that a strike was "inevitable" unless the government intervened to compel the

[55] United States Department of Labor, *Report and Recommendations of the Pacific Coast Longshore Fact Finding Board*, mimeographed (Washington, May 13, 1946), pp. 8–9.

[56] *Pacific Shipper*, vol. 20 (Jan. 14, 1946), 22.

WEPC to pay retroactive wages provided by the NWLB order of 1945. On February 6, the seven crafts met in Washington and recommended the formation of "one big maritime union," to be considered at a second meeting scheduled for May in San Francisco.[57] According to Joe Curran, president of the NMU, the crafts participating in the February meeting formed the Committee for Maritime Unity (CMU), to negotiate on a national basis, to call strikes if necessary, to engage in political action, and to publish a paper.[58] Thus the Committee acquired a complexion similar to the Joint Marine Strike Committee of 1934 and the extinct Maritime Federation of the Pacific of 1935–1941. However, there were differences: the SUP and MMP did not participate in the new organization (the SUP was not even invited), and the MEBA only sent "observers." The presence of the NMU tended to give the CMU negotiations a national coloration, while at the same time signalizing jurisdictional conflicts with the SUP.

Later in February, the ILWU membership approved by a 93 per cent vote a recommendation of their leaders for a coastwide strike on or before April 1. Negotiations with the WEPC had been suspended in January by the employers, in retaliation for illegal strikes at Port Gamble, Washington, and Portland. At Port Gamble, ILWU members refused to work under AFL foremen, although the operators were compelled to use the AFL men under contract. At Portland, the ILWU struck over refusal of the employers to use ship clerks in jobs in which they were not normally used. Arbitration yielded a decision that the Port Gamble strike was illegal. The Portland affair was settled when the ILWU capitulated after the employers canceled the ILWU clerks' contract.[59]

Negotiations were resumed on March 4, although these two incidents were indicative of the bad feeling between the parties. At this time the WEPC offered an eighteen-cent raise and overtime for Saturday work, and revived once more a group of demands aimed at increased productivity and contract compliance: restoration of steady gangs, availability of special skilled gangs, more liberal sling-load limits, the right

[57] *Dispatcher* (ILWU), vol. 4 (Jan. 11, 25, Feb. 8, 22, 1946).

[58] *Pacific Shipper*, vol. 20 (Feb. 11, 1946), 19–21.

[59] *Ibid.* (Feb. 4, 1946), 14–15; vol. 21 (March 4, 1946), 7, 9.

freely to shift individual work assignments, a pledge against make-work practices, and financial liabilities of the parties for violations of contract.[60] Contingent upon union acceptance of these demands the WEPC agreed to distribute the 1945 retroactive pay by July 1.[61]

Negotiations were hung up on these issues, but the April 1 deadline was set aside with the appointment of a Pacific Coast Longshore Fact Finding Board by Secretary of Labor Schwellenbach on April 5. It seemed evident that the strategy of the ILWU, as part of the new CMU, was to gain a favorable settlement by government intervention, in place of "economic" action through a strike.[62]

After several hearings, the board submitted its report on May 13. On the wage issue, it recommended a twenty-two-cent raise from the $1.15 per hour base rate. This increase was, in its opinion, consistent with the Atlantic Coast "pattern," given other advantages enjoyed by the Pacific Coast longshoremen. The employers had offered $1.33 and the union had asked $1.50. Regarding efficiency, the board proposed that the Department of Labor conduct a study of productivity on the docks, and that the parties themselves study the problem of improved safety. Other recommendations affecting call-pay, vacation eligibility, and the hatch-tenders' differential demanded for San Francisco left current practices either unchanged or slightly modified.

Concerning compliance with the contract, the board declared that "there had been little genuine effort to observe the spirit of collective bargaining," and expressed the hope that the parties would mend their ways. It noted that:

collective bargaining, as the term is generally understood, has met with little success in the Pacific Coast longshore industry. Strikes, lockouts, and short-lived arbitrators characterized the relations of the parties in the pre-war period. There are present signs that the improvement in collective bargaining relations which appeared during the war years, is being replaced by the familiar pattern of work stoppage and lockout. Under these circumstances, there is little to be gained by substituting punitive measures for lack of genuine collective bargaining.

---

[60] *Ibid.*, vol. 21 (March 18, 1946), 4–5.

[61] *Dispatcher*, vol. 4 (March 22, 1946), 1.

[62] The fact-finding board had power only to investigate the issues and recommend terms for settlement. James Lawrence Fly was chairman; Judge Lloyd L. Black and Fowler Harper were the other members.

Accordingly, the board rejected the employers' demand for a damage fund, and exhorted both sides to try bargaining in good faith.[63] It also urged the parties to change the status of the Coast Arbitrator to that of Impartial Chairman, and to reconstitute the Port Agent system, as ordered by the NWLB in 1945.

At the end of May, the employers accepted the $1.37 per hour proposed by the board; the ILWU continued to hold out for $1.50. At this point, Secretary of Labor Schwellenbach summoned all the maritime crafts to Washington for a national wage conference, apparently hoping to work out an over-all "pattern" to head off an impending national maritime strike threatened by the CMU unions. Thus began an almost fantastic sequence of events under federal intervention. To place them in their proper perspective, we should first consider the position of the SUP at this time.

As will be developed fully in the next chapter, from 1938 onward the SUP had rapidly evolved to become a responsible "business" union, guided by short-run aims, basing its strategy upon its own "economic" strength, and recognizing the economic needs and problems of the operators who provided the sailors their employment opportunities. In keeping with this change of orientation, Secretary Lundeberg told his members shortly after the war that now was the time for a cautious and moderate approach regarding economic demands. Citing the shipping slump of 1921, he counseled defense of the large gains recently won and temperate demands in the immediate future.[64]

Early in January, 1946, the *West Coast Sailors* colorfully described Bridges' proposed maritime industrial union as "limburger cheese."[65] The SUP was not invited to the February CMU conference, and it was quick to point out what it considered to be critical weaknesses in the CMU approach to a new federation: the member unions would lose their autonomy in negotiations and strike decisions; despite the union constitutions, the CMU heads would acquire certain central powers; the organization would be dominated by "Communist-controlled" CIO

---

[63] *Report and Recommendations of the Pacific Coast Longshore Fact Finding Board*, pp. 28–30.

[64] Lampman, *op. cit.*, p. 293.

[65] *West Coast Sailors*, IX (Jan. 25, 1946), 8.

unions; the CMU would, under such control, embark upon "Communist" political strikes. Moreover, the SUP noted that important AFL unions had been frozen out of the CMU—the Seafarers' International Union (SIU) and its affiliate, the SUP, the Radio Operators (AFL), and the Teamsters. [66] To the SUP this was a strange kind of unity— one to be avoided at all costs.

The sailors, however, found themselves in a peculiar position with the developments in the spring of 1946. For one thing, the intense rivalry between the SIU and its affiliate, the SUP, on the one side, and the ILWU and NMU, on the other, had made contract gains a measure of prestige among the rank and file, and so compelled the SUP and SIU to be prepared to strike for extreme demands, if necessary thwarting Lundeberg's earlier policy of moderation. For another, the SUP leaders were compelled to justify a waiting game to their members, who were aware of the gains produced by joint action in 1934 and 1936–1937, and who expected militant action. Here the leadership told the sailors during the impending CMU strike that a strike would be bad strategy at the time. Many ships had been laid up and unemployment was increasing. The operators could not lose in a strike because they were mainly government agents on fees, and most cargo was relief tonnage that would have to move anyway. Last, the SUP could not safely place its own fortunes in the hands of the "Communist-controlled" CMU. [67]

Then, on May 27 the Pacific Coast operators offered the SUP a basic increase of $12.50 a month, paralleling an Atlantic Coast offer to the NMU. The NMU membership rejected this increase, and the CMU prepared to strike on June 15. This led to Secretary Schwellenbach's summons to the Washington maritime conference, with the aim of developing a "national maritime wage pattern."

The SUP was invited to participate but rejected the opportunity, choosing to stick to its independent strategy and refusing to countenance a substitution of "political" bargaining for its traditional preference for direct negotiations. The Washington conference was called

[66] *Ibid.* (Feb. 22, 1946), 3, 6. In the issue of March 22, Joe Curran was quoted as saying that Communists were attempting to take over the NMU, an affiliate of the CMU.

[67] *Ibid.* (April 5, 1946), 1–2.

for May 29, and it had hardly gotten under way before the SUP made its next move, by demanding that the Pacific Coast operators return immediately to San Francisco for direct bargaining with the SUP. On June 6, the SUP members began a series of day-to-day work stoppages, to impress the operators and the government that they meant business.[68] At the same time, the SUP declared that if the CMU called a strike, its sailors would respect the picket lines of these unions.

Meanwhile, the government-sponsored conference in Washington produced a raise of $17.50 per month in the basic NMU rate for the Atlantic lines, which that union accepted. This agreement also reduced the straight-time week at sea from fifty-six to forty-eight hours, and in port from forty-four to forty hours, with fifty-six hours' work guaranteed at sea.[69] The ACA and MEBA won similar gains, and the "pattern" seemed set.

But not for long. For within a few days, the SUP won a basic increase of $22.50 per month ($5.00 more than the NMU) from the Pacific operators, by direct negotiations. Other gains included a four-hour reduction in the straight-time week in port and an eight-hour day at sea.[70] For the time being, the SUP had won the contest for prestige with the maritime rank and file. The timely assistance from the employers was probably not fortuitous. Lundeberg's strategy of independence had paid off, and temporarily, at least, the CMU unions found themselves in the uncomfortable position of having settled for less.[71] For Bridges, the pill was a bitter one, but it was sweetened to some extent by the prospect of negotiations for the new contract of October 1.

The first coastwide strike. Government intervention had headed off a CMU strike on June 15, by achieving a temporary "stabilization" of the situation. However, all of the settlements had to be approved by federal agencies. In addition, several of the crafts were now about to

[68] *Ibid.* (June 20, 1946), 1, 2, 4.

[69] Lampman, *op. cit.,* p. 294.

[70] *West Coast Sailors,* IX (June 27, 1946), 2–3.

[71] Although the ILWU participated in the Washington conference, the latter was really the NMU's show. In the outcome, the ILWU leaders agreed to recommend that the membership accept the recommendations of the Longshore Board (*Dispatcher,* vol. 4 [June 28, 1946], 1).

be involved in new negotiations, once more carrying the threat of a maritime strike.[72] By early July, the situation grew even more precarious when the NMU demanded additional increases to match the differential gains of the SUP and SIU. Next, the War Shipping Administration approved the SUP and SIU June settlements. On August 23, however, the National Wage Stabilization Board eliminated the SUP and SIU $5.00 differential, to maintain the "pattern" set by the earlier NMU settlement.

Infuriated, the SIU-SUP leaders took a strike vote, and on September 4 called out the sailors in the first of the national maritime strikes. On September 11, the MFOWW—which had also gained the contested $5.00 differential increase—joined the strike. Two days later, the chaos was further increased when the NMU also walked out, to gain parity with the SIU and SUP.

On September 12, John W. Steelman, federal Director of Stabilization and Reconversion, amended the wage controls to permit approval of the SUP differential, and that union officially ended its strike. However, the sailors stayed out until September 25, when their contract was finally signed. The CMU unions remained officially on strike after September 12, and on the 20th, Arbitrator James L. Fly awarded them additional increases to attain parity with the SIU-SUP. To do so, he had to extend his jurisdiction, thereby catching the Atlantic operators by surprise.[73]

This twenty-one-day national shipping strike was an impressive show of power by the maritime unions, especially the SUP and SIU. Even without the official concurrence of the Pacific Coast longshoremen, the ports were closed down tight. For the Pacific operators, however, the crisis did not end on September 25. On the contrary, it was

---

[72] On June 30, jurisdictional warfare broke out between the SUP and ILWU at the lumber port of Coos Bay, Oregon, in a strike lasting until mid-November, 1946. This stoppage began when Bridges ordered his longshoremen not to load the SS *Mello Franco* or other ships of the American Pacific Steamship Co., formerly a tanker line that had now entered the dry-cargo trade, extending its SUP contract to cover dry-cargo ships. In retaliation, Lundeberg froze the entire port. A government panel upheld the SUP's claims, but the boycott continued until November, when the ILWU capitulated to the SUP's threat to tie up the entire coast. (*West Coast Sailors,* IX [Nov. 15, 1946], 1, 8.)

[73] *West Coast Sailors,* IX (Sept. 20, 1946), 5; *Pacific Shipper,* vol. 21 (Sept. 23, 1946), 3, 14–17; *Dispatcher,* vol. 4 (Sept. 20, 1946), 1, 8; Lampman, *op. cit.,* p. 298.

just beginning, for exactly six days' grace remained before the expiration of the ILWU contract at 12:01 A.M. on October 1. On that date, the second group of coastwide strikes began.

The second coastwide strike. Negotiations for the ILWU contract revealed that Bridges was seeking a basic rate of $1.70 per hour in place of $1.37, no doubt to recoup the prestige he had lost in June. Lesser objectives involved revival of his earlier demands concerning four hours' minimum call-pay, more liberal eligibility provisions for paid vacations, application of the ten-cent hatch-tender's differential to San Francisco, and clarification of the ILWU's jurisdictional rights on schooners in the coasting trade.

Before October 1, the offshore employers were negotiating with the MMP and MEBA, which were seeking pay increases and a preferential hiring clause. In addition, the MCS was back for an additional increase over the amount awarded it in September by Arbitrator Fly.[74]

All of these negotiations broke down, and on October 1 the ILWU, MMP, and MEBA all went on strike. Once more the ports and ships of the Pacific Coast were completely tied up. By the middle of the month, controversy with the SUP also developed over the ILWU's demand concerning schooner jurisdiction. In a letter to the SUP, Bridges declared he was merely seeking a separate contract for this specialized trade, to cover only the ILWU's "own" work. In reply, the SUP charged that the ILWU was attempting to "move in" on the sailors' work, and had refused to supply front men to the sailors' hatch or to work in the same hold, while also trying to dictate the hatches and times the SUP men could work.[75] The SUP threatened to strike to protect its claims, and the employers refused to agree to a separate ILWU contract because it carried the threat of a jurisdictional conflict.

After the sixth week of the tie-up, Bridges complained that the strike had really become a lockout. On November 20, the ILWU and MEBA officially settled for new contracts. This isolated the MMP, and on November 23 it also settled. The fifty-two-day shutdown was over.

In the ILWU settlement, Bridges obtained a fifteen-cent increase in

---

[74] *Pacific Shipper,* vol. 21 (Oct. 7, 1946), 3, 27–29.
[75] *West Coast Sailors,* IX (Oct. 18, 1946), 1–3.

the basic rate (to $1.52), improved provisions regarding call-pay and eligibility for vacations, the ten-cent hatch-tender's differential for San Francisco, the creation of an advisory longshore safety commission, and arbitration of the definition of a steam schooner. The employers also agreed to distribute retroactive pay due under the interim settlement of June 15. All that the employers obtained in return was agreement that the Impartial Chairman would restore the Port Agent system, and that disputes involving work stoppages currently before the Coast Committee or the Impartial Chairman would have precedence over all other issues.

Although the MEBA and MMP got wage increases, neither succeeded in winning a preferential shop. This latter had been a long-standing issue, intensified for the Pacific Coast during the strike when the Atlantic and Gulf operators agreed to such provision in their contracts with these unions.[76]

This second group of strikes culminated in considerable ill-feeling toward Bridges, and the disintegration of the CMU. The CMU was represented in this strike only by the ILWU and MEBA, and the tie-up was really Bridges' affair. Other labor leaders held that little was really gained over the initial offers of the employers, and Bridges' skill as a strategist was now openly questioned. V. J. Malone of the MFOWW took his union out of the CMU, declaring the strike to be "a notorious fiasco" that gained "exactly nothing." The MMP periodical charged that Bridges had "sold out" the MEBA and MMP, and the SUP asserted that Bridges had forced the MEBA to settle by threatening that otherwise the union could not survive the strike. The climax to these recriminations was reached in a few weeks when Curran took the NMU out of the CMU, charging that the Bridges group had used the strike as a weapon against the AFL maritime unions.[77]

In any event, Bridges now found himself further away from maritime unity than at any time since 1934. Nationally, the NMU was now openly opposed to him. On the Pacific Coast, he faced the active and implacable hostility of the SUP, with the MMP and MFOWW em-

---

[76] *Pacific Shipper*, vol. 21 (Nov. 4, 25, 1946).

[77] *Ibid.* (Dec. 2, 1946), 12–14; *West Coast Sailors*, IX (Nov. 29, 1946), 1–2; Lampman, *op. cit.*, p. 298.

bittered against him by the outcome. As faithful satellites, he could now only count upon the MCS and ACA, with the MEBA a dubious ally. All the maritime unions might still unite in a crisis, but Bridges could not dominate their bargaining strategy. Last, the hoped-for maritime industrial union now had no prospects whatever.

● *The Coastwide Strike of 1948.*—Neither side desired another trial of strength in 1947, given the losses they had imposed upon themselves in 1946. As a result, new agreements were made in 1947 without strikes. But so far as the WEPC and ILWU were concerned, the forces of irrepressible conflict were still active, and 1948 witnessed a climactic showdown, preceded by eight months of preliminary skirmishing. Although the Pacific American Shipowners Association and the SUP were to negotiate a new contract effective March 1, and PASA and the MCS, MEBA, and MFOWW had contracts expiring June 15, the 1948 affair was also primarily a WEPC-ILWU show. And once more that show was to be a costly production.

Events preceding the strike. One important new element appeared in the background of the 1948 strike—the passage in 1947 of the federal Labor-Management Relations (Taft-Hartley) Act. This statute affected the conflict in three major ways. First, it outlawed the closed shop in industries in interstate commerce, placing in question the existing registration and dispatching system of the maritime hiring halls. This system was the basis of union power over the employers. Second, the law established a special class of disputes involving national emergencies, for which the President is empowered (a) to appoint special boards of inquiry, and (b) to seek a temporary (approximately eighty days) injunction from a district court, to prevent a stoppage or to compel resumption of operations. Third, the law provided that before a union could have legal standing in representation cases before the National Labor Relations Board, its officers must first have filed affidavits with the board that at that time they were not members of the Communist party, or members or supporters of organizations dedicated to the overthrow of the government of the United States by illegal or unconstitutional methods. In each of these three respects, the Taft-Hartley Act played a major role in the 1948 conflict.

So far as the SUP was concerned, the threat posed by the closed-shop ban was at least temporarily overcome early in the fall of 1947, by a formula devised by Harry Lundeberg and Gregory Harrison (PASA counsel) for incorporation in the SUP-PASA contract. In essence, the new clause provided that: (1) the operators would "prefer" men previously employed on their vessels in hiring deck personnel for future voyages, and the union would respect this preference in referring applicants; and (2) if the supply of such experienced men were short, then the SUP would refer graduates of the Furuseth School. Since the experienced men were all SUP members, and the Furuseth School was an SUP enterprise, the union's security, job-control, hiring hall, and rotation system could all be retained intact without explicitly requiring SUP membership as a condition of employment.[78]

Negotiations between the ILWU and WEPC commenced in February, with the employers taking the offensive. Using the Taft-Hartley proscription of the closed shop as a basis, they demanded: (1) elimination of employment preference for union members; (2) elimination of the ILWU's authority to refuse registration to new men; and (3) a change in the selection of the hall dispatchers (currently chosen by the union). On the ILWU's part, Bridges declared that complete retention of the existing hiring hall system was the union's "number one demand," and that the "Lundeberg formula" was unacceptable. As negotiations progressed, Bridges also asked for: (1) vacations with pay for all longshoremen; (2) the elimination of all disciplinary powers and penalties from the contract, and explicit provision that individual or group stoppages were not violations of the agreement; (3) one scheduled day off per week, plus four hours' minimum call-pay; (4) an eight-hour maximum day at current levels of take-home earnings; (5) the incorporation in the contract of the recommendations of the Longshore Safety Commission; and (6) a two-year contract.[79]

As the *Pacific Shipper* had suggested with considerable acumen, the WEPC's demands furnished Bridges with a badly needed pretext for a strike. First, they could be construed as "union-busting" in the sense

---

[78] Lampman, *op. cit.*, p. 304.

[79] *Pacific Shipper*, vol. 23 (March 29, 1948), 22–23; *Dispatcher*, vol. 6 (April 16, 1948), 1.

of a complete destruction of the union's basis of power, which lay in control of the hall, the dispatcher, and the registration list. Very likely, this was not the employers' real purpose. In fact, they declared at the time that they believed the hall itself was legal, that they could continue to give first call to the registered men, to practice rotation, and not to discriminate against ILWU members. Their real motives appear to have been different: to protect their legal position under the Taft-Hartley law and, if possible, to bring about a weakening and eventual elimination of the Bridges leadership.[80]

Second, the ILWU, as an organization, and its members, personally, had suffered serious financial losses in the 1946 strikes. Bridges himself had lost considerable prestige at that time, and the necessary morale for another strike was lacking among the rank and file. In this context, Bridges could use another strike to rehabilitate his leadership by closing ranks once more within the organization. Yet at the same time, the strike had to seem to be forced upon him from without. On this interpretation, the WEPC played right into his hands with its demands, for they could readily be propagandized as just another attempt to wreck the union. This alone was the basis on which Bridges could justify a strike to the membership and, in so doing, prove his own insight and indispensability as a leader. In fact, this is exactly what eventually happened.

By late March, Bridges once again was making "unity" overtures, to prepare for a possible strike. This time the call was made to the NMU, MCS, MEBA, MFOWW, and ACA. In a subsequent meeting in April, the NMU, MEBA, and ACA (now temporarily a division within the MEBA) reached agreement that if the operators refused to bargain with any one of the group, this would become the top demand of the other unions. The MFOWW sent "observers" to this meeting.[81]

In the meantime, the PASA reached amicable settlements with the SUP and MMP, providing for wage increases of about 8 per cent and long-term (eighteen months) contracts expiring in September, 1949. The SUP contract met the closed-shop problem by inclusion of the

---

[80] *Pacific Shipper*, vol. 23 (Feb. 23, 1948), 10, 14; (March 29, 1948), 22–23.

[81] *Dispatcher*, vol. 6 (April 2, 1948), 1, 10; (April 16, 1948), 1.

"Lundeberg formula," but the MMP was exempt from the statute because of the supervisory status of its members. In connection with this settlement, the *West Coast Sailors* took occasion to praise the superiority of "direct free collective bargaining."[82]

During April and May, the ILWU-WEPC negotiations were hung up on the hiring hall issues, and a strike loomed for June 15, involving the ILWU, MEBA, MEBA-ACA, MFOWW, and possibly the MCS. To forestall this shutdown (which also involved the NMU and hence would have been nationwide) President Truman on June 3 established a Board of Inquiry, using his authority under the Taft-Hartley law.[83] The board was to investigate all of the outstanding maritime disputes in the United States and to report to the President by June 11. In its preliminary report, the board declared that the "over-riding issue" in the WEPC-ILWU dispute involved the employers' demands affecting the hiring hall. The same basic issue divided the PASA and MCS. The board found that the MEBA and MFOWW negotiations had not sufficiently advanced to crystallize the issues.

On June 14, the threatened strike was temporarily forestalled when the Attorney General obtained a ten-day restraining order, requiring both sides to continue operations under the *status quo ante*. Subsequently, this order was superseded by an eighty-day Taft-Hartley injunction, enjoining a tie-up before September 2 and applicable to all parties to unsettled disputes.[84]

At the time the first order was issued, feeling was intense between the WEPC and ILWU. F. P. Foisie declared false the union's charge that the hiring hall and the members' jobs were at stake. Attorney Richard Gladstein of the ILWU countered by accusing the employers of refusing to bargain.[85] Within a week of the issuance of the order, Bridges was quoted as telling his men that they "need not break their

[82] *West Coast Sailors*, X (April 16, 1948), 1; *Pacific Shipper*, vol. 23 (April 12, 1948), 8–9; (April 26, 1948), 24.

[83] This board consisted of Harry Shulman, chairman; Andrew Jackson, Jesse Freidin, A. P. Allen, and George Cheney. The last two were unable to participate in all of the proceedings and did not sign the report. (10 *Labor Arbitration Reports*, 451–469; 859–883.)

[84] *Pacific Shipper*, vol. 23 (June 21, 1948), 5, 8, 16–17; (July 5, 1948), 5, 7, 20; *Dispatcher*, vol. 6 (July 9, 1948), 1–2.

[85] *Pacific Shipper*, vol. 23 (June 14, 1948), 19.

backs" at work, while Hugh Bryson of the MCS was emphasizing a "special safety campaign."[86] Then toward the end of June, relations worsened when the operators filed a complaint with the NLRB charging the ILWU with unfair labor practices.[87]

The eighty-day injunction failed to elicit constructive negotiations so far as the ILWU-WEPC and MCS-PASA were concerned, so that by the eve of the strike the Board of Inquiry had to report (August 13, 1948) that the "controversies on the Pacific Coast between the employers and the ILU and the MCS provided little basis for a conclusion other than despair. If deterioration in so bad a situation is possible, the situation has deteriorated."[88]

This was the context in which the WEPC made its final offer (August 10): a five-cent wage increase, a nine-hour shift, one scheduled day off each week, five cents per hour in lieu of increased vacation allowances; all contingent upon prior changes in the hiring hall system. Here the board noted that the employers appeared to want these latter changes not merely because they considered them mandatory under Taft-Hartley, but because they were dissatisfied with the existing system. The ILWU, in turn, held that the existing system should be retained pending determination of its legality by a court of last resort.[89]

Shortly after, Bridges told a meeting of longshoremen that "we're hitting the bricks September 2nd." On August 30, the NLRB conducted a referendum vote among the ILWU membership concerning the employers' last offer, and not a single longshoreman cast a ballot. On September 2, the second longest strike in Pacific Coast maritime history officially began, with the ILWU, MCS, and MFOWW participating.[90]

The strike itself. On the eve of the strike, the *Pacific Shipper* out-

[86] *Ibid.* (June 21, 1948), 5, 13, 16–17. During July, employers at Seattle and San Pedro were complaining bitterly that longshore output had been greatly reduced.

[87] *Dispatcher*, vol. 6 (June 25, 1948), 1–3. Ultimately, this proceeding appears to have been dropped without action, probably by the NLRB. It was indicative of the legalistic state of mind toward collective bargaining developed by the WEPC leaders over the years.

[88] 10 *Labor Arbitration Reports*, 867. In its report, the board revealed the acute perception that the hatred of the parties for each other was by now as much of a barrier to settlement as the issues themselves.

[89] 10 *Labor Arbitration Reports*, 868.

[90] *Pacific Shipper*, vol. 23 (Sept. 6, 1948), 5–6, 9.

lined editorially what in fact became the employers' strategy, by suggesting that in a major strike "the industry can break the back of Communist domination of a minority of the maritime unions . . . notwithstanding previous defeats."[91] Their aim was to bring about the removal of the Bridges-Bryson group from leadership of the ILWU and MCS, in order to achieve a transition to what the operators conceived to be responsible trade unionism. As a central feature of this purpose, the operators sought major revision of the existing hiring hall system, which, undoubtedly, was the primary basis of Bridges' power. To achieve their objective, the operators sought to identify the Bridges-Bryson group with the anticapitalist program of the Communist party. At the same time, the employers attempted to justify their approach by citing their legal obligations under the Taft-Hartley law.

In essence, then, the employers' opening strategy involved an attack upon the ILWU-MCS leadership and upon the security of these unions as provided in past contracts. The strike began, therefore, as a struggle for power rather than as economic warfare for more limited aims. Naturally, Bridges and Bryson found themselves compelled to fight on these terms. Fortunately for these two leaders, the employers' strategy handed them the one weapon that could effectively unite their wavering union memberships for a fight to the finish.

The WEPC and PASA began their offensive by withdrawing all previous offers and announcing that they would conduct no further negotiations and make no new agreements with unions (ILWU, MFOWW, and MCS) whose officers had not signed and filed non-Communist affidavits.[92] As one of their spokesmen declared, "Up to now we've tried buying peace . . . we're through now with appeasement." Shortly after, F. P. Foisie attributed the strike to the Communist party line against relief shipments. Almon Roth of the San Francisco Employers' Council claimed there was "positive evidence" that Bridges was actively collaborating in left-wing efforts to create European unrest. At the NLRB hearings in the employers' complaint

---

[91] *Ibid.* (Aug. 30, 1948), 18–19.

[92] Technically, the Taft-Hartley Act does not unconditionally require such affidavits. They are only necessary if a union wishes to have legal access to NLRB proceedings.

case, the WEPC representative, Frank Gregory, according to the ILWU *Dispatcher*, said that there would be no further negotiations with the present union leadership. About this time, the operators placed advertisements in the press charging Bridges with sabotaging the industry on behalf of the USSR, implying that he was a member of the Communist party. Bridges responded by filing a $750,000 libel suit.[93]

The events of the first month revealed clearly that the parties were at a complete impasse, locked in a death battle. So long as the operators rested on their chosen position, and so long as there was no rank-and-file revolt against Bridges and Bryson, negotiations were blocked and settlement was impossible. A war of attrition was the only prospect.[94]

Early in October, the first sign of restiveness appeared in the employers' ranks. An editorial in the *Pacific Shipper* referred to "differences" within the industry concerning "method and timing" in the conflict. It was stressed that though all agreed it was necessary to remove party-line union leaders, some operators manifested an attitude of "a plague on both your houses."[95]

By the fifth week of the strike, F. P. Foisie and J. B. Bryan, the chief negotiators for the two employer groups, felt obliged to make public a detailed statement of management's position. The move was probably partly defensive, occasioned by Bridges' publicly expressed willingness to resume negotiations, and by the operators' need to show a united front. They declared that the associations were "ready and willing to negotiate a contract with responsible union leadership," but that the ILWU and MCS were not responsible organizations, having "consistently followed the Communist Party line." In their view, even signed affidavits were not proof of union responsibility. At the same

---

[93] *Pacific Shipper*, vol. 23 (Sept. 6, 1948), 5–6, 9; (Sept. 13, 1948), 5–6, 9–10; (Sept. 20, 1948), 5–6, 9–10; *Dispatcher*, vol. 6 (Oct. 1, 1948), 1–3.

[94] The only minor break in the deadlock at the time involved the MFOWW, whose Pacific Coast officials had signed Taft-Hartley affidavits just after the strike had begun, and later asked PASA to resume negotiations. Malone, the MFOWW leader on the Pacific Coast, all along had exhibited a conciliatory attitude. PASA's response to his request was to ask if he were free to make a contract, given his obligations to the other striking unions. *Pacific Shipper*, vol. 23 (Sept. 27, 1948), 5–6, 9.

[95] *Ibid.* (Oct. 4, 1948), 18–19. Cleavages could and probably did emerge between certain member companies and the employer associations. Centralization of authority in the associations was becoming a serious issue at the time.

time, both officials emphasized that they were not attempting to break the unions; rather, they firmly subscribed to the principle of maintenance of all hiring halls.[96]

At this time, events began moving toward a crisis. It began with a request by four hundred ILWU longshoremen to President Philip Murray of the CIO, asking that he intervene. News reports indicated that he was under similar pressure from the Truman Administration.[97] Within a week, Murray responded by dispatching two emissaries— Allan Haywood and R. J. Thomas—to San Francisco, to offer the employers a guarantee by the national CIO that the ILWU and MCS contracts would be observed. Bridges accepted the idea, but the employers reacted in cool fashion, asking what force such a guarantee would have. Murray then attacked the employers for refusing to bargain and placed the full force of the CIO behind the two embattled unions.[98]

The employers stood fast, and their strategy seemed to be beginning to pay off when the MEBA officials joined the MFOWW in filing signed affidavits, and then proceeded to break Bridges' already thin unity front by reaching agreement with the PASA.[99]

The Murray proposal, however, was the beginning of an attempt to get the operators to abandon their original position and to resume negotiations with the ILWU and MCS. During the first week of November, rumors developed that the CIO representatives and the San Francisco Employers' Council had devised a formula for breaking the deadlock. In the week following, these rumors were confirmed when the "Roth-Murray formula" was announced. In principle, it called for: (1) participation by the national CIO in ILWU-MCS negotiations, (2) underwriting of the eventuating contracts by the CIO, and (3) peaceful settlement of all ILWU disputes with no support by the SFEC of any lockout not approved by the Council, and with no support of any ILWU strike by the CIO unless the latter had approved the strike and the ILWU had given prior notice.[100]

[96] *Ibid.* (Oct. 11, 1948), 5–6, 9–10.

[97] *Ibid.*, pp. 9–10.

[98] *Ibid.* (Oct. 18, 1948), 5–6, 9–10; *Dispatcher*, vol. 6 (Oct. 15, 1948), 1; (Oct. 29, 1948), 1, 3.

[99] *Pacific Shipper*, vol. 23 (Nov. 1, 1948), 5–6.

[100] *Ibid.* (Nov. 8, 1948), 6, 9; *Dispatcher*, vol. 6 (Nov. 12, 1948), 8.

Acceptance of this new approach by the WEPC and PASA signalized the crystallization of the earlier internal conflicts within those organizations. Foisie and Harrison were supplanted by Dwight Steele as chief WEPC negotiator, and entirely new negotiating committees were named by both associations. The employers' front was broken, and once more they found themselves attempting to deal with the Bridges-Bryson leadership, this time with what the *Pacific Shipper* called "new faces and new approaches." To these developments, the term "new look" began to be applied.[101] More skeptical observers wondered whether the operators were merely right back where they started.

Negotiations between the WEPC, PASA, and the four unions still officially on strike (ILWU, MCS, MFOWW, and MEBA-ACA) were resumed, and in the final two weeks of November rapid progress was made toward a general settlement. Early in December, all of the parties reached agreements, but actual termination of the strike was delayed by ratification of the contracts. In addition, the SUP threatened to strike if the ILWU settlement affected its steam-schooner jurisdiction. Both of these hurdles were overcome, and on December 6 work was finally resumed, after a tie-up of ninety-five days.

The 1948 settlements and the "new look." The new agreements provided wage increases and other benefits that need not be recounted here. The ILWU contract was the most interesting one and is noteworthy in four respects: (1) the hiring hall issue was resolved; (2) the grievance machinery was decentralized and improved; (3) the ILWU pledged an end to outlaw strikes, and the CIO underwrote this pledge; and (4) for the first time, a long-term contract was made—for three years.

The parties met the problem posed by the Taft-Hartley law by providing in reserve a substitute procedure for hall administration if the regular procedures were suspended by legal action. In essence, the substitute clause gave preference to registered men, who were almost all ILWU members anyway. If legal action compelled resort to this clause, the parties agreed to negotiate a new clause within 120

[101] *Pacific Shipper*, vol. 23 (Nov. 15, 1948), 5, 6, 9.

days. Failing agreement, the substitute clause remained in effect. And if legal action impaired this clause also, the parties provided another 120 days for additional negotiations. If these negotiations were abortive, or if the agreement reached were also nullified, either party then became free to cancel the contract on five days' notice.[102]

The nub of this compromise was to preserve the existing hiring and dispatching system intact until it was legally attacked, and to extend maximum possible security to the ILWU in the event of such attack. This, obviously, was a major retreat by the WEPC from its original stand.

The grievance machinery was also radically overhauled. Here the intent was to get more prompt settlements at the local level. To do so, the contract now provided seven successive steps for the adjudication of grievances arising on the job: (1) to the walking boss or foreman, (2) to a bipartisan two-man committee, (3) to the Port Committee, (4) to the Area Committee, (5) to the Area Arbitrator for decision, (6) to the Coast Committee if either party held that the decision at steps (3), (4), or (5) conflicted with the main contract, (7) to the Coast Arbitrator for final decision. Both the Coast Committee and the Coast Arbitrator were explicitly denied jurisdiction over issues concerning the halls, port rules, continuance of work during local disputes, pay rates, or sling-load limits. This provision was intended to strengthen the position of the Area Arbitrator, by permitting greater decentralization and more prompt resolution of these issues at the local level.

The new contract included a no-strike-no-lockout clause, and provided that pending settlement of issues arising on the job, work was to continue according to the agreement, or if the agreement were silent, then as directed by the employer. The "agreement" was defined to include work rules already agreed to, minutes of the Port Committees regarding work rules, final written rulings of the former Port Agents, outstanding arbitration awards, and orally understood practices. The no-stoppage requirement maintained the exception that work could cease if the health and safety of the men were involved.

In addition, a new exception was added, to deal with the problem

---

[102] All references to the settlements are based on the contracts themselves.

of picket lines. The longshoremen were not required to cross a "legitimate" picket line, defined as one established independently by another union in connection with a direct dispute over wages, hours, or working conditions, when this union was the majority bargaining representative. A variety of picket lines were proclaimed "illegitimate": those involving hot cargo, secondary boycotts, or political demonstrations.

The ILWU had undertaken commitments in the past against "quickie" strikes, but these commitments had not been respected in a responsible fashion, and the employers had never before been able to obtain penalties against the union itself for noncompliance. Nor had they ever been able to get the union itself to apply penalties against its members for outlaw strikes. These stoppages had dogged the employers for fourteen years, contributing in a major way to the understandable bitterness of their attitude.[103]

With this contract, "something new" was added. First, the national CIO had pledged its moral force to compliance by the ILWU. The latter organization itself now came under a kind of "discipline" by the parent body. Second, the employers had made a sincere effort to forget the past in the settlement negotiations. They had introduced "new faces and new approaches," in an earnest effort to make collective bargaining a method of solving problems rather than a field for industrial warfare. It seemed evident that the entire future position of the Bridges leadership rested upon its willingness to respond in good faith. As events turned out, this not negligible moral pressure proved unusually effective in resolving the "quickie" strike problem during the life of the 1948–1951 contract.[104]

The upheaval within the employers' ranks during the strike proved to be the beginning of a change in their leadership and policies. Shortly

---

[103] Our tabulation of the PMA data shows eighty-eight such stoppages in 1946, and ninety-two in 1947. These totals were the highest since 1939, and show the persistent use of the tactic up to the eve of the 1948 strike.

[104] According to a study released by the PMA, there were only twenty-seven local stoppages during the whole of 1949–1951—three involving a thousand men or more, and twenty-four involving at least one gang for one day. Pacific Maritime Association, *Research Report*, "Strikes and work stoppages in the West Coast maritime industry," mimeographed (San Francisco, Dec. 13, 1951), pp. 2–3.

after the end of the shutdown, one of the San Francisco papers carried an article highly critical of the WEPC executives, charging them with responsibility for the strike.[105] The view expressed was extreme and probably unfair, and was repudiated by the WEPC directors. Editorially, the *Pacific Shipper* declared that the WEPC deserved reëxamination, not for its "culpability" but for its "futility." "The old era has passed, not because the WEA [WEPC] has been wrong in principle, but because it has been wrong in practice." Yet, "barring the original guilt of the shipowners in the ancient hard-boiled days, the responsibility for West Coast shipping's 14 years of labor strife lies primarily with the left-wing unions captained by Harry Bridges."[106]

Two developments emerged: a reorganization of the WEPC and PASA, which were consolidated to become the Pacific Maritime Association in early 1949, under new leadership; and what came to be called the "new look" in maritime labor relations.

In some respects, this "new look" was as much a change of attitude as it was a shift of policy. Its advocates believed that collective bargaining could be made to work as a technique of problem-solving if the employers could begin to view it that way. Such a change of view called for several things: acceptance of the unions in the fullest sense, recognition of their legitimate organizational needs and interests, and a determination to deal with issues in a constructive and conciliatory spirit. Emphatically, it meant abandonment of formalism, of reliance upon the letter of the contract, of stress upon legal rights and claims, and of dependence upon legislative and juridical remedies for fancied or real wrongs. The employers' theory was that with this change of view, even Bridges could be brought to responsible unionism, and it must be admitted that to a degree this actually occurred.

Although the view of the partisans of the "new look" is sound in some respects, they cannot claim too much. Low efficiency and very high loading costs continue to plague the industry, and its competitive position has grown steadily weaker during the postwar years. Moreover, the comparative peace of 1948–1951 was purchased with a greatly increased outlay in money wage costs. Peace is always avail-

---

[105] *Pacific Shipper*, vol. 23 (Dec. 13, 1948), 5, 50.   [106] *Ibid.* (Dec. 20, 1948), 16–17.

able at a price. In this instance, we have a case of payment deferred. For in June, 1950, Pacific Coast shipping was blown out of the doldrums of torpid decline by the outbreak of the Korean war. Many ships were again put back into service, and once more wartime cargoes filled the docks. Best of all, the increase of operations was financed entirely by the taxpayers. In the spirit of the "new look," generous concessions could be made and the unions placated, because the industry was not required to foot much of the bill.

War once more had replaced famine with feast, but the ensuing peace could hardly be credited in full to the "new look." The acid test of the new approach will come if and when the overseas troubles end, and the industry once again has to fight for survival in a commercial market.

● *Basic Issues in the Coastwide Strikes.*—The 1934 strike was a struggle for power between the reborn unions and a highly autocratic group of employers. The essential issues were recognition, coastwide bargaining, and the hiring hall. Summed up, the conflict turned upon two conceptions of job-control. With the settlements, the conflict was only partly resolved.

The incomplete outcome in 1934 made almost inevitable the second trial of strength in 1936–1937. The second tie-up could have been averted only if the employers had voluntarily conceded to the offshore crafts advantages paralleling those already possessed by the longshoremen. This they were unprepared to do.

By the end of the second strike, a split was evident between Bridges and Lundeberg. As the next chapter will show, this split was the beginning of a "polarization" of the unions into two groups, one led by Bridges, and the other by Lundeberg. In the decade that followed 1937, the unions associated with the SUP found it possible to reach a *modus vivendi* with the employers, and collective bargaining shifted from its earlier status as a theater of conflict, to become a means for living together in relative peace. In this same period, however, the ILWU and MCS remained locked in conflict with the operators, and collective bargaining with these unions largely failed to fulfill its constructive promises.

The issues underlying the second and third coastwide strikes (1946) were both economic and political. Union security was no longer an issue. Large and inflationary increases in wages were now very much in the foreground. The operators were worried about soaring costs in a tight and unpromising competitive market. The unions felt the political necessities of making wage gains comparable to national "patterns" of the time. The first of the two strikes had its inception in an inept attempt of the federal government to cut back the increase gained by the SUP and SIU in collective bargaining. When this attempt inevitably failed, the CMU unions joined the strike to obtain an additional increase to match that of the SUP and SIU. Within a week after the resolution of the first strike, Bridges followed with the second. Again the basic cause was political. Bridges had settled in June for much less than the SUP had subsequently obtained. He badly needed a show of strength to recover his prestige—among his own men and among the other unions. The second strike occurred, ending with Bridges getting little more than had originally been offered by the employers.

The showdown in 1948 (like 1934) was once more a basic struggle for power. Perhaps not too adroitly, the employers had elected to challenge the longshore hiring hall system, which was the basis of Bridges' power. Bridges chose to fight on this line, probably because it was the one issue on which he could unite his membership in his own support. The employers then centered their attack upon the Bridges-Bryson leadership in the ILWU and MCS, charging it with Communist orientation and refusing further negotiations. Thus the strike became an irreconcilable conflict, ending in the capitulation of the operators. This took nearly a hundred days to occur, and resulted in a fundamental shift of employer strategy—to that of the "new look."

CHAPTER X

Job-Action Strikes and Other Issues

● *Introduction.*—The five coastwide strikes were the most dramatic form of labor-management conflict from 1934 to 1948. There were other manifestations as well. One of these was job-action or "quickie" strikes, which numbered more than 1,300 in these years. Another concerned employee discipline. Still another involved the productivity of longshoremen. In addition, there were serious jurisdictional controversies between some of the unions themselves, with indirect effects upon the employers.

In this chapter, we shall begin with a description of the evolution of the industry's complex bargaining structure. This is essential to a clear understanding of the issues. Then we shall consider the issues themselves, where necessary centering attention upon the relevant provisions of the contracts.

● *Changes in the Status of the Bargaining Parties.—Evolution of employer organizations.* The attainment of monopoly power over labor supply by the Pacific Coast maritime unions rested, first, upon recognition by the employers and, second, upon coastwide bargaining agreements. Without coastwide bargaining units, negotiations would have been much more difficult, and strikes much less effective. Tonnage then could have been diverted to other lines or other ports. Strikes

221

against single employers or local port associations could have been easily broken, even if the union itself were a highly centralized, coastwide organization.

Once the employers had conceded the principle of coastwide negotiations and agreements, however, as occurred in the settlements of 1934 and 1937, power relationships were radically altered. No longer could they cling to single-company and local port bargaining. Instead it now became imperative to establish and maintain a common front all along the coast, for negotiations and disputes and for the administration of contracts. Centralized power on the union side, coupled with coastwide bargaining units, called for formal consolidation of the employers' ranks as well. Ultimately, the solution was to call for a single peak employer association, to unify the conduct of labor relations in both the longshore and offshore parts of the industry. At that time, so far-reaching a move was not possible. It was practicable, however, to link up the port stevedore associations on a coastwide basis, and to match this principle with a similar organization for the steamship lines engaged in offshore and intercoastal operations. Between 1935 and 1937, events culminated in these developments.

For them, there was some precedent. Long before 1934, multiple-employer organizations had emerged in the industry, but these were restricted in scope. The various port associations of stevedoring employers and the Shipowners Association of the Pacific Coast (SAPC) for lines in the coastwise schooner trade were limited bodies of this kind. Originally, they had been created for the narrower type of collective bargaining existent before 1919. During the open-shop period, they continued to administer labor relations.

With the emergence of coastwide bargaining in 1934, these local bodies proved unwieldy for purposes of a common front. In the 1934 strike, their coördination was achieved in an informal way, not too satisfactory to the employers. Instead of a centralized organization, they were a loose confederation. The first step toward centralization was taken in May, 1935, when the longshore port associations created the office of Coast Coördinator and appointed Frank P. Foisie of Seattle to the post. At that time it was understood that member firms could not make separate agreements with the ILA.

Early in 1936, the longshore employers took the second step, by creating the Coast Committee for the Shipowners, to carry on negotiations in that critical year. This move, in part, was probably inspired by the formation of the Maritime Federation of the Pacific in 1935, which brought about a united front of the maritime unions. The MFP, of course, also included the offshore crafts. Thus at about the same time as the appearance of the Coast Committee, the offshore and intercoastal ship operators created the Pacific American Shipowners Association (PASA), as a central organization to deal with the seafaring unions.

Following the settlement of the second coastwide strike in early February, 1937, the Coast Committee was converted to a permanent organization, the Waterfront Employers Association of the Pacific Coast (WEPC). This body was a peak association, bringing together the four port associations under a common leadership, although these latter organizations retained their separate identities. According to statements of Almon E. Roth, first president of the WEPC, and Gregory Harrison, its counsel, the WEPC was to negotiate and administer the longshore contracts and to formulate labor policies for the stevedore groups.[1]

The WEPC gave the longshore branch of the maritime industry a coastwide multiple-employer association for the first time. PASA provided a similar organization for the offshore and intercoastal ship operators, as did the SAPC for the coasting schooner group. Formal coördination for the maritime industry as a whole on the coast was still to be achieved. Yet there was very close liaison between the three main employer associations, and, indeed, some executives and directors in common. Likewise, there was close parallelism in labor policies. This structure remained intact until early 1949. At that time, the peak bodies were merged to become the Pacific Maritime Association (PMA).

Multiple-employer bargaining is a method by which a relatively large number of individual employers can meet the power of highly

---

[1] *National Labor Relations Board*, 1014–1021 (1938) ; Joint Committee on Labor-Management Relations, *Labor-Management Relations: West Coast Maritime Industry*, pp. 7–9.

centralized unionism. It prevents the union from exercising divide-and-conquer tactics. With the emergence of coastwide bargaining, the employers were compelled to create appropriate coastwide multiple-employer associations. The process meant centralization of the power to negotiate and to administer contracts. As a process, it stripped the individual employer of his independence in labor relations. With this progressive loss of individual autonomy, power and authority to act in such matters shifted to the associations. Long-distance bargaining of a highly inflexible and bureaucratic kind was the inevitable result. With these developments, the area of disputes in the main now involved the entire coast, instead of the port or the single-ship operator.

Union representation of longshoremen. In these same years, important changes occurred on the union side as well. Harry Bridges became president of the Pacific Coast district of the ILA in 1936. Early in 1937, Bridges began preparations for detaching this district from the ILA, so that it could affiliate with the CIO as a new longshoremen's union. ILA locals on the coast began passing resolutions favoring the move. At a district convention in May, Bridges recommended that member locals refuse payment of any assessments levied by the national ILA to finance jurisdictional conflict with the CIO. In June, the Bridges-controlled MFP recommended that its member unions conduct referenda concerning CIO affiliation. Shortly after, the ILA members on the coast voted for CIO affiliation by a 3 to 1 majority. On July 18, 1937, ILA District 38 applied for a CIO charter. On August 11, the charter was delivered, and on the same day the district took the name International Longshoremen's and Warehousemen's Union (ILWU-CIO).[2]

In a sense, then, the Pacific Coast ILA at this point passed into history. But not quite. The waterfront employers were not prepared to transfer recognition from the old ILA to the new ILWU. Rather, as President Roth of the WEPC phrased it in a letter to Henry Schmidt of the San Francisco ILWU, the employers took "a position of neutrality" in the matter.[3] By this stand, the employers called into question the place of the ILWU as bargaining agent and, in effect, refused

[2] *7 National Labor Relations Board*, 1010–1014.   [3] *Ibid.*, pp. 1027–1028.

to accord it formal recognition for bargaining purposes. Perhaps the intent of the employers was merely to avoid charges of unfair labor practices under the National Labor Relations Act. Whatever their motive, however, the effect was to suggest to the leaders of the new ILWU that management hoped for its destruction—an interpretation that served those leaders well as propaganda for closing union ranks and at the same time contributed to the ill-feeling already existent between the parties.[4]

As a result, the ILWU raised the question of its representation rights with the National Labor Relations Board in January, 1938. In this proceeding, the union pleaded for a coastwide bargaining unit, and the employers proposed separate units for each employer. Local 38 of the old ILA objected to the board's taking jurisdiction of the case, on the grounds that a bargaining contract already existed between Local 38 and the employers. The NLRB found in favor of the coastwide unit, and in an ensuing election the longshoremen favored ILWU representation by a majority of 3 to 1. The board then certified the ILWU as bargaining agent on June 21, 1938.

This decision is of interest for two reasons. First, in establishing a coastwide bargaining unit, the NLRB gave color of legality to one of the union's basic objectives from 1934. Of particular importance, the board stressed the inability of the longshoremen to bargain effectively on a single-employer or port-by-port basis, because the employers could always divert cargo in case of a strike. Moreover, the board noted that in the evolution of bargaining relations, the employers themselves had moved to a consolidated coastwide policy and in their agreements from 1934 had conceded successively uniform coastwide standards respecting basic rates, overtime pay, penalty rates, and maximum sling loads. The decision thus gave permanent effect to the industry-wide multiple-employer bargaining system that had arisen under union pressure.

Second, by awarding the ILWU sole bargaining rights along the entire coast, the board swept into the unit certain locals whose mem-

---

[4] See Paul Eliel, "Labor peace in Pacific ports," *Harvard Business Review*, XIX, no. 4 (Summer, 1941), 431.

bers had not signed cards designating the ILWU as their bargaining
agent—notably Tacoma, Olympia, Port Angeles, and Anacortes,
Washington; Bandon, Oregon; and Eureka, California, where no
ILWU cards were returned. In a few other ports, the ILWU returns
were either a minority of those eligible to vote (Santa Barbara, Ven-
tura, and Monterey, California), or the majority favoring the ILWU
was not a substantial one (Aberdeen, Washington; Astoria and St.
Helens, Oregon).[5] The board's interpretation of majority rule and its
decision to establish a coastwide unit in effect overrode the wishes of
these longshoremen. Moreover, this fact gave rise to a second representation proceeding, initiated by Local 38 of the old ILA on September 12, 1940.[6]

In this proceeding, the ILA sought representation elections for
longshoremen at the ports of Tacoma, Anacortes, and Port Angeles,
Washington. The evidence revealed that locals at these ports and at
Olympia, Washington, had never applied for or received ILWU
charters, and instead had retained their affiliations with the ILA.
Moreover, in a memorandum agreement dated July 15, 1938, the
WEPC and ILWU had stipulated that these four ports were to be
excepted from the change of name to ILWU in the contract of February 4, 1937. Later agreements between the WEPC and ILWU continued this policy of "exceptions" as regards these ports. In addition,
the board found that at no time did the ILWU have any members at
Tacoma, Anacortes, and Port Angeles, and in fact longshoremen at
these ports were hostile to the Bridges union. Accordingly, while the
board reaffirmed its earlier principle that a coastwide longshore bargaining unit was appropriate to the industry, it also recognized that
under its "Globe doctrine"[7] the longshoremen in these three "exception
ports" were entitled to new representation elections. Here, the board

---

[5] 7 *National Labor Relations Board*, 1040.

[6] 32 *National Labor Relations Board*, 668. Actually, three cases were involved, with Ship-
owners Association of the Pacific Coast, Waterfront Employers Association of the Pacific
Coast, Waterfront Employers of Washington, *et al.*, and International Longshoremen's
Association (AFL), Locals 38–83, 38–86, and 38–97 as parties to the proceedings.

[7] In the matter of *Globe Machine and Stamping Company* and *Metal Polishers Union*,
etc., and *United Automobile Workers of America*, 3 *National Labor Relations Board*, 294.
The "doctrine" here established was that where there was no clear proof that a particular
bargaining unit was more appropriate than another, the desires of the employees themselves should govern the unit actually to be set up by the board.

noted that the fact that the ILWU itself had recognized these ports as "exceptions" proved controlling in the decision to retreat from the coastwide principle. In the elections that followed, the three ILA locals each won a majority vote, and in 1941 the board certified them as bargaining units in these ports.

Thus District 38 of the ILA did manage to survive on the Pacific Coast in these three small ports.

Developments affecting the SUP. Changes of even greater significance involved the offshore unions in the later 'thirties. In greater part, they centered upon the SUP and the dissolution of the ISU in June, 1937. It will be recalled that the ISU had expelled the SUP in January, 1936, temporarily tied up its funds, and attempted to replace it with a rival organization. About the same time, Joe Curran led a revolt of the Atlantic Coast sailors against the ISU, in a move that later resulted in the formation of the National Maritime Union, which affiliated with the CIO in 1937. The emergence of the NMU was to presage a bitter jurisdictional conflict with the SUP, contributing to the fatal split in the Maritime Federation of the Pacific in June, 1938.

After its expulsion from the ISU, the SUP began a fight for survival. The immediate problem for the SUP was to protect its recognition as bargaining agent for the deck departments of the Pacific Coast steamship lines. The question was crucial, for the award of 1934 had certified the ISU as bargaining agent for the unlicensed personnel, and in the agreements that followed the ISU was a co-signer along with the SUP, MCS, and MFOWW, all of which were then district unions of the ISU.[8] Now that the SUP had been expelled from the ISU, the problem was: Who was the sailors' bargaining agent, the ISU or the SUP?

By almost unanimous return cards, the deck personnel chose the SUP as their representative. The SUP then requested representation rights of the NLRB on May 21, 1936, to cover thirty-two steamship companies on the Pacific Coast. At about this time, Lundeberg learned from the operators that they did not consider themselves free to negotiate new contracts with the SUP because they had continued to rec-

---

[8] *2 National Labor Relations Board*, 214.

ognize the ISU and did not feel free to shift recognition to the SUP pending the NLRB proceeding. Shortly afterward, however, the operators did notify the ISU and the SUP of their desire to open negotiations. Lundeberg replied that the SUP was no longer a part of the ISU, hence that the ISU could not negotiate in the SUP's behalf. At the NLRB hearings, the offshore operators, represented by T. G. Plant, declared their willingness to recognize and to negotiate with the SUP providing the ISU was willing to withdraw from the picture. The steam-schooner operators went even further, initiating negotiations with the SUP alone in September, 1936, before the board had made its decision.

The whole issue was resolved at the hearings when the ISU representatives removed their organization from the SUP's negotiations, asserting their willingness to let the SUP make its own contracts on the Pacific Coast. As a result, the board found *de facto* that the operators had recognized the SUP, that the ISU was not contesting the representation rights of the SUP, hence that no question of representation really existed.

Thus the SUP made secure its status as bargaining representative for the deck personnel, in this way winning the first engagement in its battle for survival.

The SUP won a second major victory in the strike of 1936–1937, when the employers agreed to hire deck personnel exclusively from the SUP's union-controlled hall, thereby giving the SUP a closed shop. However, the split between Lundeberg and Bridges now posed a new threat to the SUP's existence because of Bridges' close relations with Curran and the NMU, and the strategic position of the longshoremen in the maritime industry. As a defensive measure, the SUP officials in the spring of 1937 entered negotiations with John L. Lewis, looking toward affiliation with the CIO. Actually, the SUP membership voted for such affiliation, but Lundeberg held off because of his fears for the traditional autonomy of the SUP and concerning the jurisdictional relationships between the SUP and the NMU.[9]

---

[9] Lampman, *Collective Bargaining of West Coast Sailors, 1885–1947: A Case Study in Unionism*, pp. 197–199.

As conflicts with the NMU developed in 1937 and 1938, in which Bridges' ILWU members passed through SUP picket lines, the SUP shifted its strategy to the development of friendly relations with the AFL once more. This was a natural alliance for two reasons: (1) Dave Beck's Teamsters (AFL) were in conflict with Bridges concerning the organization of warehousemen, while the SUP and the ILWU were locked in battle over loading jurisdictions on steam schooners and over the role of the NMU on the Pacific Coast; (2) the ISU had ceased to function effectively as an AFL affiliate in 1937, and the AFL now desired to recoup its position in the maritime industry and so deal a fatal blow to the aspirations of Curran and Lewis.[10]

Matters came to a head in June, 1938, when the SUP made its first move by formally quitting the Maritime Federation of the Pacific. Contributing causes to this action were the jurisdictional conflicts with both the ILWU and the National Maritime Union (NMU) (whose delegates were present at the MFP convention), and the deep personal split between Bridges and Lundeberg, now widened by evident ideological differences. The SUP's second move came in the same month when its members voted to affiliate with the AFL. In October, 1938, the AFL reciprocated by revoking the ISU charter, and by assigning to the SUP a charter for a new Seafarers' International Union (SIU), within which the SUP was to be an autonomous and controlling body. With the SIU as the instrument, the AFL and the SUP were now armed for making war on the CIO and the NMU throughout the maritime industry in the United States.[11] Even more, the SUP now had powerful new allies in its Pacific Coast struggle with Bridges, whose own position had been seriously weakened by the split in the Maritime Federation of the Pacific and the consequent collapse of his "unity" program.

Other unions. What happened to the other maritime unions? The demise of the ISU in the spring of 1937 had left two other orphan unions to go it alone. One, the National Union of Marine Cooks and Stewards (MCS), had been a department within the ISU since 1901, though it became inactive in the organization in 1936. Controlled by

---

[10] *Ibid.*, pp. 198–203; Liebes, *Longshore Labor Relations on the Pacific Coast, 1934–1942*, p. 204.

[11] Lampman, *op. cit.*, pp. 205–206.

Bridges' followers, the MCS affiliated in 1938 with the CIO.[12] The other, the Pacific Coast Marine Firemen, Oilers, Watertenders and Wipers Association (MFOWW), formed in 1883, became an independent union in 1937 and has since continued in that status.[13]

The radio operators had been originally organized in 1931, in an independent union known as the American Radio Telegraphists Association (ARTA). In 1937, this organization became the American Communications Association (ACA) and under the control of Bridges' followers affiliated with the CIO.[14] As the ACA, this union remained intact as Pacific Coast bargaining agent until 1946. At that time, the Brotherhood of Electrical Workers (IBEW-AFL) supplanted it on the Alaska lines. Thereafter, the ACA underwent changes of organization and has been badly weakened by jurisdictional conflicts.

Of the two licensed crafts, the National Marine Engineers' Beneficial Association (MEBA) has a history extending back to 1875. It affiliated in 1918 with the AFL, but withdrew in 1923.[15] In 1937, the MEBA affiliated with the CIO.[16] The National Organization of Masters, Mates and Pilots of America (MMP) was originally formed in 1887, gained its present title in 1916, and has been affiliated with the AFL to the present time.[17]

By the end of 1938, the pattern of unionism in the industry had largely crystallized. The employer associations were dealing with no less than nine craft unions—four then affiliated with the CIO (ILWU, MEBA, MCS, and ACA),[18] four with the AFL (SUP, IBU, MMP, and three ILA locals in Washington), and one independent (MFOWW). This complex bargaining structure was further confused by bitter personal rivalry between Bridges and Lundeberg, by jurisdictional con-

[12] Florence Peterson, *Handbook of Labor Unions* (Washington, American Council of Public Affairs, 1944), p. 221.

[13] *Ibid.*, p. 225.

[14] *Ibid.*, pp. 89–90.

[15] United States Department of Labor, Bureau of Labor Statistics, *Handbook of Trade Unions*, bull. no. 618 (Washington, Government Printing Office, 1936), pp. 234–235.

[16] Peterson, *op. cit.*, p. 223.

[17] *Handbook of Trade Unions*, p. 238.

[18] In late 1949, the national CIO charged the ILWU and MCS and their international officers with adherence to the Communist party line. A special investigating board of the CIO sustained these charges, and in 1950 both the ILWU and MCS were expelled. Since that time, both organizations have been independent unions. These events are discussed in the next chapter.

flicts between their two unions, and by sporadic efforts of the NMU to invade SUP territory. In place of the solidarity so strongly exhibited in 1934 and again in 1936, there now existed a "polarization" of the unions. This division was occasioned by jurisdictional and ideological strife. For the employers, now largely committed to collective bargaining and stripped of their original power, the situation was difficult, unstable, and constantly threatened with explosion. This, then, was the environment of labor-management relations that was to dominate the industry for the next decade, with great costs to all concerned.

● *Longshore Labor Relations.*—Between the end of the lengthy coast-wide strike of 1936–1937 and that of 1946, only one major strike involved the longshoremen—a fifty-three-day strike of dock checkers in San Francisco from November 10, 1939, to January 3, 1940. It would be a mistake, however, to infer that peaceful labor relations had finally been achieved by the parties during these years. They remained bitterly at odds over several issues, and guerrilla warfare in the form of "quickie" strikes and retaliatory lockouts was frequent throughout the period. In this section we shall present a brief chronological account of those issues that directly affected the economic position of the industry.

The issue of employee discipline. The 1934 award gave the employers the right to discharge longshoremen for incompetence, insubordination, or failure to perform work as required. However, as the employers observed in the 1945 National War Labor Board case, this right was "illusory."[19] A discharged man remained on the registered list at the port, retained his rights in the rotation of new jobs, and in fact even could be redispatched to the same employer. "Under this system every incentive to good work was destroyed; the last vestige of loyalty or responsibility to the employer was gone."[20] In the 1936 negotiations, the employers tried to strengthen their disciplinary powers, but in the settlement of February 4, 1937, they achieved but little success. In this contract, the union pledged its members to work "conscientiously and with sobriety," but succeeded in getting exclusive

---

[19] 26 *War Labor Reports*, 541–542.
[20] Joint Committee on Labor-Management Relations, *op. cit.*, p. 47.

control of the disciplinary function. The employer could lodge a complaint against an offender, but the union alone was to try the case and to determine the penalty (if any)—fine, suspension, or expulsion. Although the employer could carry his grievance to the Port Labor Relations Committee, that bipartisan body could divide as to action, and in any event could not penalize the union for improper disciplinary actions.

In the contract of 1938, the employers gained the right to carry disciplinary grievances to the Coast Arbitrator. In addition, the Port Committee in the first instance, and the Coast Arbitrator in the second, were allowed to impose specific penalties against individuals. These were: (1) removal from the registered list for pilferage or broaching of cargo; (2) ineligibility for work for one week for drunkenness. Significantly, no penalties were provided for deliberate slowdowns— a basic issue in these years. Nor was the union as a body held responsible for the proper exercise of its own disciplinary authority.[21]

No new agreement was reached in 1939. The old one was continued during some fourteen months of difficult negotiations. A new contract became effective December 20, 1940. Two new provisions were added to the existing system in this contract. First, the Port Committee was given "the power and the duty" to penalize individual longshoremen for work stoppages in violation of contract, refusal to work cargo according to the agreement, departure from job before provision of relief, pilferage, broaching of cargo, drunkenness, or other violations of the agreement or any award or decision of the Coast Arbitrator or his agents. Second, and more important, grievances unresolved at the port level now were to go to the new Coast Labor Relations Committee (bipartisan) established by the 1940 contract. Failing resolution here, the issue was to be decided finally by the Coast Arbitrator. This broadened the arbitrator's scope for penalizing individuals by including the offenses listed for the first time in the 1940 agreement.

Less than a year later, the employers complained that even this procedure was unsatisfactory. They claimed that discipline was non-

---

[21] Unless otherwise cited, assertions concerning disciplinary practices have been based upon study of the main contracts between the parties.

existent, citing as evidence that during the entire seven years of contractual relations[22] no man or no gang had ever been removed from the registered list for wilful slowdowns.

Except for wage matters, the parties lived by their 1940 contract until it was importantly modified by directive order of the National War Labor Board on August 18, 1945. That order settled a dispute emerging with the expiration of the previous contract on September 30, 1944. In that dispute, the employers had sought thoroughgoing revision of the disciplinary procedure, including a demand that the arbitrator be given the power to assess money damages against the union and to penalize offending individuals in certain disciplinary cases.[23] The NWLB denied this demand, and also a demand for a penalty of thirty days' suspension for all violations of working requirements. The employers also asked that no discharged longshoremen be redispatched to any employer until his case had been disposed of by the Coast Committee, a proposal that the board modified to provide that the discharged employee was not to be redispatched to the discharging employer pending final disposition of his case. Finally, the employers also had demanded certain specific penalties: for pilferage, cancellation of registration; for drunkenness or smoking in prohibited areas, thirty days' suspension for first offense, and cancellation of registration for repeated offenses. These the board modified to become: for pilferage, first offense, six months' suspension as a minimum penalty, and discretionary determination of the maximum; for second offense, mandatory cancellation of registration; for drunkenness or smoking, first offense, fifteen days' suspension; for second offense, thirty days' suspension, and for succeeding offenses a minimum of sixty days' suspension, and discretionary determination of the maximum.

On July 16, 1946, the parties incorporated these disciplinary provisions in their first postwar contract, an interim agreement ending on September 30. In the settlement of the longshore strike in 1946, these provisions were retained. They were renewed once more in the 1947–1948 agreement. This contract expired on June 15, 1948, but the

---

[22] Joint Committee on Labor-Management Relations, *op. cit.*, p. 48.

[23] *Ibid.*, pp. 48–49. A similar demand proved abortive in the 1940 negotiations. We find no reference to the 1945 demand in the board's 1945 decision and directive order.

status quo was maintained until September 2 by a series of injunctions. During this time, negotiations were undertaken looking toward a new agreement. As on most matters, however, the parties split radically on the issue of discipline. The ILWU proposed, first, the elimination of all disciplinary and penalty clauses, and, second, that work stoppages by the men individually or in groups no longer be considered a violation of contract. This, of course, would have destroyed all formal protec-

TABLE 13

MINOR LOCAL STOPPAGES INVOLVING LONGSHOREMEN, TOTALS FOR FOUR MAJOR PORTS, PACIFIC COAST MARITIME SHIPPING, 1934–1947

Year	Total	Year	Total
1934[a]	71	1941	37
1935	295	1942	15
1936	161	1943	66
1937	126	1944	38
1938	59	1945	65
1939	121	1946	88
1940	82	1947	92

[a] Part year only.
SOURCE: Tabulated from records compiled by the Pacific Maritime Association, and corrected to eliminate all known "one-man" strikes. See Appendix, table 18.

tion of the employers' disciplinary rights. Even these formal protections were frail enough, given the union's irresponsible conception of discipline. The employers thus countered the demand by asking, first, for elimination of the union from the assessment of all disciplinary penalties, and, second, for the right to impose penalties themselves, subject to review under the grievance procedure.[24]

Taken together, the proposals of both sides exhibited a kind of sham bargaining that revealed deep hostility and distrust. The employers had not wanted to deal with the union in the early years. In turn, this had enabled the union leaders to cultivate rank-and-file dislike for the employers. The ILA (later ILWU) leaders took no real interest in disciplining their own ranks to bring about a respect for contracts—the essential element of good relations. Had these officials invoked such discipline themselves, as the leaders of the SUP had

[24] Joint Committee on Labor-Management Relations, *op. cit.*, p. 49.

done after 1937, the employers would have had no reason to seek redress by loading the contracts with complex clauses. Irresponsible unionism, therefore, helped to poison bargaining relations, worsening them as time went on.

The issue of strikes in violation of contract. Job-action strikes became an issue between the parties almost from the inception of the 1934 award. Table 13 indicates the frequency of these stoppages over most of the period.

In the beginning, these strikes reflected resentment against pre-1934 conditions. In addition, the reëstablished unions had difficulties at that time in settling down to responsible conduct. Then the situation was made worse when the Maritime Federation of the Pacific formally endorsed job-action tactics early in 1935.

Study of the "quickie" strike record reveals that the leading causes of these strikes were refusal to pass picket lines, refusal to work as directed, or disputes over pay rates, sling loads, size of gangs, or work assignments.[25] During these years, the employers bitterly charged that strikes to respect picket lines were a violation of contract, and that the union was following a "planned slow-down" policy, using these strikes to gain concessions either directly or from ensuing arbitration awards.[26] With the closing of employer ranks in 1935, the companies for a time adopted the retaliatory tactic of locking out the port. This proved successful, but was ruled a violation of contract by the arbitrator.[27] Thereafter, the employers were compelled to attempt to control these strikes by arbitration and contract negotiations.

The longshore award of 1934 provided for timely reopening of negotiations before the expiration date of September 30, 1935, and for automatic renewal for an additional year if neither party sought revision. In addition, the award empowered the port labor relations committees "to investigate and adjudicate all grievances and disputes relating to working conditions." If the committee could not agree "on any matter," it was given the option of referring the issue to outsiders for settlement or of handing the question to an arbitrator for decision.

---

[25] These are tabulated in Appendix, table 19.

[26] Eliel, "Labor peace in Pacific ports," pp. 429–432.

[27] *Ibid.*, pp. 430–431.

The arbitrator was to be appointed by the Secretary of Labor or his authorized agent. Finally, the award established the obligation of the longshoremen to "perform all work as ordered by the employer," with any emergent grievances to be processed according to the procedure described above.

From these provisions, it would appear that the award contemplated only one class of legitimate stoppage: where, after timely notice, the parties had failed to negotiate a new agreement prior to the expiration date. Clearly, "quickie" strikes were not sanctioned. Quite the contrary. Work was to proceed as ordered, with disputes concerning working rules, pay rates, sling loads, or picket lines of other unions to be resolved peacefully under an orderly procedure with formal arbitration as the terminal step. Nevertheless, local stoppages continued to occur with high frequency. An early arbitration award, however, found that "hot cargo" strikes not directly involving the longshoremen were a violation of contract.[28]

With the 1937 contract, a new clause was added to provide that, in case of a dispute, work was to continue according to conditions prevailing before the dispute had arisen. Representatives of each party were to attempt settlement within twenty-four hours, and failing here, either party could refer the issue to the Port Committee and the previous procedure then would come into operation.[29] An additional new clause pledged all members of the then ILA to work conscientiously. Any man allegedly guilty of "deliberate bad conduct" or of an "illegal stoppage of work" causing sailing delays could be tried by the union and, if found guilty, penalized accordingly. Moreover, the employer could lodge the complaint and, if need be, bring it up in the Port Committee.

Since the union obtained the exclusive right to administer discipline to individuals and was itself exempted from all penalties, union leaders themselves could instigate "quickie" strikes. Further, they could fail to penalize adequately, or fail to penalize at all, indi-

---

[28] Liebes, *op. cit.*, pp. 112–115. "Hot cargo" strikes are sympathetic strikes.

[29] The 1937 contract provided for joint committees to negotiate coastwide penalty rates on certain classes of cargo and maximum limits for sling loads. Penalty rates and sling loads were a frequent issue in job-action strikes.

vidual members who had invoked such strikes, without being subject to penalty for violating the contract. At most, the arbitrator or his agents could only find the union in noncompliance.[20] The job-action tactic was the union's to use as it desired, free of all redress.

This unilateral power of the union was so great, and its irresponsible exercise so menacing, that the employers fought hard to curb it in contracts after 1937. But they proved unable to make much headway in the contract of October 1, 1938. The earlier procedure for resolving disputes arising during the contract was retained, but the arbitrator was now authorized to decide whether issues brought before him were "basic interpretations" of the agreement and, if not, whether they were coastwide or local in application. More important, the union local was now obliged to notify the Port Committee within ten days concerning its decision in employer complaint cases involving illegal strikes. If the employers believed that discipline was warranted and none was meted out by the union, or that the discipline was inadequate, they could then carry the issue to the arbitrator.

However, the contract still carried no explicit penalty upon individuals for illegal strikes or slowdowns, and none against the union for instigating or condoning such acts of the membership. Conceivably, the employers could carry such grievances to the arbitrator, but a 1939 decision by Arbitrator Wayne L. Morse limited his penalty powers to pilferage and drunkenness, the only offenses carrying specific penalties in the contract.[31] As a result, job-action strikes remained beyond redress. The union had exclusive control of discipline. The arbitrator held he could not penalize individuals for such acts, and that his jurisdiction was limited to the authority to find the ILWU local not in compliance, but without penalty. The employers could not combat these strikes with lockouts, nor could they eliminate offenders from the registration list if the union were to oppose such a move. Indeed, the offenders could claim their regular turns in work assignments. Insofar as job-control was concerned, the ILWU was in complete power.

[20] Joint Committee on Labor-Management Relations, *op. cit.*, p. 40.

[31] The case involved refusal of Los Angeles longshoremen to pass demonstration pickets protesting scrap iron shipments to Japan. Bridges declared flatly the union's unwillingness to penalize members for respecting such demonstration picket lines. (*Ibid.*, pp. 46–47.)

Upon entering the protracted negotiations eventuating in the 1940 contract, the employers declared that they would make no concessions of any kind until the union had satisfied their two basic demands: (1) an end to illegal strikes, and (2) an end to the allegedly deliberate slowdown of work.[32] In detail, the employers described the first demand as calling for a joint deposit of cash by both parties to cover damages arising from contract violations, and for the power of the arbitrator to assess penalties against individuals.[33] On its side, the union asked for the preservation of all basic gains won from 1934, a five-year contract, the existing language concerning the exclusive disciplinary rights of the union, and the right to refuse to pass picket lines so far as allowed by arbitration awards.[34]

On December 20, 1940, the parties agreed to a contract extending to September 30, 1942. This agreement is significant for the "quickie" strike problem in two respects: (1) illegal strikes, refusals to work cargo according to the provisions of the agreement, and any other violations of the agreement or of awards or decisions of the Coast Arbitrator[35] were proscribed, and (2) the adjudication of disputes and grievances was radically overhauled.

Arbitrator's agents were provided for each of the major ports, to replace the cumbersome local arbitrator system. A new body, the Coast Labor Relations Committee, was created to review the acts of the port committees and to handle disputes unresolved at the local level. The Coast Arbitrator was given the power to hear and determine any complaint of either party regarding alleged contract violations, and to designate Port Agents to act in local matters.

As in the earlier contract, local strikes were outlawed. But here the union gained a concession. If the men involved in a job dispute believed in good faith that their health and safety were threatened by continuance of operations, work was to cease until the Port Agent could order an emergency change in work methods, pending resolution of the issue at higher levels. Either party could carry disputed issues or

---

[32] We consider the issue of declining efficiency in the section immediately following.
[33] Liebes, *op. cit.*, p. 228.
[34] *Ibid.*, p. 227.
[35] The position of Coast Arbitrator was formally established by the agreement of 1938.

alleged violations of contract successively to the Port Committee, the Coast Committee, and finally, to the Coast Arbitrator. Thus a complete procedure for peaceful adjudication of disputes was provided.

Further, the new contract assigned the port committees "the power and the duty" to impose penalties upon individual longshoremen for, among other offenses, strikes in violation of contract, refusal to work cargo according to contract provisions or arbitration awards, or otherwise breaking the agreement. The port committees, however, were only to act on complaint of the employer that the ILWU local had failed to penalize or had penalized inadequately.

From all this, it would appear that "quickie" strikes were effectively proscribed and an equitable adjudication procedure provided for peaceful settlement. However, a serious loophole remained. If the union leadership encouraged or condoned job-action strikes, discipline by the local would be at best inadequate, and remedial action by the bipartisan port and coast committees could effectively be stymied. The issue would then have to go to the Coast Arbitrator for decision. But here the contract failed to provide specific penalties for strikes in violation of contract and related offenses, though specific penalties were provided for pilferage and drunkenness. On the precedent of the Morse award of September 11, 1939, the arbitrator could not impose specific penalties upon individuals for strikes in violation of contract, because the contract had failed to provide such penalties. To have done so would have placed the arbitrator in the position of amending the contract, hence exceeding his jurisdiction. On this construction, the arbitrator could do no more than find the union in noncompliance— essentially an empty gesture.[36]

The contract therefore left the employers about in the same position as the Joint Committee on Labor-Management Relations described for the 1938 agreement.

... The employers had no effective means of enforcing proper working directions, no power to impose penalties for any reason. The arbitrator was limited to cases of pilfering and drunkenness. For any other offense the longshoreman was subject only to such discipline as his own union might care to impose.... This union control has been used most effectively to enforce whatever policies

---

[36] The employers' 1940 demand for a damage fund was lost in negotiations.

and practices the union officials chose to impose . . . the slowdowns, the steady reduction of sling loads, refusal of jitney drivers to move out of turn, opposition to use of swing boards, refusal to handle hot cargo or pass demonstration picket lines.[37]

It is thus obvious that no matter how detailed a contract may be, and no matter how well-conceived its formal adjudication procedure, job-action strikes cannot be controlled unless *both* parties really desire to control them. Given an irresponsible union, with leaders motivated by purposes other than the building of good labor-management relations and possessed of almost unparalleled power, a serious "quickie" strike problem would be likely. This was the case, particularly with the ILWU, for many years.

Nor was the problem overcome by the 1940 contract, despite the high hopes of the employers.[38] True, there were fewer job-action strikes in 1941 than in 1940, but even in 1941 complaints about bad discipline arose once more. With the beginning of World War II, however, the situation improved. The union suddenly developed a keen interest in production and volunteered to relax certain working rules in order to increase efficiency. Significantly, too, the number of job-action strikes fell very sharply from eighty-two in 1940 to thirty-seven in 1941 and only fifteen in 1942.

In 1943 and 1944, however, the number of these strikes rose markedly once more, and in the contract negotiations of the latter year the employers were again asking for strong measures of control. For this purpose, they proposed that the arbitrator be given power to assess money damages against the union for violations of contract, and that the employers be allowed to suspend individuals from registration for misconduct.[39]

---

[37] Joint Committee on Labor-Management Relations, *op. cit.*, p. 47. It is, of course, difficult to prove conclusively that the ILWU officials directly encouraged job-action strikes. However, there is some evidence: the job-action resolution of the MFP of 1935, Bridges' support of the refusal to pass demonstration pickets for loading of scrap for Japan, the lack of disciplinary penalties by the union, and the marked decline in "quickie" strikes in later 1941, when Russia and then the United States had entered the war. Significantly, too, the number of these strikes rose markedly again in 1946 and 1947.

[38] Eliel, "Labor peace in Pacific ports," p. 47. This time Eliel believed he had discerned a determination to abandon guerrilla warfare and to replace "the will to power" by "the will to peace."

[39] Joint Committee on Labor-Management Relations, *op. cit.*, pp. 48–49.

In its decision on the case, the War Labor Board ordered no basic changes in the existing controls so far as strikes in violation of contract were concerned. Discipline for such offenses was left with the union in the first instance, with the employers retaining the right to follow the 1940 grievance procedure. The employers' demand for the right to suspend individuals for misconduct was denied. However, accepting a union proposal, the board did alter the position of the arbitrator in one respect: he was now made an Impartial Chairman to preside over the Coast Committee and to vote in case of a tie. On request of the parties, he could appoint a Port Arbitrator to settle purely local disputes not resolved by the Port Committee. The first change was to expedite arbitration of coastwide issues; the second change was to speed decisions concerning purely local questions.[40]

Even before the end of World War II, job-action strikes had again become a serious problem, rising once more to prewar levels. The problem remained acute until all work ceased with the 1948 strike. During 1946–1948, therefore, the employers continued their efforts to overcome the difficulty by attempting to strengthen the contracts. This was essentially a formal approach, probably dictated by the irresponsibility of the ILWU leaders. These efforts met with failure until the settlement of December 6, 1948. The WEPC was unable to modify the pertinent basic provisions of the 1940 agreement, either by NWLB directive order (1945) or by negotiations with the union, before the 1948 settlement. The crucial weakness of the 1940 agreement was that the Coast Arbitrator was not provided with a schedule of penalties for job-action strikes. This weakness remained, despite formal changes in the grievance procedure after 1940.

The 1948 settlement likewise did not contain a schedule of penalties for these strikes. Yet there were differences. The parties now pledged themselves to a no-strike-no-lockout clause, and this pledge was underwritten by the CIO, so far as the ILWU was concerned. Moreover, the agreement defined "legitimate and *bona fide*" picket lines and outlawed demonstration strikes and various kinds of secondary boycotts. These latter had been an important source of "quickie" strikes.

[40] 26 *War Labor Reports*, 519. Case decided August 18, 1945.

Finally, the agreement revised the grievance procedure, to stress prompt and final local settlement of job disputes.

The real significance of the 1948 agreement lay not in its formal provisions, but in a change of attitudes. With the employers' adoption of the "new look" philosophy and the intervention of the national CIO, the ILWU leaders were put under strong pressure to adhere to the contract in good faith. What they were expected to do was to turn their organization into a responsible union. In the practical sense they did so. Job-action strikes ceased to be a problem in the years that immediately followed.

The issue of declining efficiency of longshoremen. Probably no issue has contributed more to conflicts between the WEPC and the ILWU than what the parties themselves have termed the "efficiency" of longshore operations.[41] During the years between 1935 and 1948, the employers repeatedly charged that the productivity of longshoremen was seriously declining, and they blamed this result mainly upon an alleged "deliberate" slowdown by the men on the job, encouraged by the union itself. To these charges, the union replied that the operators really desired to restore the 1934 "speedup," and to disrupt if not to destroy the work rotation system.

In the controversy over the productivity of longshoremen, three problems were involved. One concerned the effects of innovations in labor-saving equipment and work methods upon employment and earnings. Another concerned the impacts of changes in dispatching and working rules upon employment and output. Still another concerned

---

[41] "Efficiency" is too loose a term for describing what the parties were talking and disputing about. Properly used, "efficiency" refers to the human factor in work: intensity of effort put forth, quality of work performed, and availability for work. "Productivity," in turn, relates to the quantitatively realized results of human work, usually expressed as "output" relative to "input" measured in man-hours (or sometimes gang-hours) of actual working time. As defined, "efficiency" obviously directly affects "productivity," but so also do other factors. Among these must be considered the kind and quality of capital equipment supplied for longshore operations (a marked variable by port, dock, and ship), and the working rules established by port practice or contract. These rules affect both input and output, and in a complex manner affect both efficiency and productivity. They include the size of sling loads, the number of men in a gang, flexibility in the assignment of jobs to the gang and its individual members. Finally, productivity is also affected by the nature of the commodity being handled. Given all these influences, it is very difficult to isolate primary causes in appraising responsibility for changes in the productivity of longshoremen; above all, for analyzing the basic causes of changes in the money costs of stevedoring operations.

alleged "make-work" practices of the longshoremen—slowdowns in speed of operations, lightening of sling loads, requiring unnecessary men, etc. Each of these types of change led to many job-action strikes and to arbitrations concerning contract rights and provisions.

The award of 1934 gave the employer the right, without interference or restraint by the union, "to introduce labor-saving devices and to institute such methods of discharging and loading cargo as he con-siders best suited to the conduct of his business," so long as his loading and discharging methods were compatible with the health and safety of the men. The succeeding contract of 1937 preserved this clause intact, but added a pledge of the employers to provide safe gear and conditions, and an agreement to negotiate a coastwide safety code. A committee was also established to negotiate coastwide sling-load maxima for standard commodities.

With the 1938 agreement, these maximum sling-load limits were incorporated in the contract, with express provisions that the em-ployers were not to regard the maxima also as minima if such involved "unreasonable speed-ups," and the union pledged itself not "to resort to subterfuges to curtail production." As a result, loads were sharply reduced from pre-1934 levels.

During the life of the 1938 agreement, several issues affecting the efficiency and productivity of longshoremen came to a head. In the latter 'thirties, the employers had been making increasing use of lift-boards, Ross lumber carriers, loading cranes on certain industrial docks, and mechanical trimmers for handling cargoes in bulk.

In the 1939 proceeding concerning the liftboard in particular, the union argued that wages were fixed in the 1934 award on the basis of an estimated volume of total available work which was to be distrib-uted by rotation in such a manner as to realize a certain level of annual earnings. The same principle of balance was invoked in setting the sling-load maxima in 1937, which presumed a reasonable loading or discharging rate and a correlative given number of men. In the union's view, the liftboard, the Ross carrier, and the dock crane all upset this balance, increasing the productivity per man while reducing the total work available and the earnings per man. Accordingly, the union wanted the arbitrator to award an increase in pay such that the old wage bill total would still be paid to a gang of reduced size. In his decision, however, Arbitrator Morse found that under the contract the employers were free to expand the use of the liftboard or other labor-saving devices.[42] On similar grounds, Morse upheld the employers on the use of the mechanical trimmer, even though it reduced the number of men required.[43]

During these years, the operators also made other changes in methods of working: direct ship-to-ship cargo transfers, use of a "third board" to get continuous production from divided hold gangs, shifting of gang men on the job between hold and dock and vice versa, shifting of gangs between hatches at mealtimes, and attempts to set sling loads at the maxima. On these questions, the employers again won in arbitration, with the exception of sling loads. There, the arbitrator ruled that the maximum load was not necessarily a "reasonable" one under the contract; hence the operators were not free to fix any load they wished up to the maximum.[44]

The union's purpose in these proceedings was to prevent technological changes from reducing the total volume of available work. One response was to contest these changes in arbitration. As noted, this could involve one of two approaches: (1) to demand wage adjustments that would increase the costs of the change and reduce the incentive to make it; or (2) to block the change on the ground it would reduce the work opportunity. Alternatively, the other response open to the union was to compel the employment of unnecessary men, either by attempting to tighten up on working rules through arbitration, or by slowing down the pace of operations on the job. Regarding unnecessary men, the union's tactics took two forms: (1) attempts to compel the continued employment of "extras" until the gang itself had completed the job, regardless of the need for the "extras";[45] and (2) attempts to re-

---

[42] Award of September 15, 1939, cited in Liebes, *op. cit.*, pp. 247–254.

[43] Award of September 16, 1939; *ibid.*, pp. 258–260.

[44] *Ibid.*, pp. 257, 262–268, 274–277.

[45] At all ports except San Francisco, the standard gang then consisted only of shipmen (ten in Seattle and Los Angeles; eleven or thirteen at Portland, depending on the operation). In San Francisco, the standard gang then numbered sixteen, because at this port alone dockmen were included. At the other ports, dockmen were "extras" to be used when

strict the flexibility of the employer in shifting the assignment of gang members between hold and dock, and in shifting gangs between hatches. In connection with the first tactic, the union sought to extend to all ports the San Francisco practice of having extras on the dock included in the standard gang. This effort failed in negotiations, as did the union's attempt in arbitration to compel the retention of extras until the gang had finished. Moreover, Arbitrator Morse also ruled against the union regarding the employers' flexibility in individual assignments, affirming the latter's right so long as it was consistent with the safety clause.[46]

In spite of these apparent gains in arbitration, the employers charged that the productivity of longshoremen continued to fall throughout 1935–1939. This they blamed mainly upon the decreasing "efficiency" of the force because of an asserted "slowdown" to "make" more work. Such slowdowns were possible, because the gang could control such factors as winch speeds, time spent in preparation, time spent in building loads, or time between movements of loads between the dock and the hold.

In the lengthy 1939–1940 negotiations, the employers made the restoration of efficiency one of their two basic conditions precedent to any concessions to the union. In elaboration, they interpreted this demand to mean the restoration of "steady" gangs,[47] the elimination of the dispatching of unneeded men, and the end of the alleged slowdown.

Although the employers were unsuccessful in obtaining the inclusion of specific measures to meet these demands in the 1940 contract, they did obtain some important concessions from the union. Foremost,

and as needed, separately from the ship gang. At San Francisco, "extras" then applied to men in excess of sixteen. 26 *War Labor Reports*, 538–539.

[46] Liebes, *op. cit.*, pp. 270–276. Award on flexibility of gang-member assignments dated August 19, 1939.

[47] "Steady" gangs referred to gangs made up of permanent personnel on continuous assignment to a single employer. These gangs had been eliminated at Portland, Seattle, and Los Angeles in 1935, because the 1934 award had provided explicitly that all men were to be hired and dispatched through the hall. Continuous assignment was incompatible with rotation to equalize work opportunities. However, steady gangs continued as a local practice in San Francisco until 1939, when the union took the issue to arbitration. Arbitrator Morse ruled that the ILWU was free to urge its members to refuse continuous assignments and to insist upon rotation, though not to "coerce" the members for this purpose. In any event, steady gangs disappeared from San Francisco at about this time.

the ILWU tacitly admitted a decline of efficiency since 1935, in agreeing to have the Coast Labor Relations Committee study means for "the restoration of reasonable efficiency" and "reasonable compliance" with the terms of the agreement. If by February 1, 1941, reasonable efficiency were restored and reasonable compliance obtained, the employers agreed to make a five-cent increase in the basic wage.

Moreover, the innovation clause was importantly modified. The *members* of the union were now also pledged not to interfere with innovations. More significant, the employers conceded that under certain conditions the union could make the continued use of an innovation a negotiable and even arbitrable issue. To become such an issue, the innovation had to injure earnings and employment "materially." There had to be proof of reasonable compliance with the contract. Further, there had to be a showing that use of the labor-saving device had materially increased, that the ILWU and its members had not obstructed its introduction and use, and that productivity had markedly improved. As a result, the union succeeded in making innovations a bargainable issue, but this right was contingent upon prior respect for management's right to innovate.

Finally, the contract authorized the Coast Committee to negotiate coastwide working and dispatching rules. Either party could take disputed issues to the Coast Arbitrator for decision.

On February 1, 1941, the employers granted the contingent wage increase, but were careful to assert that so far there had been "no appreciable restoration" of productivity, and that "the slowdown still continues."[48] The union accepted the increase but denied the charges.

Between February and August, the employers maintained their position, and then the second wage reopening occurred. In the same period, the parties were deadlocked in negotiations for coastwide working and dispatching rules.[49] The second wage increase was refused by the employers, so the matter went to arbitration. In this proceeding, the ILWU contended that it had relaxed many working rules, and that

---

[48] Award of Coast Arbitrator Morse, January 31, 1942, pp. 3–4.

[49] The ILWU here petitioned the arbitrator for a hearing on these issues. In the hearing the employers contended that many rules proposed by the union exceeded the area agreed to for arbitration. The ILWU failed to follow up with argument on the merits of its case, so this arbitration was never concluded. *Ibid.*, pp. 6–7; 26 *War Labor Reports*, 537.

the employers were insisting upon "living in the past," keeping alive old controversies. The union dismissed the employers' evidence of falling productivity (known as the "Price-Waterhouse survey") as inadequate, prejudicial, and based upon noncomparable data.[50]

Arbitrator Morse also found himself "not impressed" by the employers' evidence, noting that the findings rested upon a diversity of methods, admitted limitations and qualifications, and unreliable and noncomparable data. In awarding a ten-cent increase in the basic rate, however, he declared: ". . . there is merit in the employers' contention that the longshoremen have not fully performed their work efficiency obligations under their collective bargaining contract." Expressing his intention of calling "a spade a spade," Morse added that at the time the 1940 agreement was signed, "there was a need for restoration of reasonable efficiency in the performance of longshore work and a need for more reasonable compliance" with contracts.[51]

By the time of the 1944 negotiations, longshore productivity was once more a bitterly disputed issue. The WEPC contested demands for increased wages by citing evidence of a continuing decline in productivity, and in turn submitted several demands aimed to reverse the alleged trend.[52] In its final determination of the case, on August 18, 1945, the National War Labor Board upheld its panel on the main wage issue, deciding that the ILWU's wage demand should be considered independently of the productivity question.

To the employers' demand that steady gangs be restored because continuity of employment increased efficiency, the panel recommended denial because it would upset equalization through rotation—a basic principle of the hiring hall. The board upheld the panel on this point. Another WEPC demand called for ten-man ship gangs along the entire coast, with extras to be dispatched only as ordered. This would have abolished the eleven-man ship gang at San Francisco, the compulsory five dockmen in standard gangs at that port, and the special thirteen-

---

[50] Award of January 31, 1942, mimeographed (San Francisco, Jan. 31, 1942), p. 10.

[51] *Ibid.*, pp. 20–21.

[52] The evidence referred to sugar-discharging rates for bags of sugar at Crockett, California; for copra at various ports; and to lumber loading. For the first two, comparisons between 1935 and 1944 showed large declines in units handled per gang-hour. 26 *War Labor Reports*, 535–536.

man gangs at Portland. Instead, the board ordered that all standard gangs should consist of ship gangs only, with size to be governed by present port practice (eleven men at San Francisco, ten men elsewhere except for special cases at Portland), and with dock extras to be dispatched only as ordered by the employer.

Regarding the employers' demand for greater flexibility in the assignment of gang members to various tasks, the panel found that this would compromise the contract right of the men to select their jobs. The employers now could eliminate unneeded extras at the dock, and the board upheld the panel's recommendation to deny this additional request.

The employers had also requested that the men be required to report at the halls during dispatch times each day except Saturday and Sunday, to reduce absenteeism. Here the panel noted the union's argument that the operators had offered no stand-by fee and no guarantee of a job, together with testimony attributed to Frank Foisie of the WEPC that longshoremen usually chose their occupation because its casual nature gave them the right to decide when to take time off. The panel, however, did recognize that absenteeism of men already assigned jobs was a costly and punishable offense. Accordingly, the board ordered a progressive scale of individual penalties.

To increase productivity directly, the WEPC asked the board to abolish the 1937 sling-load limits, and to give the employers the right to set their own limits compatible with health and safety requirements. The union expressed willingness to examine these limits on their merits, but objected in principle to the unilateral nature of the employers' proposal. The board denied the request and directed the parties to renegotiate the limits in effect.

Finally, the WEPC attempted once more to alter the selection of the hall dispatcher. From the inception of bargaining relations in 1934, the employers had been dissatisfied with the award to the union of the right to select the dispatcher. The dispatcher is the key man in the selection of longshoremen for jobs, and in acquiring the exclusive right to name him, the union had solidified its practically unilateral job-control powers. Thus in 1936, Gregory Harrison, attorney for the employers, while accepting the hall as an institution, pleaded for a jointly controlled hall with an impartial dispatcher.[53] At stake were such issues as discipline, selection of men, compliance with the contract, and, indirectly, the attainment and maintenance of efficiency and productivity.

By 1944, the employers were insisting that dispatching required an experienced man. Although they now declared they had no objection to the dispatcher's being a union man, they held that the halls were being inefficiently administered because of the great turnover among dispatchers. For remedy, they asked that the dispatcher be selected by the Port Committee or, failing this, by an arbitrator; also that each party be allowed to have a representative continuously present at the halls. On its side, the ILWU admitted that the dispatchers should serve for a fixed and uniform term. Admitting also that the job calls for special qualifications, the union stressed that the position is one of particular trust, since the dispatcher assigns men to "blind jobs." The longshoremen must have confidence in him and, to protect their interests, a voice in his selection. In the union's view, these ends required union election of the dispatcher. Regarding the presence of bipartisan observers, the union had no comments.

Upholding its panel, the NWLB ordered that: (1) the port committees were to fix standards for eligibility of candidates; (2) the union was to elect the dispatchers; (3) they were to hold office for one year; (4) disputes over standards or qualifications of candidates were to be resolved by the Impartial Chairman (replacing the Coast Arbitrator) or, at his option, by the Port Agent; and (5) each party was authorized to have a representative at each of the halls.

The NWLB directive order of 1945 ended attempts of the employers to increase longshore productivity by amendment of the contracts. During 1946–1948, the issue itself remained alive, but relations between the WEPC and ILWU deteriorated so far that more basic questions now dominated negotiations. Even the "new look" settlement of 1948 left the provisions affecting productivity largely intact. The sling-load limits negotiated in 1937 in all essentials were left un-

---

[53] Joint Committee on Labor-Management Relations, *op. cit.*, p. 40.

changed. The innovations clause of 1940 was also retained. Any subsequent improvement in longshore productivity thus depended upon mutual consent in the administration of the 1948 agreement. Whether such improvement has actually occurred has yet to be determined.

Other issues. Discipline, job-action strikes, and productivity were central issues making for conflict between the waterfront employers and the longshoremen between 1934 and 1948. To be sure, there were other issues also, such as control of the dispatcher and rotation of monthly employees. These were mainly reflected in the more basic questions we have just considered. Another issue concerned management control of supervisory employees, in particular "walking bosses." The walking boss is a foreman who oversees the work of several gangs. In the earlier years, the employers seemed to show little interest in bringing these men into the managerial structure. Most of them turned to the union, and in 1947 the NLRB certified the ILWU as their bargaining agent in California, Oregon, and the Columbia River ports in Washington. The employers refused to bargain with this unit of the ILWU, stressing the supervisory role of the walking boss and the anomaly of his being represented by a union made up primarily of employees under his supervision. The issue was resolved by the subsequent passage of the Taft-Hartley Act, which exempted employers from the duty to bargain collectively with unions of supervisors.[54]

● *Offshore Labor Relations.*—In a sense, the longshoremen were the focal point of conflict between labor and management after 1937. Bargaining relations involving the seafaring unions were less complex and, in the main, not marked by deep or extensive differences. Except for the MMP and MEBA, these unions were now secure and very powerful, and their primary objectives centered upon higher wages and improved conditions, although in the case of the SUP there was bitter conflict with the ILWU and NMU over jurisdictional issues.

The SUP. By 1937, the SUP had become completely alienated from the Maritime Federation, and Lundeberg had recognized the necessity for strengthening internal discipline and centralized control of the SUP, to deal effectively with the threats of the NMU and ILWU. Job-

---

[54] Joint Committee on Labor-Management Relations, *op. cit.*, pp. 51–52.

action ceased to be official policy, and responsible unionism now became the goal of the SUP leadership. On its own, the union introduced penalties for individual violations of contracts. "Bum beefs" (job-action disputes without merit) were condemned, and the leadership promised strict discipline for such offenses. With the development of shortages in available sailors from 1939, the SUP opened its ranks to new members and developed the use of "trip carders" (permit men) to supplement the force, taking steps to see that these temporary men lived up to the union's obligations.[55]

Together, these moves toward responsible policies marked the beginnings of the SUP's return to the hard-headed and conservative business unionism of Andrew Furuseth and the old ISU in its heyday. Reaffiliation with the AFL in 1938 symbolized this change. Not that the SUP became softer in its economic demands than the ILWU. Rather, the SUP was rapidly returning to the traditional AFL philosophy: tough bargaining aimed at short-range economic goals and based upon the independent strength of the organization, coupled with respect for contracts and recognition of the economic problems and needs of the steamship operators.[56]

In keeping with this change of outlook, the SUP regarded government intervention in shipping operations with contempt and hostility. In the union's view, the federal government's role in shipping was limited to safety-at-sea legislation, the promotion of free collective bargaining, the promotion of the American merchant marine, and the restriction of jobs in the merchant marine to American citizens. Since the federal agencies concerned with shipping affairs in those years envisaged a much broader scope for their activities, it was inevitable that they would come into conflict with the SUP.[57]

One basic issue concerned hiring—which was fundamental to job-control. In 1936, Congress passed the Copeland-Bland Act, requiring continuous discharge books for seamen (known colloquially as "the Copeland fink books"). The SUP claimed these discharge books could

---

[55] Lampman, *op. cit.*, pp. 208–216.

[56] Except for the proscription of job-action tactics, the "new philosophy" of the Sailors' Union of the Pacific was quite consistent with the short-run aspects of the syndicalist tradition.

[57] Lampman, *op. cit.*, p. 257.

become a black-listing system and succeeded in getting the law revised to make their use optional. Then, in 1938, the United States
Maritime Commission started the practice of requiring subsidized
operators to recruit personnel exclusively from government halls. The
first move was made on the Atlantic Coast, with NMU support, despite an SUP picket line. After a strike by the SUP in Seattle in the
summer of 1939, the Maritime Commission abandoned this inept
policy.[58]

Issues related to hiring and job-control involved the training of
seamen and the right to strike. The SUP bitterly opposed government
training schools, holding that they would increase the work force ex-
cessively, contribute to dilution of the SUP's ranks, and weaken the
union. In their place, the SUP created its new Furuseth School of Sea-
manship, as an adjunct of the union.[59]

For many years the right of sailors to strike has been circumscribed
by the mutiny laws. A Supreme Court decision in 1942 held that an
employer was justified in refusing to rehire men who had struck in
violation of shipping articles and the mutiny laws. On this decision,
strikes by seafaring employees were legal only after the men had left
the payroll and had refused to sign articles for another voyage.[60]

Jurisdictional conflicts with the NMU and the ILWU were a major
factor in SUP experience during 1938–1945. The battle between the
SUP and the NMU in major part was fought over the Pacific Coast
tanker trade. Between 1934 and 1937, the tanker lines successfully
had fought off unionism. In the latter year, both unions undertook
organizing drives, and between 1938 and 1942, the NLRB conducted
a series of representation elections. In some instances, the board set
up the deck department as an appropriate bargaining unit; in others,
the deck, stewards', and engine departments were consolidated. The
MFOWW and MCS in effect withdrew from the field, giving the NMU
(which had a consolidated three-department structure) the advantage,
and forcing the SUP to develop a broader bargaining unit for the
tanker lines—in which sailors, firemen, and cooks were combined.
Prolonged court proceedings delayed the emergence of effective col-

---

[58] *Ibid.*, pp. 245–254.   [59] *Ibid.*, p. 257.   [60] *Ibid.*, pp. 256–257.

lective bargaining in the tanker trade until late 1942. By 1943, the SUP claimed agreements with all operators except Union Oil (which had recognized the NMU) and Standard Oil of California, which succeeded in fighting off unionism until 1945. In that year, the SUP negotiated its first agreement with Standard and, except for Union Oil, now dominated the tanker trade on the Pacific Coast.[61]

Conflicts between the SUP and ILWU concerned claims to loading and unloading work by sailors in the coastwise schooner trade and to ship-scaling work as part of vessel maintenance. The schooner issue was an old one, and in these years it provoked several local strikes and a number of arbitrations. Their result was further to inflame the hostility developing between the two unions after the 1937 maritime strike. The ship-scaling issue emerged in January, 1939, when the Dollar Line hired ILWU men for such work in San Francisco. Pickets from the SUP, MFOWW, and MMP appeared, and the company transferred the work to the SUP. The issue arose again in 1940 at San Francisco, this time with Lundeberg leading his sailors through an ILWU picket line, at the cost of a fractured jaw. There were other clashes of similar nature in this period.[62]

Unlike the ship-scaling controversy, the steam-schooner question stayed alive for some years to come. On June 30, 1946, it emerged in dramatic form at the lumber port of Coos Bay, Oregon. Earlier, the SUP had gained a contract with the American Pacific Steamship Company, originally a tanker line. Subsequently, the line entered the dry-cargo trade and agreed to extend SUP jurisdiction to include this work. These sailors engaged in loading and unloading operations and so competed with the longshoremen. Bridges challenged the SUP, by ordering his men not to load the SS *Mello Franco* at Coos Bay. In retaliation, Lundeberg struck all ships in the port. A prolonged tie-up followed. Arbitration later upheld the rights of the SUP, but the strike continued. In mid-November, 1946, Bridges capitulated when the SUP threatened to extend the strike to the entire coast.[63]

The schooner issue arose once more on the eve of the longshore

[61] *Ibid.*, pp. 269–272.
[62] *Ibid.*, pp. 276–278.
[63] *West Coast Sailors*, IX (Nov. 15, 1946), 1, 8.

settlement in 1948. The ILWU had asked for inclusion of a definition
of steam schooners in the agreement. Lundeberg immediately declared
that the sailors would strike to protect their jurisdictional rights
against possible infringement. Protective guarantees were undertaken
by the operators, and the issue was temporarily resolved, though the
underlying causes were by no means overcome.[64]

The MEBA and MMP. Two important issues divided the operators
and these two unions of the licensed personnel. One concerned preferential employment of their members, and the other, rotation of the
officers under a hiring hall system. Throughout the 1934–1948 period,
the Pacific Coast operators insisted strongly that these officers were
supervisory personnel and should be selected individually for permanent posts with the various lines. Except for the Alaska lines, the
companies were unwilling to concede more than sole bargaining rights
to the two unions. Instead, they clung to individual contracts with their
permanent officers. In November, 1946, the Atlantic and Gulf operators granted both unions a preferential shop, but the PASA group
continued to hold out.[65] After the 1948 strike, the PMA (successor to
PASA) compromised the issues. Regarding the MEBA, the operators
conceded a union shop in exchange for the unconditional right to
select chief and first assistant engineers. Engineers in junior classifications were to be supplied in rotation through the hall, but the operators retained the right to reject unqualified men and to retain preferred
men in continuous employment.[66]

In relations with the MMP, the operators retained the unconditional
right to select masters and chief officers, and granted that these men,
upon becoming union members, would have to maintain their membership in good standing as a condition of continued employment. All
nonmember officers were required to join the union within thirty days

[64] In September, 1948, the ILWU and MCS attempted unsuccessfully to tie up the SS
Rolando at Coos Bay, by picketing, though the line was not on strike. When the ship
subsequently arrived with a full load at San Pedro, her lines were cut, and a pitched battle
occurred between the sailors and longshoremen. She was unloaded the next day by the
sailors, under AFL and police protection. (*West Coast Sailors*, X [Sept. 17, 1948], 1–3;
[Dec. 10, 1948], 1, 3.)
[65] *Pacific Shipper*, vol. 21 (Nov. 4, 1946), 3–4; Joint Committee on Labor-Management
Relations, *op. cit.*, pp. 28–29.
[66] From a copy of the agreement between the PMA and MEBA (Nov. 1, 1951), p. 2.

after the signing of the contract. Officers below the rank of master or chief officer were now to be supplied by rotation through the hall, with the operators retaining rights of selection and of continuous employment of preferred men.[67] Thus the MMP obtained a union shop, but only a limited application of the principle of rotation.

● *The Significance of These Developments.*—This labyrinth of organizations and conflicts had implications of the highest importance for the economic performance of the Pacific Coast maritime shipping industry from 1934 onward. In sum, these developments reflected two harsh economic facts for the operators: extensive loss of control over costs and increasing inability to maintain scheduled services for shippers. Both facts adversely affected performance.

The rebirth of unionism involved the emergence of nine organizations. Some of these unions were strategically situated and possessed great power. Their memberships were fanatically loyal, their leaders militant and resourceful, and in some instances unusually hostile to management. The unions had achieved coastwide bargaining units, and strikes could now tie up almost all operations in the industry. Given nine aggressive unions, it was not surprising that the initial solidarity soon gave way to intense rivalry. Rivalry became most acute between the ILWU and the SUP. It was further inflamed by the ideological differences of their leaders and by repeated attempts of the ILA-ILWU to invade the SUP's jurisdiction.

Viewed as a whole and without neglect of management's own deficiencies, these factors created a difficult environment for the practice of successful collective bargaining. Obviously, management was required to undergo a radical change in its original concepts of labor relations, to accommodate itself to a completely different power structure. Inevitably this took much time and improvisation, not to mention an arduous process of learning.

Thus it was hardly surprising that the water lines found relatively little opportunity in these years to make notable improvements in technical operations or in the quality of services offered their customers.

---

[67] From a copy of the agreement between the PMA and MMP (Nov. 14, 1951), pp. 4–5. The American-Hawaiian Steamship Company, an intercoastal operator, and the Oliver Olson Line, a contract coastwise carrier, were not parties to the PMA agreement.

Much of management's time and energies were absorbed in a struggle to stabilize its labor relations. It had to adjust itself to the return of collective bargaining, and so found itself fighting to hold what it could of its former autonomy, developing more effective organizations and policies for dealing with the host of pressing new problems that were now presented. If its success in labor relations was not spectacular, at least in good part this was attributable to the difficult bargaining environment, much of which lay beyond effective managerial control.

Job-action strikes were formally adopted as a calculated tactic of the unions in 1935. Later, the SUP abandoned the tactic and developed a respect for its contracts. The ILA-ILWU continued to resort to job-action throughout the period, however, in spite of its contractual obligations. These strikes meant sailing and unloading delays, which undoubtedly cost much shipper good will. They also frequently meant the extortion of costly concessions from the operators. Given a union that was determined to use the tactic, there was little the industry could do to prevent it.

Jurisdictional strikes were less numerous, but in the postwar years their effects were very expensive to the firms surviving in the coastwise and intercoastal lumber trade. In this instance, too, the problem could not be overcome by management. It was a helpless bystander, a victim of conflict between two powerful unions.

Moreover, the reappearance of unionism meant loss to the employers of most of their former authority in the administration of personnel relations. This was inevitable with collective bargaining, and the change brought valuable benefits to the maritime workers: job security and grievance procedure. In time these gains might even have led to increased efficiency and productivity of labor, but in this case their immediate effect was to increase costs. Five important unions, including the ILWU and the SUP, gained what was in fact a closed shop coupled with a system of rotating work opportunities. There is a case for the closed shop and rotation in casual industries, but we shall not examine it here; we are concerned only with economic effects. The closed shop ended the employers' freedom to select men on the basis of competence. Rotation made it impossible for the individual operators to select and develop a force of permanent employees. They were now compelled to take the inefficient along with the efficient, unless the unions themselves coöperated to increase efficiency.

Furthermore, the employers on the docks lost the power to discipline the worker in the interests of efficient operations. They were no longer free to eliminate the incompetent and the recalcitrant, to select and to retain the better qualified men. In itself, the employers' loss of disciplinary authority might not have been important, given respect for contractual obligations and recognition of the legitimate economic interests of the operators. In the case of the very powerful ILA-ILWU, however, these were lacking, and there was little that the employers could do to change the situation.

Finally, one of the outstanding elements of management's labor relations problem was the emergence of the ILA-ILWU as a very powerful union with a leadership that was deeply and bitterly hostile toward management. That hostility was not concealed. Indeed, the leaders of the union cultivated and exploited it for their own ends. From the record, it is evident that it represented more than the conventional antagonisms of the bargaining table. As it actually found expression, it revealed contempt for contractual obligations, indifference to and probably contempt for the economic interests of the employers and of the industry itself, and a determination to use the union as the vehicle for purposes well beyond collective bargaining in its familiar sense. Whatever may have been the justice of the longshoremen's original grievances, it was soon made clear that their leaders had acquired a vested interest in continued conflict, without regard to its costs. They had institutionalized hostility, to make it a political asset.

CHAPTER XI

Underlying Causes of Conflict

IN THE last two chapters, we presented a brief history of labor-management relations in the Pacific Coast maritime shipping industry between 1930 and 1948. It is a story of deep and extreme conflict.

Why were there nearly fourteen hundred strikes? Why were the five coastwide tie-ups so prolonged? Why were employers and employees alike so uncompromising? Why did collective bargaining fail to bring peace and mutual acceptance to *all* the unions and employers? Why were the intervals between major strikes frequently characterized by guerrilla warfare, instead of harmonious relations? What primarily covert forces lay back of the overt forms of conflict?

There are no simple answers to these questions. The underlying causes of conflict were complex and interrelated. Four of them stand out in the record: historical circumstance, ideologies and attitudes, union rivalries, and economic pressure. What role did each play in the bitter conflict during these years?[1]

● *Historical Circumstance.—Introduction.* In any industry, the process of collective bargaining will be shaped in part by the setting in

---

[1] Others have also considered this problem: the Joint Committee on Labor-Management Relations of the 80th Congress; Paul Eliel; Clark Kerr and Lloyd Fisher. We have drawn valuable suggestions from their publications, which are cited in chap. ix, p. 175, n. 1.

which the bargaining takes place. Peace or conflict, in their many possible variants, will depend not alone upon the goals of the bargaining groups, but also upon the strategies they employ in the pursuit of these goals.[2] In turn, goals and strategies themselves are powerfully influenced by the particular environment and its history. Historical circumstance embraces the experience of the people in the industry, as workers and union members, as union leaders, and as employers. Through experience, men come to formulate their problems and objectives, and to derive their conceptions of their opponents. For Pacific Coast maritime shipping, the historical setting is highly important to an explanation of the fifteen years of strife between 1934 and 1948.

The system of casual labor. Longshoring and seafaring work is casual. The term of employment is often short and the men shift from employer to employer. The demand for men fluctuates widely. Casual work attracts men who prefer the freedom involved. It also tends to preclude the development of loyalties between the men and their employers. The very fluidity of the market forbids it. The employers themselves in the years before 1934 showed but limited interest in building a stable and loyal force. Instead, they used the casual market to their utmost advantage. Bred to an intensely individualistic and competitive tradition, the operators gave no quarter and treated their men accordingly.

Yet there was an exception: the employers did attempt to develop a relatively large group of "steady" longshoremen and a regular corps of licensed officers. The result was a division of the labor market into first- and second-class members. The second-class group probably formed the majority. In their ranks were gathered the militants, the floaters and drifters, the part-timers, and the down-and-outers. They drew the leavings, suffered the vices of the casual system, and grew to hate it.

Here were all the ingredients for rank-and-file revolt and militant unionism: a body of workers who were natural radicals and a tough-minded group of employers fighting to survive in a shrinking and unstable market. Five years of depression made the mixture explosive.

---

[2] Frederick H. Harbison and John R. Coleman, *Goals and Strategy in Collective Bargaining* (New York, Harper, 1951).

Once the unions had reappeared, it was inevitable that they would capture the unattached loyalties of the men. With their early great successes, the unions turned these loyalties into a fanatical kind of fighting morale. The men came to identify all of their interests with the unions. Any differences with the employers could be and were construed as attempts to destroy the unions. And partly to make sure that the employers could not capture the loyalties of the men, the unions extended the rotation principle as rapidly and extensively as possible. "Steady" jobs and monthly employees were largely abolished. Although the labor market was now closed to floaters, in another sense casualization was actually increased by the elimination of the old distinction between first- and second-class members.

As a result, the unions became a peculiar kind of labor contractor. By veto power over the registration of new members, they acquired a monopoly control over labor supply. By control of rotation, they actually controlled all work opportunities. In a nontechnical sense, the unions now really "owned" the jobs and assigned them to the men. The unions therefore contracted with the employers and arranged to carry out the work. The men were made completely dependent upon the unions, and under rotation they could form no permanent attachments to a particular employer. In the case of the ILWU, even disciplinary functions and the direction of gangs became prerogatives of the union. In all these ways the unions and their leaders in particular gained power far beyond that characteristic of most industries.[3] Much depended upon how those leaders exercised that power.

The influence of history. Between 1919 and 1921, the important unions were broken in an open-shop drive. In the years that followed, the men lost all organized protection of their interests. Here was an industry with an aggressively individualistic tradition, subject to the relentless competitive pressures of shrinking markets. The results were large cuts in wages, longer hours, and worsened conditions. Men were black-listed for union activity. Favoritism, extremely unequal treatment, and the speedup became the rule. In their fifteen-year develop-

---

[3] The MMP and MEBA were exceptions. These men are supervisory in status, and the operators succeeded in preserving some measure of individual contracting and in staving off rotation up to 1948.

ment, these policies thoroughly alienated the men from the employers, making them perfect material for militant, and at times even irresponsible, unionism. From 1934 onward, a union leader could close ranks and strengthen his own position on any matter simply by citing the employers' past record.

In essence, this past record provided powerful, practical support for the view that the interests of the employers and those of the men were deeply opposed. Even where labor-management relations are friendly and constructive, some such opposition of interests will exist, if only because in any labor contract one party is buyer and the other is seller. To admit this is elementary wisdom and requires no acceptance of the Marxian thesis of class struggle, or no denial of the principle that labor and management also have basic interests in common.[4] In this case, the maritime labor markets on the Pacific Coast during 1919–1934 were largely casual. They were highly competitive on the labor supply side. On the demand side, they were subject to the ruthless pressures of a shrinking industry. In such a context, the labor policies of the employers stressed to an extreme degree this opposition of interests. This provided unusual support for the doctrine of class conflict and a valuable propaganda weapon for certain of the union leaders.

Then came the events of the year 1934. With appropriate exploitation for class war purposes, those events acquired great symbolic importance for the period that followed. The setting was one of extreme depression, severe suffering of nearly five years' duration, and badly strained loyalties toward the enterprise system. Unionism offered a method of practical action and so became a symbol of hope for better times. In turn, the 1934 strike afforded a means of venting long pent-up grievances and a way to redress the balance of interests. At this stage, the unions were fighting against strong odds for the right to exist. Ranged against them were well-organized employers, the press, and at a critical point, the power of government. Violence occurred, and in the "Battle of Rincon Hill" two longshoremen were killed in a melee with the police.

---

[4] Even in a socialized enterprise the interests of management and of the workers are opposed at certain points, in essence similar to those in capitalistic enterprise.

This episode and its surrounding setting gave dramatic emphasis to the clash of interests. Once more, the differences could be propagandized as class war, and for years afterward hatred of the employers could be kept alive.[5] With this shrewd exploitation of the facts, the ILWU leaders could and did succeed in polarizing the positions of the union and the WEPC. For fifteen years, war was the normal state, and collective bargaining merely a form of combat.

Inevitably, the employers responded in kind. Until the 1937 settlements, it is likely that they continued to cherish hopes of dislodging the unions. Even after 1937, their hostility at least to the ILWU and MCS continued to be evident. Rather than take the admittedly risky gamble of unreserved acceptance of these two unions, they chose the course of formalism and legalism in contracts, and devious tactics to meet the wily moves of the Bridges group. Relationships were thus poisoned with mutual distrust and scarcely concealed hatred.

Peculiarities of the bargaining system. The bargaining pattern itself may well have contributed to bad relations and open conflict. The spirit of mutual distrust and dislike inevitably led the ILWU and WEPC to make their contracts bulky and complex legal documents, intended to cover all conceivable possibilities and to fix firmly the rights and obligations of each party. Collective bargaining can be a technique for living together, in which the contract expresses the basic intent to do so, and direct and frequent contact between the parties serves to make the contract work. Or collective bargaining can be a state of war, and the contract at best a kind of mutually repugnant cease-fire agreement. Direct relations then will be unsatisfactory, and each side will take refuge in the contract in the ensuing conflict. This was what happened from 1934 to 1948.

Arbitration played a peculiar role from the start, so far as the ILWU and WEPC were concerned. Relations were so bad at the beginning that the first contract itself was imposed by arbitration. This contract prescribed the *modus vivendi* for the next several years. Yet its terms

---

[5] The ILWU leaders termed this incident "Bloody Thursday" and began their exploitation of it with a well-publicized funeral procession. For fourteen years thereafter, ILWU locals up and down the coast held annual stop-work meetings to "commemorate" the event, and incidentally to keep class feeling tense.

were imposed rather than bargained out, a fact basic to the whole period, for often these terms were less the product of mutual accept- ance than of external constraint. This had an important consequence. It led to further arbitration of the provisions of the original contract. In essence, amendment by arbitration, rather than by genuine bargain- ing, became the main method of changing the contract. Again, the method was external constraint. In this spirit of distrust, legalism, and compulsion, mature bargaining simply could not germinate, let alone flourish.

Then the bargaining system itself acted as a kind of barrier to good relations, particularly in the longshore part of the industry. As Eliel has noted, the system really involved long-distance bargaining, in several senses.[6] The stevedore employer for whom the longshoreman works is actually a kind of labor contractor who usually serves an ultimate employer, the steamship company. These stevedoring firms in turn were organized into port associations, and the individual port associations themselves were combined in a coastwide organization— the WEPC until 1949, and thereafter the PMA. Given the rotation system and this complex form of management representation, the men could not become permanent employees of a single employer, and the union itself could not deal directly with the single employer in basic bargaining. Instead, the system was of necessity impersonal, indirect, and bureaucratic. And it was made all the more so by its coastwide structure. The coastwide contracts themselves made necessary a long- distance system of representation, negotiation, and administration on both sides. They also created the difficult problem of uniformity versus local differences.[7]

In consequence, the peculiar nature of the bargaining system largely thwarted the constructive possibilities of direct bargaining and com-

---

[6] Eliel, "Industrial peace and conflict: a study of two Pacific Coast industries," pp. 490– 495.

[7] Thus the ILWU and WEPC shifted back and forth between decentralized and cen- tralized arbitration of local issues, torn between the desire for prompt settlement and an urge for uniformity under central coastwide control.

With the emergence of the PASA as the management association for the offshore and intercoastal steamship operators, representative bargaining became characteristic of this part of the industry as well. The SAPC performed a similar role in the coasting trade.

munication between a given union and a single employer. Instead, the basic relationship was indirect. It was conducted by intermediaries, acting through a complex system of representation and circumscribed (especially in the longshore case) by elaborate contracts, awards, and understandings.

On the management side, the association officials had the task of negotiating and administering contracts for their employer constituents. At times, however, they seem to have lacked adequate authority for executing those basic responsibilities. Instead, their hands were often tied by a large and frequently divided group of operators. This cumbersome system precluded prompt and clear settlements. Inevitably, it bred distrust and want of understanding, needlessly exacerbating existing differences.

We conclude, therefore, that the historical and institutional setting of the industry has been, and may well continue to be, an important cause of labor-management conflict; but that setting in essentials was not unique to Pacific Coast shipping. Other industries have also initiated collective bargaining against a background of the open shop, casual labor markets, depression, and violent conflict. Yet they were able ultimately to reach a genuine *modus vivendi.* Why was this largely not true of maritime shipping? Clearly, because additional causes of conflict stultified in great part the growth of mature bargaining relations.

● *Ideologies and Attitudes.—Introduction.* Peace or conflict in union-management relations turns upon more than historical background, institutions, or bargaining systems. It also depends upon the ideologies and attitudes of the leaders participating in the bargaining process. By "ideology" we mean the system of guiding ideas or principles by which each side defines and conceives the bargaining relationship, interprets the actions and aims of the other side, and formulates its own objectives and tactics. By "attitude" we have in mind the emotional temper, the bearing, or feelings expressed by the bargainers toward each other.

Quite clearly, ideology influences the attitude taken. An ideology premised upon irreconcilable conflict, for example, will invoke an attitude of calculated and devious hostility. The relationship between the parties will be limited to "bargaining" as such, with bargaining a synonym for conflict and no more. No real meeting of minds can occur. Relations will exhibit intransigence, distrust, and guile. The controlling purpose will not be to find an area of agreement, but to gain the advantage. The emotional posture will of necessity be hostile—now open, now artfully concealed. Usually, such an attitude will induce or reinforce a similar pattern of behavior by the opposite party. Only rarely does the other side deliberately refuse the gauge of battle, and instead attempt to convert its opponents by unwonted affection to a philosophy of mutual survival.

Past experience may also influence the ideologies adopted and the attitudes derived. Coupled with bad economic conditions, employer indifference or hostility to the welfare of employees lends plausible support to a philosophy of irreconcilable interests. By a kind of selection, union leaders will emerge who stress conflict and who fix this conception in the minds of the rank and file. Each successive hostile act of the employer then reinforces the union's ideology of conflict. Also important, union leaders who come to power in this environment may well acquire a vested interest in the perpetuation of conflict.

What, then, was the influence of ideologies and attitudes upon conflict in Pacific Coast shipping? To answer the question, we shall begin with the employers, since their policies between 1919 and 1934 were crucial in shaping the response of the unions in the latter critical year.

The employers. Beyond doubt, the employers followed an open-shop policy after 1919. This policy was initiated with the destruction of the previous collective bargaining system. It rested upon deliberate warfare against independent unionism and a marked affection for an extreme version of the philosophy of individual self-reliance—as applied to labor. Its aim was power to determine the labor contract, and so to administer labor relations, unchecked by the restraints of independent unionism. It called for deep hostility toward any manifestations of unionism. As we have shown, the system led to a division of the labor market into two parts: a group of "steady" employees whose loyalties as individuals were strongly cultivated; and a larger group of "casuals" whose services were viewed primarily if not exclusively as a commodity.

Like unionism, the open shop is a philosophy of power—power over the determination of the contents of the employer-employee relationship, so far as possible within the limits of a free labor market. As a philosophy, the open shop was peculiarly consistent with the tough individualism of the maritime tradition. In active expression this doctrine viewed the union as a natural enemy and gave rise to policies consistent with this conception. With the reappearance of unionism, conflict was inevitable. Initially, at least, collective bargaining could hardly flourish in this environment.

This was the central fact in the background of 1934. So far as the employers were concerned, the revival of independent unionism was a challenge to their power. They attempted to meet that challenge, and in the end collective bargaining was imposed upon them from the outside—by arbitration. The open-shop philosophy was not thereby destroyed. It died hard, and for some of the employers, indeed, may never have really died at all.

By 1937, however, the power of the employers was completely broken by the unlicensed unions. A tremendous shift of power had taken place. By practical unilateral control of the hiring halls, these unions could now call the turn. The employers were in their grip. They had largely lost their powers of selection and discipline. Even their authority to direct operations was crippled in essential respects. To deal effectively with the extreme power of the unions, the individual operators themselves were now compelled to surrender most of their remaining "sovereignty" to multiple-employer bargaining associations.

It could hardly be said that even by 1937 the open-shop philosophy had ceased to exist. Yet there is ample reason to believe that by that time the associations and many of the employers as well had resigned themselves, formally at least, to acceptance of unionism and collective bargaining. Hostile attitudes no doubt remained to complicate the new relationships, for it is hard to change men's minds, particularly when their power is at stake. Still, from 1937 onward, the emphasis clearly was aimed at shaping the contracts rather than at destruction of the unions themselves.

At this point, much depended upon how the unions would use their new-found power. The situation had reached a critical juncture. Between 1934 and 1937, attitudes on both sides had remained basically hostile, and the prevailing philosophies were essentially ones of irreconcilable conflict. The unions had frankly embraced the tactic of the outlaw strike. The employers had fought back with the lockout. For the union, arbitration was a weapon of conflict; for the employers, it was the only means of "springing ships loose." In this atmosphere, mutual distrust and dislike were obvious.

Defeat in 1937, however, had placed the employers in the uncomfortable predicament of having to learn to live with some very formidable unions. There is evidence that they were at last ready to make the attempt. If the unions were to respond in kind, a *modus vivendi* was possible. If not, the growth of collective bargaining would be stunted from birth, to remain simply a form of continuing warfare.

It is here that a polarization of the unions became determinative for the employers. Many factors made for this split within the union group, some of them quite fortuitous. Bridges and Lundeberg had fallen out, the SUP was engaged in jurisdictional warfare with the ILWU and NMU, and the AFL and CIO had become bitter rivals in an attempt to gain the adherence of the maritime unions. In any event, the SUP from 1937 onward abandoned its syndicalist tactics against the employers, to become a conservative business union of the traditional AFL type. In contrast, the ILWU maintained what was in fact an ideology of class warfare and stayed hostile from the leaders down.

In consequence, the employers and the SUP group of unions gradually developed a mature system of relations. Not that they ever moved all the way to the idyllic stage of union-management coöperation. Rather, they came to respect one another's interests, and so to live together without continuous conflict. In short, the SUP group responded favorably to the change in the employers' outlook in 1937, and thereafter ideology and attitude lost their force as factors making for conflict, so far as these groups were concerned.[8]

---

[8] Three episodes suggest that the employers knew what they were doing. In the 1936–1937 strike, they succeeded in reaching a separate settlement with the SUP—opening the road to a general settlement. In June, 1946, they again settled separately with the SUP in

With the ILWU and MCS, the situation was radically different. By 1937, the union front had been broken at last, but the ILWU and MCS continued as a hard core of implacable opposition. Apparently, the employers' ideology respecting ILWU relations was now no longer a matter of the open shop and what Bridges inveterately called "union-busting." Given the SUP precedent, it appears that the employers had finally accepted unionism and the hiring hall for the longshoremen, but completely distrusted and disliked the Bridges leadership. If that leadership could not be removed, then strategy required that it be hedged in by contract. Thus emerged the curious legalism and formalism of the employers' approach, of which complex contracts and frequent dependence upon arbitration were the natural products. Needless to add, the employers' attitudes in bargaining relations were hostile, suspicious, and artful.[9]

This kind of management-union relationship was tenuous at best, almost inevitably fated to lead to a critical showdown. With the war, the crisis was deferred. With Russia's entry, the ILWU leaders became as eager for peace and production as were the employers, but for quite different reasons. Then, with the passage of the Taft-Hartley law in 1947, the employers may have seen an opportunity to expose the Bridges leadership, and perhaps to eliminate it. The attempt was made in 1948, and failed. Shifting to the "new look," the employers changed their bargaining representatives and turned to an extreme type of conciliation. This continued to be their attitude toward the ILWU to the end of our account. Perhaps purely for tactical reasons, the union responded in kind, and though the ultimate philosophies of both sides may well remain deeply opposed, this ideological opposition has for the time being ceased to figure as an immediate factor in conflict.

The unions. Although there were nine unions in the industry during these years, only two were real leaders—the ILWU and the SUP. The remainder were either satellites or allies, or minor independents. And because the ILWU and SUP by their vigorous leadership largely

---

direct bargaining—on terms more favorable than Bridges had obtained with the help of government intervention. In April, 1948, PASA reached long-term agreements with the SUP and MMP, providing wage increases and resolving the hiring hall problem of the SUP without a strike.

[9] Eliel makes the same point. "Industrial peace and conflict . . . ," p. 496.

shaped and expressed the patterns of behavior of all the unions, we shall center attention upon them.

The ranks of the reborn maritime unions of 1934 were made up of bitterly discontented men. In part, their attitude was the direct product of their experience under the open shop. In part, too, it was a natural expression of the native syndicalism of casual workers everywhere. In any event, here was the raw material for a militant kind of unionism, indispensable for the protracted and uncompromising struggle that lay ahead. It was natural, too, for an explosive situation of this kind to produce new and radically minded rank-and-file leaders. Harry Bridges met these specifications to the full. So also did Harry Lundeberg, though his rise to prominence was not to occur until over a year later.

There is warrant for saying that the times make the leaders. Yet it is equally true that leaders can and do mold events. Bridges and Lundeberg rose to leadership in difficult times. In large part, their policies were wholly consistent with the orthodox aims and practices of practical trade unionism, given an extremely difficult setting. Consider those policies: joint strike action against recalcitrant employers to gain recognition and collective bargaining; control of the hiring hall as the basis of union security; and multiple-employer bargaining to cover the entire product and labor markets, to give the unions maximum power. In all respects these ideas were those of the most conservative "business" unions—for example, the construction trades. If there were differences, they lay in the uncompromising militancy invoked by the special problem of creating a durable unionism in an extremely hostile and difficult environment.

The events of 1934–1937, however, suggest strongly that something more was at work to guide the actions of these two men than merely the pragmatism of pure and simple unionism, and it is this missing element that requires explanation. From the nature of the case, the explanation must be tentative, because the evidence is inherently circumstantial. Moreover, the case of Lundeberg was at all times markedly different from that of Bridges, and in justice to both men this should be pointed out at the start.

There is no doubt that in these early years both men were radicals in their economic views. In 1934, they shared a common, complete dislike of the employers. At the time, each apparently adhered to a point of view that looked to the eventual disappearance of the employers as a class. Thus the leadership that they initially supplied to a discontented and rebellious rank and file probably rested upon an unusual combination of short- and long-range objectives. For the short run, the purpose was the formation of powerful trade unions for orthodox bargaining objectives. In this respect, both men could be interpreted as aggressive trade unionists in the typical American style—epitomized by the names of Gompers, Furuseth, or Lewis. For the long run, however, the aim was a society without private employers. Here Lundeberg and Bridges could be classed as unorthodox—in the tradition of Eugene V. Debs.

On this interpretation, there was no necessary clash between the short- and long-run objectives during 1934–1937. The environment fitted well with the doctrine of irreconcilable interests between employers and employees, from the point of view of both orthodox trade unionism and longer-range objectives. However, once the unions had gained the security required for effective bargaining—which they did by 1937—the thesis of irreconcilable conflict clashed with the principles of pragmatic unionism. The reason is clear: pragmatic unionism does not aim at the destruction of the private employer. Indeed, it cannot exist without him.

At the outset, both Lundeberg and Bridges were identified with philosophies of class conflict. Yet the evidence indicates clear differences in their doctrinal orientations. To the extent that Lundeberg's views in 1934–1937 are known and admit of philosophical interpretation, they exhibit the typical qualities of late nineteenth-century syndicalism. According to formal syndicalist teaching, the working class and the employing class have nothing in common. Conflict between unions and management is inevitable and ineradicable. To resolve this conflict and to satisfy fully the workers' interests, it is necessary to build a coöperative society whose industries will be managed by trade-union syndicates, free of state coercion. To achieve this world, workers must first build militant and powerful trade unions, in preparation for a new kind of economic society. Very likely, Lundeberg never formulated his apparent early syndicalist leanings in these rather elaborate terms. In practice, however, his actions between 1934 and 1937 were consistent with the initial tactics required by the syndicalist program.

For the entire period of 1934–1948, Bridges' policies and activities suggest the influence of a quite different kind of guiding philosophy. In his case, the evidence is much more abundant. What it suggests is that Bridges was a Marxian, rather than a syndicalist, though the distinction is somewhat more difficult to establish for the very early years, because both philosophies then called for substantially the same type of initial trade-union program.

The Marxian philosophy, too, affirms an irreconcilable conflict between the two classes and also premises an ultimate collectivist society. This society also is to be coöperative and in final form to be free of state coercion. Yet the Marxian method differs radically from the syndicalist. Although it regards trade unionism as a fertile field in which to cultivate class consciousness and warfare, it relies primarily upon the leadership of a political party built around a central core of professional revolutionists. Instead of a quick transition by a climactic general strike, Marxism contemplates the attainment of political power by the party, followed by the imposition of a ruthless but "temporary" dictatorship. Later this dictatorship is supposed to "wither away." We do not know, of course, the extent to which Bridges accepted this doctrine. It is clear, however, that his actions throughout the period were at all times consistent with the "preparatory" stages of the Marxian program, as we shall develop more fully at a later point.

Essentially, the difference between the two ideologies lies in their ultimate conceptions of unionism—a difference that provides an adequate explanation of the divergent evolutions of the SUP and ILWU during 1937–1948. Syndicalism views the union as both the means and the end of the historical process. Marxism accepts the union as an important means, but only as one. Under Marxism, leadership belongs instead to the party; and the party, not the union, is to take power. This distinction is of vital importance, because it reveals a basic difference of loyalties. For the syndicalist, the union is his primary loyalty. For the Marxist, it is the party, and if the interests of the party and those of the union should happen to clash, the union's interests must be sacrificed.

Harry Lundeberg came to power as a rank-and-file worker with a syndicalist orientation. The responsibilities of power seem to have wrought a basic change in his outlook, a not unusual development in history. By 1937, he faced a fundamental choice. Either he could continue with a trade-union policy that was implacably hostile to the employers, as was typified by his earlier affiliation with the job-action program of the MFP. Or, having gained complete security for his union, he could shift to pragmatic trade unionism and so concede permanent existence to the private employer. The drastic changes in SUP policies from 1937 onward suggest strongly that he chose the latter course. The SUP was rapidly transformed into a disciplined and centrally controlled organization, whose whole program was now premised upon mutual survival. Thus emerged the characteristics of orthodox trade unionism: tough bargaining, scrupulous respect for contracts, rigorous internal discipline. With this change, ideology ceased to be a factor in conflict so far as the SUP's relations with the employers were concerned.

From the time of Bridges' original emergence as the real leader of the Pacific Coast longshoremen in 1934 down to the end of 1948, the record shows no evolution comparable to that of the SUP. Rather, it is a record of deep-seated, persistent, and relentless hostility to the maritime employers far beyond that engendered by conventional differences in bargaining objectives. It was a hostility rooted in contempt for contracts and disregard for those economic needs of employers ordinarily conceded by pragmatic trade unionists. For these policies, Bridges and his associates bear full responsibility. From 1937 onward, they had the power and the opportunity to develop a responsible type of unionism. This they clearly failed to do.

We do not assert that Bridges was, or is, a member of the Communist party. However, it has been said by an investigating committee of the CIO and also by others that Bridges and his colleagues during these years consistently followed the complex and twisted tactical line of the Communist party and adapted the policies of the longshoremen's union accordingly. For this the evidence is very persuasive and worth recounting, for it has a direct bearing upon the problem of continuing conflict in the Pacific Coast maritime shipping industry.

Between 1934 and 1937, Bridges' activities indicated a threefold program. (1) He began by gaining control of the old ILA on the Pacific Coast, and then attempted to extend that control over the other crafts, looking eventually to the formation of a single maritime industrial union under his leadership. The Joint Marine Strike Committee of 1934 and the Maritime Federation of the Pacific of 1935 were the initial results. In the ensuing conflict over centralization of power in the MFP, Bridges favored centralization and Lundeberg opposed it. As we noted in chapter viii, Bridges in this period drew published support from the Communist press, while Lundeberg was severely attacked. (2) Bridges sought to destroy any remaining loyalty of the longshoremen toward their employers and to monopolize that loyalty for the union. At the time, this also was Communist doctrine, and it far exceeded anything required for the existence of the hiring hall and rotation system as such. (3) Bridges succeeded in detaching the Pacific Coast ILA from the AFL in 1936 and in affiliating it with the new CIO, at a time when the leaders of the latter body were actively coöperating with Communists, and when the line of the Communist party called for unequivocal support of the CIO and industrial unionism.[10]

Though these early activities constitute strong evidence of parallel-

---

[10] On May 14, 1937, Bridges is reported to have made the following statement in a speech at the University of Washington Luncheon Club:

"We take the stand that we, as workers, have nothing in common with the employers. We are in a class struggle and we subscribe to the belief that if the employer is not in business his products still will be necessary and we will be providing them when there is no employing class. We frankly believe that day is coming.

"We use politicians as long as they benefit the labor movement and when they don't, we fight them."

Joint Committee on Labor-Management Relations, *Labor-Management Relations: West Coast Maritime Industry*, p. 59. For other evidence concerning Bridges' position at this time, see Ralph Chaplin, *Wobbly* (Chicago, University of Chicago Press, 1948), pp. 376–389.

ism between the actions of the ILA-ILWU leadership and the Communist line, between 1937 and 1948 that parallelism is even more impressive.[11] Until 1939, the Communist party line called for collective security against Hitler, and the ILWU press went right along. With the Nazi-Soviet pact of 1939, the line changed to opposition to "imperialist war," and the ILWU publications and officials took the same position. With the attack on Russia in June, 1941, the conflict became a "people's war," with all-out aid to the Soviet Union and the second front as imperatives. Again the ILWU leadership fell completely into line, now proposing maximum efficiency in longshore operations and an unconditional no-strike policy. When the war with Germany was about over, the Communist party line shifted once more—away from "Browderism" and back to "imperialism and class war." Again the ILWU fell into line. During 1947–1949, the union publications opposed the Greek-Turkish Aid Program, the European Recovery Program, and the North Atlantic Treaty Organization. By contrast, the union favored the USSR, termed its satellites "democracies," upheld the Berlin blockade, and backed Henry Wallace and the Progressive party.

Taking these singular facts of parallelism into account, together with direct testimony of ex-Communists that Bridges had participated in numerous secret Communist meetings, a special investigating committee of the CIO concluded:

... That the policies and activities of the International Longshoremen's and Warehousemen's Union, under the leadership of its international officers and executive board, have long been and are today directed toward the achievement of the program and policies of the Communist Party rather than the objectives set forth in the constitution of the CIO.[12]

---

[11] For this period, we rely mainly upon the report of an executive board committee of the CIO, appointed by President Philip Murray late in 1949 to consider charges that the ILWU was Communist-oriented in its policies. See *Communist Domination of Certain Unions*, Report of the Subcommittee on Labor and Labor-Management Relations, Committee on Labor and Public Welfare, United States Senate, 82d Cong., 1st sess., S. Doc. 89 (Washington, Government Printing Office, 1951), pp. 83–96. See also an exchange of letters between Bridges and Father Charles Rice, appearing in *West Coast Sailors*, X (Sept. 3, 1948), 8. As the CIO committee found, a study of the ILWU *Dispatcher* over these years also proves highly instructive regarding parallelism between the Communist position and that of the ILWU.

[12] *Communist Domination of Certain Unions*, p. 83. In no instance could the CIO com-

Given this finding, the very extensive array of evidence to support it, and the marked absence of facts to contradict it, what is its significance for labor relations involving the ILA-ILWU during 1934–1948?

The answer lies in the nature of Communist philosophy. Communism is an explicit program for the destruction of the capitalistic employer. This destruction is to be accomplished by class warfare, aimed ultimately at the conquest of political power and the imposition of a party dictatorship. In its preparatory phase, the program calls for unreserved support of the government of Soviet Russia and open or covert hostility to all governments not controlled by the Russian dictatorship.[13]

The result is a peculiar kind of unionism. On the surface it has many of the features of orthodox unionism, suggesting superficially that it too is guided by a concept of bargaining struggle rather than class struggle. Yet in ultimate aims, underlying policies, day-to-day tactics and attitudes of the leaders, Communist-oriented unionism is basically hostile—to independent unions, to the employer, to the public, and to the American government. Its aim is the destruction of the capitalistic system and of all associations and institutions not under its direct control. Consequently, in its trade union aspect it never develops a bargaining relationship based upon mutual survival.

The facts suggest clearly that ILA-ILWU policy was oriented to a pro-Communist ideology throughout the period under study. With this hypothesis there may be found the explanation of many things: the polarization of the maritime unions after 1937 into two antagonistic groups; the continued use of the outlaw strike by the ILWU for fifteen years; the indifference of the ILWU toward the problem of declining longshore productivity save for the years when the USSR was at war; and the attitude of chicane, distrust, and even hatred displayed by the ILWU officials toward the employers until the settlement of 1948. Plainly, between the ILWU and the WEPC there existed an unbridgeable gulf, an irreconcilable opposition, and an irrepressible conflict.

---

mittee find a clash between the position of the Communist party and that of the ILWU. *Ibid.*, p. 92. The CIO expelled the ILWU and MCS in the spring of 1950.

[13] Whenever the Soviet government requires the support of certain non-Communist states—as in 1934–1939 or 1941–1945—expediency may call for tactical concessions and a veiling of this basic hostility. The hostility, however, is always there.

It is true that the employers played into Bridges' hands. Their original policies invoked the early militant unionism and provided surface plausibility for a doctrine of class conflict. By 1937, however, the ILWU was secure from dislodgment by employer attack, and it then became possible for the ILWU to shift to a program of responsible unionism, as the SUP actually did. The failure of the ILWU leaders to do so may well be attributed to their confirmed adherence to a long-run ideology that was incompatible with orthodox trade unionism. The employers sensed this deep-seated hostility, and they too resorted to devious tactics, making no secret of their distrust of the Bridges leadership. But these were more the employers' response to the situation after 1937 than they were an initiating cause. Until the end of 1948, therefore, the ILWU-WEPC relationship continued to be one of deeply rooted conflict.

Does the so-called "new look" alter the situation? Does it prove that the troubles with the ILWU group between 1934 and 1948 could, after all, be explained more simply as the product of employer antagonism and intransigence? Were these troubles merely a matter of conventional trade unionism struggling against hostile management, uncomplicated by Marxian ideology?

We do not think so. All that the "new look" program really proves is that peace of a kind can be obtained at the price of appeasement. On the ILWU side, the heavy losses sustained by the longshoremen themselves, who were and are mostly non-Communist, in three costly coastwide strikes after the war may well have compelled Bridges to make what might be only a temporary tactical retreat, before renewing the offensive. Tactical retreats without sacrifice of ultimate aims are perfectly compatible with Marxist doctrine. Indeed, in this instance retreat was made all the easier by the broad concessions of the employers. Yet, deliberately continued conciliation by the employers—if they can afford it—might succeed in convincing the longshoremen that they are acting in good faith. If so, the ILWU leaders might then find themselves isolated from their membership, and perhaps even eliminated from office. That is for time to determine.

● *Union Rivalries.*—Pacific Coast maritime shipping has suffered se-

verely from rival unionism. In part, this rivalry was the direct result
of craft unionism. With the revival of unionism in 1934, eight organizations claimed bargaining rights—seven on the ships and one on
shore. It was inevitable that competition for leadership and prestige
would develop, particularly among the stronger groups such as the
ILWU (then ILA) and SUP. After all, craft unions are notoriously
jealous of their preserves, and their leaders extremely sensitive to
charges that their rivals have obtained more for their members.

An already highly competitive union structure was made all the
more so by attempts of outside unions to encroach upon well-guarded
territories. The leading example was the National Maritime Union, an
organization that consolidated the three unlicensed departments on
shipboard, and so threatened the SUP, the MFOWW, and the MCS.
Then, on an even broader front, rivalry was intensified by conflict
between the AFL and CIO from 1937 onward. This conflict took place
on two levels. First, the CIO attempted to raid the AFL, to get certain
of the latter's affiliates to shift allegiance to the new federation. As a
result, the Pacific Coast ILA became the ILWU and, with the MCS,
joined the CIO. Second, the AFL fought back, by inducing the SUP
to rejoin its ranks, and by creating the Seafarers' International Union
under SUP control—to fight against the CIO's NMU on the Atlantic
and Gulf coasts and on the Great Lakes. Then, as the situation developed, the AFL and CIO maritime unions on the Pacific Coast split
into two camps, fighting not only for jurisdictional advantage but for
triumphs over the operators in the battle for prestige.

During this period, the more powerful crafts in particular faced a
situation parallel to that confronting business competitors in a market
in which the sellers are few and the size of each is great. There are
three choices open: to live and let live in tacit or explicit coöperation,
to go it alone, or to attempt to exterminate the rivals. In 1934, when
craft rivalries had hardly asserted themselves, joint action was the
only practicable course, and it was followed. Joint action survived
until the 1937 settlement. It then gave way to internecine warfare, with
the ILWU and SUP as the centers of two polarized factions, each with
its allies. The two smaller independents—the MFOWW and the

MEBA—attempted to go it alone, now playing one side, now the other.

During 1934–1948 as a whole, union rivalry expressed itself in three forms. One was jurisdictional conflict. Here the issues concerned control of specific work and the right to represent the workers involved for purposes of collective bargaining. Controversy of this kind involved raids of existing "territories" and conflicts in the efforts to expand existing territories. The long-standing efforts of the ILWU to raid the SUP's steam-schooner jurisdiction is an example of the former. The fight between the SUP and NMU to organize the Pacific Coast tanker lines is an instance of the latter.

Second, union rivalry also took a political form, showing itself in several ways. Most important, the SUP and ILWU groups fought for prestige among the rank and file in winning the largest settlements. Connected with this conflict was the running battle between the two groups in 1946 over federal intervention. The ILWU group sought federal aid in achieving a desired pattern and in imposing its terms upon the SUP group. In contrast, the SUP group opposed government interference, and vigorously pursued an independent strategy.

Third, bitter personal rivalry developed between Bridges and Lundeberg from 1936 onward. In part, this conflict emerged because each was a strong personality, in command of a strategically situated union composed of intensely loyal members. In part, also, the conflict reflected a division of institutional interests. Each craft prized its jurisdiction and its freedom of action. Yet both were thrown together in a fight for survival, and so temporarily suppressed their differences. Moreover, the two men were deeply divided ideologically. Bridges, in particular, wanted to extend his power beyond the ILWU, to control the strategy and tactics of the other crafts, and eventually to consolidate them in one great industrial union. Lundeberg's basic loyalty always lay with the SUP. Although he could concede the principle of joint action in major strikes, he was never willing to surrender the autonomy of the SUP to any federation. Indeed, he believed in strengthening his own union even at the cost of jurisdictional conflict and, at times of crisis, of sacrifice of unity among the entire group.

Rivalries among the Pacific Coast maritime unions contributed to conflicts between labor and management in two main ways. For example, jurisdictional struggles between the SUP and ILWU occasioned several local strikes, particularly in the coastwise lumber trade. Probably the most serious of these stoppages was the five months' tie-up at Coos Bay, Oregon, in 1946. However, the primary impacts of union rivalry arose from the political struggle within the group, in which Bridges and Lundeberg figured personally.

This political struggle was essentially a contest for power. In union affairs, power rests in great part upon the prestige of the leaders with the broad rank and file. And prestige is won or lost by the ability to deliver tangible results—large wage gains and improved contract terms. With two aggressive leaders such as Bridges and Lundeberg, negotiations from 1936 onward were complicated by the desire of each to gain the advantage over the other. Each was jockeying for the leadership of all the unions together. To play this kind of game under the watchful eyes of militant constituents, each leader had to be resourceful, daring, and on occasion uncompromising. The results were varied: extreme demands, delaying tactics at times, and, at certain points, "necessary" strikes.

Many episodes exhibit these tactics. When Lundeberg achieved a separate settlement in 1936, Bridges may well have stalled a general return to work for six weeks, to obscure Lundeberg's victory. In May, 1946, Bridges seems to have staked his position on the probability of federal intervention and the imposition of a uniform pattern—with Bridges getting the credit for the achievement. By holding out, Lundeberg was able to wring even greater gains from the employers, which he clinched by defeating the government itself in the September strike. To recoup his position, Bridges had to bring off additional large concessions himself. Very likely, the longshore strike in October was prolonged to emphasize Bridges' ability to deliver the goods.

For the operators, these tactics made negotiations extremely difficult during most of the time. The reason lay in the interdependent positions of the unions themselves. After 1936, joint action and simultaneous general settlements proved impossible. Piecemeal negotiations and settlements, which were successive in time, meant that the unions settling first had to take the risk of having their gains exceeded in the later agreements. Those settling later were thus induced to make more extreme demands, and in any event to dramatize their achievements, perhaps by uncompromising tactics and prolonged strikes.

It would be wrong, however, to make too much of union rivalry as a factor in conflict. Undoubtedly, it created a number of local strikes, but its main effect was more in the direction of making the processes of negotiation, settlement, and administration of contracts more difficult than it was in causing strikes themselves. It could nevertheless be said that rivalry, taken in conjunction with the other influences, did increase the likelihood that disputes would culminate in major strikes and that these strikes would be protracted ones.

● *Economic Pressure.*—Economic pressure can influence bargaining relations in two main ways. From the employer standpoint, the pressure shows up in the cost-revenue relationship. The chief problem for them in this respect is control of costs, of which labor cost is a major if not predominant part. From the union point of view, the pressure exhibits itself in the demands of the members for larger wage incomes, reduced hours, improved conditions, and easier work. All of these union demands, unless offset by increased productivity, are reflected in increased costs of operations to the employers. To the latter, the problem is one of protecting profit margins. The problem was, and remains, unusually acute in Pacific Coast shipping, for two reasons. Its markets, and hence its revenues, underwent long-run decline during 1930–1948. At the same time, very intense competition developed, with foreign vessels in the foreign trade, and with railroads, trucks, and pipelines in the coastwise and intercoastal trades.

One might expect, therefore, that the maritime operators would have been extremely obstinate in resisting the economic demands of the unions during these years, so that economic pressure would have contributed significantly to conflict in the industry. For the period 1930–1936, this expectation was justified. After 1936, the situation changed. Not that economic pressure then ceased. Far from it. Rather, it changed to an inflationary form and was largely absorbed by timely federal aid of various kinds. In consequence, the balance of forces was changed. Employer resistance declined at the same time that union demands increased.

During the open-shop period of 1930–1934, the industry had suffered a very severe contraction in its markets. Costs were reduced by retrenchment or abandonment of services, and by a combination of wage cuts, worsened working conditions, and attempts to increase labor productivity. No doubt economic pressure at this time contributed powerfully to bringing about the 1934 strike—in two ways. First, cost cutting—through its impacts on the men—built up great hostility to the employers. Second, the imperative need to control costs in a shrinking market served as a strong incentive to the employers to resist unionism with all the means at their command. This resistance was evident until the 1937 settlement, when the employers were finally and decisively defeated. It would thus be correct to say that economic pressure was a highly important factor in these first two coastwide strikes.

After 1937, there was relatively little that the employers could do to resist the pressure of increasing costs. The unions were too strong. Furthermore, shipping was in the midst of a weak but badly needed recovery, which to some extent expanded revenues once more. In addition, the operators in foreign trade were now partly protected by operating subsidies. Until the entry of the United States into the war, cost pressure was overcome principally by innovations in longshore operations. These to a limited extent served to offset the slowdown tactics of the ILWU. At the same time, these changes reduced the short-run work opportunities of longshoremen. In turn, this led to conflict with the ILWU and the waterfront employers.

As World War II stepped up the volume of ocean shipping, the ship operators found themselves serving a new market—one in which the federal government made it practically impossible to lose money. On the one hand, it offered an insatiable demand for shipping at guaranteed profits. On the other, it controlled wages. Economic pressure there certainly was, but it was not the kind of pressure that makes for union-management conflict.

With the 1946–1948 period, maritime shipping—almost alone in the American economy—suffered a rapid and severe shrinkage in its markets. Yet cost pressure failed to be of great influence upon bargaining relations. There were several reasons for this. First, the domestic lines had been almost completely driven out of the coastwise and intercoastal trade by the war. For them, the question was not how to reduce costs, but whether to resume operations at all. The answer lay in a very restricted renewal of services. In other words, cost pressure was largely overcome by permanent abandonment of operations. Second, these lines were protected from foreign competition, and the more efficient ones were able to survive. Third, American vessels in foreign trade were protected from an otherwise impossible cost situation by federal operating and construction subsidies, plus the continuance of a substantial volume of government cargoes. For these operators, there was little incentive to resist union-imposed cost increases, because the taxpayers were ready to foot the bill anyway. Fourth, the Alaska-Hawaii noncontiguous lines were protected from foreign competition, and at the same time from competition of land-based carriers. Cost increases could be absorbed by raising rates. Finally, the stevedoring side of the industry could sustain increasing costs and yet survive because it would handle all tonnage available to American vessels, and in addition the tonnage carried by the foreign lines, which were better situated. To do so, of course, it also had to accept as permanent the large contraction in dry-cargo tonnage in the coastwise and intercoastal trades.

In consequence, economic pressure at this time registered its main influence in another direction. This was from the side of union demands. Effective wage controls had been abandoned in 1945, which released a great amount of accumulated inflationary wage pressure. The result was the now famous first-round cycle of wage increases in American industry in 1945–1946. The "pattern" of these increases became an imperative for the maritime unions. Failure to keep up with the procession would be viewed as a sign of incompetence of any given union leaders. This inflationary pressure made possible Lundeberg's victory in the summer of 1946, and the futile attempt to contain it was the cause of the first coastwide strike in September. The same pressure, with its political implications for Bridges, was central to the second strike in October.

Thereafter, inflationary forces largely receded. So far as the 1948 tie-up was concerned, only indirectly was it related to economic pressure. The main issue was Bridges' power, which was challenged by the employers' attack on the hiring hall. To some extent, this attack was undoubtedly impelled by Bridges' indifference to the employers' problems of cost and his irresponsible use of job-action strikes. But by this time the ILWU-WEPC conflict had become a struggle for power, originating primarily from deep ideological divisions. In contrast, economic factors were largely in the more remote background.

A final comment about economic pressure is in order. Recent experience makes it painfully clear that Pacific Coast maritime shipping could hardly survive were it not kept alive by government aid. This has taken four forms: protection of the domestic lines from competition of foreign vessels; construction and operating subsidies for American ships in foreign trade; an enormous boost in revenues and large increases in cargoes and modern floating equipment to supply the Pacific theater in World War II; and continuing substantial government cargoes for American lines in the postwar foreign and non-contiguous trades. Government support has meant that only the intercoastal and coastwise dry-cargo carriers have really been vulnerable to the postwar pressure of increased costs, because their rates are directly affected by the competition of low-cost land transportation. Even here the pressure has been eased in some degree, for the war had already eliminated permanently many marginal operators from the domestic trades, and the remaining dry-cargo tonnage is probably less than a quarter of the Pacific Coast total. Relatively little shrinkage in this tonnage remains possible, and the latter is now in the hands of the more efficient operators who were able to survive.

In the net, therefore, the industry has been saved from cost pressure by government protection. Generous advances to the unions have thus been possible without risking extinction. Indeed, government support probably reduced greatly any incentive to resist large wage concessions. As a result, cost ceased to figure as an important factor in employer resistance to union demands, hence as a major element making for union-management conflict.

● *Conclusions.*—In the study of history, it is not possible to separate controlling causes from one another, and so to explore the influence of each in isolation. There is no way to conduct such experiments. What we have in Pacific Coast maritime shipping is an instance of multiple causation, with the causes mutually interlocked. All we can do is to guess at which causes were the more predominant at certain times in the production of conflict during past years.

Between 1930 and 1936, the major influences seem to have been a combination of economic pressure, opposing ideologies, and historical circumstance. After this time, conflict seems to have centered in ILWU-WEPC relations and in jurisdictional struggles. The major factors appear to have been ideology and union rivalry. In 1946, economic pressure rejoined this pair of influences. By 1948, ILWU-WEPC relations were alone the focus of serious conflict, whose immediate cause seems to have been a struggle for power between the two groups. This power struggle had its origins in the opposing ideologies of both parties.

What were the effects of conflict as a whole in the industry during these years? First, the strikes themselves were an important cause of unstable performance. Undoubtedly, the five main strikes cost the industry much tonnage in four separate years. These losses were increased by many local port-wide strikes as well, some of which were serious. Second, to the users of ocean shipping, the strikes meant unreliable service and, at times, actual losses from resulting delays of goods in transit. To an undetermined extent, the industry probably lost some business permanently from its inability to provide continuous service. Third, unionism undoubtedly accelerated a rise in costs. Ocean transportation rates are particularly vulnerable to higher wages and reduced productivity. Although to some degree these effects were cushioned by federal subsidies, there is little doubt that in the domestic trades rail and truck transportation gained an increasing comparative advantage over water carriage after 1940. In this way, too, some business was probably permanently lost.

Nevertheless, the primary impact of conflict was in the direct losses caused by the strikes themselves. If the coastwide tie-ups could have been settled more promptly, the large direct losses would have been greatly reduced. If the many local strikes could have been resolved by peaceful negotiations, the industry would not have acquired its unenviable reputation for unreliable service. So far as tonnage and markets were concerned, therefore, labor-management conflict imposed its main losses through protracted major strikes and an excessive number of local tie-ups.

After the 1937 settlement, the factor most responsible for continuing costly conflict seems to have been the deep-seated ideological hostility of the Bridges group toward the maritime employers. Had it not been for their vested interest in class conflict, it is likely that mature bargaining relations could have developed rather rapidly in the industry, once the unlicensed crafts had won unequivocal security in 1937. Disputes and strikes undoubtedly still would have occurred, but without the uncompromising bitter-end tactics, the protracted tie-ups, and the day-to-day conflicts in contract administration that took place. Thus the failure of a general atmosphere of mutual survival to emerge seems justly attributable to the recalcitrant position of the ILWU leaders. Whether their hostile ideology has ceased to influence Pacific Coast maritime labor relations is still to be determined, for it awaits the test of time.

Part IV
An Appraisal

CHAPTER XII

Conclusions and Inferences

● *Introduction.*—To account for the changing economic fortunes of an industry requires a series of approximations by which we approach the truth. In sequence, this procedure permits the investigator to establish the major contours of industry performance, to supplement those contours with additional relevant facts of a deeper and more detailed character, and then to evaluate the influence of the governing processes he suspects have been at work. The task is one of blending the generalizations furnished by economic theory with evidence whose collection and interpretation are at all times guided by theory. By analogy, the procedure is similar to geological inquiry, in which a given region is mapped in preliminary relief, worked up in greater detail, then tested for the past operation of known processes of terrestrial change, and finally given explanation by collective assessment of proved causes.

In the case of Pacific Coast maritime shipping, we began by mapping the main contours of the industry's performance during 1930–1948, presenting our results in our first volume. These findings will bear brief repetition for a final time. In essence, they were that the industry suffered from great instability and long-run decline. More fully, instability was apparent in all of the basic trades—foreign, in-

289

tercoastal, coastwise, and noncontiguous. Decline was evident in the first three; slow growth was shown in the noncontiguous category alone. By the end of the third postwar coastwide strike in 1948, the industry found itself at a critical impasse, and the central problem of this second volume emerged: to account for the industry's postwar plight.

In what follows, we propose to bring the account into a common focus, by a series of approximations. In the first, we shall review briefly our main findings regarding the commodity structure of Pacific Coast water-borne trade and the geographical distribution of its foreign trade, where we have isolated certain focal points of instability and decline. In the second, we shall evaluate separately the main impacts of each of the major causes of instability and decline in the industry. In the third, we shall bring the analysis together, for an integrated interpretation of the industry's past experience and current predicament. Then in the final approximation we shall apply a version of Alfred Marshall's principle that "history is prediction read backwards," using our analysis to show how the major controlling forces might affect the future of the industry.

● *First Approximation: The Commodity Structure of the Trades and the Geographic Pattern of Pacific Coast Foreign Trade.—Commodity structure.* There is no need to repeat here the detailed findings in this sphere. These findings do, however, yield some very important generalizations that in turn are important clues to much of the remainder of the inquiry.

(1) In the years 1930–1948, the water-borne trade of the Pacific Coast consisted mainly of a two-way exchange of products of agriculture and of natural resources. Only in a small way did it embrace manufactured goods. In terms of output, the Pacific states were producers of certain raw materials and primary products, in which they have always enjoyed a marked comparative advantage. In terms of incoming tonnage, these states were principally consumers of foodstuffs and raw materials for further processing; the comparative advantage lay with the areas of supply.

(2) Outbound shipments from the Pacific Coast were heavily dominated by two leading commodities, lumber and petroleum. This was

true of the foreign, noncontiguous, and intercoastal trades, and also for the coastwise, which is not an "export" trade. Inbound movements (excluding coastwise) in all trades consisted almost wholly of a diverse array of dry cargo, not dominated by any particular commodities. However, in the noncontiguous category, sugar, pineapples, and fish were prominent; in the intercoastal category, iron and steel manufactures were most important.

(3) Not surprisingly, fluctuations in petroleum and lumber tonnage were the focuses of instability in total traffic. Outbound agricultural products conformed to normal expectations and were thus relatively immune to cyclical movements. By contrast, incoming raw materials and agricultural products moved rather closely with the prewar American business cycle.

(4) Outbound movements of petroleum and lumber showed marked aggregate decline postwar versus prewar, although in the noncontiguous trade slow growth occurred. In fact, the decline of petroleum and lumber shipments was central to the over-all decline of industry tonnage. Although exports of manufactures revealed modest long-run growth in the foreign and noncontiguous trades, it was not enough to offset the general decline of tonnage as a whole. On the inbound side, total tonnage in the foreign, noncontiguous, and intercoastal trades together proved stable over the long run, though highly unstable in shorter periods. Modest gains in the noncontiguous were offset by losses in the intercoastal, while imports from abroad remained steady. Given large increases in population, output, and income on the Pacific Coast during these years, it follows that the region was reducing its per capita dependence upon imports by water, especially in the foreign and intercoastal trades.

The geographic distribution of foreign trade. Examination of the changing geographic pattern of the water-borne foreign trade of the Pacific Coast also affords some useful clues for later analysis.

(1) Throughout 1930–1948, foreign trade was concentrated in the nations of the Pacific basin, both in exports and in imports. Continental Europe and the United Kingdom were markedly less important. (2) Within the Pacific basin complex, the East Indies–East Asia

region was the outstanding prewar leader in both imports and exports of the Pacific Coast. Trade with this region was subject to sharp fluctuations. (3) Postwar, the large decline of exports to the East Indies–East Asia zone was central to the fall of exports as a whole. Imports from this region also showed a sharp postwar decline.

(4) Prewar and postwar, the volume of Pacific Coast exports to and imports from the Dominion of Canada to a marked extent, and the Caribbean–Mexican–Central American region to a lesser, exhibited strong upward tendencies. (5) Exports to the Bayonne-Hamburg range of continental Europe recovered to prewar volume in the early postwar years, but exports to the United Kingdom and to South America never again attained the levels of the beginning of the 1929–1932 slump, and were even below the later 'thirties by 1946–1947. Imports from the Bayonne-Hamburg range held rather stable over the long period. Those from South America, although cyclically very sensitive in the 'thirties, showed some long-run growth.

Clues to possible causes. The following principal facts regarding tonnage patterns of the maritime shipping industry describe, rather than explain, the instability and long-run decline; however, they furnish some important leads for further inquiry.

(1) During 1930–1948, the Pacific states enjoyed very rapid growth in population, industry, and income. Outbound water tonnage was nevertheless in decline, and inbound movements failed to increase. Clearly, there was a linkage between regional development and water-borne trade, but whatever its nature its effects were apparently perverse. (2) The over-all decline in water-borne trade was centered in outbound shipments of petroleum and lumber. Regional development in the west influenced the production, use, and transportation of these two primary products, but it did so in a fashion adverse to the maritime shipping industry.

(3) Outbound shipments of lumber and petroleum, and inbound movements of all types, both revealed a prewar pattern of movement that conformed fairly well with major business movements in the United States. Maritime shipping was a cyclically sensitive industry. (4) There were enough irregularities in tonnage fluctuations, how-

ever, to indicate also that frequent and prolonged maritime strikes had depressed dry-cargo movements in certain years. (5) Postwar, outbound tonnage of petroleum and lumber in foreign trade, and outbound and inbound shipments in the East Indies–East Asia segment of that trade, all showed sharp declines, breaking off the upward tendencies of the later 'thirties. In some way, the war had worked against this traffic.

(6) During the 'thirties there were sharp fluctuations in trade between the Pacific Coast and its principal trading partners. Further, over the entire nineteen-year period (1930–1948) under study here, there were the East Indies–East Asia decline and similar tendencies relative to Europe and the United Kingdom. In contrast, trade with Canada and the Caribbean–Mexican–Central American zone underwent long-term growth. Perhaps the actions of the various governments involved had influenced the changes noted.

So much for some initial clues. We turn now to the second approximation, in which we shall review the impacts of each of the causal forces we have considered.

● *Second Approximation: Challenge and Response.—International politics and trade policies.* There were many lines of government action that affected water-borne commerce—tariffs, exchange controls, exchange depreciation, import restrictions, bilateral agreements, war preparations, wartime mobilization of shipping, and the postwar American military and civilian aid programs. With some of these measures, the effects were obvious—for example, the postwar emergency shipments to the Orient. With others, for instance, the American tariff of 1930 and retaliatory measures abroad, there is no way to isolate their effects from those produced by other concurrent forces.

However, there is warrant for the inference that international politics and commercial policies contributed to the short-run fluctuations of cargo tonnage handled by the maritime shipping industry. Their influence was limited primarily to Pacific Coast foreign trade, hence was necessarily small in over-all impact upon the industry. The effect was to increase the magnitude of upswings and downswings. Thus with the onset of depression, tariffs and other restrictive devices came into common use and probably reduced foreign tonnage below the level induced by the world-wide fall in incomes. With the recovery between 1932 and 1937, measures to increase trade with the United States may have yielded some benefit, although they were probably tempered by the American dollar depreciation in 1933. Probably, too, the Sino-Japanese war gave some impetus to the prewar East Indies– East Asia trade. Moreover, war preparations after 1938 may have increased tonnage moving between the Pacific Coast and Canada, Europe, and the Orient.

Postwar, many nations with overvalued currencies experienced balance of payments difficulties. Corrective measures to overcome the "dollar shortage" tended to restrict exports from the Pacific Coast and to expand its imports. In this respect, the United Kingdom and the Bayonne-Hamburg range were important. In contrast, the large decline of the East Indies–East Asia trade was connected with political disturbances and political ambitions in that region. Finally, Pacific shipping drew badly needed support in 1946–1948 from the American program of civilian aid and military occupation in the Far East.

In the main, then, international politics and trade policies in these years probably added to the instability of the maritime shipping industry. If the actions of governments in this broad sphere had any net influence upon the long-run fortunes of the industry's privately conducted (nongovernmental) foreign trade, it was probably adverse. After all, 1930–1948 was hardly a propitious period for international trade, dominated as it was by war, movements toward autarky, increased state trading, and the spread of inconvertible currencies.

All these developments were beyond the effective control of the industry itself. All it could do was to respond to the changes of demand involved.

Economic changes in the Pacific states. During 1930–1948, the Pacific states experienced a very large increase of population. This growth was not confined to the major port cities. Rather, it also involved the building up of many inland cities and new surrounding zones, and the emergence of several important new centers. At the same time, the coast enjoyed extensive industrialization, in basic iron and steel and in heavy and light manufacturing industry. Manufacturing grew rapidly in relative importance, as an employer of labor, a user of raw materials, and a source of income. Intimately connected with developments in population and in industry were some almost revolutionary changes in the technology of land transportation. After the end of World War I, a network of hard-surfaced roads was built up and the motor truck emerged as both a short- and long-haul carrier. In the same period, oil pipelines were extensively introduced into California. Stimulated by these new forms of competition, the railroads rationalized their techniques and improved their services, effecting some notable economies of cost.

Economic expansion in the west also gave rise to prodigious increases in total and per capita real income. The expansion of income reinforced the process of industrialization and at the same time led to increased local consumption of western raw materials and products.

Regional development, however, in all its phases was not favorable to maritime shipping. Indeed, it seems to have worked against it. The clue lies in the sources of the long-run decline of total tonnage, which was concentrated in the intercoastal, coastwise, and foreign export trades. Between the decline of these trades and regional development, there was a direct and perverse connection. The great drop in outbound intercoastal cargoes was centered in shipments of lumber and petroleum. Yet regional production of these commodities was greatly increasing at the time. In part, at least, the loss of much of this movement was occasioned by increased regional consumption that accompanied the large growth of incomes. Inbound, the decline of the intercoastal trade was less severe. Here it was centered in iron and steel manufactured goods. In part, the reason lay in increased local manufacturing. In part, too, it was connected with the inland shift of wholesale distribution points that accompanied the inflow of population and the improvement of land transportation.

Not only did the purely intraregional coastwise trade lose almost all of its dry-cargo traffic but even its always dominant petroleum tonnage failed to gain over the long period. For this trade, the rapid development of land transportation proved crucial. It offered cheaper, faster, and more flexible substitutes for water services, and it made possible a new pattern of wholesale and retail distribution.

Losses in the foreign trade of the Pacific Coast were centered in exports, while imports merely held their own over the long run. Here it is likely that regional growth, by increasing local consumption of lumber and petroleum, worked to reduce the volume of exportable surpluses. It is probable that imports failed to increase because new local sources of supply were developed and new external sources created that could be served better by land transportation.

It must be admitted that to some extent the evidence for the generally adverse influence of regional growth upon maritime shipping is circumstantial. Either the development of the west and the decline of shipping were a chance concurrence or they were causally connected. The array of proved facts on both sides is too substantial, however, to lend strength to an hypothesis of chance concurrence. Accordingly, it is more reasonable to infer a causal connection.

Regional development represented an important unfavorable change in the industry's environment. It was a factor beyond the effective control of the water carriers. Consequently, their choice was a hard one: to trim services and survive as best they could.

Business fluctuations. During the prewar decade, the American economy experienced in succession the sharp 1929–1932 slump, the weak recovery between 1932 and 1937, the recession of 1938, and the resumed advance of 1939. With the end of World War II, production and income emerged at unprecedentedly high levels, and during 1946–1948 there was a further slow advance.

In the 'thirties, shipping tonnage matched these movements fairly closely—in all trades together, in each of the trades, in the dominant commodities, and in exchanges with the principal foreign areas. Clearly, business movements in the United States were highly important to an explanation of the prewar instability of the maritime shipping industry.

Total trade suffered relatively greater declines than the fall in production during 1930–1932 and 1937–1938. Further, all trades in the first slump and all but coastwise in the second dropped more sharply than national output. Then in the 1932–1937 business recovery the intercoastal trade lagged far behind, though noncontiguous and foreign were ahead. These facts indicate a chronic underlying weakness in maritime traffic relative to general business.

For 1946–1948, there was no clear connection between American production and the instability of shipping tonnage. Business was prosperous and expanding. Yet tonnage was strongly humped around 1947, and even in that year traffic was well below the better prewar years. Obviously, other factors were also at work (strikes in 1946 and 1948, for example), some making for instability, some for long-run decline.

Once again, we observe that the industry was hard hit by powerful forces in its environment, over which it had no control.

World War II. Although the war was, in a sense, an aspect of international politics, its impacts upon maritime shipping were so great as to justify its treatment as a separate force.

Its force was felt by maritime shipping in several ways. The coastwise and intercoastal trades were compelled to suspend operations, and thereby they lost their normal customer relationships. The foreign trade was converted to the needs of war, with serious disruption of traditional import-export patterns. The industry itself was transformed to become a quasi-state enterprise, operated under very tight military and civilian control. Its operations were vastly increased, but its routes and its tonnage were now wholly governed by the requirements of warfare. Almost overnight a new fleet was brought into being, and once again the ports hummed with an activity unknown for nearly a generation.

The effects of the war were keenly felt even in the postwar years. A substantial volume of military cargoes continued to move, now supplemented by increasing civilian aid tonnage. Both were most welcome in the postwar shipping slump. Moreover, the industry was largely reëquipped with larger and faster vessels, affording badly needed cost economies for meeting ever keener competition.

There was also a negative side to the aftermath of the war. The intercoastal and coastwise trades were compelled to fight their way back into their markets against heavy odds. Old customers had to be re-gained and aggressive railroad and truck competitors dislodged, if these trades were to make a come-back.

It seems safe to conclude that the primary effect of the war was to increase the instability of the industry. The conflict demanded rapid and enormous expansion, and an equally rapid and large contraction. Over the longer run, the effects of the war were less pronounced. There was now the prop of government tonnage, which aided the Far Eastern trade. However, the political disturbances bequeathed by the war to the Orient crippled recovery in areas of vital importance to Pacific Coast foreign trade. Furthermore, although the war did not cause the great contraction in the coastwise and intercoastal trades, it certainly precipitated it. And the legacy of difficulties left by the war to these trades certainly put off any possible improvement in their fortunes.

Once more the environment imposed a difficult challenge, and once more the industry's role was limited to rather desperate adaptation.

Strikes. The five great coastwide strikes between 1934 and 1948 closed down the Pacific ports for a total of 349 calendar days, or 9 per cent of the total time available in the eleven peacetime years involved. In addition, there were seventy-eight port-wide strikes and 1,255 local stoppages during the period as a whole. Five years stand out sharply from the standpoint of losses in longshore working time: 1934 (22 per cent), 1936 (18 per cent), 1937 (12 per cent), 1946 (21 per cent), and 1948 (27 per cent). Few industries, if any, can match these losses.

The losses were concentrated in dry-cargo tonnage. When annual movements of this tonnage in these years are compared with move-ments in American production for the same years, the negative impacts of the strikes show up most clearly. Thus in 1934, national output rose 10.4 per cent, but dry-cargo tonnage advanced only 4.3 per cent. In 1936, output advanced 13.5 per cent, while tonnage fell about 1 per cent. In 1937, output increased 4.8 per cent, and dry-cargo ton-nage nearly 7 per cent. The apparently favorable comportment of ton-nage on this occasion has a wry explanation: although, considered ab-solutely, time lost in 1937 was great, it was *less so* relative to 1936. Hence maritime shipping could enjoy a phantom recovery. Postwar, the situation was even worse. Statistical frailties compelled us to use 1947, rather than 1945, as a bench mark for 1946. National production rose less than 1 per cent in 1947 relative to 1946. By contrast, dry-cargo tonnage actually increased by a third. Again it was purely a phantom recovery. Strike losses were great in 1946, and negligible in 1947. In 1948, tonnage declined by 23.4 per cent, although production advanced 3.5 per cent. Time lost from strikes in 1948 was the heaviest on record.

Beyond any doubt, strikes made a large contribution to the instability of the maritime shipping industry. The main losses they invoked were concentrated in five out of eleven peacetime years between 1934 and 1948. The losses may be compared to those occasioned by a serious trade depression. The industry was thus compelled to suffer the equivalent of a major depression during every other year of its peacetime operations.

There is also ample reason to believe that the many maritime strikes aided the slow erosion of dry-cargo traffic, by building up the industry's reputation for unreliable service. This would have been most likely in the coastwise and intercoastal trades, in which shippers had land transportation available as a substitute.

In the main, the strikes, too, were an environmental factor, so far as shipping management was concerned. They had their origin in the industry's inability to stabilize its labor relations, because of a complex and deeply rooted conflict during these years. Although a case may be made that, during the early phase of this struggle, management might have lessened its severity if it had been prepared emotionally and intellectually to do so, we shall see that in important ways the conflict lay beyond its effective control.

Costs and competition. After the revival of trade unionism in 1934, Pacific Coast maritime shipping found itself under rapidly increasing cost pressure. Wages represented nearly half of vessel operating expense and perhaps 90 per cent of loading and unloading costs. Wage rates alone nearly tripled between 1934 and 1948, and this was not all. Labor costs were also expanded by many other supplementals— for example, extremely liberal longshore overtime pay rates and an

ever-tightening network of working rules, ashore and on ship. We have
no wish to ignore the very low levels at which these gains were initiated
(for the offshore crafts), nor to discount the many benefits they entailed for those fortunate enough to attain them. But we do observe
that as time went on they well exceeded wages and conditions for comparable work in other industries, and that whatever their merits these
gains represented corresponding increases in costs to the maritime
shipping industry. Furthermore, they were extracted from an industry
whose difficulties were already great, hence one that was not well
equipped to provide them. Nor was it solely a matter of the increasing
money costs for maritime labor. These might have been borne, had
they been compensated for by reasonably comparable increases in the
physical productivity of that labor. The available evidence indicates,
however, that the productivity of longshoremen actually fell during
the decisive years of the later 'thirties, and for the period as a whole
showed no gain. Offshore, the postwar fleet of larger and faster vessels
probably yielded modest increases in productivity, but not enough to
make much over-all difference and almost certainly not enough to offset the technological advantages gained by their competitors—the railroads, trucks, and pipelines.

Here, then, was a weak industry, confronted by falling demand for
its services, and yet under extreme wage pressure, unrelieved by increasing physical productivity. The setting was not a propitious one in
which to stage a fight for survival.

The pressure was most keenly felt in the coastwise and intercoastal
trades. Operations of American vessels in foreign trade were supported by several types of federal aid, while the noncontiguous lines
were protected by statute from the competition of foreign vessels and
by geography from competition of land carriers. Coastwise and inter-
coastally, however, the industry faced the sharp and growing competition of the railroads, trucks, and other competitors. Here it found
itself at an increasing disadvantage.

There were ample reasons for this disadvantage. Wage rates rose
much faster for the water lines, and since the labor-to-total-cost ratios
of the truck, railroad, and vessel operators were rather close, the

steamship operators were the most vulnerable. Furthermore, railroading and trucking both achieved great technological improvements during these years, improvements that manifested themselves in large increases in labor productivity. Within this context, maritime shipping lagged badly from the standpoint of productivity but was far ahead in increases of wage costs. It lost both ways. Finally, shipping also suffered a unique handicap in the form of increased accessorial charges above port-to-port transportation rates. These extras pushed total water rates above those for competitive land transportation for much of the traffic in which the water carriers once had the long-haul advantage but which required transshipment to or from inland points.

It may be wondered why the maritime unions persisted in wage and related policies that increased the industry's already severe competitive handicap. One factor lay in the zeal of their leaders to produce income gains for the memberships, given the obvious political advantages of such a strategy. Another lay in opportunity costs. With or without unionism, maritime labor could be procured by the operators only at rates of pay and working conditions commensurate with comparable work in more prosperous industries ashore. However, maritime wages and working conditions, aship and ashore, ultimately came to exceed those obtainable for comparable work in other industries. Here lay a third factor—the great power acquired by the maritime unions. Through the closed shop and the job-rotation system, the union leaders could accept stagnation or even decline in total job opportunities, and do so with some complacency. By these means, the incumbent workers could be protected from permanent unemployment, even in a declining labor market partly invoked by their leaders' own policies.

In any case, cost pressure was of high importance in bringing about the long-run decline of the industry. As the reader will recognize, it was not the only factor. But it is also clear that cost pressure does much to explain the tremendous postwar drop of intercoastal dry cargo to less than two-thirds its average prewar level, and of coastwise dry cargo to one-quarter of its average prewar volume.

Cost pressure, too, was primarily an environmental influence. In the main, its origins lay in an unusually strong combination of forces:

the competitive effects of rising money wages generally, augmented by great union power. For effective response, the industry's main hope lay in increasing the productivity of its labor, but as we shall develop later, this hope was largely a vain one. It is true, however, that had the industry enjoyed a pure monopoly in all of its trades, the cost pressure would have presented no great problem. What made that pressure a critical difficulty was the competition of better situated land carriers, competing in the intercoastal and coastwise trades. From this aspect, too, the environment grew more and more unfavorable, and some steamship lines chose the one possible response, that of curtailment or abandonment of operations.

Conflict in labor relations. If the external environment for Pacific Coast maritime shipping in the main could be described as adverse during these years, it can be asserted with even greater confidence that the internal environment in which it had to conduct its labor relations was anything but a favorable one. Indeed, its difficulties in this sphere may be safely proclaimed to have been outstandingly bad. So bad, in fact, that they were central to an explanation of the industry's performance from the standpoint of internal management, as distinguished from the volume of cargo handled.

Between 1934 and 1937, two types of labor relations conflict coalesced to plague the industry. On one side it was a struggle between the maritime workers themselves and their ship and shoreside employers, a struggle born of depression conditions and the antiunion policies of the operators. On the other, it was a struggle of organizations and their leaders—nine resurgent and militant unions and, at the start, a loosely confederated group of employers. Organizationally, the conflict turned on initial recognition of the unions, the establishment of coastwide rather than single-employer or local-port bargaining units, and the creation of union-controlled hiring halls (in some instances *de facto* if not *de jure*) for the distribution of all work. In essence, these organizational issues were simultaneously the vehicle by which rank-and-file hopes could be transformed into a practical program of action, and the institutional requirements by which the unions could acquire security and strength as agencies in collective bargaining.

By early 1937, this phase of the conflict ended with victory for the unions. At this point, a new alignment of forces began to emerge. The position of the unions was now secure and their power great. Led by Harry Lundeberg and his Sailors' Union of the Pacific, one group of organizations returned to the tested traditions of strong internal discipline, respect for contracts, and tough bargaining. Another group, led by Harry Bridges and his International Longshoremen's and Warehousemen's Union, continued to maintain the bitter hostility of 1934, and used their power in a manner calculated to keep conflict permanently alive. There was thus born a struggle among the unions and their leaders, a running battle that now paralleled the controversy with the employers.

Many issues were involved, replete with adverse economic implications for the industry. Wages, of course, were the most obvious. Originally, they had been very low, and initially the aim was to redress the balance with other industries. Later it became a matter of keeping up with wage movements in general, finally emerging as an effort to get well out in front. In the intense union rivalry that soon developed, wages came to function as a symbol of leadership prestige.

There were other issues as well, however, and here the peculiar hostility of the Bridges group proved decisive. One concerned the declining efficiency of longshoremen, given the ability of the union to control loading and unloading speeds, and a growing network of restrictive rules. Another involved the employers' progressive loss of control over the direction of longshore work, which also embraced loss of the authority to assess disciplinary penalties for unsatisfactory performance. Still another issue embraced strikes in violation of contract, a tactic originally supported by the sailors but after 1937 indulged in by the Bridges-controlled unions alone. Finally, there were numerous attempts by the longshoremen to capture jurisdictional territory from the sailors, with particularly serious effects for the coastwise steam-schooner trade.

Thus the more obvious costs of conflict, frequent and prolonged strikes, were but part of the picture. They were simply the visible part of the iceberg.

Back of these badly troubled labor relations lay four principal causes. One lay in the industry and its history. Independent unionism had been broken in the early 'twenties. Coupled with falling wages, longer hours, worsened conditions, and the natural radicalism of casual workers, this fact exploded in the 1934–1937 struggle. Thereafter it largely lost force, except for its propaganda value in the perpetuation of an atmosphere of conflict. Another cause was ideological. The shipping employers came to collective bargaining in 1934 with a tradition of tough individualism. Naturally, they set out with an unfriendly attitude and appropriate concomitant tactics. On the union side, Lundeberg and Bridges originally rose to power with radical leanings, and the latter preserved this point of view throughout the period. In contrast, Lundeberg soon became a typically conservative AFL leader. This difference largely explains the interunion struggle that then developed. It also accounts for much of the employers' continuing conflict with the ILWU.

Closely linked to ideological divisions on the union side was a third factor: increasingly intense rivalry among the unions. This rivalry was fed by jurisdictional ambitions, which after 1937 were supplemented by bitter antagonism between the right-wing unions led by Lundeberg and the left-wing group under Bridges. Rivalry contributed much to the employers' difficulties, leading as it did to unstable negotiations, prolonged strikes, and extremely touchy administration of contracts. Finally, conflict was also nourished by economic pressure, first with the initial hostility of the men invoked by conditions of extreme depression, and then after the war by strong inflationary forces.

Conflict imposed heavy economic losses on all sides during these years. From the point of view of supply, it greatly increased the costs of providing maritime services. Higher costs were brought about by the extreme advance in wages, by barriers to efficiency and productivity, and by diminished employer control over operations. Strikes not only shut off the supply of maritime services entirely at times, but the financial losses they imposed upon the companies crippled their ability to finance innovations in production and in services. From the side of demand, the strikes cost the industry much shipper good will, by giving it a reputation for unreliable service. This factor has bulked large in shipper complaints and very likely it added to the losses of traffic in the coastwise and intercoastal trades.

In sum, labor-management conflict must be assigned a high place in an explanation of the instability of the industry; through its effects upon costs and shipper good will it was also important to the decline of the two domestic trades.

Had the maritime employers been better prepared mentally and emotionally during 1934–1937 to accept the return of independent unionism, they might have been able by shrewd conciliation to have tempered the initial phase of the conflict, encouraging earlier the development of a constructive unionism with responsible leaders. Possibly, too, their postwar tactics helped to drive Bridges to an even more extreme intransigency. Whatever their mistakes, however, it seems unquestionable that the operators found themselves relatively helpless in a most difficult environment of labor relations, as time went on. Foremost, there was the chronic, deep, and resourceful ideological hostility of the Bridges faction. There seems to have been no practical way to appease this hostility until it had imposed enormous costs, particularly upon the rank-and-file longshoremen themselves.

Moreover, the employers had no practical means to overcome the costly rivalry among the unions with which they were compelled to deal. Rivalry usually makes bargaining difficult, and in this instance it was also nurtured by bitter ideological differences. Finally, the employers were the focal point of converging economic pressures, particularly in the later years. On the one side, they faced the problem of survival in a market characterized by declining movements of demand. On the other, they were compelled to adjust wages and working conditions radically upward under the competitive pressures of an expanding domestic economy, pressures which were greatly augmented by the monopoly power of some unusually aggressive unions.

In the main conflict, too, there was an adverse environmental force for the industry. Once again it was a case of adapt and improvise, fighting rear-guard actions in what proved to be a prolonged retreat.

● *Third Approximation: An Interpretation of the Industry's Plight.*—
During these years, the industry suffered greatly from extreme fluctuations in the volume of its traffic. Back of them lay three primary causes and a fourth subordinate one. (1) In the prewar years, major swings in American production were of great importance. Postwar, however, the possible effects of this factor were overshadowed by the effects of others. (2) World War II disrupted normal trade but also involved an enormous expansion of operations. This expansion was succeeded by rapid contraction after 1945. Even so, the war left a generous legacy of emergency cargo tonnage. (3) Conflict in labor-management relations, expressed through a heavy burden of many strikes, was of high importance to an explanation of perverse tonnage movements in three prewar and two postwar years. (4) International politics and trade policies probably added to cyclical swings in foreign-trade tonnage, and may have aided the decline in this category.

For the period as a whole, the industry was in over-all decline. Although it recovered in some degree in the later 'thirties, it failed to match the recovery in American production. In 1947, even though it was a year without strikes, the industry operated well below the later 'thirties, indeed, at a level comparable with the worst years of the depression.

The decline was centered in three trades: intercoastal, coastwise (mainly the dry-cargo segment), and foreign exports. Again three causes provide the principal explanation. (1) Economic development of the Pacific states coupled with competitive shipments from other producing areas curtailed outbound movements of petroleum and lumber moving in the intercoastal and foreign export trades. With the great increase of population and income in the region, it became more profitable to retain larger amounts of these commodities for local use. Moreover, regional growth embraced a relative shift of population to inland centers and to port hinterlands beyond economical water transport range and also marked improvements in the range and efficiency of land transportation. Thus maritime shipping lost out in the coastwise dry-cargo trade, and to a lesser extent in inbound intercoastal tonnage.

(2) Soaring labor costs, boosted further by a prolonged running battle between shipping management and certain unions, finally put the industry at an almost fatal competitive disadvantage relative to the railroads and trucks. Maritime shipping enjoyed no significant increase in labor productivity; its rivals did. Yet wages rose faster and higher for the water lines. Coupled with ever-increasing supplemental shipping charges, cost inflation in the industry canceled out most of its few long-haul rate advantages. Here again the intercoastal and coastwise dry-cargo trades largely lost out.

(3) Finally, internal conflict caused many strikes, and these gave the industry a bad reputation among its customers. Once more, the intercoastal and coastwise trades were the victims, since there were competing alternatives available to shippers.

This, then, is the essence of the industry's story of instability and decline during these unhappy years. It is a story of unceasing challenges from a largely hostile environment, challenges that in the main were not met with success. Decline was the ultimate result.

It is worth while to pursue the matter a little further. In a system of private enterprise, the expansion or contraction of an industry is largely determined by the relationship between revenues and costs, that is to say, by the market. Revenues reflect the behavior of demand in the product market (in this case tonnage), and costs reflect the prices the industry must pay in competitive factor markets for labor and capital, costs whose final expression in product price is modified by the industry's efficiency in transforming its factor inputs into service outputs. In these respects, the industry has a two-sided economic environment: the demand for its services on the one hand, and the supply of its productive factors on the other. Ultimately, its economic success or failure rests upon its ability to adapt itself successfully to externally imposed changes coming from both sides. In maritime shipping, the complex of these imposed changes in the net was unfavorable. Decline was the outcome.

The demand side of the industry's environment was marked by extreme short-run fluctuations and a slow shrinkage of commercial, nongovernmental markets. On the supply side, the industry proved very vulnerable to aggressive unionism, which boosted its costs, crippled its ability to increase productivity, and at times closed down its services entirely. On both sides, therefore, the environment was *displacing* rather than *adopting* the industry, from a long-run point of view. Thus there came about the decline of foreign exports, the failure of foreign imports to grow, and the deep erosion of the intercoastal and coastwise trades. The tides of historical change were strongly on the ebb.

Abandoned at this point, the interpretation would be too deterministic, since between the factor and the product markets stands the industry itself. As the center of initiative in an enterprise system, management obviously has some degree of freedom in the process of influencing demand and controlling costs. Ordinarily, lines of action other than the defeatist course of passive adaptation are possible. But if they were possible in this instance, they were largely unrealized by the Pacific Coast maritime shipping industry. The question is: Why?

The answer may be found in a combination of facts. On the one hand, there were inherent weaknesses in shipping management. On the other, the adverse impinging forces were simply too strong. Central to management's weaknesses was its inability to attract adequate fresh capital. Well before 1930, the industry was in the doldrums and was thus an unpromising zone for investment. Increasingly, it came to depend upon government aid and protection. Its reputation for earning power naturally suffered. With the depression, the outlook turned bleak, never really to change. Perhaps influenced by this unpromising prospect, coupled with some inertia, political agencies in charge of port facilities along the Pacific Coast largely allowed them to languish.

In only one major way was the industry's capital position significantly improved during the period and that was through the fortunate wartime legacy of a modernized fleet. This bounty offered some opportunity for an effective attack upon costs, but it was far from enough to reverse the industry's declining fortunes.

Another weakness lay in the caliber of management itself. True, during these years the industry possessed a strong corps of experienced and competent executives. Nevertheless, there were obstacles. The times were inherently difficult, hence unfavorable to more than defensive actions in a shrinking market. Labor problems absorbed much of management's time and energies, requiring as they did endless improvisation and counter-tactics. Furthermore, the contraction of the industry involved the expulsion of many firms, severe curtailment by others, and a consequent spirit of bafflement and demoralization. New talent had neither the opportunity nor the incentive to commit its future to so unpromising a field. Pushed by events to a mood of resignation if not despair, the older officials found it enough if they could hold operations at a level that would permit survival. Bold ventures were simply not in the cards.

Moreover, the scope for initiative was badly restricted by the hostile character of impinging forces. Capital was lacking for the establishment of extensive new services to expand and create demand, and in any case the prospects were too unpromising. Here the vagaries of the business cycle and of sporadic showdowns with the unions were combined with an almost insuperable cost handicap. The complex proved a fatal obstacle to initiatives in the coastwise and intercoastal trades; in the noncontiguous category expansion had little point, given the highly inelastic demand for such service. This left the foreign trade, and here the operator had to confront all of the barriers to international trade, political disturbances in the Orient, the keen competition of low-cost foreign vessels, and the growing preference of western producers for local markets. In sum, there was little actual prospect for the creation of new demands.

What about costs? If costs could have been kept lower by marked technological improvements and high labor efficiency, the decline might have been arrested to some extent. But here again the position of the industry was almost uniquely bad. In the nature of the case, it had to pay higher money prices for its factors of production, merely to keep pace with the rest of the economy. However, this was only part of the story. Its wage costs rose much faster than those of its rivals, given the peculiar power of the maritime unions. Further, it was unable to profit from cost-savings through extensive changes in work methods, under the pattern of union control that emerged. Finally, it was largely powerless to prevent most of its many strikes, and consequently it had to absorb the severe losses these strikes entailed.

The conclusion is unavoidable, therefore, that the scope for managerial initiative was narrowly restricted at a time when unfavorable changes in the environment called for the broadest possible freedom of action. Because of this, the industry's strategy was primarily defensive, and involved the curtailment or abandonment of operations. This was the line of least resistance, and it was followed. The gradual displacement of maritime shipping from its former position in the economy of the Pacific Coast is therefore hardly a fact to occasion surprise. The logic of events made it inevitable.

● *Fourth Approximation: The Outlook for the Future.*—It seems safe to say that there will always be some economic need for the Pacific Coast maritime shipping industry, in spite of its many misfortunes. As to the nature and scope of this future need, it would be out of place to attempt a prediction here. Nevertheless, the future bears some relationship to the past, and in this past we have uncovered the effects and modes of operation of some very powerful and rather permanent forces. This knowledge permits considerable narrowing of the range of possibilities, with some description of their likely characteristics.

At the outset, it is helpful to make two important simplifying assumptions. First, we shall adopt the premise that a full-scale world war will not break out in the present decade. If open conflict were to occur, once again the industry would promptly become simply an adjunct to military operations, and as such, hardly recognizable in its normal peacetime aspects. Second, we shall assume that the effects of regional development upon maritime shipping have now largely been completed. After all, the coastwise dry-cargo trade is almost dead, while the surviving intercoastal segment has proved virile enough to meet the toughest kind of a challenge and therefore seems to have permanent viability.

On this reasoning, we are left with four main environmental forces: international politics and trade policies, business fluctuations in the United States, costs and competition, and labor-management relations. To these we must add a fifth factor, managerial initiative. To set forth what seem to be the main possibilities for the calculable future of the industry, we can now depict three alternative clusters of these primary influences: one that is optimistic, one that is pessimistic, and one that is cautious. At their own option, individual readers can devise further variations on this general theme.

We may begin by outlining an optimistic view. First, we shall assume that severe business fluctuations will not occur. Future relapses in production and income would then be modest and brief, fortified by strong underlying growth. Second, we shall suppose that labor-management relations have finally been permanently stabilized, hence that frequent and prolonged strikes now also belong to history. Third, we may add the presumption that cost pressure from the side of wages will cease to be extreme, and even that the unions will take a friendlier view of the productivity problem and so not impose barriers to promising cost-saving innovations, even if their price is some temporary unemployment. On this third general premise, it would be reasonable to infer that land carriers could not then widen their present cost advantages much further, hence that further incursions into domestic water traffic would be unlikely. Fourth, we shall assume that with steady American prosperity, coupled with vigorous measures to expand our imports and with the continued growth of relevant foreign production, barriers to foreign trade would gradually be lowered. Foreign tonnage would then slowly expand. Finally, we shall postulate a modest revival of managerial initiative, backed by adequate capital, and now willing and able to make innovations in equipment and work methods, and even some efforts to recapture former markets.

With this admittedly favorable cluster, a few tentative conclusions may now be drawn. Along with the growth of foreign trade, there would be a similar development for the noncontiguous, perhaps even augmented by the vigorous development of Alaska in particular. Intercoastal tonnage would surely hold its own, and indeed might even slowly expand. Coastwise dry cargo would remain necessarily small in the over-all total, but with the development of specially designed vessels to handle packaged lumber and loaded truck-trailer combinations, there would even be reasonable hope for some growth in this category.

In fact, if the water lines could attack successfully their shoreside and accessorial costs, they could recapture considerable long-haul dry cargo in bulk, in both the intercoastal and coastwise trades.

A pessimistic view would imply the converse of these general assumptions, with results that may quickly be summarized. With the recurrence of a major and prolonged depression, all trades would quickly drop and in time some marginal operations would be eliminated. With a revival of labor-management conflict on the former scale, major strikes would again be the order of the day, and wage pressure would be renewed at an extreme relative degree. Barriers to innovations would not be lowered. If anything, they would be raised. Although further significant losses of coastwise and intercoastal tonnage would hardly be possible, these trades could not look forward to any tangible improvement in their circumstances or their prospects. Foreign trade would likely be repressed further, with a renewal of beggar-thy-neighbor policies. Noncontiguous tonnage would expand over the long run, but probably at a slower rate. There would be little incentive and less scope for managerial initiative, hence no prospects for creating new markets or revitalizing old ones. The industry would merely continue to stagger along indefinitely at the halting gait of 1934.

On a cautious view, we would have to assume, first, that if the business cycle is not yet extinct, at least its swings would be less extreme and less prolonged. This would enable the industry to take its slumps in stride, and even to look forward to modest long-term growth. Second, we could assume that the idyllic picture of complete union-management coöperation is something reserved for the next world, hence that some conflict would continue. This would mean occasional coastwide strikes, though certainly a better record than that of 1934–1948. It would also mean some wage pressure and fairly stiff obstacles to cost-saving innovations in work methods and equipment; hence there would be rather small opportunity or incentive for major new services or recapture of lost traffic. Foreign trade would slowly expand, probably unhampered by major new restrictions. Noncontiguous commerce would grow with the Territories and the home economy.

Intercoastal trade would possibly enjoy very modest increases, but hardly more. Coastwise dry-cargo movements would remain negligible.

We believe that the cautious view is the safest one to take. It offers no great comfort, but at least it posits the survival and slow expansion of the industry, and it rests upon reasonably safe premises.

Man is never wholly the passive creature of his environment. Quite the contrary. His history is largely a record of spontaneous actions to transform and to control that environment. In its own modest way and in its more remote and more romantic past, the maritime shipping industry itself has shown a remarkable degree of creative power. There is no reason to suppose that today the industry lacks all opportunity for creative action to strengthen its position in the economy of the west. The principal tasks are to reduce costs and to enlarge the demands for shipping services. Various practical possibilities are in the offing.

The ability of the industry to enlarge its markets and to compete more effectively with its rivals is principally a problem of costs. In turn, the major difficulties concerning costs center in cargo-handling at the docks. In this connection it has been pointed out that substantial potential savings could be had from the introduction of generally adaptable loading pallets for uniform-package shipments, and from consolidation of diverse-package shipments into "unitized" gross loads.[1] These innovations, however, rest mainly upon labor saving, and their introduction would first require important concessions from the longshoremen's union regarding sling-load limits and dock labor requirements.

Other possibilities affecting cargo-handling involve improved dock facilities and specially adapted vessels. While some progress has been made recently in the construction of modern freight terminals at the Pacific Coast ports, many docks are obsolete, lacking cranes, modern conveyor systems, and short-loading devices. Many of them are badly arranged for access by motor trucks, which leads to congestion and costly delays. These limitations greatly inflate the costs of freight

---

[1] State of California, San Francisco Bay Ports Commission, *A Report on Intercoastal Shipping Problems, with Special Reference to the San Francisco Bay Ports Area*, prepared by J. A. Stumpf (San Francisco, June, 1953), pp. 21–24.

handling, by necessitating excess labor and overtime wage charges, and by increasing the turn-around time of vessels in port.[2] By contrast, rail and truck transportation have made impressive advances in the technology of freight handling at their terminals, relatively unhampered by union rules affecting craft jurisdictions and labor requirements. Within maritime shipping itself, the specialized tanker lines have clearly proved capable of holding their own during two decades of hard times in the industry, and in notable contrast to the faltering dry-cargo group. The principal reason is that the tankers carry a very limited range of uniform types of cargo, which can be handled at very low terminal costs. Handling costs are low because the cargoes can be transferred by mechanical methods requiring very little labor. If similar improvements, now available, could be introduced in the technology of dry-cargo transfers, the prospects for these lines could become much brighter.

For these advances to be practical, private investors and public bodies would have to be induced to overcome their pessimism regarding the future of the industry, while the longshore union would have to be willing to relax its stringent working rules if the potential savings in labor costs were to be realized.

Three types of specially adapted vessels also offer promise, especially in the coastwise trade: those for carrying loaded freight cars, truck-trailer combinations, and pre-packaged lumber. All three are innovations to eliminate costly labor at the docks, now required for the placement, assembly, movement, stowage, unloading, and transfer of dry cargoes. Again the obstacles are reluctance to invest and union obstructions, with the latter complicated by conflicting jurisdictional claims to the types of work involved in dock operations.

Of somewhat lesser importance from the standpoint of costs are the transit tolls for intercoastal ships using the Panama Canal and the scheduling of voyages relative to seasonal fluctuations in available tonnage. In recent years, Canal tolls have run as high as $9,000 per

---

[2] State of California, San Francisco Bay Ports Commission, *A Report on Pacific Coastwise Shipping, with Special Reference to the San Francisco Bay Ports Area*, prepared by R. F. Burley (San Francisco, June, 1953), p. 40; *Final Report of the Senate Fact-Finding Committee on the San Francisco Bay Ports* (Sacramento, California State Printing Office, 1951), pp. 22–23, 375–376.

voyage, which is substantial relative to total revenue.[3] It may well be that these tolls are excessive relative to the economic costs of providing Canal facilities to these carriers. Even if this were not the case, the national interest in conserving the merchant marine might well justify concessions in toll costs. Regarding scheduling of intercoastal vessels, it would be advantageous for the carriers to follow the model of the railroads and establish a shipper-carrier advisory board, to forecast future traffic requirements, so that schedules could be more closely related to available tonnage through the year.

On the side of demand, the attainment of durable peace between management and the unions would be of the greatest importance, particularly if it could lead to some measure of coöperation to reduce costs. We have remarked many times that such a *rapprochement* is vital to effective solution of the cost problem. This peace would be no less important to the recovery of shipper confidence, if it made sailings no longer subject to sudden and frequent interruptions.

Demand might also be stimulated in the coastwise and intercoastal trades if rate structures could be revised and simplified. In the intercoastal trade, for example, the establishment of through rates and through bills of lading (to include coöperating land carriers) would overcome the present disadvantages in the port-to-port system of water rates, while the water lines themselves could then attain substantial economies in accounting costs.[4] Moreover, careful study of competitive rail rates in these two trades would be desirable, to determine if they are uneconomically low relative to rail transportation costs, as the water carriers have repeatedly claimed.

In any case, there undoubtedly exist several significant ways by which ocean shipping might reverse its declining fortunes. In good part, the job involves the formidable task of attaining a fuller reconciliation of the interests of management and of the unions and their members, to bring about a more plastic environment for cost-saving innovations and for the creation of new demands for steamship serv-

---

[3] State of California, San Francisco Bay Ports Commission, *A Report on Intercoastal Shipping Problems . . .* , p. 31.

[4] *Ibid.*, pp. 25–28; Stanford Research Institute, *An Economic Analysis of Pacific Coast Trans-Pacific Shipping* (Stanford, Stanford [University] Research Institute, 1950), p. 2.

ices. More is required here than a mere truce to reduce strikes as such.
However, the over-all task also calls for vision, confidence, and the
willingness to invest fresh capital in what has hitherto proved to be
an unpromising field. No miracles are likely, but the opportunities are
there, obscure as they may sometimes seem to be.

It is fitting to close our account with an appropriate quotation from
an editorial appearing in the *Pacific Shipper* for October 31, 1949,
under the title, "What's Holding Shipping Up?"

After all the unmerciful beating that West Coast water transportation has
taken at the hands of longshore and maritime unions, and from global economics, why doesn't it fall to the canvas and take the count? What keeps it on
its feet? Punchdrunk as it certainly has been at times, why doesn't it go down?

Perhaps not all, but certainly a large part of the answer lies in the resolution
with which the operators pursue the formidable task of providing steamship
service. To be sure, their approach [is] often grim, but at the same time there
is an essential element of confidence and courage, of determination to do business and damn the torpedoes. . . .

The moral seems to be that Pacific Coast Shipping has a strong will to live,
a potent determination to survive. In the highest tradition of the pioneering
West, it dies hard.

The West Coast as a community, which in many respects has failed to provide a favorable climate for shipping, ought to be grateful for as much.

APPENDIX

APPENDIX

20. Coastwide and major local strikes for which losses can be computed, Pacific Coast maritime shipping industry, 1934–1948.
21. Total losses in man-days from coastwide and major local strikes, longshoremen and seamen, Pacific Coast maritime shipping, 1934–1948.
22. Dry-cargo tonnage handled by Pacific Coast maritime shipping industry, by trades, 1930–1939, 1946–1948.
23. Man-days available for work and percentage of time lost in strikes, longshoremen and seamen, Pacific Coast maritime shipping, selected years, 1934–1948.
24. Indexes of basic wage rates by occupations and craft groups, Pacific Coast maritime shipping industry, 1935–1948.
25. Indexes of the cost of living for moderate income families in large cities and of straight-time hourly earnings of employees of Class I railways, 1935–1948.
26. Indexes of estimated average hourly earnings, exclusive of overtime, of production workers in manufacturing and of basic wage rates in Pacific Coast maritime shipping, 1939–1948.
27. Estimated total dry-cargo tonnage handled by Pacific Coast longshoremen, 1935–1939, 1946–1948.
28. Rail rates for shipping selected commodities between certain Pacific Coast ports, 1929–1948.
29. Water rates for shipping selected commodities between certain Pacific Coast ports, 1929–1948.
30. Tons of revenue freight carried by steam railroads in California, Oregon, and Washington, 1930–1948.
31. Tons of freight carried in intercity service by motor carriers reporting tonnage to state public utilities commissions, California and Washington, 1930–1948.

TABLE 1

Pacific Coast Water-borne Foreign Trade Exports by Selected Commodity Groups, 1930–1940, 1946, and 1947[a][b]

(in tons of 2,240 lbs.)

Grp. no.	Commodity group[c]	1930	1931	1932	1933	1934	1935	1936	1937	1938	1939	1940	1946[d]	1947[e]
1	Grains and grain products	1,172,248	1,053,758	510,286	413,320	707,890	206,414	232,479	445,224	758,403	1,150,612	524,915	608,776	706,567
2	Animals, fruits, vegetables, and products	597,789	737,851	667,492	658,161	656,381	756,945	559,275	532,630	844,978	695,821	315,143	699,026	471,576
3	Cotton	68,785	92,865	59,173	45,800	75,732	93,137	69,021	164,317	135,941	90,771	99,406	16,643	26,581
4	Paper stock and manufactures	100,092	114,489	101,475	136,837	201,669	211,470	204,014	282,099	149,159	158,665	320,032	60,697	84,833
5	Logs and lumber	2,265,385	1,921,007	1,125,124	1,413,381	1,594,552	1,461,714	1,458,676	1,331,606	681,596	851,729	784,598	511,736	1,149,932
6	Iron, steel and manufactures	95,826	36,349	53,679	139,744	302,179	300,766	251,780	445,683	438,233	611,951	537,008	477,894	551,557
7	Ores, other metals, and manufactures	80,346	70,565	65,533	86,421	68,285	56,099	54,203	93,434	116,143	131,572	79,341	10,407	43,557
8	Pigments, chemicals, and manufactures, n.e.s.	108,447	109,310	98,867	97,036	127,991	134,119	124,343	168,055	108,401	135,881	132,500	140,253	113,160
9	Coal and coke	5,393	335	1,599	6,133	646	1,065	528	562	20,543	25,005	44,018	504,381	748,764
10	Petroleum and products	7,214,988	5,504,005	5,008,499	4,564,771	5,418,427	6,128,749	6,182,487	8,449,998	8,236,638	7,497,670	6,093,107	2,983,655	3,881,187
11	Other	255,217	240,034	155,935	303,409	265,521	288,390	247,981	270,168	256,493	319,722	383,419	467,532	1,517,286
	Total	11,964,516	9,880,568	7,847,662	7,865,013	9,419,273	9,638,868	9,384,787	12,183,776	11,746,528	11,669,399	9,313,487	6,481,000	9,295,000

ᵃ This table represents an attempt to join three separate commodity tonnage series. (See source note below.) Perfect matching of all commodity groupings is impossible. However, by consulting the commodity code tables showing the commodity composition of the Maritime Commission series for 1930–1937 and 1938–1940, these series have been sufficiently aligned to permit the analyses desired. Postwar statistics (compiled by the Bureau of the Census) have been adjusted to conform as closely as possible with prewar data by using the Bureau's *Schedule B, Statistical Classification of Domestic and Foreign Commodities Exported from the United States*, *Schedule S, Statistical Classification of Domestic and Foreign Merchandise Exported from the United States Arranged in Shipping Commodity Classifications Shown During 1937 Through 1945* in *Schedule B*. Detailed notes regarding certain of the matching difficulties appear below. Commodities or commodity groups accounting for very small tonnages are not shown separately in this table.

Broad export categories have been included in this table because the analytical purpose of the table is to depict the general commodity characteristics of Pacific Coast exports. Where necessary, the tonnage of certain components of the broad categories is cited separately in the text. They are not included in this table because there is a large number of them and their descriptions are not consistent throughout the period 1930–1947. To include the components would require much additional space in the table itself and voluminous footnotes to explain the reconciliations. Further, for our purposes, their inclusion would probably serve to obscure rather than clarify our basic analysis.

The data in this table cover commercial cargoes only. Military and relief program cargoes are not included.

ᵇ Figures for 1948 are available from the same source used to obtain 1947 data. The clerical expense involved in transcribing and segregating the information was beyond our limited means.

ᶜ Not all of the commodity groupings are those employed by the Maritime Commission and/or the Bureau of the Census. Some categories have been broadened to facilitate matching the statistical series used. Generally speaking, the 1930–1937 groupings have been used, with modifications to accommodate changes in the coverage under certain groupings. For example, part of the apparent increase in cotton exports (Group 3) during 1938–1940 as compared with the earlier and later years is attributable to changes in coverage. From 1930 to 1937 only raw cotton was included. During the period 1938–1940, linters and waste were added, and in 1946–1947, linters, but not waste, were included. Reference to other discrepancies is made in the text treatment of particular export groups. So far as can be determined none of them is sufficiently grave to invalidate the general inferences drawn from these export data.

ᵈ These tonnage figures do not include all shipments in the designated categories. *Foreign Commerce and Navigation of the United States, 1946* shows shipping weights by commodities by port, only if the total weight of the commodity passing through a Pacific Coast port in 1946 was 1,000,000 pounds or over or its value was $100,000 or more.

ᵉ These tonnage figures do not include all shipments of the designated items. The statistics were taken directly from the coded machine record, unpublished monthly reports. Lack of funds prevented using the selection criteria employed in *Foreign Commerce and Navigation....* (See above.) Instead, only commodities accounting for 1,000,000 pounds or more in a month in a customs district were included. This means that all of the annual tonnage of a commodity may not be accounted for if the exports of the item fell below 1,000,000 pounds in any customs district during any month. Comparison of 1946 and 1947 figures, however, suggests that, after allowance for the over-all increase in the export tonnage handled on the Pacific Coast in 1947, the discrepancies attributable to the different bases for selection are probably not large. For our purposes, the data are adequate though not precise.

SOURCE: For commodity and total tonnages, 1930–1937, United States Maritime Commission, Division of Research, "Waterborne foreign commerce of the United States," *Report No. 275*, annual (Washington, Government Printing Office, 1931–1938). For commodity and total tonnages, 1938–1940, United States Maritime Commission, Division of Research, "Waterborne foreign and noncontiguous commerce and passenger traffic of the United States," *Report No. 2610* (Washington, Government Printing Office, 1939–1941). For commodity tonnages, 1946, United States Department of Commerce, Bureau of the Census, *Foreign Commerce and Navigation of the United States, 1946*, Vol. II (Washington, Government Printing Office, 1950), pp. 237–255, 269–271, 343–347. For commodity tonnages, 1947, January–June, United States Department of Commerce, Bureau of the Census, "United States exports of domestic and foreign merchandise by vessel," *MC714*, monthly, unpublished. For 1947, July–December, United States Department of Commerce, Bureau of the Census, "Value and shipping weight of United States general exports on dry cargo vessels by domestic port of lading by foreign port of unlading by *Schedule S* commodity," *MC703*, monthly, unpublished; United States Department of Commerce, Bureau of the Census, "Value and shipping weight of United States general exports on tanker vessels by domestic port of lading by foreign port of unlading by *Schedule S* commodity," *MC703*, monthly, unpublished. For total tonnage, 1946, Department of Commerce, Bureau of the Census, *Foreign Commerce and Navigation of the United States*, annual, as quoted in the *Statistical Abstract of the United States, 1948*, p. 565. For total tonnage, 1947, Bureau of the Census, Foreign Trade Division, "Water-borne trade by United States port," *Summary Report FT 972*, 1948, as quoted in United States Department of Commerce, *Foreign Commerce Weekly*, XXVI (1949), 6.

TABLE 2

PACIFIC COAST WATER-BORNE FOREIGN TRADE IMPORTS BY SELECTED COMMODITY GROUPS, 1930–1940, 1946, AND 1947 [a][b]

(in tons of 2,240 lbs.)

Grp. no.	Commodity group [c]	1930	1931	1932	1933	1934	1935	1936	1937	1938	1939	1940	1946 [d]	1947 [e]
1	Coconuts and copra	225,025	165,460	184,725	240,375	164,479	204,056	162,872	206,915	184,439	184,577	222,179	265,914	399,567
2	Sugar and molasses	122,421	95,455	89,934	90,835	209,779	76,001	130,196	116,597	81,476	71,163	66,285	f	9,918
3	Coffee and cocoa	92,669	90,468	80,364	85,364	84,789	100,353	90,887	104,662	127,636	122,645	129,361	156,805	148,484
4	Grains and grain products	37,598	14,881	5,567	15,724	26,268	267,703	382,762	228,777	7,377	21,932	31,551	2,264	f
5	Fruits, vegetables, and products	420,870	351,832	282,025	337,351	357,927	524,733	478,882	516,039	321,295	362,657	429,451	59,816	119,636
6	Jute, jute manufactures, and other vegetable fibers and grasses	87,333	55,058	50,362	55,556	59,147	61,128	61,963	74,502	64,806	74,066	73,963	43,159	54,289
7	Paper and paper stock	197,242	153,100	195,811	185,347	199,088	244,369	254,210	273,475	212,831	264,190	207,072	178,983	247,807
8	Logs and lumber	365,214	242,367	205,087	199,532	185,802	333,188	303,162	389,734	390,671	405,618	458,537	214,564	247,830
9	Petroleum and products	6,263	6,535	6,511	9,302	3,386	5,021	47,307	60,761	4,952	10,336	53,536	90,722	17,279
10	Coal and coke	101,689	62,355	48,410	41,623	50,879	79,218	97,642	109,649	80,756	57,790	42,663	27,747	7,291
11	Metallic ores and manufactures	489,348	308,562	226,056	175,759	230,211	400,072	398,796	400,509	344,881	386,044	404,258	170,667	287,770
12	Nonmetallic minerals and manufactures	326,813	136,042	68,952	108,711	132,475	193,628	182,225	205,680	132,163	163,193	150,839	84,195	207,498
13	Pigments, chemicals, and manufactures, n.e.s.	95,303	61,836	45,197	38,460	48,218	41,750	22,659	25,087	66,349	57,447	39,427	6,175	37,913
14	Fertilizers	119,036	117,592	87,092	105,301	93,905	72,891	120,175	137,194	73,911	71,010	73,556	35,756	42,443
15	Other	218,051	194,508	147,561	163,013	166,362	191,508	242,686	228,263	136,436	195,792	193,432	803,233	362,275
	Total	2,904,875	2,056,051	1,724,254	1,852,253	2,012,715	2,795,619	2,976,424	3,077,844	2,229,979	2,448,460	2,576,110	2,140,000	2,190,000

[...] matching of all commodity groupings is impossible. However, by consulting the commodity code tables showing the commodity composition of the Maritime Commission series for 1930–1937 and 1938–1940, these series have been sufficiently aligned to permit the analyses desired. Prewar statistics (compiled by the Bureau of the Census) have been adjusted to conform as closely as possible with prewar data by using the Bureau's *Schedule A, Statistical Classification of Imports into the United States,* and *Schedule T, Statistical Classification of Imports into the United States Arranged in Shipping Commodity Groups.* Detailed notes regarding certain of the matching difficulties appear below. Commodities or commodity groups accounting for very small tonnages are not shown separately in this table.

The import commodity group categories were selected on the basis of their contribution to the analytical purpose of this table. Some groupings are therefore broader than others. Some of the components of the broad classifications are cited separately in the text. They are not included in this table because there is a large number of them and their descriptions are not consistent throughout the period 1930–1947. To include them would require much additional space in the table itself and voluminous notes to explain the reconciliations. Further, for our purposes, their inclusion would probably serve to obscure rather than clarify our basic analysis.

The data in this table cover commercial cargoes only. Military and relief program cargoes are not included.

b Figures for 1948 are available from the same source used to obtain 1947 data. The clerical expense involved in transcribing and segregating the information was beyond our limited means.

c Not all of the commodity groupings are those employed by the Maritime Commission and/or the Bureau of the Census. Some categories have been broadened to facilitate matching the statistical series used. Generally speaking, the 1930–1937 groupings have been used, with modifications, to accommodate changes in their scope or description in the two later series. So far as can be determined, there are only minor (from the standpoint of this study) discrepancies attributable to differences in the commodities included under each commodity group in each of the series used. There are some discrepancies between pre- and postwar figures because of differences in methods of data collection. (See below, note e.)

d These tonnage figures do not include all shipments in the designated categories. *Foreign Commerce and Navigation of the United States, 1946* shows shipping weights by commodity by port, only if the total weight of the commodity passing through a Pacific Coast port in 1946 was 1,000,000 pounds or over or its value was $100,000 or more.

tistics were taken directly from the coded machine record, unpublished monthly reports. Lack of funds prevented using the selection criteria employed in *Foreign Commerce and Navigation. . . .* (See above.) Instead, only commodities accounting for 1,000,000 pounds or more in a month in a customs district were included. This means that all of the *annual* tonnage of a commodity may not be accounted for if the imports of the item fell below 1,000,000 pounds in any customs district during any month. Comparison of 1946 and 1947 figures, however, suggests that, after allowance for the over-all increase in the import tonnage handled on the Pacific Coast in 1947, the discrepancies attributable to the different bases for selection are probably not large. Again, for our purposes, the data are adequate though not precise.

f There may have been imports in this category, but the selection process (see above, notes d and e) excluded them from the statistical series.

SOURCE: For commodity and total tonnages, 1930–1937, United States Maritime Commission, Division of Research, "Waterborne foreign commerce of the United States," *Report No. 275,* annual (Washington, Government Printing Office, 1931–1938). For commodity and total tonnages, 1938–1940, United States Maritime Commission. Bureau of Research, "Waterborne foreign and noncontiguous commerce and passenger traffic of the United States," *Report No. 2610* (Washington, Government Printing Office, 1939–1941). For commodity tonnages, 1946, United States Department of Commerce, Bureau of the Census, *Foreign Commerce and Navigation of the United States, 1946,* Vol. II (Washington, Government Printing Office, 1950), pp. 321–331, 341, 348–351. For commodity tonnages, 1947, January–June, United States Department of Commerce, Bureau of the Census, "United States imports of merchandise by vessel," *MC 814,* monthly, unpublished. For commodity tonnages, 1947, July–December, United States Department of Commerce, Bureau of the Census, "Value and shipping weight of United States general imports on dry cargo vessels by domestic port of unlading by foreign port of lading by *Schedule T commodity,*" *FT 308,* monthly, unpublished. United States Department of Commerce, Bureau of the Census, "Value and shipping weight of United States general imports on tanker vessels by domestic port of unlading by foreign port of lading by *Schedule T commodity,*" *FT 308,* monthly, unpublished. For total annual tonnages, 1946, Department of Commerce, Bureau of the Census, *Foreign Commerce and Navigation of the United States,* annual, as quoted in the *Statistical Abstract of the United States, 1948,* p. 565. For total tonnage, 1947, Bureau of the Census, Foreign Trade Division, "Waterborne trade by United States port," *Summary Report FT 972,* 1948, as quoted in United States Department of Commerce, *Foreign Commerce Weekly,* XXVI (1949), 6.

TABLE 3—Pacific Coast Water-borne Trade with Alaska and Hawai

Group no.	Commodity group[b]	1930	1931	1932	1933
		Imports			
1	Sugar and molasses.......................................	854,707	766,225	663,143	681,38?
2	Fruits, vegetables, and products...........................	216,339	200,170	89,023	143,90(
3	Fish and products[e].....................................	177,687	187,321	180,026	176,17?
4	Fertilizers..	12,914	8,277	10,447	11,29(
5	Nonmetallic minerals.....................................	189,836	130,480	87,767	57?
6	Metallic ores and manufactures...........................	74,652	37,539	22,601	11,08?
7	Other[g]..	36,252	31,300	26,648	30,35?
	Total..	1,562,387	1,361,312	1,079,655	1,054,76?
		Exports			
1	Animals, fish, vegetables, and products[h]..................	30,225	36,372	38,541	52,53
2	Animal feeds and fodder, grains and grain products[h]........	119,256	126,393	116,557	114,36
3	Logs and lumber..	152,404	132,687	107,575	116,19
4	Paper stock and manufactures[i]...........................	25,122	30,966	21,773	31,32
5	Iron, steel and manufactures.............................	81,705	60,512	49,226	55,38
6	Nonmetallic minerals and manufactures....................	74,230	67,749	55,012	42,10
7	Fertilizers (excluding phosphates).........................	22,475	26,920	14,869	31,3€
8	Coal and coke..	31,771	27,787	24,459	22,95
9	Petroleum and products..................................	581,195	474,780	369,183	398,22
10	Other..	156,681	134,573	130,060	123,3?
	Total..	1,275,064	1,118,739	927,255	987,79

[a] This table represents an attempt to join several separate commodity series. Perfect matching of all commodi groupings is impossible. However, by consulting the commodity code tables showing the commodity composition the Maritime Commission series for 1930–1937 and 1938–1940, these series have been sufficiently aligned to pern the analyses desired. Postwar statistics (compiled from unofficial sources—see source note below) have been fitted the commodity groupings derived from the joining of the prewar Maritime Commission statistics. Detailed no regarding certain matching difficulties appear below.

Commodities or commodity groups accounting for very small tonnages are not shown separately in this tab

The data in this table cover commercial cargoes only. Military and relief program cargoes are not included.

The discrepancies between postwar total export-import figures in this table and those shown in Gorter and Hil brand, *op. cit.*, Vol. I, Appendix II, table 7, are attributable to the receipt of additional information after Volum was accepted for publication.

[b] For the most part, the commodity groupings are based upon the 1930–1937 classifications employed by the Ma time Commission. They have been adjusted to facilitate matching the later series with the series covering the earl years. The components of the broad categories are not included in the table because there is a large number of the and their descriptions are not consistent throughout the period 1930–1948. To include the components would requ much additional space in the table itself and voluminous footnotes to explain the reconciliations. Further, for c purposes, the inclusion of the components would probably serve to obscure rather than clarify our basic analys

[c] The figures for 1946 and 1947 (except as noted below) are in revenue tons and cover trade with Hawaii only lifted by Matson Navigation Company vessels.

[d] Exports for 1948 include, in addition to Matson Navigation Company cargoes, shipments by the Alaska Stea ship Company to Alaska. In this addition we have assumed that revenue tons are the equivalent of long tons.

[e] In matching the 1930–1937 series with the 1938–1940 series four different components have been reconciled. T 1930–1937 series includes "Salmon" and "Fish and products." In 1938–1940, the two categories used are "Anim fish, and dairy products, edible" and "Oils, animal, fish and vegetable." For trade with Hawaii and Alaska, 1930–1937 statistics show no imports of animal or dairy products or of vegetable oils. A substantial importation of th items during 1938–1940 appears, therefore, to have been unlikely. By inference, then, the 1930–1937 and 1938–1 commodity groupings are sufficiently comparable for our purposes.

[f] Not available.

ʙʏ Selected Commodity Groups, 1930–1940, 1946–1948[a] (in tons of 2,240 lbs.)

1934	1935	1936	1937	1938	1939	1940	1946[c]	1947[c]	1948[d]
				Imports					
614,319	684,852	649,054	709,181	655,654	708,495	640,275	586,861	823,352	675,184
189,624	188,421	261,121	237,688	189,674	254,047	201,492	225,295	290,543	185,321
226,655	167,639	269,962	208,433	221,589	185,298	138,171	f	f	f
13,503	15,636	14,219	19,697	14,744	13,177	6,763	f	f	f
522	126,790	91,897	129,775	102,430	176,798	135,819	f	f	f
9,841	28,032	32,623	61,184	55,044	24,771	23,252	f	f	f
41,926	48,556	49,457	50,944	40,499	39,675	46,635	192,367	178,364	108,172
1,096,390	1,259,926	1,368,333	1,416,902	1,279,634	1,402,261	1,192,407	1,004,523	1,292,259	968,677
				Exports					
56,157	58,335	65,504	62,173	68,829	80,521	100,632	f	35,654	36,509
105,796	110,603	99,718	100,117	110,363	106,985	116,933	125,421	153,977	103,947
121,224	135,203	169,087	245,843	175,328	176,464	224,412	58,970j	198,570	125,914
38,464	37,555	42,337	49,583	35,294	40,217	46,100	f	8,293	42,983
68,814	68,432	78,519	81,683	47,387	50,426	88,833	95,818	152,987	139,438
58,996	58,411	62,768	66,647	67,979	76,353	167,072	31,271	24,797	26,074
9,498	11,290	10,147	12,290	9,749	12,817	14,351	74,578k	94,251k	71,626k
25,625	24,783	23,026	20,513	19,424	14,924	14,263	f	f	2,978
536,479	552,031	634,277	735,557	639,746	699,544	993,083	899,303l	1,071,567l	1,321,775m
140,239	163,993	164,642	178,205	246,814	272,523	380,563	278,583n	53,500n	623,903n
1,161,292	1,220,636	1,350,025	1,552,611	1,420,913	1,530,774	2,146,242	1,563,944	1,793,596	2,495,147

ᵍ For 1946, 1947, and 1948 "other" refers to Matson Navigation Company "general merchandise."

ʰ These categories differ from the foreign trade classifications. Animal feeds and fodder have been included with ʳains and grain products to make possible prewar and postwar comparisons.

ⁱ The 1930–1937 components include wood pulp, which is not included in the 1938–1940 components. The assumpᵗⁱon is, however, that wood pulp did not move in significant quantities to Alaska and Hawaii.

ʲ This figure was estimated by multiplying total lumber tonnage to Alaska and Hawaii from Oregon and Wash-ᵢⁿgton in 1947–1948 by the percentage of total shipments (from Oregon and Washington to Alaska and Hawaii) atᵗributable to Matson shipments to Hawaii only in 1947–1948.

ᵏ Includes shipments from British Columbia, Canada. Includes phosphates.

ˡ Postwar shipments are reported only for Alaska and Hawaii combined. The figures shown are estimates for ᵃwaii only. Estimates made by multiplying total annual shipments by weighted average annual ratio of shipments ᵗᵒ Hawaii to total shipments to Alaska and Hawaii combined for the period 1930–1940.

ᵐ Alaska and Hawaii combined.

ⁿ This figure may include tonnage of commodities ordinarily included in other categories. The descriptions in ᵗʰe basic records used (see below) were not clear enough to permit us to classify them as falling within the other cateᵍories used.

Source: For commodity and total tonnages, 1930–1937, United States Maritime Commission, Division of Re-ᵉarch, "Waterborne foreign commerce of the United States," *Report No. 275*, annual (Washington, Government ᵖʳinting Office, 1931–1938). For commodity and total tonnages, 1938–1940, United States Maritime Commission, ᴰivision of Research, "Waterborne foreign and noncontiguous commerce and passenger traffic of the United States," *ᵣeport No. 2610* (Washington, Government Printing Office, 1939–1941). For commodity tonnage, 1946 and 1947 (except ᵤmber, 1946), records of the Matson Navigation Company, San Francisco. For 1946 lumber, Pacific Lumber Inspec-ᵗⁱon Bureau, "Waterborne shipments of lumber as reported to this Bureau," *Circular*, no. 808, 823, 841 (Seattle, ᵂashington, n.d.). For petroleum and products tonnage, 1946–1948, compiled for the authors by the Standard Oil ᶜompany of California from United States Department of Interior, Bureau of Mines, Petroleum Economics Branch, "The petroleum situation in the Pacific Coast territory," *Statistical and Economic Surveys* (Los Angeles, monthly), ᵖʳocessed. For commodity tonnage, 1948, records of the Matson Navigation Company, San Francisco, records of the ᴬlaska Steamship Company, Seattle. For total export tonnage, 1946 and 1947, United States Department of Com-ᵐerce, Bureau of the Census, "Annual tabulation of monthly noncontiguous summary cards," *EA 699*, unpublished.

TABLE 4—Pacific Coast Inbound Intercoastal Trade by Selected

Group no.	Commodity group[b]	1930	1931	1932	1933
1	Iron, steel and manufactures.................	941,361	626,783	322,779	482,622
2	Machinery..............................	46,913	39,832	28,706	27,465
3	Automobiles and autotrucks..................	48,038	51,400	35,170	35,193
4	Textiles................................	40,379	50,234	40,288	49,765
5	Tinplate................................	119,815	85,926	53,334	14,945
6	Miscellaneous manufactured goods, n.e.i.......	71,501	107,337	57,387	48,745
7	Soap and products........................	25,839	28,980	27,709	25,160
8	Nitrates................................	....	....	15,326	22,214
9	Sulphur................................	131,286	117,566	93,830	128,625
10	Chemicals, n.e.i..........................	....	30,844	29,032	35,013
11	Liquors................................	....	....	....	....
12	Corn..................................	....	....	127,457	70,815
13	Canned and preserved goods.................	67,266	81,121	80,665	87,849
14	Glass and glassware.......................	....	22,770	29,607	34,390
15	Paper, paper scrap, and paper products........	68,287	67,865	66,092	77,390
16	Metals.................................	30,073	20,653	12,661	....
17	Oils, mineral............................	92,158	111,575	115,874	147,486
18	General[d]..............................	527,930	335,904	216,086	224,782
19	Other.................................	484,674	369,462	349,844	388,977
	Total...............................	2,695,520	2,148,252	1,701,847	1,901,436

a The war years, 1941–1945, omitted because intercoastal trade almost disappeared during this period.
b *The Panama Canal Record* (see below) contains detailed commodity breakdowns too numerous to warrant reproduction here. Only the commodities and/or commodity groups contributing at least 1.5 per cent of annual inbound tonnage in any year are included in this table. Where no entry appears for a given category this indicates that either no tonnage was reported or the tonnage was so small that it was obviously less than 1.5 per cent of total inbound tonnage for that year and therefore not included in the tabulations upon which this table is based. The postwar figures are all-inclusive because they were obtained by specific request direct from The Panama Canal (see below) by the categories shown and The Panama Canal did not employ the 1.5 per cent criterion.

TABLE 5—Pacific Coast Outbound Intercoastal Trade by

Group no.	Commodity group[b]	1930	1931	1932	1933
1	Sugar.................................	119,242	195,705	198,789	272,566
2	Fruit, dried.............................	106,457	147,284	168,894	154,562
3	Flour.................................	....	66,696	84,552	173,653
4	Wheat................................	....	....	....	96,647
5	Canned goods...........................	583,662	495,562	537,314	579,962
6	Beans, edible, dry.......................	53,020	65,836	59,102	71,415
7	Paper, paper scrap and products.............	102,285	85,898	79,074	82,653
8	Wood pulp.............................	98,112	105,814	105,180	101,983
9	Lumber and hardwoods....................	1,902,717	1,852,675	1,073,707	1,289,908
10	Oils, mineral............................	3,152,233	2,040,517	1,505,378	2,552,311
11	Asphalt and tar.........................	....	....	....	....
12	Metals................................	121,957	88,954	62,145	88,424
13	General[c]..............................	159,956	134,887	84,944	91,292
14	Other.................................	466,537	371,312	338,885	401,921
	Total...............................	6,866,178	5,651,140	4,297,964	5,957,297

a The war years, 1941–1945, omitted because intercoastal trade almost disappeared during this period.
b *The Panama Canal Record* (see below) contains detailed commodity breakdowns too numerous to warrant reproduction here. Only the commodities and/or commodity groups contributing at least 1.5 per cent of total annual outbound tonnage in any year are included in this table. Where no entry appears for a given category this indicates that either no tonnage was reported or the tonnage was so small that it was obviously less than 1.5 per cent of total outbound tonnage for that year and therefore not included in the tabulations upon which this table is based. The postwar figures are all-inclusive because they were obtained by specific request direct from The Panama Canal (see below) by the categories shown and The Panama Canal did not employ the 1.5 per cent criterion.

Commodity Groups, 1930–1940, 1946–1948 [a] (in tons of 2,240 lbs.)

1934	1935	1936	1937	1938	1939	1940	1946	1947	1948
559,105	719,138	912,637	1,146,645	675,527	931,281	1,155,750	478,159	788,161	567,100
32,424[c]	55,850	43,124	38,828	....	31,177[c]	....	9,741	20,932	12,822
20,388	32,304	59,730	35,573	15,105	30,351	....	3,376	3,854	3,080
45,253	55,119	46,521	45,453	38,843	44,789	45,364	4,258	4,856	3,531
54,865	70,803	55,983	53,826	55,936	56,217	71,482	5,093	14,775	7,157
25,382	36,891	40,285	81,189	77,603	109,390	133,614	71,806	107,560	83,899
21,605	....	....	....	24,840	....	28,767	6,305	6,246	3,419
28,169	....	27,615	26,265	18,677	24,665	21,584	602	2,696	63
126,362	127,983	143,188	202,755	93,481	181,949	164,113	57,030	76,451	87,751
40,513	49,584	46,676	47,480	44,006	54,827	49,938	19,677	16,312	18,444
24,897	40,849	34,675	36,376	39,536	40,085	21,584	6,475	8,705	9,052
73,318	....	....	....	....	16,531	....	40	....	....
83,605	94,442	89,706	107,929	85,641	102,670	106,827	35,802	28,399	42,347
28,892	35,690	....	....	....	....	....	621	766	229
93,515	109,211	103,018	119,436	122,856	125,779	136,270	61,485	81,251	85,346
....	....	34,027	33,304	26,423	43,009	38,698	....	....	....
122,696	121,449	147,891	155,397	157,285	127,248	125,616	168,913	132,411	140,463
215,715	245,732	227,541	211,853	181,346	170,091	154,440	140,034	119,504	117,811
390,051	514,383	491,034	478,958	488,765	582,415	615,024	197,518	230,565	185,402
1,986,755	2,309,428	2,503,651	2,821,267	2,145,870	2,672,474	2,869,071	1,266,935	1,643,444	1,367,916

[c] *The Panama Canal Record* notes that this tonnage does not include electrical machinery.
[d] "General" refers to small miscellaneous shipments, according to information furnished to the authors by The Panama Canal.

SOURCE: For commodity tonnages, 1930–1940, *The Panama Canal Record*, Vol. XXIII, no. 28—Vol. XXXIV, no. 6 (Balboa Heights, C.Z., The Panama Canal, Feb. 12, 1930–Jan. 30, 1941). For commodity tonnages, 1946–1948, letter, E. C. Lombard, Executive Secretary, The Panama Canal, Office of the Governor, Canal Zone, February 28, 1951. For total annual inbound tonnage, letter, E. C. Lombard, Executive Secretary, The Panama Canal, Executive Department, Canal Zone, September 27, 1949.

Selected Commodity Groups, 1930–1940, 1946–1948 [a] (in tons of 2,240 lbs.)

1934	1935	1936	1937	1938	1939	1940	1946	1947	1948
220,890	287,605	230,761	112,207	177,174	211,323	178,794	18,930	298	1,015
147,519	144,683	114,632	121,046	154,138	134,887	138,619	4,548	18,936	16,835
229,344	328,109	242,148	221,550	145,585	92,527	127,045	28,368	19,918	2,977
168,180	90,120	91,716	95,628	15,375	987	24,865	51,019	16,813	357
607,535	623,838	675,218	667,387	642,932	747,142	691,745	190,844	297,967	238,592
68,300	71,152	56,097	58,251	64,669	66,048	56,843	1,180	2,193	2,771
74,250	87,900	66,703	80,678	69,330	81,982	81,169	16,558	16,381	27,507
82,921	108,867	125,724	191,488	170,475	218,306	149,451	21,968	39,078	33,890
918,398	1,282,333	1,424,543	1,413,200	1,240,294	1,729,367	1,679,677	462,850	910,999	791,701
3,429,489	1,154,339	931,348	668,504	630,130	1,077,765	789,471	161,879	184,669	305,584
11,026	75,157	49,690	62,831	74,315	75,769	90,974	11	3	....
88,961	119,697	122,570	60,797	59,493	62,009	37,055	13,618	31,192	7,875
101,928	108,529	101,276	65,423	52,697	59,112	....	33,080	58,661	31,003
503,064	580,762	455,252	412,137	354,441	423,813	359,463	458,576	284,425	291,484
6,651,805	5,063,091	4,687,678	4,231,127	3,851,048	4,981,037	4,405,171	1,463,429	1,881,560	1,751,591

[c] "General" refers to small miscellaneous shipments, according to information furnished to the authors by The Panama Canal.

SOURCE: For commodity tonnages, 1930–1940, *The Panama Canal Record*, Vol. XXIII, no. 28—Vol. XXXIV, no. 6 Balboa Heights, C.Z., The Panama Canal, Feb. 12, 1930–Jan. 30, 1941). For commodity tonnages, 1946–1948, letter, E. C. Lombard, Executive Secretary, The Panama Canal, Office of the Governor, Canal Zone, February 28, 1951. For total annual outbound tonnage, letter, E. C. Lombard, Executive Secretary, The Panama Canal, Executive Department, Canal Zone, September 27, 1949.

TABLE 6

PACIFIC COAST COASTWISE TRADE BY PRINCIPAL COMMODITY GROUPS,
1930–1940, 1946–1948[a]

(in thousands of 2,240-lb. tons)

Year	Total (1)	Lumber (2)	General cargo (3)	Petroleum (4)
1930	24,790	1,646	1,072	22,072
1931	22,983	1,187	1,120	20,676
1932	17,018	737	1,012	15,269
1933	17,188	896	1,092	15,200
1934	14,339	720	929	12,690
1935	16,323	1,179	1,056	14,088
1936	19,221	1,312	731	17,178
1937	23,903	1,420	635	21,848
1938	24,211	1,427	652	22,132
1939	23,662	1,485	652	21,525
1940	25,951	1,446	b	a
1946	19,000[a]	219	124	a
1947	19,247	304	a	18,768
1948	22,172[a]	359	a	21,773

[a] The missing figures for 1946–1948 (petroleum in 1946 and general cargo in 1946 and 1947) cannot be estimated or derived from the available data in a manner that would make them consistent with the 1930–1940 figures. The 1946–1948 total tonnage figures were estimated by adding the known or estimated petroleum tonnages to the dry-cargo tonnage estimates provided by the Pacific American Steamship Association. (See Gorter and Hildebrand, *op. cit.*, Vol. I, p. 28 and Appendix II, table 8.) Had these total tonnage figures been available from the same or as reliable a source as the prewar data we should have been willing to derive and include in this table the missing postwar figures for petroleum and general cargo.

[b] Not available.

SOURCE: *Column 1*, 1930–1940, 1946–1947, Gorter and Hildebrand, *op. cit.*, Vol. I, Appendix II, table 8; 1948, petroleum tonnage (see column 4 source note below) and dry-cargo tonnage as provided by Pacific American Steamship Association (*ibid.*, p. 28). *Column 2*, Pacific Lumber Inspection Bureau, "Waterborne shipments of lumber as reported to this Bureau," *Circular* (Seattle, Pacific Lumber Inspection Bureau, n.d.), mimeographed. *Column 3*, 1930–1939, Gorter and Hildebrand, *op. cit.*, Vol. I, Appendix II, table 6 (converted to long tons); 1946, *ibid.*, p. 28. *Column 4*, 1930–1940, derived as follows: column 1 − [column 2 + column 3]; 1947, United States Maritime Commission, Bureau of Government Aids, Research Division, *Tankship Traffic in United States Domestic Trade*, summary report prepared in the Trade Routes Branch (Washington, 1948), p. 1; 1948, Department of the Army, Corps of Engineers, South Pacific Division, special tabulation for the authors, unpublished, San Francisco, September 12, 1952.

TABLE 7—Pacific Coast Water-borne Foreign Trade Cargo Tonnage by

Region no.	Foreign trade region[b]	1930	1931	1932	1933
		Imports			
1	Caribbean, Central America, Mexico......................	265.2	197.9	153.1	162.2
2	East coast of South America............................	87.1	79.4	65.7	81.6
3	West coast of South America...........................	167.7	71.3	37.9	68.5
4	United Kingdom..	86.1	49.9	33.4	39.7
5	Baltic Scandinavia, Iceland, Greenland..................	64.9	43.7	47.3	55.2
6	Bayonne-Hamburg range, Portugal, Spanish Atlantic......	384.7	260.9	186.0	170.1
7	Azores, Mediterranean, Black Sea.......................	20.6	14.2	12.7	13.9
8	South, East, and West Africa...........................	0.6	c	c	......
9	Australasia, Antarctica................................	82.0	56.5	35.8	34.3
10	India, Persian Gulf, Red Sea...........................	62.1	36.4	34.2	35.8
11	East Indies, East Asia.................................	868.9	722.2	625.9	781.9
12	Canada..	814.9	523.6	492.3	409.1
	Totals[d]...	2,904.8	2,056.0	1,724.3	1,852.3
		Exports			
1	Caribbean, Central America, Mexico......................	1,092.1	731.5	495.4	515.9
2	East coast of South America............................	293.6	76.7	66.7	56.2
3	West coast of South America............................	857.0	529.7	125.7	236.3
4	United Kingdom..	2,146.6	1,311.0	1,080.3	867.0
5	Baltic Scandinavia, Iceland, Greenland..................	39.5	71.1	44.0	55.3
6	Bayonne-Hamburg range, Portugal, Spanish Atlantic......	861.7	646.6	521.6	452.2
7	Azores, Mediterranean, Black Sea.......................	64.6	40.6	136.9	79.2
8	South, East, and West Africa...........................	34.4	29.9	17.5	25.5
9	Australasia, Antarctica................................	1,080.3	693.3	823.7	688.8
10	India, Persian Gulf, Red Sea...........................	104.7	104.5	25.6	34.9
11	East Indies, East Asia.................................	4,325.4	4,685.8	3,620.1	4,030.5
12	Canada..	1,064.6	959.8	890.2	823.4
	Totals[d]...	11,964.5	9,880.5	7,847.7	7,865.2

a Imports only, for 1948. Our limited funds did not permit tabulation of export tonnages.
b These foreign trade regions are not precisely the same as those appearing in any one of the sources from which the above data were taken. This is unavoidable. In 1938, the United States Maritime Commission altered the nomenclature as well as the geographic boundaries of the foreign trade regions in their reports. The postwar data, obtained from the Bureau of the Census, show foreign trade by commodity by domestic and foreign port of lading or unlading.

We have used a regional instead of a country breakdown of foreign trade for two reasons. First, the regional breakdown involves fewer entries, thus simplifying the analyses without undue sacrifice of their significance. Second, the expense involved in the compilation of statistics by country for the entire period would have been beyond our limited financial resources.

Our decision, however, to use only regional figures did not simplify the methodological problem of matching the different regions used by the Maritime Commission during 1930–1940. By inspection of the components of the 1930–1937 and 1938–1940 regions used by the Commission, we have developed regional classifications that, with minor exceptions, yield a consistent series from 1930 to 1940.

Joining the postwar statistics to this series involved a different problem: domestic and foreign port data were available and had to be combined into regional totals. To save time and financial expense we tabulated the unpublished monthly foreign trade statistics for 1947 by customs districts and by foreign country of origin or destination instead of by foreign port of unlading or lading. Then we combined the country totals to derive foreign trade region figures. For 1946, the data were different. They showed annual totals by ports, foreign and domestic. We combined foreign port totals by country and then derived foreign trade region totals. These procedures created unavoidable discrepancies between prewar and postwar regional totals, because in the prewar series some countries were included in more than one foreign trade region.

Once, for the postwar years, we did segregate a country (Russia) total into subtotals appropriate to particular trade regions. Russia imported substantial cargoes from the Pacific Coast for delivery to ports in Asiatic Russia. For 1946, we have accurate data showing shipments to Russia by Russian port. Two regions received these cargoes—region no. 11 (East Indies and East Asia) and region no. 7 (Azores, Mediterranean, and Black Sea). For 1947 we know only the total tonnage of Pacific Coast exports to Russia. We estimated the share going to region no. 11 and region no. 7 by multiplying the 1947 total cargo tonnage of Pacific Coast exports to Russia as a whole by the percentage of 1946 total tonnage that went to each of these regions.

The discrepancies remaining after the adjustment of the figures for exports to Russia are not detrimental to our analysis. The following is an example of the type of discrepancy that remains. Colombia has ports in the Caribbean and on the west coast of South America. Our figures credit the Caribbean with all of Colombia's foreign trade—roughly 80,000 long tons of the Caribbean's over 1 million long ton total for 1947.

FOREIGN TRADE REGIONS, 1930–1940, 1946–1948 [a] (in thousands of 2,240-lb. tons)

1934	1935	1936	1937	1938	1939	1940	1946	1947	1948
Imports									
196.0	211.2	196.9	271.6	252.3	271.8	318.0	205.3	331.7	388.4
68.9	308.2	437.4	326.4	79.5	118.1	123.4	103.4	106.5	113.9
116.4	128.2	115.5	152.6	135.6	135.9	190.9	130.0	217.9	212.1
56.4	51.4	76.0	49.9	45.1	35.0	65.0	3.1	46.6	48.2
69.2	166.0	156.2	138.1	97.3	109.0	20.1	18.2	65.6	118.1
157.3	230.3	272.8	286.0	207.8	141.4	7.7	4.3	15.7	37.2
11.3	49.7	86.0	11.4	9.8	11.6	4.8	0.5	8.0	13.1
......	......	c	4.4	c	c	......	0.2	6.6	0.7
23.0	41.0	35.0	48.8	42.4	50.5	56.1	133.4	52.1	54.0
37.9	38.9	50.1	63.5	51.9	55.5	59.1	78.0	60.0	57.9
842.7	930.7	967.3	927.3	597.3	685.3	802.7	286.1	542.7	536.6
433.5	640.0	583.3	797.9	711.0	834.4	928.3	518.9	629.6	929.1
2,012.6	2,795.6	2,976.5	3,077.9	2,230.0	2,448.5	2,576.1	1,481.4 [e]	2,083.0 [f]	2,509.3 [f]
Exports									
705.0	525.5	740.3	1,247.0	935.7	1,058.6	826.6	304.6	786.4	
168.8	123.9	69.3	81.9	73.5	101.0	112.1	80.6	341.7	
319.8	348.3	336.7	610.9	521.5	460.5	499.0	159.8	244.1	
788.8	1,007.8	828.7	965.3	1,202.7	1,112.0	524.0	276.8	1,216.3	
51.3	55.5	53.4	64.0	114.2	98.6	44.1	172.0	203.4	
490.1	539.0	539.9	625.1	775.4	531.6	63.5	661.7	774.5	
68.2	72.5	57.7	82.1	115.0	35.8	20.8	557.0	277.4	
42.0	44.9	52.5	79.1	41.6	68.5	87.5	62.8	157.3	
670.6	667.2	532.0	550.8	512.6	324.7	296.1	580.4	982.7	
30.0	44.6	35.1	69.2	52.6	59.6	118.4	67.1	434.1	
5,143.5	5,270.7	5,131.0	6,717.3	6,390.1	6,743.0	5,554.1	2,081.9	2,143.1	
941.0	939.1	1,008.2	1,091.0	1,011.7	1,075.4	1,167.4	1,364.7	1,733.1	
9,419.1	9,638.8	9,384.8	12,183.7	11,746.6	11,669.3	9,313.6	6,369.4 [e]	9,294.1 [f]	

[c] Less than 50 tons.

[d] Except where otherwise noted, totals vary from those shown in Gorter and Hildebrand. *op. cit.*, Vol. I, Appendix II, table 1, because of rounding and/or errors in source tables.

[e] The discrepancy between this total and that shown in Vol. I, Appendix II, table 1, is attributable to the preliminary nature of the figure appearing in the first volume and the inclusion of Alaska, Hawaii, and Puerto Rico in the Pacific Coast regional totals. At the time table 1 (in Vol. I) was constructed only the figures appearing in the *Statistical Abstract* were available.

[f] The discrepancy between this total and that shown in Vol. I, Appendix II, table 1, is attributable to revisions made after the completion of the tabulations from which we obtained our data and possibly to errors in the transcription and manipulation of the data contained on the code sheet tabulations. All our figures have been checked at least twice, but with thousands of calculations and transcriptions, errors occur.

SOURCE: For 1930–1937, United States Maritime Commission, Division of Research, "Waterborne foreign commerce of the United States," *Report No. 275*, annual (Washington, Government Printing Office, 1931–1938). For 1938–1940, United States Maritime Commission, Bureau of Research, "Waterborne foreign and noncontiguous commerce and passenger traffic of the United States," *Report No. 2610* (Washington, Government Printing Office, 1939–1941). For 1946, United States Department of Commerce, Bureau of the Census, *Foreign Commerce and Navigation of the United States*, Vol. II (Washington, Government Printing Office, 1950), pp. 235–255, 269–271, 321–331, 341. For imports, 1947, January–June, United States Department of Commerce, Bureau of the Census, "United States imports of merchandise by vessel," *MC 314*, monthly, unpublished; July–December, United States Department of Commerce, Bureau of the Census, "Value and shipping weight of United States general imports on dry cargo vessels by domestic port of unlading by foreign port of lading by *Schedule T* commodity," *FT 303*, monthly, unpublished; United States Department of Commerce, Bureau of the Census, "Value and shipping weight of United States general imports on tanker vessels by domestic port of unlading by foreign port of lading by *Schedule T* commodity," *FT 303*, monthly, unpublished. For exports, 1947, January–June, United States Department of Commerce, Bureau of the Census, "United States exports of domestic and foreign merchandise by vessel," *MC 714*, monthly, unpublished; July–December, United States Department of Commerce, Bureau of the Census, "Value and shipping weight of United States general exports on dry cargo vessels by domestic port of lading by foreign port of unlading by *Schedule S* commodity," *MC 703*, monthly, unpublished; United States Department of Commerce, Bureau of the Census, "Value and shipping weight of United States general exports on tanker vessels by domestic port of lading by foreign port of unlading by *Schedule S* commodity," *MC 703*, monthly, unpublished.

TABLE 8—Distribution of Pacific Coast Water-borne Foreign Trade

Region no.	Foreign trade region	1930	1931	1932	1933
1	Caribbean, Central America, Mexico	9.1	9.6	8.9	8.8
2	East coast of South America	3.0	3.9	3.8	4.4
3	West coast of South America	5.8	3.5	2.2	3.7
4	United Kingdom	3.0	2.4	1.9	2.1
5	Baltic Scandinavia, Iceland, Greenland	2.2	2.1	2.7	3.0
6	Bayonne-Hamburg range, Portugal, Spanish Atlantic	13.2	12.7	10.7	9.2
7	Azores, Mediterranean, Black Sea	0.7	0.7	0.7	0.8
8	South, East, and West Africa	a	a	a	....
9	Australasia, Antarctica	2.8	2.7	2.1	1.9
10	India, Persian Gulf, Red Sea	2.1	1.8	2.0	1.9
11	East Indies, East Asia	30.0	35.1	36.3	42.2
12	Canada	28.1	25.5	28.6	22.1
	Totals[b]	100.0	100.0	99.9	100.1
1	Caribbean, Central America, Mexico	9.1	7.4	6.3	6.6
2	East coast of South America	2.5	0.8	0.9	0.7
3	West coast of South America	7.2	5.4	1.6	3.0
4	United Kingdom	17.9	13.3	13.8	11.0
5	Baltic Scandinavia, Iceland, Greenland	0.3	0.7	0.6	0.7
6	Bayonne-Hamburg range, Portugal, Spanish Atlantic	7.2	6.5	6.6	5.7
7	Azores, Mediterranean, Black Sea	0.5	0.4	1.7	1.0
8	South, East, and West Africa	0.3	0.3	0.2	0.3
9	Australasia, Antarctica	9.0	7.0	10.5	8.8
10	India, Persian Gulf, Red Sea	0.9	1.1	0.3	0.4
11	East Indies, East Asia	36.2	47.4	46.1	51.2
12	Canada	8.9	9.7	11.3	10.5
	Totals[b]	100.0	100.0	99.9	99.9

a Less than 0.1 per cent.
b Rounding accounts for totals more or less than 100.
Source: Computed from Appendix, table 7.

CARGO TONNAGE BY FOREIGN TRADE REGION, 1930–1940, 1946–1948

1934	1935	1936	1937	1938	1939	1940	1946	1947	1948
				Imports					
			(Per cent of total Pacific Coast import cargo tonnage)						
9.7	7.6	6.6	8.8	11.3	11.1	12.3	13.9	16.0	15.7
3.4	11.0	14.7	10.6	3.6	4.8	4.8	7.0	5.1	4.4
5.8	4.6	3.9	5.0	6.1	5.5	7.4	8.8	10.5	8.5
2.8	1.8	2.6	1.6	2.0	1.4	2.5	0.2	2.2	1.9
3.4	5.9	5.2	4.5	4.4	4.4	0.8	1.2	3.1	4.7
7.8	8.2	9.2	9.3	9.3	5.8	0.3	0.3	0.8	1.5
0.6	1.8	2.9	0.4	0.4	0.5	0.2	a	0.4	0.5
.....	.....	a	0.1	a	a	.....	a	0.3	.....
1.1	1.5	1.2	1.6	1.9	2.1	2.2	9.0	2.5	2.2
1.9	1.4	1.7	2.1	2.3	2.3	2.3	5.3	2.9	2.3
41.9	33.3	32.5	30.1	26.8	28.0	31.2	19.3	26.1	21.4
21.5	22.9	19.6	25.9	31.9	34.1	36.0	35.0	30.2	37.0
99.9	100.0	100.1	100.0	100.0	100.0	100.0	100.0	100.1	100.1
				Exports					
			(Per cent of total Pacific Coast export cargo tonnage)						
7.5	5.4	7.9	10.2	8.0	9.1	8.9	4.8	8.5	
1.8	1.3	0.7	0.7	0.6	0.9	1.2	1.3	3.7	
3.4	3.6	3.6	5.0	4.4	3.9	5.4	2.5	2.6	
8.4	10.5	8.8	7.9	10.2	9.5	5.6	4.3	13.1	
0.5	0.6	0.6	0.5	1.0	0.8	0.5	2.7	2.2	
5.2	5.6	5.8	5.1	6.6	4.6	0.7	10.4	8.3	
0.7	0.8	0.6	0.7	1.0	0.3	0.2	8.7	3.0	
0.4	0.5	0.6	0.6	0.4	0.6	0.9	1.0	1.7	
7.1	6.9	5.7	4.5	4.4	2.8	3.2	9.1	10.6	
0.3	0.5	0.4	0.6	0.4	0.5	1.3	1.1	4.7	
54.6	54.7	54.7	55.1	54.4	57.8	59.6	32.7	23.1	
10.0	9.7	10.7	9.0	8.6	9.2	12.5	21.4	18.6	
99.9	100.1	100.1	99.9	100.0	100.0	100.0	100.0	100.1	

TABLE 9

ESTIMATED TOTAL POPULATION, CALIFORNIA, OREGON, WASHINGTON,
AND THE UNITED STATES, 1930–1948[a]

Year	California	Oregon	Washington	United States
1930.............	5,711,188	955,994	1,568,078	123,076,741
1931.............	5,823,910	966,200	1,581,003	124,039,648
1932.............	5,894,295	972,232	1,584,096	124,840,471
1933.............	5,962,561	977,692	1,592,129	125,578,763
1934.............	6,059,628	985,236	1,610,056	126,373,773
1935.............	6,174,939	1,001,257	1,629,131	127,250,232
1936.............	6,341,328	1,025,373	1,653,214	128,053,180
1937.............	6,527,521	1,047,646	1,681,351	128,824,829
1938.............	6,655,647	1,066,724	1,698,128	129,824,939
1939.............	6,784,591	1,080,584	1,715,249	130,879,718
1940.............	6,982,000	1,100,000	1,741,000	131,936,000
1941.............	7,405,000	1,131,000	1,792,000	133,058,000
1942.............	7,951,000	1,147,000	1,909,000	133,752,000
1943.............	8,508,000	1,233,000	2,058,000	133,971,000
1944.............	9,001,000	1,282,000	2,162,000	132,622,000
1945.............	9,491,000	1,294,000	2,274,000	132,137,000
1946.............	9,925,000	1,398,000	2,334,000	139,893,000
1947.............	10,194,000	1,473,000	2,279,000	143,375,000
1948.............	10,467,000	1,482,000	2,326,000	146,045,000

[a] Estimates include persons in the armed forces stationed in each state and exclude members of the armed forces overseas.

SOURCE: For 1930–1939, United States Department of Commerce, Bureau of the Census, "Estimated population of the United States, by states: 1910–1944," *Population—Special Reports*, Series P–45, no. 9 (Washington, Oct. 1, 1945). For 1940–1948, United States Department of Commerce, Bureau of the Census, "Provisional intercensal estimates of the population of regions, divisions, and states: July 1, 1940 to 1949," *Current Population Reports*, Series P–25, no. 47 (Washington, March 9, 1951).

TABLE 10

Population and Number of Places by Urban and Rural Place Size-Groups, Pacific Coast,[a] 1920–1950[b]

Place size-group	Population				Number of places			
	1920	1930	1940	1950	1920	1930	1940	1950
Urban territory								
Places of 100,000 or more	1,977,647	3,336,261	3,819,651	5,218,011	6	9	10	12
Places of 25,000 to 100,000	601,276	852,265	1,038,739	1,692,146	12	19	24	35
Places of 10,000 to 25,000	316,205	608,512	664,482	1,341,397	21	42	47	90
Places of 5,000 to 10,000	269,241	431,615	492,514	471,641	41	61	66	68
Places of 2,500 to 5,000	295,737	306,228	340,523	382,370	83	90	94	108
Totals	3,460,106	5,534,881	6,355,909	9,105,565	163	221	241	313
Rural territory								
Incorporated places of 1,000 to 2,500	245,979	233,231	253,879	277,553	154	148	158	169
Incorporated places under 1,000	160,480	145,728	145,015	136,373	344	336	316	281
Unincorporated places	1,700,306	2,280,593	2,978,459	4,967,036	c	c	c	c
Totals	2,106,765	2,659,552	3,377,353	5,380,962	498	484	474	450

a California, Oregon, and Washington.

b The 1950 figures are based upon the 1940 Census definitions of urban and rural. With minor exceptions (insofar as our study is concerned) these definitions are consistent with those used in 1930 and 1920. For information regarding these definitional matters, see L. E. Truesdell, "The development of the urban-rural classification in the United States: 1874 to 1949," United States Department of Commerce, Bureau of the Census, Current Population Reports, Population Characteristics, Series P-23, no. 1 (Washington, Government Printing Office, 1949); and United States Department of Commerce, Bureau of the Census, "Population of the United States, urban and rural, by states, April 1, 1950," 1950 Census of Population, Preliminary Counts, Series PC-3, no. 10 (Washington, Feb. 16, 1951), pp. 1–2.

c Not available.

Source: For 1920–1940, Washington, United States Department of Commerce, Bureau of the Census, Sixteenth Census of the United States: 1940, Vol. II, pt. 7 (Washington, Government Printing Office, 1943), p. 303. For Oregon, ibid., pt. 5, p. 963. For California, ibid., pt. 1, p. 515. For 1950, Washington, United States Department of Commerce, Bureau of the Census, "Number of inhabitants of Washington," 1950 Population Census Report P-A 47 (Washington, Government Printing Office, 1951), p. 47–7. For 1950, Oregon, United States Department of Commerce, Bureau of the Census, "Number of inhabitants of Oregon," 1950 Population Census Report P-A 37 (Washington, Government Printing Office, 1951), p. 37–11. For 1950, California, United States Department of Commerce, Bureau of the Census, "Number of inhabitants of California," 1950 Population Census Report P-A 5 (Washington, Government Printing Office, 1951), p. 5–8.

TABLE 11

INDEXES OF NUMBER OF PRODUCTION WORKERS AND VALUE ADDED BY MANUFACTURE, UNITED STATES, CALIFORNIA, OREGON, AND WASHINGTON, 1947

(1939 = 100)

Census group code no.	Industry group	United States		California		Oregon		Washington	
		Number of production workers	Value added by manufacture	Number of production workers	Value added by manufacture	Number of production workers	Value added by manufacture	Number of production workers	Value added by manufacture
20	Food and kindred products.........	137.1	259.0	134.7	288.9	146.3	319.7	155.3	277.1
21	Tobacco manufactures.........	118.0	183.2		205.8	147.6	284.1	111.1	293.7
22	Textile mill products.........	106.1	293.8	102.3	413.7	106.4	271.1	123.2	275.0
23	Apparel and related products.........	129.2	320.6	173.3	376.6	152.1	518.0	106.1	302.9
24	Lumber and products, except furniture.....	140.9	341.5	147.2	352.7	127.3	271.5	162.9	344.9
25	Furniture and fixtures.........	149.3	329.8	165.9	369.4	131.8	320.8	140.6	355.6
26	Paper and allied products.........	143.9	323.6	190.3	260.0	138.6	243.6	136.6	258.1
27	Printing and publishing industries.........	135.1	241.9	151.6	371.7	268.5	677.2	164.3	230.8
28	Chemical and allied products.........	169.2	295.0	194.6	239.9	a	a		
29	Petroleum and coal products.........	157.5	289.0	181.3					
30	Rubber products.........	177.7	320.8	204.4	447.2	144.6	306.5	160.2	352.7
31	Leather and leather products.........	106.5	263.0	215.4	345.0	194.2	396.1	191.1	203.4
32	Stone, clay, and glass products.........	151.9	269.4	203.2	407.1	483.9	984.2	307.6	724.0
33	Primary metal industries.........	150.2	265.8	240.3	402.8	243.8	416.7	187.7	349.8
34	Fabricated metal products.........	182.3	351.3	317.4	464.4	264.6	455.4	226.7	430.9
35	Machinery, except electrical.........	232.1	383.5	365.6	615.4	774.0	1780.6	450.3	689.8
36	Electrical machinery.........	257.8	413.6	326.9	550.2	531.4	133.9	349.8	493.4
37	Transportation equipment.........	181.3	331.1						
38	Instruments and related products.........	214.4	324.0	264.2	419.2	196.0	288.4	117.7	191.9
39	Miscellaneous manufactures.........	164.5	331.8	250.6	342.5	a	a	170.1	306.1
...	All other major industry groups.........								

a Index not calculable because 1939 data withheld to avoid disclosing figures for individual companies.

SOURCE: Computed from United States Department of Commerce, Bureau of the Census, *Census of Manufactures, 1947*, Vol. III (Washington, Government Printing Office, 1950), pp. 22, 92, 505, 627.

TABLE 12

PERCENTAGE OF TOTAL PRODUCTION WORKERS AND TOTAL VALUE ADDED BY MANUFACTURE ATTRIBUTABLE TO SELECTED INDUSTRY GROUPS, UNITED STATES, CALIFORNIA, OREGON, AND WASHINGTON, 1939 AND 1947

Census group code no.	Industry group	United States Number of production workers 1939	1947	United States Value added by manufacture 1939	1947	California Number of production workers 1939	1947	California Value added by manufacture 1939	1947	Oregon Number of production workers 1939	1947	Oregon Value added by manufacture 1939	1947	Washington Number of production workers 1939	1947	Washington Value added by manufacture 1939	1947
20	Food and kindred products	10.3	9.2	14.2	12.1	26.0	17.9	26.3	21.3	17.3	15.8	21.5	16.0	16.8	17.3	20.1	17.0
23	Apparel and related products	9.6	8.2	5.7	6.0	8.2	7.3	4.1	4.7	2.7	1.8	1.9	1.2	2.4	2.0	1.4	1.2
24	Lumber and products, except manufactures	5.4	5.0	3.0	3.4	8.9	6.7	5.3	5.7	55.0	52.2	44.8	53.8	46.0	32.5	34.5	32.0
25	Furniture and fixtures	2.4	2.4	1.7	1.9	3.6	3.1	2.3	2.3	4.4	3.5	3.6	2.3	2.1	2.3	1.4	1.5
26	Paper and allied products	3.5	3.3	3.6	3.9	2.0	1.9	1.9	2.0	5.3	4.4	6.9	5.1	9.9	9.3	14.5	15.7
27	Printing and publishing industries	4.2	3.7	7.2	5.7	5.9	4.6	8.9	6.5	3.0	2.6	6.4	3.6	3.4	3.1	6.2	4.9
28	Chemicals and allied products	3.5	3.9	7.4	7.2	3.6	3.6	6.7	7.0	0.5	0.9	1.1	1.7	1.0	1.1	2.5	1.8
29	Petroleum and coal products	1.4	1.4	2.8	2.7	3.5	3.2	7.9	5.3	...	...	...	...	...	...	...	...
32	Stone, clay, and glass products	3.4	3.4	3.5	3.1	4.1	4.5	4.0	3.9	0.9	1.1	1.1	1.0	1.8	2.4	3.2	2.0
33	Primary metals industries	8.6	8.5	8.9	7.7	4.7	4.9	3.9	4.4	0.9	2.8	1.3	2.9	3.0	6.1	3.3	7.2
34	Fabricated metal products	5.8	6.9	5.7	6.6	7.0	8.6	6.4	7.3	2.3	3.6	3.2	3.1	2.5	3.1	2.9	3.1
35	Machinery, except electrical	6.9	10.4	8.3	10.5	4.7	7.5	5.5	7.1	2.0	3.3	2.7	2.0	2.3	3.4	2.2	2.9
37	Transportation equipment	7.0	8.3	7.2	7.9	9.7	16.3	9.0	13.9	0.8	2.5	0.6	2.0	6.4	15.0	5.8	8.8
	Other	28.1	25.4	20.7	21.4	8.1	9.9	7.7	8.5	4.9	5.6	4.9	4.4	2.4	2.4	2.1	1.9
	Totals[a]	100.1	100.0	99.9	100.1	100.0	100.0	99.9	99.9	100.0	100.1	100.0	100.0	100.0	100.0	100.1	100.0

[a] Rounding accounts for totals more or less than 100.

SOURCE: Computed from United States Department of Commerce, Bureau of the Census, Census of Manufactures, 1947, Vol. III (Washington, Government Printing Office, 1950), pp. 22, 92, 505, 627.

TABLE 13

PACIFIC COAST PRODUCTION AND WATER-BORNE SHIPMENTS [a] OF LUMBER,
1930–1940, 1946, AND 1947

(in thousands of 2,240-lb. tons)

| Year | Shipments by trade | | | | | Production [c] |
	Foreign	Non-contiguous	Inter-coastal	Coastwise [b]	Total	
1930	2,625	152	1,903	1,646	5,966	15,258
1931	1,921	133	1,853	1,187	5,094	10,716
1932	1,125	108	1,074	737	3,044	6,501
1933	1,413	116	1,290	896	3,715	8,790
1934	1,595	121	918	720	3,354	9,236
1935	1,462	135	1,282	1,179	4,058	8,800
1936	1,459	169	1,425	1,312	4,365	14,725
1937	1,332	246	1,413	1,420	4,411	15,503
1938	682	175	1,240	1,427	3,524	12,301
1939	852	176	1,729	1,485	4,242	12,292
1940	785	224	1,680	1,446	4,135	16,734
1946	512	59 [d]	463	219	1,253	17,776
1947	1,150	199	911	304	2,564	20,329

[a] Except for coastwise trade, shipment figures are for outbound cargoes only. Shipments include logs and lumber. No 1948 figures were included because of their lack of comparability with earlier years.

[b] Covers only shipments from Washington and Oregon to California.

[c] Lumber production, in board feet, was converted to long tons on the basis of 3.2 pounds per board foot, the conversion factor for fir lumber. Lumber production tonnage is therefore understated slightly because of the output of California redwood (3.5 pounds per board foot). Except for 1937, Pacific Coast production includes lumber produced in Nevada. California and Nevada are combined in the source tables from which these data were taken.

[d] Estimated by multiplying the Pacific Coast Lumber Inspection Bureau data for shipments to Alaska and Hawaii by the ratio of the tonnage of these shipments in 1947 and 1948 to the tonnage of lumber shipments carried by the Matson Navigation Company during these years.

SOURCE: For shipments, Appendix, tables 1, 3, 5, 6. For production, 1930–1946, United States Department of Agriculture, "Lumber production in the United States, 1799–1946," *Miscellaneous Publication No. 669* (Washington, Government Printing Office, 1948), pp. 16–18. (See *ibid.*, pp. 230–233, for primary source.) For production, 1947, United States Department of Commerce, Bureau of the Census, *Census of Manufactures, 1947*, Vol. II (Washington, Government Printing Office, 1949), p. 263.

TABLE 14

PACIFIC COAST WATER-BORNE SHIPMENTS OF PETROLEUM AND PRODUCTS[a] BY TRADE, AND CALIFORNIA CRUDE OIL PRODUCTION, 1930–1940, 1946–1948

(in millions of 2,240-lb. tons)

Year	Pacific Coast water-borne shipments by trade					California crude oil production[c]
	Foreign	Non-contiguous[b]	Inter-coastal	Coastwise	Total	
1930	7.2	0.5	3.2	22.1	33.0	33.0
1931	5.5	0.5	2.0	20.7	28.7	27.4
1932	5.0	0.4	1.5	15.3	22.2	25.9
1933	4.6	0.4	2.6	15.2	22.8	25.0
1934	5.4	0.5	3.4	12.7	22.0	25.3
1935	6.1	0.6	1.2	14.1	22.0	30.2
1936	6.2	0.6	0.9	17.2	24.9	31.2
1937	8.4	0.7	0.7	21.8	31.6	34.7
1938	8.2	0.6	0.6	22.1	31.5	36.3
1939	7.5	0.7	1.1	21.5	30.8	32.6
1940	6.1	1.0	0.8	....	....	32.5
1946	3.0	1.2	0.2	d	....	45.7
1947	3.9	1.4	0.2	18.8	24.1	48.4
1948	3.3	1.3	0.3	21.8	26.7	49.4

[a] Includes all coastwise shipments and only outbound foreign, noncontiguous, and intercoastal. Military shipments not included.

[b] Alaska and Hawaii only.

[c] Converted from barrels at rate of 6.88 barrels per long ton. This is based upon the unweighted average specific gravity of California crude oil as stated in the National Research Council of the United States of America, *International Critical Tables of Numerical Data, Physics, Chemistry and Technology* (New York, McGraw-Hill, 1927), pp. 137–138.

[d] Not available.

SOURCE: For shipments, foreign, 1930–1947, Appendix, table 1; 1948, compiled for the authors by the Standard Oil Company of California from United States Department of Interior, Bureau of Mines, Petroleum Economics Branch, "The petroleum situation in the Pacific Coast territory," *Statistical and Economic Surveys* (Los Angeles, monthly), processed. For shipments, noncontiguous, 1930–1940, Appendix, table 3; 1946–1948, "The petroleum situation in the Pacific Coast territory," *op. cit.* For shipments, intercoastal, Appendix, table 5. For shipments, coastwise, Appendix, table 6. For production, United States Department of Interior, Bureau of Mines, *Minerals Yearbook* (Washington, Government Printing Office, annual). Note: In 1930 and 1931, *Minerals Yearbook* was titled *Mineral Resources of the United States* and was issued by the United States Department of Commerce which, until 1934, included the Bureau of Mines.

TABLE 15

COMPARATIVE INDEXES OF REAL GROSS NATIONAL PRODUCT AND TOTAL, FOREIGN,
INTERCOASTAL, NONCONTIGUOUS, AND COASTWISE CARGO TONNAGES, PACIFIC COAST
MARITIME SHIPPING, 1930–1940, 1946–1948[a]

(1930 = 100)

Year	Real gross national product	Total cargo tonnage	Foreign tonnage	Inter-coastal tonnage	Non-contiguous tonnage	Coastwise tonnage
1930	100.0	100.0	100.0	100.0	100.0	100.0
1931	92.6	86.8	79.9	81.3	89.3	92.7
1932	79.3	66.4	64.4	62.5	71.4	68.5
1933	78.7	70.6	65.1	82.3	71.4	69.4
1934	86.9	70.4	76.5	89.6	82.1	57.7
1935	94.6	74.1	83.2	77.1	89.3	65.7
1936	107.4	79.7	82.6	75.0	96.4	77.4
1937	112.6	94.4	102.7	74.0	107.1	96.4
1938	107.6	88.1	94.0	62.5	96.4	97.6
1939	116.9	94.8	94.6	80.2	103.6	95.6
1940	128.0	93.1	79.9	76.0	117.9	104.8
1946	177.2	65.6	57.7	28.1	139.3	76.6
1947	177.5	74.7	77.2	36.5	164.3	77.8
1948	183.7	72.7	59.7	32.3	132.1	89.4

[a] The real gross national product series was converted from a 1939 to a 1930 base.
The total cargo and foreign tonnage series do not include emergency government or army dry-cargo tonnage.

SOURCE: Real gross national product was taken from United States Department of Commerce, *Survey of Current Business*, supplement, "National income and product of the United States, 1929–1950" (Washington, Government Printing Office, 1951), table A, p. 146. All of the tonnage series were derived from Gorter and Hildebrand, *op. cit.*, Vol. I, Appendix II, table 8.

TABLE 16

INDEXES OF IMPORTS AND EXPORTS IN FOREIGN TRADE,
PACIFIC COAST MARITIME SHIPPING INDUSTRY,
1930–1940, 1946–1948

(1930 = 100)

Year	Imports	Exports
1930...................	100.0	100.0
1931...................	72.4	83.2
1932...................	58.6	66.4
1933...................	65.5	66.4
1934...................	68.9	78.9
1935...................	96.6	80.7
1936...................	100.0	78.9
1937...................	106.9	102.5
1938...................	75.9	99.2
1939...................	86.2	98.3
1940...................	89.7	78.2
1946...................	72.4	54.6
1947...................	75.9	78.2
1948...................	89.7	52.1

SOURCE: Gorter and Hildebrand, *op. cit.*, Vol. I, Appendix II, table 1.

TABLE 17

Sᴛʀɪᴋᴇs ɪɴ ᴛʜᴇ Pᴀᴄɪꜰɪᴄ Cᴏᴀsᴛ Mᴀʀɪᴛɪᴍᴇ Sʜɪᴘᴘɪɴɢ Iɴᴅᴜsᴛʀʏ, 1934–1948[a]

| Year | Coastwide strikes (1) | Local strikes | | | | Total (all) |
		Major local (of known extent) (2)	Major local (other) (3)	Minor local (of known extent) (4)	Minor local (other) (5)	
1934	1	0	0	7	65	73
1935	0	4	0	42	254	300
1936	1	1	0	42	122	166
1937	0	2	1	10	115	128
1938	0	2	1	3	56	62
1939	0	7	0	10	110	127
1940	0	1	2	2	95	100
1941	0	0	1	0	37	38
1942	0	0	0	0	21	21
1943	0	0	0	2	96	98
1944	0	0	0	5	38	43
1945	0	0	6	9	54	69
1946	2	4	27	2	58	93
1947	0	5	12	18	56	91
1948	1	2	0	0	0	3
Totals	5	28	50	152	1,177	1,412

[a] *Column 1* includes strikes involving one or more unions along the entire Pacific Coast. *Column 2* includes strikes involving 1,000 men or more, usually at a single port. *Column 3* includes port-wide strikes whose length was unknown. *Column 4* includes strikes known to involve at least one longshore gang for at least one eight-hour shift. *Column 5* includes all local longshore strikes for which the number of men and/or the length of the strike was unknown.

Sᴏᴜʀᴄᴇ: The occurrence and dates of the coastwide strikes were established from sources cited in chap. viii. For 1934–1947, the major and minor local strikes were collected, with elimination of duplications, from the Report of the Joint Committee on Labor-Management Relations, *Labor-Management Relations: West Coast Maritime Industry*, 80th Cong., 2d sess., S. Rept. 986, pt. 5 (Washington, Government Printing Office, 1948), pp. 15–16; and from mimeographed tabulations, by port, prepared by the Waterfront Employers Association of the Pacific Coast (now part of the Pacific Maritime Association). For 1948, the two major local strikes were obtained from Pacific Maritime Association, *Strikes and Work Stoppages in the West Coast Maritime Industry*, mimeographed (San Francisco, Pacific Maritime Association, Dec. 13, 1951), p. 4.

TABLE 18

LOCAL LONGSHORE STRIKES BEFORE AND AFTER REMOVAL OF KNOWN ONE-MAN
STRIKES, PACIFIC COAST MARITIME SHIPPING, 1934–1948[a]

Year	Total local strikes	Known one-man strikes	Adjusted total
1934	72	1	71
1935	297	2	295
1936	164	3	161
1937	126	0	126
1938	60	1	59
1939	121	0	121
1940	99	17	82
1941	38	1	37
1942	21	6	15
1943	98	32	66
1944	43	5	38
1945	69	4	65
1946	88	0	88
1947	94	2	92
1948	0	0	0

[a] One-man strikes refer to cases reported in which a single man failed to report, left early, or got drunk on the job and was sent home. Such cases are more accurately treated as individual personnel problems rather than as strikes.

It cannot be said that the corrected total eliminates all these instances, for in many cases the facts reported precluded determination.

SOURCE: Mimeographed tabulations for the ports of Seattle, Portland, San Francisco, and Los Angeles, for 1934–1947, prepared by the former Waterfront Employers Association of the Pacific Coast (now PMA).

TABLE 19

MINOR STRIKES CLASSIFIED BY CAUSE, PACIFIC COAST
LONGSHOREMEN, 1934–1947[a]

Asserted cause	Number of strikes
Refusal to work with nonunion men	66
Wage rate and/or allowances payable	60
Refusal to pass picket lines	128
Size of sling load	96
Size of gang	92
"Hot" ship or cargo	81
Sympathetic strike	61
Stop-work meeting	66
Refusal to work as directed	368
Demonstration strike	34
Jurisdictional dispute	47
Protest of work assignment	68
Slowdown on job	43

[a] In each case, the assigned cause was that given by the Waterfront Employers Association of the Pacific Coast, which collected the original tabulations for the four major ports. We eliminated all known "one-man" strikes from the list. The ILWU has challenged the accuracy of the WEPC list.

SOURCE: Mimeographed reports prepared by the WEPC in 1948.

TABLE 20

Coastwide and Major Local Strikes for Which Losses Can Be Computed, Pacific Coast Maritime Shipping Industry, 1934–1948[a]

Year	Group involved	Area	Number involved	Issues	Calendar length
1934....	All crafts	Coastwide	17,300	Recognition, working conditions, wages	83 days
1935....	Longshoremen	Seattle	1,400	Union matters	1 day
	Longshoremen	Portland	1,132	Demonstration	1 day
	Seamen	San Francisco	3,750	Wages	94 days
	Longshoremen	San Francisco	2,800	Sympathetic strike	40 days
1936....	Longshoremen	San Francisco	1,650	Union matters	7 days
	All crafts	Coastwide	17,968	Offshore hiring halls, working conditions	98 days[b]
1937....	Longshoremen	Los Angeles	2,649	Sympathetic strike	59 days
	Longshoremen	San Pedro	2,040	Various	3 days
1938....	Longshoremen	Seattle	1,350	Union matters	8 days
	Longshoremen	Los Angeles	2,546	Various	9 days
1939....	Longshoremen	Los Angeles	2,494	Wages, hours	3 days
	Longshoremen	San Francisco	4,700	Sympathetic strike	2 days
	Seamen	San Francisco	1,050	Various	5 days
	Seamen and longshore-men	Portland	1,500	Discrimination	15 days
	Longshoremen, dock checkers	San Francisco	5,050	Elimination of monthly employees	13 days
	Sailors and firemen	Coastwide (steam schooners only)	1,250	Wages	10 days
	Longshoremen, dock checkers	San Francisco	4,500	Elimination of monthly employees, closed shop	53 days[c]
1940....	Seamen	Coastwide (steam schooners only)	1,330	Wages	60 days

1946....	Longshoremen	San Francisco	Stop-work meeting	4,667	1 day
	Longshoremen	Los Angeles	Wages, hours, other	1,000	1 day
	Longshoremen	Los Angeles	Bargaining tactics	3,185	1 day
	All crafts	Coastwide	Wage increase denied by government	45,854	21 days[d]
	All crafts	Coastwide	Wages[e]	45,854	52 days
	Longshoremen, dock checkers	Seattle	Jurisdictional rights	1,747	15 days
1947....	Seamen	Unknown	Unknown	1,020	3 days
	Longshoremen	Los Angeles	Stop-work meeting	2,936	1 day
	Seamen	Seattle	Recognition	1,160	9 days
	Longshoremen	Los Angeles	Stop-work meeting	979	2 days
	Longshoremen	Los Angeles	Union membership of walking bosses	2,936	6 days
1948....	All crafts	Coastwide	Union security, control of longshore halls	26,496	95 days

[a] Wherever possible, we used our own estimates of the number of men involved, which were usually lower than those cited in other sources. For the coastwide strikes in particular, we included members of all crafts among those directly involved, regardless of which union or unions were actually on strike. This is logical, since picket lines are respected. However, seamen at sea cannot legally strike, and so they become directly involved only slowly and cumulatively, as the ships return to home port. There is no way to correct accurately for this. Also, there is no way to estimate the wider impacts of local port strikes involving a single union. In these latter cases, only those in the union were counted as directly involved.

Actually there were eighty-three coastwide or major local strikes during these years, of which only thirty-one were tabulated above. The remaining fifty-two were either of unknown length, or unknown scope, or both together.

[b] This strike actually extended into 1937, for thirty-five of the ninety-eight total calendar days it lasted. To maintain a calendar year tabulation, we have listed the entire ninety-eight days as occurring in 1936.

[c] This strike extended two days into 1940, but was counted in 1939 in its entirety.

[d] This strike began as a sailors' strike, but immediately paralyzed the entire coast. It was settled formally nearly two weeks before contracts were actually signed and pickets withdrawn. In the meantime, the firemen, and sailors belonging to the National Maritime Union, also struck, and set up picket lines. All crafts were directly involved throughout.

[e] This strike was primarily a longshore strike, but it paralyzed the entire coast, affecting all crafts. Although the ostensible issue was wages, it was also a "prestige" strike for Bridges, to attempt to reëstablish his leadership of the Pacific Coast maritime crafts.

SOURCE: Except for the coastwide strikes, those cited were obtained from the Report of the Joint Committee on Labor-Management Relations, *Labor-Management Relations: West Coast Maritime Industry*, *op. cit.*, pp. 15–16; and mimeographed tabulations by the four major ports, prepared by the former Waterfront Employers Association of the Pacific Coast (now PMA). Wherever usable, numbers involved in these strikes were obtained from Gorter and Hildebrand, *op. cit.*, Vol. I, Appendix II, tables 14–17.

The occurrence and dates of the coastwide strikes were established from sources cited in chap. ix. Estimates of the numbers involved were taken from Gorter and Hildebrand, *op. cit.*, Vol. I, Appendix II, tables 18 and 19.

TABLE 21

Total Losses in Man-Days from Coastwide and Major Local Strikes, Longshoremen and Seamen, Pacific Coast Maritime Shipping,
1934–1948[a]

Year	Longshoremen Man-days lost	Seamen Man-days lost	Total Man-days lost
1934	456,000	493,000	958,000
1935	114,000	248,000	362,000
1936	411,000[b]	388,000	799,000
1937	348,000[b]	211,000	559,000
1938	34,000	0	34,000
1939	225,000	31,000	256,000
1940	0	57,000	57,000
1941	0	0	0
1942	0	0	0
1943	0	0	0
1944	0	0	0
1945	0	0	0
1946	743,000	1,624,000	2,367,000
1947	22,000	11,000	33,000
1948	847,000	928,000	1,775,000
Totals	3,200,000	3,991,000	7,191,000

[a] These figures apply to the thirty-one coastwide or major local strikes (out of a total of eighty-three) for which length in calendar days and number involved were known. If losses could have been computed for the remaining fifty-two major local strikes and for the 152 minor local strikes of known extent, the over-all loss totals undoubtedly would have been larger.

To calculate the losses, the numbers involved in each of the thirty-one strikes were multiplied by the length of the strikes. However, the length of each strike was first adjusted, to remove from the total calendar days (1) any regular holiday (six) occurring during the strike, and (2) two days out of every seven to allow for regular time off. This corresponds with the procedure of the Bureau of Labor Statistics, as set forth in United States Department of Labor, Bureau of Labor Statistics, *Techniques of Preparing Major BLS Statistical Series*, bull. no. 993 (Washington, Government Printing Office, 1950) pp. 8–12. Since seamen actually work seven days a week at sea, this understates the loss for this group. In contrast, seamen cannot legally strike until the ship returns to home port, hence in this respect the loss for this group is overstated. Finally, longshore local strikes lasting one full day (twenty-four hours) or less were converted to equivalents in shifts (each shift figured at eight hours arbitrarily). Thus if the strike lasted but one shift, the number of longshoremen registered at the port was divided by three to determine the number actually involved. This recognizes that longshoring is a twenty-four-hour operation, and assumes that the full force is divided equally among the three shifts per day.

[b] The total losses for 1936 and 1937 include the effects of the ninety-eight-day coastwide strike, which extended to February 4, 1937. To distribute the loss between the two years, the adjusted times for each year were multiplied by the corresponding numbers involved.

Source: Appendix, table 20.

TABLE 22

DRY-CARGO TONNAGE HANDLED BY PACIFIC COAST MARITIME SHIPPING INDUSTRY,
BY TRADES, 1930–1939, 1946–1948 [a]

(in millions of 2,240-lb. tons)

Year	Foreign	Noncontiguous	Intercoastal	Coastwise	Total
1930	7.7	2.3	6.3	2.7	19.0
1931	6.4	2.0	5.7	2.3	16.4
1932	4.6	1.6	4.4	1.7	12.3
1933	5.1	1.6	5.2	2.0	13.9
1934	6.0	1.8	5.1	1.6	14.5
1935	6.3	1.9	6.1	2.2	16.5
1936	6.2	2.1	6.1	2.0	16.4
1937	6.9	2.3	6.2	2.1	17.5
1938	5.8	2.1	5.2	2.1	15.2
1939	6.6	2.2	6.5	2.2	17.5
1946	5.6	2.7	2.4	0.2	10.9
1947	7.6	3.2	3.2	0.5	14.5
1948	5.6	2.4	2.7	0.4	11.1

[a] For 1930–1939, the trade totals were obtained by deducting shipments of petroleum and products from the over-all totals for these trades. For 1946–1948, the same method was used to obtain dry-cargo totals for the foreign, noncontiguous, and intercoastal trades. The coastwise dry-cargo totals for 1946–1948 were obtained directly, from data collected by the Pacific American Steamship Association from reports of the Interstate Commerce Commission.

The 1930–1948 totals for the foreign and noncontiguous trades include small quantities of inbound petroleum shipments that could not be deducted because their absolute amounts were unknown. The 1946–1948 dry-cargo totals do not include dry cargo shipped for army account or in connection with emergency government relief programs. The coastwise totals for 1930–1939 do not include small amounts of dry cargo carried within California or between Oregon and Washington ports.

SOURCE: For all trades except intercoastal, 1930–1939, petroleum and products were obtained from Appendix, table 14; intercoastal from Appendix, tables 4 and 5; gross totals for all trades from Gorter and Hildebrand, *op. cit.*, Vol. I, Appendix II, table 8. For 1946–1948, these sources were used for the foreign, noncontiguous, and intercoastal trades; coastwise dry-cargo totals were obtained from Pacific American Steamship Association, *Year End Report of Pacific Coast Shipping*, mimeographed (San Francisco, March 28, 1950), p. 2.

TABLE 23

Man-Days Available for Work and Percentage of Time Lost in Strikes, Longshoremen and Seamen, Pacific Coast Maritime Shipping, Selected Years, 1934–1948[a]

Year	Longshoremen		Seamen		Total	
	Man-days available (in millions)	Per cent of time lost	Man-days available (in millions)	Per cent of time lost	Man-days available (in millions)	Per cent of time lost
1934...................	2.0	23.3	2.3	21.4	4.3	22.3
1935...................	2.1	5.4	2.4	10.3	4.5	8.0
1936...................	2.3	17.9	2.2	17.6	4.5	17.8
1937...................	2.4	14.5	2.2	9.6	4.6	12.2
1938...................	2.4	1.4	2.4	0.0	4.8	0.7
1939...................	2.5	9.0	2.3	1.3	4.8	5.3
1946...................	3.5	21.2	7.9	20.6	11.4	20.8
1947...................	3.3	0.7	4.9	0.2	8.2	0.4
1948...................	3.2	26.5	3.5	26.5	6.7	26.5

[a] To calculate man-days available, it was assumed that each man would normally work 250 days each year. This allows two days off per week, plus an extra two weeks for vacation and holidays. The figures for man-days available, for each year for each group, were the products of the numbers in each group times 250. For 1936–1948, the numbers in the two groups were taken from records of the Pacific Maritime Association. For 1934–1935, we used our own estimates.

Source: Gorter and Hildebrand, *op. cit.*, Vol. I, Appendix II, tables 18 and 19. Man-day losses were taken from Appendix, table 21, this volume.

TABLE 24

INDEXES OF BASIC WAGE RATES BY OCCUPATIONS AND CRAFT GROUPS, PACIFIC COAST MARITIME SHIPPING INDUSTRY, 1935–1948

(1935 = 100)

Craft and occupation	1935	1936	1937	1938	1939	1940	1941	1942	1943	1944	1945	1946	1947	1948
Longshoremen:														
Longshoremen	100.0	100.0	100.0	100.0	100.0	100.0	105.3	115.8	115.8	121.1	144.2	160.0	173.7	191.6
Hatch tenders	100.0	100.0	100.0	100.0	100.0	100.0	104.9	114.6	114.6	119.5	140.9	158.0	170.7	187.3
Winch drivers	100.0	100.0	100.0	100.0	100.0	100.0	104.9	114.6	114.6	122.0	143.4	158.0	170.7	187.3
Lift-truck jitney drivers	100.0	100.0	100.0	100.0	100.0	100.0	105.0	115.0	115.0	120.0	142.0	157.0	170.0	192.0
Average	100.0	100.0	100.0	100.0	100.0	100.0	105.0	115.0	115.0	120.7	142.6	158.2	171.3	189.6
Sailors:														
Boatswains	100.0	100.0	118.7	118.7	118.7	131.3	153.1	153.1	153.1	153.1	209.4	265.6	325.0	381.3
Able-bodied seamen	100.0	100.0	116.0	116.0	116.0	132.0	160.0	160.0	160.0	160.0	232.0	276.0	316.0	361.6
Ordinary seamen	100.0	100.0	122.2	122.2	122.2	144.4	183.3	183.3	183.3	183.3	283.3	333.3	355.6	413.3
Average	100.0	100.0	119.0	119.0	119.0	135.9	165.5	165.5	165.5	165.5	241.6	291.6	332.2	385.4
Firemen:														
Oilers	100.0	100.0	113.8	113.8	113.8	127.6	151.7	151.7	151.7	151.7	213.8	244.8	283.4	311.7
Firemen-watertenders	100.0	100.0	113.8	113.8	113.8	127.6	151.7	151.7	151.7	151.7	213.8	244.8	283.4	311.7
Wipers	100.0	100.0	120.0	120.0	120.0	140.0	175.0	175.0	175.0	175.0	265.0	350.0	405.1	446.1
Average	100.0	100.0	115.9	115.9	115.9	131.7	159.5	159.5	159.5	159.5	230.9	279.9	324.0	356.5

Cooks and stewards:													
Chief stewards	100.0	108.7	108.7	108.7	119.6	135.0	135.0	135.0	135.0	174.1	191.3	221.4	249.0
Chief cooks	100.0	110.0	110.0	110.0	121.0	137.5	137.5	137.5	137.5	182.5	205.0	237.3	258.5
Second cooks	100.0	112.5	112.5	112.5	131.3	153.1	153.1	153.1	153.1	209.4	231.3	267.7	293.6
Messmen–utilitymen	100.0	120.0	120.0	120.0	140.0	175.0	175.0	175.0	175.0	265.0	300.0	347.3	386.9
Average	100.0	112.8	112.8	112.8	128.0	150.2	150.2	150.2	150.2	207.8	231.9	268.4	297.0
Radio officers:													
Radio officers	100.0	108.7	108.7	108.7	119.6	150.0	150.0	150.0	150.0	189.1	220.9	255.7	281.2
Engineers:													
Chief engineers	100.0	105.1	105.1	105.1	115.6	124.8	124.8	124.8	134.2	149.5	199.3	222.5	236.8
First assistants	100.0	108.3	108.3	108.3	125.3	137.4	137.4	137.4	147.8	172.9	227.9	253.5	271.0
Second assistants	100.0	109.7	109.7	109.7	124.2	137.3	137.3	137.3	140.7	178.7	212.9	239.2	251.9
Third assistants	100.0	110.7	110.7	110.7	125.7	139.6	139.6	139.6	152.9	185.0	217.1	244.0	256.9
Average	100.0	108.5	108.5	108.5	122.7	134.8	134.8	134.8	146.2	171.5	214.3	239.8	254.2
Officers (deck):													
First officers	100.0	108.6	108.6	117.1	128.9	141.3	141.3	141.3	152.0	177.7	234.3	245.0	278.8
Second officers	100.0	110.0	110.0	116.7	128.3	141.8	141.8	141.8	154.7	184.7	220.0	231.0	260.3
Third officers	100.0	111.1	111.1	118.5	130.4	144.8	144.8	144.8	158.5	191.9	225.2	236.4	266.4
Average	100.0	109.9	109.9	117.4	129.2	142.6	142.6	142.6	155.1	184.8	226.5	237.5	268.5
Over-all averages:													
Seagoing crafts	100.0	112.7	112.7	113.9	128.5	149.6	149.6	149.6	154.2	204.3	244.4	276.1	306.5
All maritime crafts	100.0	110.4	110.4	111.4	123.3	141.5	143.3	143.3	148.1	193.1	228.8	257.0	285.2

SOURCE: For longshoremen, United States Department of Labor, Bureau of Labor Statistics, "Pacific Coast longshore industry, 1934–1949," mimeographed (Washington, n. d.). For seagoing personnel, tabulations prepared by the Pacific American Shipowners Association, covering basic wage rates for each occupation in each craft, in the foreign and intercoastal operations of member companies. Rates for engineers, boatswains, and deck officers apply to Type B vessels. Those for cooks, stewards, and radio officers apply to freighters.

TABLE 25

INDEXES OF THE COST OF LIVING FOR MODERATE INCOME
FAMILIES IN LARGE CITIES AND OF STRAIGHT-TIME HOURLY
EARNINGS OF EMPLOYEES OF CLASS I RAILWAYS, 1935–1948

(1935 = 100)

Year	Cost of living[a]	Railway hourly earnings[b]
1935.......................	100.0	100.0
1936.......................	101.0	100.6
1937.......................	104.7	103.5
1938.......................	102.8	109.2
1939.......................	101.3	109.2
1940.......................	102.1	109.5
1941.......................	107.2	113.9
1942.......................	118.9	124.1
1943.......................	126.1	133.0
1944.......................	128.1	138.5
1945.......................	131.1	138.8
1946.......................	142.2	166.4
1947.......................	162.7	175.0
1948.......................	175.2	193.6[c]

[a] Converted from 1935–1939 base to 1935. Technical title of series is "Index of consumers' prices."
[b] Converted to relatives on a 1935 base from actual earnings in cents per hour. Excludes earnings of executives, officers, and assistants.
[c] September, 1948, only.
SOURCE: Cost of living from United States Department of Labor, Bureau of Labor Statistics, *Handbook of Labor Statistics, 1950 Edition*, bull. no. 1016 (Washington, Government Printing Office, 1951), p. 100. Railway earnings for 1935–1946 from J. Elmer Monroe, *Railroad Men and Wages* (Washington, Association of American Railroads, July, 1947), Appendix C, p. 123; for 1947–1948 from *Ex-Parte No. 168, Increased Freight Rates, 1948*, 276 I.C.C. 21 (Washington, Government Printing Office, 1950).

TABLE 26

INDEXES OF ESTIMATED AVERAGE HOURLY EARNINGS, EX-
CLUSIVE OF OVERTIME, OF PRODUCTION WORKERS IN MANU-
FACTURING AND OF BASIC WAGE RATES IN PACIFIC COAST
MARITIME SHIPPING, 1939–1948

(1939 = 100)

Year	Manufacturing hourly earnings	Maritime wage rates[a]
1939	100.0	100.0
1940	.....	110.7
1941	110.9	127.0
1942	127.2	128.6
1943	141.2	128.6
1944	149.6	132.9
1945	152.1	171.7
1946	166.0	205.4
1947	189.3	230.7
1948	207.0	256.0

[a] Converted from 1935 to 1939 base.

SOURCE: Hourly earnings in manufacturing from United States Depart-
ment of Labor, Bureau of Labor Statistics, *Handbook of Labor Statistics, 1950
Edition*, bull. no. 1016 (Washington, Government Printing Office, 1951), p. 80.
Maritime wage rates from Appendix, table 24.

TABLE 27

ESTIMATED TOTAL DRY-CARGO TONNAGE HANDLED BY PACIFIC COAST LONGSHOREMEN,
1935–1939, 1946–1948

(million long tons)

Year	Total tonnage, all trades[a]	Adjustment for coastwise[b]	Emergency tonnage[c]	Army dry cargo[d]	Total tonnage handled
1935	16.5	2.2	....	....	18.7
1936	16.4	2.0	....	....	18.4
1937	17.5	2.1	....	....	19.6
1938	15.2	2.1	....	....	17.3
1939	17.5	2.2	....	....	19.7
1946	10.9	0.2	1.8	2.7	15.6
1947	14.5	0.5	2.7	3.3	21.0
1948	11.1	0.4	1.8	2.5	15.8

[a] Total for foreign, noncontiguous, intercoastal, and coastwise trades together.
[b] Since coastwise cargo is both loaded and unloaded on the Pacific Coast, the actual tonnage moved must
be counted twice.
[c] Figures obtained by multiplying average over-all tonnage (including petroleum and products) for
1935–1939 (44.9 million long tons) by .803 for 1946, .925 for 1947, and .815 for 1948, and subtracting over-all
tonnage totals for each year from the corresponding products obtained.
[d] Figures obtained by deflating original magnitudes, which were in measurement tons, by a divisor of
1.75. This divisor is the quotient of 70 cu. ft./40 cu. ft., use of which was suggested by official evidence that on
the average army dry cargo required 70 cubic feet per (long) weight ton, instead of the standard 40 cubic feet.
SOURCE: Total dry-cargo tonnage for all trades from Appendix, table 22; adjustment for coastwise tonnage
from Appendix, table 6; emergency cargo tonnage from data in Gorter and Hildebrand, *op. cit.*, Vol. I, p. 35;
army dry cargo from *ibid.*, p. 37.

TABLE 28

Rail Rates for Shipping Selected Commodities between Certain Pacific Coast Ports, 1929–1948

(in cents per 100 lbs.)

Commodities and rates between ports shown

Year[a]	Beverages San Francisco		Canned goods San Francisco		Canned goods Los Angeles	Fruit, dried San Francisco		Salt in packages San Francisco		Sugar San Francisco		Wood pulp Los Angeles
	Portland	Seattle	Portland	Seattle	Portland	Portland	Seattle	Portland	Seattle	Portland	Seattle	Seattle
1929[b]	88.0	89.0	85.0	101.5	....	103.5	117.5	55.0	....	88.0	....	....
1931	33.0	42.0	26.5	35.0	38.0	31.5	42.0	23.5	31.5	24.0	31.5	40.0
1932	31.5	39.0	27.0	....	38.5	....	....	....	....	....	....	....
1934	....	....	30.0	33.0	....	....	39.0	....	....	....	....	....
1936	33.0	....	32.0	35.0	40.0	35.0	....	25.0	29.0	26.0	29.0	39.5
1940	42.0	44.0	38.0	41.0	46.0	....	....	....	....	....	....	....
1941	38.0	....	....	....	....	....	....	....	....	....	....	....
1942	....	39.0	....	....	....	....	....	30.5	30.5	32.0	34.0	....
1944	....	....	....	....	....	43.0	46.0	....	....	....	....	38.5
1948	64.0	67.0	65.0	72.0	86.0	80.0	91.0	44.0	49.0	55.0	59.0	59.0

[a] Not all rate changes shown. Rate is last rate in effect during a given year. In a few instances rates changed sooner than indicated. These are not shown in order to avoid, where possible, single entries for a given year. The figures shown trace the principal contours of rate behavior for the period shown.

[b] Rates not shown in 1929 were not included in source from which data were taken. See source note below.

SOURCE: For 1929, I.C.C. Docket No. 10245, *Fourth Section Cases*, Exhibit 10, witness, Hallmarks, as transcribed in *Final Report of the Senate Fact Finding Committee on San Francisco Bay Ports* (Sacramento, California State Printing Office, 1951), p. 278. For 1931–1944, *Statement Showing Changes Made in Rail Rates* (In Cents per 100 lbs.) *Between November 10, 1931 and September 20, 1945, Both Inclusive on Representative Commodities . . ., Before the Interstate Commerce Commission.* [*Docket No. 29721, All-Rail Commodity Rates Between California, Oregon, and Washington; and* [*Docket*] *No. 29722, Pacific Coastwise Water Rates*, Exhibit 15, witness, Nickerson. For 1948, table 10, p. 159.

TABLE 29

WATER RATES FOR SHIPPING SELECTED COMMODITIES BETWEEN CERTAIN PACIFIC COAST PORTS, 1929–1948 [a]

(in cents per 100 lbs.)

Commodities and rates between ports shown

Date rate effective [b]	Beverages		Canned goods			Fruit, dried		Salt in packages		Sugar		Wood pulp
	San Francisco		San Francisco		Los Angeles	San Francisco		San Francisco		San Francisco		Los Angeles
	Portland	Seattle	Portland	Seattle	Portland	Portland	Seattle	Portland	Seattle	Portland	Seattle	Seattle
Oct. 15, 1929....	21.0	23.0	20.0	23.0	31.5	21.0	23.0	16.0	17.5	19.0	21.5	25.0
Dec. 1, 1931....	23.0	23.0	15.0	15.0	20.0	20.0	20.0	16.0	15.0	19.0	15.0	20.0
Nov. 1, 1932....	18.0	19.0	20.0	23.0	31.5	22.5	25.0	17.5	17.5	19.0	21.5	20.0
Dec. 26, 1934....	22.5	24.0	23.0	26.0	32.5	26.0	29.0	17.5	17.5	21.0	23.5	20.0
June 15, 1936....	26.0	28.0	25.0	28.0	33.0	28.0	31.0	19.0	19.0	22.0	24.0	25.0
Sept. 21, 1938....	29.0	31.0	28.0	31.0	36.0	31.0	34.0	21.5	21.5	24.0	26.0	25.0
Aug. 15, 1940....	32.0	34.0	31.0	34.0	39.0	34.0	37.0	24.5	24.5	26.0	29.0	28.0
June 30, 1946....	28.0	29.0	31.0	34.0	39.0	34.0	37.0	24.5	24.5	26.0	29.0	28.0
July 1, 1946....	30.0	31.0	33.0	36.0	41.0	36.0	39.0	26.0	26.0	27.0	30.0	30.0
Sept. 26, 1946....	36.0	37.0	38.0	41.0	54.0	52.0	55.0	27.0	32.0	28.0	35.0	45.0
Jan. 1, 1947....	41.0	42.0	43.0	47.0	61.0	59.0	62.0	30.0	36.0	33.0	41.0	50.0
April, 1948....	49.0	50.0	52.0	56.0	73.0	71.0	74.0	33.0	39.0	46.0	49.0	50.0

[a] Unless otherwise noted, rates apply to shipments carried on freight vessels.

For the period October 15, 1929–August 15, 1940, the "Rates applied from or to Regular Terminals of the carriers and included charges for wharfage and handling at such terminals and unloading from cars, except when unloading is done at the request of the shipper or consignee for the purpose of sorting, weighing, marking, etc.

"Exception to this Rule: Rates do not include toll charge at . . . San Francisco, Cal.; or carloading or storage at all ports; . . ." (For source of this statement, see source note below.)

For the period June 30, 1946–April, 1948, the rates do not include wharfage charges.

None of the rates in this table include charges for switching, marine insurance, and carloading at destination.

[b] Not all rate changes have been included since in some cases only one or two rates changed as of a given date.

SOURCE: For October 15, 1929–August 15, 1940, Statement Showing Changes Made in Water Rates (In Cents per 100 lbs.). Between October 15, 1929 and December 31, 1945 on Representative Commodities, . . . , Before the Interstate Commerce Commission, [Docket] No. 29721, All-Rail Commodity Rates Between California, Oregon, and Washington; and [Docket] No. 29722, Pacific Coastwise Water Rates, Exhibit 16, witness, Nickerson (mimeographed statement [n.d.] obtained from records of the hearings on file at the offices of the Western Pacific Railroad Company, San Francisco). For June 30, 1946–January 1, 1947, Representative Statement to Reflect the Proposal of the Pacific Coastwise Water Lines (With Respect to Port-to-Port Traffic) and to Modify the Material Contained in Exhibits Nos. 10, 11 and 12 (In Part) In Order to Explain in More Detail [sic] Particularly Some of the Questions Developed in the Hearing Held in Washington, D. C. on April 28, 29 and 30, 1947, Before the Interstate Commerce Commission, op. cit., Exhibit 20, witness, Burley (mimeographed statement [n.d.] obtained from records of the hearings on file at the offices of the Western Pacific Railroad, San Francisco). For April, 1948, table 10, p. 159, above.

TABLE 30

Tons of Revenue Freight Carried by Steam Railroads
in California, Oregon, and Washington, 1930–1948 [a]

(in millions of 2,000-lb. tons)

Year	California	Oregon	Washington [b]
1930	33.6	23.2	21.3
1931	27.9	16.7	15.3
1932	21.1	11.5	11.1
1933	21.0	12.0	12.3
1934	26.3	16.3	14.2
1935	28.0	19.1	15.8
1936	33.9	21.8	20.1
1937	35.2	23.8	25.1
1938	30.1	21.2	21.3
1939	31.5	24.3	25.2
1940	34.6	26.0	25.8
1941	46.4	34.0	33.7
1942	58.8	45.4	36.4
1943	64.1	51.1	53.8
1944	73.9	52.6	56.1
1945	72.1	48.4	53.4
1946	62.1	43.8	42.6
1947	48.9	47.9	47.4
1948	62.3	44.4	39.3

[a] These figures overstate the amounts carried because most carriers report transfers from other carriers as well as freight originating on their own lines.

[b] Class I railroads only.

Source: For California, 1930, *Annual Report of the Railroad Commission of the State of California* (Sacramento, California State Printing Office, 1932), p. 339; 1931–1948, *Annual Report of the Public Utilities Commission of the State of California*, unpublished photostatic copy on file in San Francisco office. For Oregon, records of the Public Utilities Commissioner, Salem, Oregon. For Washington, 1930–1936, 1942, 1948, transcribed for the authors by the Secretary of the Washington Public Service Commission from reports available in his office; 1937–1941, 1943–1947, State of Washington, Department of Transportation, *Statistics of Steam and Electric Railways* (Olympia, annual), mimeographed. Note: This is the 1947 title and issuing agency. Some earlier reports (same title) were credited to the Department of Public Service.

TABLE 31

TONS OF FREIGHT CARRIED IN INTERCITY SERVICE BY MOTOR
CARRIERS REPORTING TONNAGE TO STATE PUBLIC UTILITIES
COMMISSIONS,[a] CALIFORNIA AND WASHINGTON, 1930–1948

(in millions of 2,000-lb. tons)

Year	California	Washington[b]
1930	2.0	...
1931	1.4	...
1932	1.2	...
1933	1.8	...
1934	1.6	...
1935	2.3	...
1936	2.8	...
1937	2.8	...
1938	2.6	...
1939	2.8	...
1940	3.8	...
1941	5.0	...
1942	6.5	...
1943	10.6	3.5
1944	7.2	3.8
1945	5.8	4.1
1946	5.5[c]	4.6
1947	6.3	5.5
1948	6.2	6.8

[a] In Washington the appropriate organization is the Washington Public
Service Commission.

[b] Data for 1930–1942 not available.

[c] Local not separated from intercity.

SOURCE: For California, 1930, *Annual Report of the Railroad Commission
of the State of California* (Sacramento, California State Printing Office, 1932),
pp. 187 and 293; 1931–1948, *Annual Report of the Public Utilities Commission
of the State of California*, unpublished photostatic copy on file in San Francisco office. For Washington, transcribed for the authors by the Secretary of
the Washington Public Service Commission from reports available in his
office.

SELECTED BIBLIOGRAPHY

Selected
Bibliography

~~~~~~~~~~~~~~~~~~~~~~~~~~~~~~~~

As THE TITLE indicates, this bibliography is not all-inclusive. It contains only references especially pertinent, in large measure, to the Pacific Coast maritime shipping industry as we have defined it. Among the excluded items are those which are primarily statistical. Readers interested in statistical matters will find complete source annotations in the major statistical tables. In addition, Appendix I, Volume I, contains a detailed description and evaluation of many statistical series. The purpose of this bibliography is to provide a handy reference to important sources of information. Many additional references appear in relevant footnotes in both volumes.

GENERAL

Coman, E. T., Jr., and H. M. Gibbs. *Time, Tide and Timber*. Stanford: Stanford University Press, 1949.

Mears, E. G. *Maritime Trade of the Western United States*. Stanford: Stanford University Press, 1935.

Radius, W. A. *United States Shipping in Trans-Pacific Trade, 1922–1938*. Stanford: Stanford University Press, 1944.

Stanford Research Institute. *An Economic Analysis of Pacific Coast Trans-Pacific Shipping*. Stanford: Stanford [University] Research Institute, 1950.

State of California. San Francisco Bay Ports Commission. *A Report on Inter-*

coastal Shipping Problems, with Special Reference to the San Francisco Bay Ports Area, prepared by J. A. Stumpf. San Francisco: 1953.

——. *A Report on Pacific Coastwise Shipping, with Special Reference to the San Francisco Bay Ports Area*, prepared by R. F. Burley. San Francisco: 1953.

——. Senate. *Final Report of the Senate Fact-Finding Committee on San Francisco Bay Ports*. Sacramento: California State Printing Office, 1951.

U. S. Congress. Senate. Subcommittee of the Committee on Interstate and Foreign Commerce. *Merchant Marine Study and Investigation*. Hearings, 81st Cong., 1st and 2d sess., on S. Res. 50. Washington: 1949 and 1950.

——. Committee on Interstate and Foreign Commerce. *Merchant Marine Study and Investigation*. Final Report, 81st Cong., 2d sess., S. Rept. 2494, on S. Res. 50. Washington: 1950.

U. S. Maritime Commission. *Economic Survey of Coastwise and Intercoastal Shipping*. 76th Cong., 1st sess. H. Doc. 209. Washington: 1939.

COSTS, RATES, AND COMPETITION

Alderman Reporting Service. *Stenographers' Minutes Before the Interstate Commerce Commission, Docket No. 29721 and 29722: in the Matter of All-Rail Commodity Rates Between California, Oregon, and Washington; Pacific Coastwise Water Rates*. Washington: Alderman Reporting Service, 1947.

U. S. Interstate Commerce Commission. *Ex Parte No. 165, Problems in the Regulation of Domestic Transportation by Water*, by C. S. Morgan. Washington: 1946.

——. *All-Rail Commodity Rates Between California, Oregon, and Washington*, Docket No. 29721; *Pacific Coastwise Water Rates*, Docket No. 29722. Interstate Commerce Commission Reports, vol. 277. Washington: 1950.

——. *Pacific Coast Fourth Section Applications*, Fourth Section Application No. 13457; *Los Angeles Chamber of Commerce vs. Southern Pacific Et Al.*, Docket No. 21918. Interstate Commerce Commission Reports, vol. 165. Washington: 1930.

——. *Transcontinental Rail Rates*, Docket No. 29663. Interstate Commerce Commission Reports, vol. 268. Washington: 1947.

——. *Motor-Water Commodity Rates Between California and Oregon-Washington*, Investigation and Suspension Docket No. M-1230. Motor Carrier Cases, vol. 30. Washington: 1942.

LABOR RELATIONS

Eliel, P. "Industrial Peace and Conflict: A Study of Two Pacific Coast Industries," *Industrial and Labor Relations Review*, 2 (July, 1949).

————. "Labor Peace in Pacific Ports," *Harvard Business Review,* XIX (Summer, 1941).

————. *The Waterfront and General Strikes San Francisco, 1934.* San Francisco: Industrial Association of San Francisco, 1934.

Hopkins, W. S. "Employment Exchanges For Seamen," *American Economic Review,* XXV (June, 1935).

International Longshoremen's and Warehousemen's Union. *Dispatcher.* San Francisco.

Keller, M. *Decasualization of Longshore Work in San Francisco; Methods and Results of the Control of Dispatching and Hours Worked, 1935–1937.* Report No. L-2. Philadelphia: WPA National Research Project on Reëmployment Opportunities and Recent Changes in Industrial Techniques, 1939.

Kerr, C., and L. H. Fisher. "Conflict on the Waterfront," *Atlantic Monthly* (Sept., 1949).

Lampman, R. J. *Collective Bargaining of West Coast Sailors, 1885–1947: A Case Study in Unionism.* Unpublished Ph.D. dissertation. University of Wisconsin, 1950.

Liebes, R. A. *Longshore Labor Relations on the Pacific Coast, 1934–1942.* Unpublished Ph.D. dissertation. University of California, 1942.

Pacific Maritime Association. *Shoreside Report.* San Francisco.

Pacific Shipper.

Palmer, D. L. *Pacific Coast Maritime Labor: A Study in Industrial Relations Before and Under the N. R. A.* Unpublished Ph.D. dissertation. Stanford University, 1935.

Quin, M. *The Big Strike.* With a postscript by Harry Bridges. Olema, California: Olema Publishing Company, 1949.

Sailors' Union of the Pacific. *West Coast Sailors.* San Francisco.

Schneiderman, W. *The Pacific Coast Maritime Strike.* San Francisco: Western Workers Publishers, 1937.

U. S. Congress. Senate. Committee on Labor and Public Welfare. *Communist Domination of Certain Unions.* Report of the Subcommittee on Labor and Labor-Management Relations, 82d Cong., 1st sess., Doc. 89. Washington: 1951.

————. *Hiring Halls in the Maritime Industry.* Hearings before the Subcommittee on Labor-Management Relations, 81st Cong., 2d sess. Washington: 1950.

————. Joint Committee on Labor-Management Relations. *Labor-Management Relations: West Coast Maritime Industry.* 80th Cong., 2d sess., S. Rept. 986. Washington: 1948.

U. S. Department of Labor. *Report and Recommendations of the Pacific Coast Longshore Fact Finding Board.* Washington: 1946.

INDEX

Index

Jackson, Andrew, 210 n.
Job-action program. *See* Strikes: "quickie"
Job-control. *See* Labor relations, major issues
Johnson, Harry, xii
Joint Committee on Labor-Management Relations, on longshore employee discipline, 1938, 239–240
Joint Marine Strike Committee, formation of, 184–185

Kerr, Clark, xi, 175 n., 258 n.
Kindleberger, C. P., 67 n.

Labor, demand for, 140–141, 146–147
Labor-Management Relations Act: effect on Pacific Coast conflict, 207; Board of Inquiry, 210–211; injunction, 1948, 210–211
Labor relations, major issues
representation and jurisdiction: *See* Conflict, labor-management, causes of: rival unionism
longshore: hiring halls, 177–182, 189–191, 215–216; employee discipline, 231–234; strikes in violation of contract, 235–242; efficiency of longshoremen, 242–250; "walking bosses," 250; significance for industry, 255–257
offshore: hiring and job-control, 251–252; SUP jurisdictional conflicts, 252–254; MEBA and MMP issues, 254–255; significance for industry, 255–257
Labor supply, control of, by unions, 144–148
Lampman, Robert J., xii, 175 n.
Lary, Hal B., 68 n.
Leonard, J. L., 180 n.
Letiche, J. M., 63 n.
Lewis, John L., 228, 229, 270
Liebes, Richard A., 175 n.
Lombard, E. C., xii
Longshore Safety Commission, 208
Longshoremen's Association, International: organization of Pacific Coast, 1933, 180; 1934 strike, 180–191; 1936–1937 strike, 194–197; supplanted by ILWU, 224–227
Longshoremen's Association of San Francisco and the Bay District, 176, 177 n.
Longshoremen's Union of the Pacific, 176 n.
Longshoremen's and Warehousemen's Un-

ion, International: and CMU, 198–200; 1946 strike, 205–207; 1948 strike, 207–215; formation, 224; certified by NLRB, 225. *See also* Conflict, labor-management, causes of: rival unionism
Lumber, production and shipping of, 93–99
Lundeberg, Harry: economic gains for sailors, 138, 141; emerges as leader, 1935, 193; and MFP, 192–197; CMU and 1946 strike, 201–204; 1947–1948 agreement with PASA, 208, 209–210; wins representation rights for SUP, 227–229; union policies, 250–252; summary, 303–304. *See also* Conflict, labor-management, causes of: ideologies and attitudes

McGrady, Edward F., 185
Malone, V. J., 206, 213 n.
Marine Cooks and Stewards, National Union of: 1934 strike, 181, 188, 190–191; 1936–1937 strike, 194, 197; joins CMU, 198; 1948 strike, 211–215; affiliates with CIO, 230
Marine Engineers' Beneficial Association, National: 1934 strike, 181, 186, 188, 190–191; 1936–1937 strike, 194, 197; 1946 strike, 205–207; 1948 strike, 214–215; affiliates with CIO, 230
Marine Firemen, Oilers, Watertenders and Wipers Association, Pacific Coast: 1934 strike, 181, 188, 190–191; 1936–1937 strike, 194, 197; joins CMU, 198; 1946 strike, 204; 1948 strike, 211–215; becomes independent, 230
Marine Service Bureau, 177, 181, 190
Maritime Federation of the Pacific, 1935–1941: formation, 191–192; policy on job-action, 193, 235; 1938 split, 227, 229
Marshall, Alfred, 290
Masters, Mates and Pilots of America, National Organization of: 1934 strike, 181, 186, 188, 190–191; 1936–1937 strike, 194, 197; 1946 strike, 205–207; affiliated with AFL, 230
Matson Navigation Company, xii, 34 n., 37, 39 n.
Mears, Eliot G., xi, 107 n.
Merriam, Frank F., 185
Mitchell, Wesley C., 111
Morse, Wayne L., 237, 244, 245, 246 n., 247